The Official History of

MIDDLESEX
COUNTY
CRICKET CLUB

THE CHRISTOPHER HELM
COUNTY CRICKET HISTORIES

Series Editors:
Peter Arnold and Peter Wynne-Thomas

HAMPSHIRE
Peter Wynne-Thomas, with a personal view by
John Arlott

KENT
Dudley Moore, with a personal view by
Derek Underwood

The Official History of

MIDDLESEX
COUNTY
CRICKET CLUB

David Lemmon

With a personal view by
Denis Compton

CHRISTOPHER HELM
London

© 1988 David Lemmon and Denis Compton
Christopher Helm (Publishers) Ltd, Imperial House,
21–25 North Street, Bromley, Kent BR1 1SD

ISBN 0-7470-2007-8

A CIP catalogue record for this book is available from the
British Library

Typeset by Cotswold Typesetting Ltd, Gloucester
Printed and bound by Biddles Ltd, Guildford, Surrey

CONTENTS

A PERSONAL VIEW
by Denis Compton

MIDDLESEX COUNTY CRICKET CLUB has been part of my life for over 50 years. And as I scored most of my 38,942 first-class runs and 123 hundreds with them I feel part, even if only a small part, of its history.

I make that point because it means, inevitably, that this introduction must be personalised. I aim to get dates and facts right. Statistics there will have to be in places to explain the stature of certain men and situations. But, here and now, I confess that I have never been one to revel in statistics. I hardly ever knew, or cared, about my batting average.

To me people, players, personalities have always been more important. They are the true stuff of sporting history. Maybe I see it that way because that is how the old-timers got it over to me when, as a lad of 14, I first started my long and happy cricket career at Lord's.

So that is the only way I can tell my story of this great club, a County Club that lives and breathes, yet, geographically, with boundaries re-drawn, no longer exists; a Club more than 120 years old that has come through the devastations of two world wars with traumas and ups and downs that have somehow mirrored the changing social life of the country itself in the last century.

By that I mean that the Club started and thrived in the sedate times of the Victorians and Edwardians when the gentry, even Royalty, were patrons. Then cricket was the splendid sport of the aristocracy with the time and money to display their skills (with just a little help from one or two professionals!) and they set the standards and traditions which still hold today. These standards keep the Club thriving and successful in one of the toughest and most competitive, commercialised, professional decades any of us have seen.

That is character for you. Those early amateurs built well. For I believe their old demands for attractive, sporting cricket have been maintained.

The fact that Lord's, the greatest cricket ground in the world, has been the home of the Club for over 100 years has meant a great deal. It has its own standards and traditions. Some will dispute my claim that Lord's is the greatest venue of them all. They will talk of Melbourne with its towering stands able to take 90,000 spectators; or Newlands for its beauty in the shadow of Table Mountain.

But ask any Australian, South African, West Indian, or any cricketer from any other country, where he would most like to make a century . . . and the answer would be Lord's. After all Lord's is the headquarters of cricket the world over and the quality, tradition, feeling, and all that cricket stands for is there. You can feel it. I have felt it on every one of the hundreds of times I have walked through the famous Long Room and out on to the middle with a bat in my hand. And I still feel it to this day whenever I pass through those Grace Gates in St Johns Wood.

I suppose I feel the magic more than most because the very first time I walked on to the middle (I was only 13) I scored what may well have been the most momentous century of my life.

I was captaining the London Elementary Schools against Mr C. F. Tufnell's Public Schools Eleven. I opened the batting with Arthur McIntyre (who later played for Surrey and England) and our century opening stand virtually won the match. The momentous bit was that the 114 I scored so impressed 'Plum' Warner, a pillar of MCC and Middlesex for over 60 years, that he immediately asked my Mun and Dad if I could join the Lord's ground staff. Dad, a good club cricketer, was as keen as I was on the idea. But Mum argued that a four-month season as a cricketer had no security, and she felt that a job in the town hall would be safer.

Her view held until, a few weeks later, Herbert Chapman, the famous manager of Arsenal, liked so much of what he saw of my footballing ability in an England *v* Wales schools match, that he offered me a job on the Highbury staff. When Dad and I confronted Mum with the fact that I would now have full employment, cricket in the summer and football in the winter, she had no chance. And that is exactly how my sporting career had lift off!

At that time, of course, I had no feelings about the history of Middlesex County Cricket Club, and certainly knew nothing about its formation way back in 1864. But I soon had the whole story drilled into me by dear old George Kenner and Archie Fowler. They were the two coaches in charge when I joined the Lord's staff a few weeks short of my 15th birthday and they soon made me understand that there was more to cricket at Lord's than the mere manipulation of bat and ball. And although they were no great men of letters they knew all about the sense of history that oozed from every stick and stone and blade of grass of their beloved Lord's. And in their view, it was essential I should know, and feel it, too.

I did, but a more immediate impression was made on me by two giants near the end of their Middlesex careers. In my view, the influence of Jack Hearne and Patsy Hendren on Middlesex cricket, in terms of consistency of top level performance through good times and bad, has been greater than that of any other two men in the whole 120-odd years existence of the Club.

As a player, a producer of runs and centuries, and as a personality radiating all that is best in the game, I rate Patsy as one of the greatest cricketers of my time, or any other time for that matter. And as I now hear youngsters in the frenzy of the modern game asking 'Patsy who?' I want to give a great man his due place.

The only way I know how to put Patsy's power into its proper perspective is to resort to a few basic statistics. In his career . . . and he was still hitting hundreds at 48 . . . he scored no fewer than 57,611 first-class runs and came through with an average of 50.80. Only Sir Jack Hobbs with 61,760 at 50.66, and Frank Woolley, with 58,959 at 40.77, have scored more in the whole history of the game.

In that massive total he hit 170 centuries; and only Hobbs, with 199, has scored more. The point I want to stress is that he was at his best in the 19 years he played after the First World War. In eight of those seasons he scored well over 2,000 runs, and in three well over 3,000. In 1923 and 1927 he hit 13 hundreds in each season and in 1928 he hit 12 for the County alone. He played in 51 Tests and was as regular at No 4 for England as he was for Middlesex.

Jack Hearne, two years younger than Patsy, made the England side before him. That was just before the First World War. But for Middlesex their careers ran in tandem right through till their retirement in the middle 1930s. I reckon they were regarded as the 'Middlesex twins' long before that title fell on Bill Edrich and me in the 1940s and 1950s.

Hearne did not match Hendren's incredible capacity for making massive scores. But he was a classic and quite superbly elegant player who included 96 hundreds in his career total of 37,252 runs. Put those with Hendren's runs, and add Hearne's additional contribution of 1,839 wickets, and you will understand my admiration for what these two greats did for Middlesex and cricket generally.

The stronger, and much the more out-going of the two, Patsy somehow radiated joy and fun in everything he did. Thickset and incredibly strong, he was one of the fastest movers and strongest throwers from the outfield I have ever seen. And when he went out to bat as the Middlesex or England No 4 he naturally conveyed a sense of challenge and action that brought the crowds from the bars and set them buzzing. For he was a great

'Patsy' Hendren. There was always fun when he was playing and no cricketer has been more loved.

driver of the ball, a fierce square cutter, and probably the best hooker the game has seen. He also had the gift of humour, and whether at the crease or patrolling the outfield he had the knack of establishing a rapport with the spectators that spread universal delight. In the dressing room, too, he was the constant joker in the pack.

If you gather from this that I regarded Patsy as very special to me, as well as to cricket, you would be right. You see, his last two years with Middlesex coincided with my first two, and as we played at Nos 4 and 5 day after day his influence on my early development, and probably my whole career, was enormous.

Looking back I think the nicest thing was that he never attempted the old-timer act of heavy-handed coaching of the new boy. Although there were 30 years between us he simply said: 'Don't let anybody try to change your style or attitude Denis . . . you have a great talent of your own. Just play to it.'

I remember another thing he said: 'Whenever I take guard I look at the bowlers and tell myself it's either them or me . . . I get on top of them or they get on top of me . . . so I aim to take them on early to establish who is boss.' I never forgot that and found it a priceless piece of advice.

But the real education I got from him was by simply watching him from 22 yards range during those first two important years of my career. He had such perfect balance, such power, such calm authority. And he enjoyed every minute. For that, he believed, was what cricket was all about. He was a genial genius and valued friend.

It was the arrival of another very special character of Middlesex cricket, in 1934, that started the upturn of fortunes for the club after the blues of the early 1930s. I refer to Big Jim Smith, who specialised in fast bowling and big hitting.

In his first season, 1934, he captured 172 wickets (143 of them for Middlesex) and his success and exuberance gave the side the lift and smell of better things it so badly needed. My old Arsenal soccer mate, Joe Hulme, produced 1,258 runs and matched Hendren's return of four centuries. Fred Price, that tough and splendid batsman-wicket-keeper, also hit 1,200 runs.

In 1935 things moved even faster and better. That was when Walter Robins came back to regular cricket and started to crack the whip in his first year as captain. Jim Sims, that tall, lovely character, who bowled effective leg-breaks and kept everybody amused with his dry cockney wit, took 109 Championship wickets to Big Jim's 94 and skipper Robins' 64.

With Patsy still topping the batting, with five more hundreds in his 1,688 runs, things were coming together and third place in the Championship was achieved. The sad note was that after Nigel Haig had retired in 1934 it was now the time for maestro Jack Hearne to call it a day and move over to coaching.

In effect that left a hole in the batting line-up I was destined to fill the following year of 1936. As a stripling of 18 I was called in for the Whitsun match against Sussex, hoping for the best, I suppose, but fearing the worst.

I shouldn't think any player ever forgets his baptism in the first team and I certainly will never forget mine. The issue was that we badly needed about 15 or 20 runs for first innings lead when I went in at No 11. That great Sussex and England bowler Maurice Tate had already taken six of our wickets and anybody could see that he fancied the new boy as an easy seventh.

Gubby Allen was batting at the other end and he met me with a quiet word of advice: 'Just remember one thing . . . this fellow Tate comes off faster than you expect, so play forward to him and you'll be all right.'

'Right, sir,' I said . . . and immediately played back, was beaten all ends up, and was lucky to see the ball miss my off stump by a whisker.

As I have no wish to see my best friend stripped of his recently awarded and much deserved knighthood I will draw a veil over Sir Gubby's comments as he came down the pitch for a short and decidedly one-sided conversation. Enough to say that it worked. We got the lead we wanted; I held my place in the team. And within three weeks I made my first hundred, against Northants, and from then on I was up the order—with my idol Patsy at No 4 and me at No 5.

It was very much a case of the Master and his apprentice for he was in his 48th year and I was 18, and still wondering what it was all about. But I can still recall the sheer delight I felt as I watched this remarkable, bubbly man hit eight hundreds in his 1,912 runs for that season. I like to feel that some of his magic rubbed off for I was pleased to complete my 1,000 in my first season in his shadow. And he was just as pleased for me.

This was the season when Gubby Allen made nearly 500 runs, average 50.66, and took 54 wickets, average 16.64, in only nine matches. Joe Hulme scored four hundreds and was still a greyhound in the deep field. It was also when big Jim Smith took another century of wickets, Jim Sims 97, skipper Robins 58 and Laurie Gray 43. These were the men who took us to the first of four consecutive second places in the Championship up to the start of the Second World War.

The two big events of 1937 were the arrival of Bill Edrich and, sadly, at the end the retirement of Patsy. Both played superb cricket, with Patsy, at 48, determined to bid farewell in style, hitting five hundreds in his final 13 games, including a lovely 113 v Surrey in his last match of all. An exciting, rock solid No 4 to the very end.

It struck me then, as it does now, as either ironic or prophetic, depending on how you look at it, that when I won my first Test cap that year against New Zealand, I found myself stepping into Patsy's place at No 4 in the England order. He had held it pretty well throughout his 51 Tests; and I was destined to hold it for the 78 that lay ahead of me. I made 65 in my only knock in that first Test and he was as pleased as I was. I was 19.

For the County Bill Edrich showed his class and courage with three century innings, I managed two, and the two of us and Patsy all had well over the 1,000 runs. And yet again Big Jim took over 100 wickets, Jim Sims took 95, Robins 70, Laurie Gray 65 and the power balance of runs, wickets, quality fielding and aggressive leadership took us to second place again.

There was an odd feeling in the dressing room in the early days of 1938. It seemed strange with both 'JW' and Patsy gone. There were fewer jokes, although Big Jim and Jim Sims tried to make up. At Bristol Big Jim had us all agog with one of the fastest big-hitting sprees I remember. He hit 66 in 18 minutes, the first 50 in a record 11 minutes. And the whole extravaganza would have been a lot faster if the Gloucestershire fielders could have retrieved some of his eight sixes more quickly. Most of them travelled huge distances, landing the ball in the car park where there was much scrambling under the parked vehicles.

Bill Edrich and I were flattered, and not a little apprehensive, when we were constantly being told that the mantle of Hearne and Hendren had now fallen on us. I can only report that we did our best. Bill came up with four big hundreds in his 1,705 runs, I had three in my 1,264, and we were both called into the Test side against the Australians.

I was lucky enough to make 102 in my first innings against them. Then it was six and 76 not out in the second Test, 14 and 15 in the third, and then, at the Oval, where Len Hutton made his famous record 364, Maurice Leyland 187, and Joe Hardstaff 169 not out in a massive 903 for seven, I was clean bowled by Waite for one!

But for Middlesex it was another good second place in the table with the bonus of Jack Robertson and Syd Brown settling in as a solid opening pair, Big Jim Smith taking another hundred wickets and Ian Peebles a useful 38.

That was the prelude for Ian to take over the captaincy in 1939 and improve his contribution to 49 wickets. He also kept the minds of the whole team on the job in spite of the growing feeling of apprehension about the obvious approach of war. And again we finished second to Yorkshire.

Bill and I consolidated our form. He hit seven hundreds, I hit six, we both scored around 2,000 altogether and averaged over 50. Jack Robertson also improved with every match to get 1,755 runs, including four good century knocks. Jim Sims rocked in on his gentle run to be a real match winner with 143 wickets. Big Jim's 86 wickets was modest stuff by his standards, but there was nothing very modest about the hundred he slammed against Kent at Canterbury. Three interruptions for rain didn't bother him one bit. Some of his seven sixes were the biggest ever seen on that famous ground. His unbeaten 101 came in 81 minutes, and he had 98 of the last-wicket stand of 116 he shared with his captain. Was it any wonder the crowds loved this splendid character?

It was significant, perhaps, that Gubby Allen and Walter Robins could make only four appearances. But their influence was still immense. Gubby, still one of the fastest bowlers in the country, had gained stature by speaking out against 'bodyline' as a member of Douglas Jardine's team to Australia in 1932–33: and from his own captaincy of the image-repairing tour that followed in 1936–37.

So, with this lively cricket-wise backing, and an ability to retain a solid match-winning balance of talent on the field, there was a confident feeling all round that we could soon take that top place from our great Yorkshire rivals.

But Mr Hitler decreed a long, long interval. He simply pulled up stumps. Bill went off to win his DFC as a bomber pilot with the RAF; George Mann, who had just made the side, to win a DSO and MC with the Scots Guards; I went to sweat through the Far East and the rest were scattered at the whims of the Army, Navy or Air Force for the next six long, anxious years.

The pattern of the club's success and failure after the Second World War has borne an astonishing likeness to that achieved after the First World War. In the first era there was a splash of instant success, then a period of mediocrity, and then another burst of success.

In this, the second era, we had instant successes from 1946 to 1949 (some called it the Robins-Compton-Edrich era) then 27 years in a mid-table wilderness, and then, in the mid-1970s and 1980s, another heady splurge of triumphs. That could be called the Brearley, Barlow, Edmonds, Emburey, Daniel and Gatting era, when no fewer than five

Championships were hauled in with three Gillette/NatWest triumphs and two Benson & Hedges Cups.

If that sequence proved anything it was that while this splendid club might have been slow to get the hang of the new age of sponsorship and commercialisation it did a great deal better than most when it did.

The most astonishing thing in the whole of this post-war period was how swiftly and dramatically Middlesex burst into action, with quite outstanding cricket, after those six harrowing years of war. We came second in the Championship in 1946, blasted record after record to take the Championship in 1947, and then, after being third in 1948, we were back to share top place with Yorkshire in 1949.

I would be less than honest if I were not to say that I had some part in the blazing cricket of those four years which had the crowds packing every ground where we played. They were four of the most exciting years of my cricketing life. And I think I can say the same for Bill Edrich, Jack Robertson, Syd Brown, skipper Walter Robins . . . and indeed the whole Middlesex side. It seemed that we were all, players and public alike, expressing our relief and joy that we had survived those six years of bombs and bullets and, come hell or high water, we were all determined to enjoy ourselves.

Walter Robins was back as captain and he set the tone for the all-out action the team provided. Although he was then turned 40, this short, slightly bandy, terrier of a man was still one of the fastest and best cover fielders in the game. He also had the knack of getting runs when they were most needed and, although he had trouble with contracting tendon leads to his spinning fingers, his leg-breaks still got wickets. There was certainly nothing wrong with his shrewd tactical sense or the high-pitched voice that left nobody in doubt about who was in charge. He was a demanding but fair and brilliant leader.

Whether it was the fact that I had 'grown up' in those six years of war I don't know, but as a player I felt stronger and more sure of myself than ever before. The ball seemed to fly from the middle of my bat every time I went to the wicket.

With a Squadron Leader's rank behind him, and a DFC won for bravery in pressing home low-level attacks on the enemy as a highly skilled bomber pilot, it was the same for Bill Edrich. Jack Robertson and Syd Brown were also back with a new maturity.

With this new confidence I came up with nine centuries in over 2,000 County runs in that first summer of 1946. Bill and Jack hit five hundreds apiece. Jack and Syd gave us no fewer than six opening partnerships of over a hundred. It was small wonder that Robins never compromised on his most notable demand. Match after match, whenever we were batting first, he would announce to us all: 'I want 350 plus on the board by five o'clock. Anybody unable to keep the runs coming get out and let somebody in who can.'

Clearly he wanted to give his attack of the much improved Laurie Gray (95 wickets), Bill Edrich (68), Jim Sims (98) and slow left-armer Jack Young (101) time to get at the enemy in the last 90 minutes of the day. A breakthrough then and victory could be set up. He usually got his way.

Amazingly the snappy action in the dampness of 1946 was merely a prelude to the unbelievable fireworks of the sun-drenched Championship summer of 1947. Walter Robins still cracked the whip, we jumped through the hoops, and packed crowds made every day a cricket carnival.

We knew we were a good side and Robins never forgot to remind us of that fact. But he also hammered into us that there could be no let up. He demanded all-out effort from everybody all day and every day. And, somehow, we just couldn't go wrong.

Jack Robertson and Syd Brown gave us one record opening partnership of 310 (against Notts), two double century partnerships, and seven of a hundred or more.

Then, without boasting in any way, Bill and I destroyed every attack we met in one of the most remarkable batting sprees ever recorded. In Middlesex matches alone I put together 13 centuries, scored 2,468 runs and averaged 102.79. I hit five more hundreds against the South Africans and finished with a record season total of 3,816 runs, 18 hundreds, and an average of 90.85.

Bill also beat the existing records with 2,650 runs, 10 hundreds, and an average of 85.48 for Middlesex. And his all-match total was 3,539 at an average of 84.48. Jack Robertson's tally was 11 hundreds and a run aggregate of 2,328, and Syd Brown had four hundreds in a total of 1,990.

These were staggering performances. We all seemed to be seeing the cricket ball as big as a football. Basically, I was always a back foot player, but this was where I found a new delight in disturbing a bowler's rhythm by advancing three or four yards down the pitch to hit the ball to any part of the field I wanted. If he put his cover point straight I took a sadistic pleasure in angling the bat a bit open and hammering the next shot square.

And such was my luck, or clarity of sight, that on one occasion, when I slipped on my backside four yards down the track, I still managed to get the ball on to the middle of the bat and steer it down to fine leg for four. It was during the tea break in that same match that skipper Robins tauntingly brought up the great straight hitting of Albert Trott, the only man ever to clear the Lord's pavilion, and Frank Mann who once hit a ball so hard that it was still rising when it hit the top tier seats behind the bowler's arm.

'When you can play all those other fancy shots, why is it that a big fella like you doesn't seem to have the big straight hit in his locker?' he queried. I knew he was deliberately trying to needle me. So I merely said: 'Why bust a gut when I don't need to?'

But then, as I was going through the door for the restart, I found myself saying: 'Watch out for the third ball of the first over.' On the way to the wicket I thought Damn it, Robby has done me again. I'm committed. I've got to give it the treatment.' And when I saw most of the lads waiting on the balcony it became a sort of 'dare'.

So when the third ball came up I was out of the crease smartly. The bowler saw me coming and tried to pull the ball short. That suited me for I was well down, caught it beautifully on the up, and the ball smacked into the pavilion brick work just to the right of the dressing room. It wasn't quite an Albert Trott or Frank Mann shot but it was a pretty good answer to Robby who was roaring his head off, delighted that his needling had worked. I just waved my bat at him and got on with the job of hitting the ball where I wanted, rather than where he wanted.

But don't think that our staggering batting performances were the whole show that year. Far from it. That Championship was won by a massive team effort. We had bags of fun but Robins never relaxed his disciplines very far. If a daring declaration was called for he made it. If extra runs were needed then he and Alec Thompson, George Mann and my brother Leslie, who was then wicket-keeper-batsman, came up with them.

And, most important of all, although Bill and I seemed to grab most of the headlines, the men who pushed through for the victories we needed were the bowlers. Bill, often after a quick shower and rub down following a big innings, was then catapulting himself into action as a genuinely fast opening bowler. And he and Laurie Gray, with over 150 wickets between them, usually got the opposition openers. And that was when the spinners mopped up. Jack Young took 139 wickets. Jim Sims, defying his 44 years, rocked his way to 120 victims with his leg-breaks. And, believe it or not, I had 63 wickets with my mixture of left-arm googlies and anything else I could think of as I ran up to the wicket.

As final proof that Middlesex really were the team of the year, we took on 'The Rest' and beat them by nine wickets at the Oval with the Middlesex 'twins' Compton and Edrich making 246 and 180. I have often wondered if any other team of Champions has ever matched the figures, or the cricket, we presented in that astonishing year.

It seems to me that any side winning top place has to command five vital ingredients:

(1) Batting strength to get big runs quickly.
(2) Bowling with the variety to ensure the penetration needed to get through the opposition twice on any type of pitch.
(3) A captain with the personality to maintain strong discipline, high fielding standards, and the know-how to take sound tactical decisions.
(4) Reserve strengths to cover for star men called into the Test side.
(5) And, as important as anything else, a generous modicum of luck with the run of the ball.

Looking back over the 40 years since it all happened I suppose we were lucky enough to have the formula exactly right . . . right down to the last detail.

Amid all this sunshine and glory none of us had the remotest idea that the post-war period would see the whole cricket scene revolutionised. The very idea that a professional, Len Hutton, would be captaining England by 1952, that dear old Len would be knighted by 1956, and that the whole system of amateurs and professionals would be abolished by 1962, would have seemed like fantasy. So would the thought of us embracing wholesale one-day cricket as a regular fact of life, or of even thinking of Test Matches being sponsored for millions of pounds with every ball being televised in colour to millions every single day. Or of the Championship being sponsored for vast sums and players hurtling round the circuit in cars supplied by yet more sponsors.

The idea that we would see the first millionaire cricketer, or that a player's benefit would reach a tax-free £163,000 as Graham Gooch's did in 1986, would seem to be out of cloud-cuckoo land.

From even further out in space would have seemed the idea that an Australian millionaire called Kerry Packer would try to take over the whole game as cannon fodder for his TV stations. One might as well believe we would see a man playing a golf shot on the moon!

Yet these 'fantasies' were to become realities in a brave new world of hurry, hurry, money, money. Some of my friends tell me that I should not have been surprised by any of these things. For I was the one who started the whole sponsorship business in cricket.

They refer to those days between 1947 and 1949 when I was dubbed the 'Brylcreem

Boy' and had my face plastered across every advertising hoarding in the country. Today, I suppose, for that saturation exposure an agent would be asking, and getting, anything up to £250,000 a year for his client. Me? In my naivety, and the sheer joy of just playing the game, I had no idea what that sort of company publicity was worth. I got nearer £500.

As I was getting a national hero-sized post-bag of hundreds of letters a day I suppose I should have been very much smarter. Test players today collect more than that for simply turning up at a single sporting dinner.

But, as I say, in those heady days so close to the war, the Middlesex team were happy enough the way things were. In 1948, with Don Bradman over here with the best Australian side ever put together, and with George Mann taking over the County captaincy from Walter Robins, we again thought we were the best side on the circuit. But Test calls were heavy and we finished in third place in the Championship.

At the risk of over-doing my Editor's directions to 'personalise' this period, I should report that Bill and I hit one of the most violent purple patches of our long association in the Somerset game of that year. In straight figures we shared a record unbroken stand of 424 for the third wicket . . . all scored in just four hours. We saved the best of it for the 70 minutes after tea when we put on 209, of which I made 139. I don't think even Ian Botham has matched that sort of scoring. Not very often, anyway.

Jack Robertson, a superb opener who should have played for England far more often than he did, provided one of the high spots of 1949 when he hit a glorious 331 not out in a day against Worcestershire. At season's end we shared top place with Yorkshire.

That was the year John Warr came in to help our attack which still had Jack Young, and the incredible Jim Sims, then 46, claiming a hundred wickets apiece. But it was also the year when a great side began to creak. The following year the club started that 27-year span in the mid-table wilderness.

A quick check shows that between top places in 1949 and 1976 we roller-coasted from a best of two third places (in 1960 and 1961) to depths as low as 13th, 14th and even 16th. But we had four years in fifth place and five years in sixth. If you ask me why, I can only say that one, two or even three of the vital ingredients I mentioned earlier for any Championship-winning side were missing.

I know that from 1950 until I had to pack up in 1957 I was in and out of hospital far too often with surgeons digging bits of broken bone out of very painful places in my right knee. Those were black disruptive days, I can tell you. I was only in my thirties and my eyes and reflexes were so good that I thought I should be able to carry on, as Patsy Hendren did, until well into my forties. Yet every time the knife went in I wondered if I would ever play again. And when I did, and was back in the runs, I wondered how long the repair job would last.

I can't tell you how often I came off the field after a longish stint at the wicket to unstrap my pads and find the knee the size of a balloon. Yet Bill Tucker, and the physios, helped get it down and when I went out again to face the bowlers I seemed to be able to get into the right position and collect enough hundreds to keep my England place. It was when they whipped my knee cap off altogether that I had to call it a day.

The incredibly tough Bill had few physical problems but he went through quite an odd time as we came up to our big year in 1947. That was when he decided to change from a

Bill Edrich. He lived life to the full and played his cricket the same way.

professional to an amateur. I never thought he was wise to do it for it meant for one thing throwing away his benefit. But Bill was his own man. He had tasted a senior officer's life style in the war, had won his DFC, had the encouragement of a wife who had also reached Squadron Officer rank in the WAAF and had seen Wally Hammond turn amateur and get the England captaincy.

That, I am sure, was his great ambition. Well, later he captained Middlesex but he never got the big one. And the more is the pity, for no bigger-hearted cricketer ever drew breath and few men ever dared more for King and country. Certainly he merited the honour more than some who received it.

I am certain it was all a bitter disappointment. But Bill was never one to mope or whine. He lived life to the full. He just got stuck in, giving everything he had every time he stepped on to a cricket field. I saw him smashed in the ribs, cracked on the head, and bruised in all parts by the fastest bowlers in the business. But never once did I see him back away. The faster they came at him and the harder they hit him the more resolutely he got behind the line for his favourite hook shot. He was a great mate.

Mention of Bill sacrificing his benefit reminds me that I didn't have the best of experiences in that direction. I was awarded my benefit in 1949 and the public were kind enough to subscribe to the tune of £12,600, which was a substantial sum in those days. One of my City friends advised me to put it into the security of Marks and Spencer shares.

I thought that sound enough. But an item of club policy was that 'in the best interest of the player' a substantial proportion of any benefit money should be withheld and invested on his behalf, presumably by those who knew better, to give him security when his playing days were over. Too many old pros, they said, had simply taken their benefit cash and blown it.

So I was allowed to take £3,000 of my £12,600 and the balance was 'shrewdly' invested on my behalf. When I enquired of its progress, five years later, I was informed, with suitable regret of course, that my £9,600 was then worth exactly £1,500. I demanded that the £1,500 be handed over and, ever since, I have wondered just how much that £9,600 would have been worth today if it had been invested with 'Marks and Sparks'.

Getting back to that lean period for Middlesex, between 1949 and 1976, some of the uncertainties must have stemmed from the top with the captaincy rarely settled until Mike Brearley was lured back to the fold in 1971. In 1950 Walter Robins tried a holding operation at the ripe old age of 44. Then, for the next two years, Bill Edrich and I shared the job. Next came J. J. Warr for three years. Then Ian Bedford for two years. Then Colin Drybrough for two years. Then Fred Titmus. Then Peter Parfitt. Then Brearley. Overall, too many straws in the wind.

Even so, when you recall the constant procession of top-quality talent that flowed through the club in that time it is astonishing that we did not achieve more. On a rough count I reckon that about 20 of us were called upon to play in well over 200 Test Matches in that period.

The 117 Tests Bill and I shared were both before and during that time. I am thinking more of men like Fred Titmus, one of the greatest all-round talents in the history of the club, who played in 53 Tests, Peter Parfitt with 37, Mike Brearley, 39, and that splendid world-class wicket-keeper, J. T. Murray, 21.

Others who won their England places were Jack Robertson, at his best near Hutton's class as an opener, Eric Russell, Alan Moss, John Price, Mike Selvey, Clive Radley, Jack Young, J. J. Warr and George Mann.

There were so many others of high quality who played their hearts out year after year. Men like Don Bennett, whose middle name was 'Courage' and who is still doing fine work bringing on our younger players, Bob Gale, Ron Hooker, Harry Sharp, and so many more. Maybe the right mix never came together in those lean times.

I suppose the latest climb back for Middlesex must have started when Mike Brearley interrupted his academic career to return as captain in 1971. But even he took a full five years to get the formula right. In fact, when Parfitt left the club in 1972, after a season in which he played three Tests against Australia and topped the averages for the County, things looked very unpromising. Especially as Eric Russell, with a record of 25,000 runs, 41 hundreds and ten England caps, followed him through the door. So it was back to 13th place in 1973.

But with Mike Selvey and Phil Edmonds new elements in the attack and Brearley, Clive Radley, Mike Smith, Norman Featherstone and later Graham Barlow all getting runs, a winning look was developing. We were runners-up in both the Gillette and Benson & Hedges Cups in 1975.

In 1976 it all came together. Barlow had a tremendous year with the bat. Brearley and Smith both topped the 1,000, and Radley and Featherstone scored well. Selvey and Allan Jones were the strike bowlers with spinners Titmus (as ever), Edmonds and Featherstone superbly effective in support. With Brearley keeping discipline the 'mix' was right, and the Championship was back at last.

Not only that, the greatest run of success in the history of the Club was on its way. The arrival of Wayne Daniel, John Emburey and a young man called Mike Gatting produced a new powerhouse of talent that made further success almost inevitable.

So, with the perfect combination of solid batting, brilliant fielding, the strongest bowling balance of pace and spin in the country, the Club shared top place with Kent in 1977, and won the Championship outright again in 1980, 1982 and 1985. Add three Gillette/NatWest Trophies and two Benson & Hedges Cups and you have a decade of triumphs that will be hard to follow.

In the darker days I was frequently asked if I thought the modern youngsters were as good as we were. My answer was always that of course they were. I think the great players of yesteryear would be just as good if playing today—and vice versa.

Individuals will always shine through and be identified as heroes. But, as I said before, a successful *team* has to have the right mix of all the talents, held together and directed, and all producing their best at the same time. Middlesex has had such teams, and the latest triumphs demonstrate how splendidly the Club has adapted to the new, hectic, mix of one-day and three-day cricket demands. I look forward to more successes in the future.

MIDDLESEX AND THE WALKERS

OF THE ORIGINS OF THE COUNTY OF MIDDLESEX little is known. In early records, it is impossible to isolate, and it was generally regarded as a piece of sparsely inhabited country through which some important trackways ran. For the period of its existence, the County found difficulty in securing recognition. Most who lived within its boundaries called themselves Londoners rather than Middle Saxons, and even the name Middlesex itself was something of an afterthought, appearing for the first time some hundred years after the Saxon invasion began. The area could claim no royal dynasties, and in the Middle Ages, it could boast few baronial homes.

In his 20th-century version of the Domesday Book, Arthur Mee, the historian, could write: 'This small county on the edge of London has given birth to only a small number of people on our roll of fame, but it is a remarkable group of people who have found their last resting place in Middlesex.' Indeed it is a remarkable group of people, ranging as it does from Karl Marx to John Walter, the coal merchant who founded *The Times*; from W. S. Gilbert to Sir Stamford Raffles, the founder of the Regent's Park Zoo; and from Sir Henry Irving to Dr Barnado.

In the mid-17th century, Izaak Walton delighted in the country walks and the abundance and variety of birds to be found in Tottenham, Edmonton and Bruce Grove. Seventy-five years later, Daniel Defoe was complaining that the same areas were 'one continued street'.

London continued to spread so that, in 1888, the map was redrawn and parts of Middlesex became attached to the County of London. Middlesex had originally occupied that area north of the Thames bounded by the River Colne in the West and the River Lea in the East. It extended north as far as Uxbridge, Harrow, Hendon and Potters Bar. It never included the City of London within its domain. The Local Government Act of 1888 deprived Middlesex of those areas closest to London, like Westminster, Fulham and Islington, while the Local Government Act of 1972 decreed that Middlesex, the second smallest county in England, like Rutland, the smallest, should cease to exist.

A decade after it had disappeared from the map, Middlesex still excited contempt. Barry Norman, the television personality and fervent follower of Middlesex cricket, wrote of it as 'a sort of unscheduled disaster of a place, the only county in the land that consists entirely of suburbs'. He suggested that the name Middlesex produced in the mind's eye 'only an endless vista of Tescos' and that nobody could possibly feel any loyalty for Middlesex the geographical area. Yet that area has encompassed the greatest rugby ground, soccer ground and the cricket ground in the country, and in sport, at least, the name Middlesex conjured a sense of excitement and, for many, a spirit of loyalty and passion.

When the county was obliterated in 1972 the Committee of the County Cricket Club issued the statement that Middlesex would continue as a county cricket team. There was a defiant simplicity in the statement that echoes the strength and vision of men who, more than a hundred years earlier, had brought the Club into existence.

None can be sure when cricket was first played in Middlesex. The *Weekly Journal*, 12 January 1717, mentions that Mr Lambeth was the groundsman at the Angel Inn in Islington, and cricket was certainly played in Islington the following year, at the White Conduit Fields when Eleven London Gamesters met the Punch Club Society from Kent for half a guinea a man. The contest ended in dissension. The Londoners accused three of the men from Kent of running away before the match could be decided. The Punch Society insisted that the game had been brought to an end by pouring rain. A law suit ensued, and honour was satisfied when the match was replayed the following year, and the London Gamesters won.

The earlier part of the 18th century also provides records of matches played in Sunbury, Brentford, Acton, Ealing, Fulham and Hampton. In June 1730, there is the first record of a game involving Middlesex: 'A great cricket-match was played at Richmond Green between Surrey and Middlesex, which was won for the former.'

One must be wary of the county titles, for it is highly unlikely that either side was a truly representative one. It was customary at the time for elevens from a particular area within a county to adopt or have bestowed upon them the name of that county. The match at Richmond Green in 1730 was probably between men of Richmond and men of Brentford, an active cricket area at the time.

There was certainly no county association at the time, but the following year, Middlesex played Kent on Kennington Common a few days before Hampton met Brentford at Moulsey Hurst. Matches advertised as being between Middlesex and Surrey caused great interest over the next few years. In July 1733, 'A great cricket-match was played at Moulsey Hurst, in Surrey, between eleven Surrey men and eleven of Middlesex, which were hard matched. The Surrey men beat by only 3 notches; at which were present the Prince of Wales, accompanied by several persons of distinction, and his Royal Highness was pleased to order a guinea to be given to each man for their great dexterity, &c.'

Two years later, the Prince fielded his own side in a match at Moulsey Hurst and included three Middlesex men in his team. The others were from the London Club.

By 1740, cricket was being played on Uxbridge Common, and at this period, Cook of Brentford was considered to be one of the best cricketers in England. Middlesex now had the ascendancy over Surrey, and, on Monday, 9 June 1746, the *General London Evening Mercury* reported that: 'In the Artillery Ground, Middlesex beat Surrey by a considerable number of notches'. The Artillery Ground was at Finsbury, then in Middlesex. It was the first Mecca of cricket. It had been presented to the Honourable Artillery Company in 1638 and thrived in the middle of the 18th century when it was the home of the London Club, a dominant force in the game. The importance of the Club and of the Artillery Ground diminished as the century progressed. The Hambledon Club moved to a position of pre-eminence while the White Conduit Club, from its home in Islington fields, held a position of some supremacy in the London area.

Formed in 1782, the White Conduit Club was an offshoot of a West End Club called the *Je-ne-sais-quoi*. Members of this club frequented White Conduit House and played cricket matches in the adjoining Islington fields. They employed as bowler and general attendant Thomas Lord, a Yorkshireman who had arrived in Islington via Norfolk. His family were Roman Catholics and had been deprived of their lands following the rebellion in 1745.

The members of the White Conduit Club tired of playing at the Islington site and agreed to guarantee Thomas Lord against loss if he would set up a new private ground. Assured of support, Lord quickly got to work and opened the first of the three grounds that were to bear his name on what is now

Dorset Square. The *Daily Universal Register*, later to be known as *The Times*, announced the event on 29 May 1787:

> A Grand Match will be played on Thursday, 31st of May, 1787, in the new Cricket-ground, the New Road, Mary-le-bone, between nine gentlemen of the county of Essex, with two given men, against eight gentlemen of the county of Middlesex, with two gentlemen of Berkshire, and one of Kent, for One Hundred Guineas a side.
>
> The wickets to be pitched at ten o'clock, and the match to be played out.
>
> No dogs will be admitted.

'Given' men were guest players who were brought into sides to balance the odds when money was at stake. The two Berkshire gentlemen in the Middlesex side were G. Louch and G. Boult, both renowned cricketers of the time. Thomas Lord was also in the Middlesex side which won by 93 runs after trailing by 72 on the first innings. The match lasted for two days. The majority of the Essex side was from the Hornchurch club.

This was the first *county* match to be played on the first Lord's ground, but Middlesex had also participated in the first match to be played on the ground. This was on 21 May when they met the White Conduit Club for 500 guineas a side. There are notices of two other matches between Middlesex and the White Conduit Club, the acorn from which the MCC grew, in 1787, and when Middlesex, with two given men, won by eight wickets in mid-June they fielded six of the side that had beaten Essex. They also had a comfortable win in the return match with Essex at Hornchurch.

The earliest notice of a match involving MCC also occurs in 1787 when it was announced that the Marylebone Club would play Islington, most certainly Middlesex, at Lord's on 30 July.

Sides bearing the label 'Middlesex' featured in several important encounters over the next few years. In 1789, Middlesex met England at Lord's. 'The weather was so cold that Lord Winchilsea did not play, but took upon himself the unpleasant task of being umpire.' (*Middlesex Journal*)

Surrey were faced in the following year, and before the end of the century there were matches against Waltham Abbey and 22 of the Homerton and Whitehall Clubs. The Clubs' side lost 13 wickets in scoring the 90 runs that they needed to win.

Highgate, Kentish Town, Finchley, Whetstone and Uxbridge were all active cricketing areas by the end of the century, and a Middlesex side met MCC at Uxbridge in August 1790. Homerton was also a strong club, and, on occasions, had Lord Frederick Beauclerk and Nyren in their eleven. In 1804, the Islington Albion Club was formed. They played initially at White Conduit Fields, but, in 1834, moved to Copenhagen House, which was to be the first home of the Middlesex County Club. Islington Albion lasted well into the latter part of the 19th century and, for a time, was a powerful side, hiring leading players for its matches. There are two interesting items concerning its matches which have been gleaned by Buckley, the noted cricket historian. The first, which probably occurred during the middle part of the Club's existence, concerned a remarkable fielding performance. It was stated that a slip fielder caught all ten of his opponents, off the same bowler, standing at the same end. The second item is noted from a contemporary source in 1828: 'The appearance of the Albion fielding was such as delighted the vast concourse who had assembled, each gentleman dressed in white with light hats.' This was most certainly one of the earliest occasions of a cricket team adopting white for its dress.

Middlesex cricket offered other eccentricities. In September 1835, Eleven Single Women played Eleven Married Women at Parson's Green. The Single Women won by seven runs so earning themselves £20 and a hot supper.

But the world of cricket was in a state of radical change. In 1807 came the first mention of round-arm bowling. Two years later, Thomas Lord opened his second ground a few hundred yards to the west of Dorset Square. The original ground had been swallowed up by the property developers, and the second was to fall foul of an act of parliament which decreed that the Regent's Canal should pass through the centre of it. Lord obtained a lease on a parcel of land alongside St John's Wood Church, which was then being erected, and successfully moved his turfs from the two earlier grounds to the site where Lord's has remained ever since.

Eton and Harrow first met at Lord's in 1805, and the Gentlemen and Players the following year. The Varsity match was inaugurated in 1827, and six years later, Charles Cowden Clarke collected and edited John Nyren's *The Young Cricketer's Tutor* and his memories of the men of Hambledon, the first great classic in cricket literature.

In the wider world, changes were even more radical and were to affect the development of cricket as they were to affect all else. One of the greatest periods of artistic creativity in English history was allied to political reform and to a sense of national energy which was finding outlet in invention. The advent of the railways brought about the most significant changes in daily life, for man made a more sudden leap than before or since, and the face and mind of England were altered drastically in a very short space of time.

In his *Cricket Memories*, Edward Rutter talks of his days at Rugby School when the 'Old Rugbeian match was a pre-railroad fixture', but 'with railroads they soon began to bring two teams'. Rutter says:

> I should think that the decade between 1860 and 1870 saw a greater development in cricket than any other in its history. Local clubs were springing up in all directions. The two England Elevens, the *'All England'* and *'United'*, composed of the best professionals with the occasional inclusion of one or two crack amateurs, had helped by their matches against local 'twenty-twos' or 'eighteens', to carry a greater interest in the game into all parts of the country. The rivalry, too, between these famous combinations, which played one another annually in London or elsewhere, was a matter of interest to the public, which took very little in such county matches as there were, and gave furthest zest to their tours.

The All England XI had been organised by William Clarke, a Nottinghamshire bricklayer and a great slow bowler with a sharp business acumen, in 1846 and played until 1879 although it undertook fewer matches as the years passed. In 1852, John Wisden and Dean established the United All England XI in opposition to Clarke's side, and they lasted until 1869. These teams introduced to a wide public cricketers of the calibre of Felix, Caffyn, Daft, Parr, Mynn, Pilch, Lillywhite and Box, and they became famous throughout the land.

County cricket was in its infancy, and we turn to Rutter again for a comment on its early years:

> County cricket, as the term then implied, began in the fifties and early sixties. In the South the teams were mostly composed of amateurs with a stiffening of professionals. In Yorkshire, Stockton-on-Tees was an important centre of

the game. For a short time Cambridgeshire, almost all pros., turned out one of the strongest sides, and then collapsed for good into less than what would now be called a moderate second-class county. Nottinghamshire became a regular nursery for young cricketers. A small army of bowlers was reared there. After a few years there were so many that places could not be found for them in the county eleven. So, under the increasing demand all over England, they were absorbed by other districts under engagements with clubs and schools. County cricket was then in its infancy. It had no rules to guide it, and the consequence was that regulations were very lax. A player, after representing one county, might in the next match be found playing against it for another! No questions were asked. The public was not sufficiently interested, for these matches attracted comparatively few spectators, though much of the best talent in England was engaged. The Press had not as yet excited people to study records and averages.

The seeds had been sown, however, for the telegraph score-board had been introduced at Lord's in 1846, and score-cards were sold for the first time that season. By the mid-19th century, there were county cricket organisations in Northamptonshire, Hampshire, Kent, Leicestershire, Surrey, Sussex, Warwickshire, Worcestershire and Nottinghamshire who, in 1853, were recognised as the Champion County.

Rutter was quoted earlier as noting that 'local clubs were springing up in all directions' in the 1860s, but one that had sprung up before then was the Southgate Club, which was founded in 1855. Cricket had been played at Southgate before that time by the Southgate Albert Club, and they were assisted on occasions by members of the Walker family, but it was John Walker who decided 'to make a proper cricket ground' and 'to beat and roll it' so that it became 'a perfect ground for fieldsmen, as it never becomes iron-bound in the hottest weather, and one's poor feet found it a haven of rest after the cracked and baked ground at Lord's'. The speaker is Vyell Edward Walker, the fifth of seven brothers known with affection as the Walkers of Southgate.

The eldest of the brothers, John, was born in 1826. Alfred was born a year later, and Frederic in 1829. Arthur Henry was born in 1833, Vyell Edward in 1837, Russell Donnithorne in 1842, and Isaac Donnithorne in 1844. All were fine

Vyell Edward Walker. 'The best all-round cricketer in the world' and a captain second to none.

cricketers, and all of them played for Middlesex. None of them married, although their five sisters all did. They inherited from their father the house Arnos Grove, adjacent to the Walker ground at Southgate, and it became one of the most celebrated of gathering places for cricketers in the whole of England.

John Walker was master in the house until his death in 1885 when, briefly, it passed to Frederic before Vyell Edward controlled it from 1889 until his death in 1906. The last surviving brother was Russell Donnithorne who died in 1922.

27

Arnos Grove was noted as one of the most splendid houses in Middlesex. It was a 'noble residence' designed in the 17th century by Sir John Weld and boasting the best stairway in Middlesex, painted in 1723 by Lancroon. It backed onto the New River, and Rutter, a frequent visitor, recalled it with affection in 1925:

> The house was a spacious one with a great hall surmounted by a beautifully painted ceiling, the work of an Italian artist. The gardens were extensive and the grounds and park covered three hundred acres or more. Moreover, the old course of the New River formed a lake within them, and before the houses were built around as Southgate became more or less a suburb, thirty brace of pheasants, besides crowds of rabbits, made quite a good day's sport. The pride of Arnos Grove was the great oak tree. It was immense and covered more space than any other in a district where great oaks were plentiful. It was known as the Chandos Oak, and very particular care was taken of it.

Within his grounds John Walker laid down his cricket field, emphasising, as his brother noted, the quality of the outfield, for John Walker was most vehement about the importance of fielding. The ground remains the home of Southgate Cricket Club, and the nearby inn is called now as it was in John Walker's day, *The Cherry Tree*. Arnos Grove itself passed from the Walker family, whose home it was for 130 years, and into the possession of the Electricity Board who renamed it Northmet House. It still stands on Cannon Hill, outwardly a neo-Georgian block of offices and now owned by the Legal and General Assurance Society.

The Walkers' wealth had come from their famous brewery, and when John died he left £463,502. Vyell's fortune was even greater, and one cannot imagine that any cricketer left more than the £1,598,177 he left in 1906. Like all his brothers, John Walker played cricket because he loved the game passionately, and he played it in a way that had no hint of selfishness about it. Like Alfred and Frederic, he went to Cambridge University. Before the formation of the Middlesex Club he played for Cambridgeshire, Bedfordshire and Surrey Club and Ground. For a time he served on the Surrey committee. He was tall and broad, an excellent wicket-keeper and a slow round-arm or under-arm bowler. He was a powerful batsman, a straight hitter of the ball and strong on the off side. W. G. Grace met him first at The Oval in 1864 when he was playing for Surrey against South Wales:

> I can remember now the impression his tall, strongly built figure made upon me as I watched him make his 44 by vigorous hitting. He was then in his 38th year. My brothers Henry and E.M. had often talked to me about the family reputation, and I was pleased when he hit our bowling all over the field, as I desired to see him score.

John Walker was an outstanding captain although he had the reputation for being rather a martinet on the field. He spent much money establishing the ground at Southgate in order to encourage cricket in the village. As professional, he engaged George Hearne who, with his elder brother Tom, was to be first of the Middlesex–Hearne connection, although both, in fact, were born in Buckinghamshire.

For the first three seasons, the matches played by Southgate were mostly against local teams. The first season saw them play and win seven matches. Five were against minor sides, but there was a victory over a Hertfordshire side that included Robert and Edward Grimston and Hughes, the noted bowler. At the end of the season, at the urgent request of Alfred Mynn, Southgate travelled to Maidstone and beat Mynn's side by four wickets. There were five Walkers in the Southgate side. Maidstone were beaten by an innings a year later, and there was also an innings victory over the Surrey Club and Ground side.

It was at the end of the 1858 season that John Walker arranged the first of the Southgate matches with the United All England XI. The game was played on 23, 24 and 25 August, and it was splendid festive occasion which attracted large crowds. Rutter, who played in the last of the great matches at Southgate, against the United South in 1868, estimated that the crowd on that occasion was in excess of 10,000, so there is no reason to believe that it was much less in 1858 when the event was a great novelty.

Having broadened the Southgate fixture list with the match against the United All England XI in 1858, John Walker took another significant step the following season. Middlesex had no ground, no organisation and no matches, but John Walker was unwilling to see the county remain idle, and, at this own expense, arranged home and away fixtures with Kent. The first match was played at Southgate on 16 and 17 June, and Middlesex won by 78 runs.

There were five Walkers in the Middlesex side, but they were supplemented by Tom Hearne, George Wells, John Wisden and John Lillywhite. Wisden was a Sussex man, but he was imported to play for Middlesex on three occasions, and like Lillywhite, another Sussex man, who played six times for Middlesex, he played for almost anybody on the basis of a professional engagement.

Wisden took four for 14 as Kent were bowled out for 47 in their second innings, but Vyell Edward Walker was the star of the match, taking six for 31 in that second innings. The local press was ecstatic about V.E.'s bowling performance, noting that he had 'a peculiar style of his own' and that he lured batsmen forward so that they were stumped by brother John.

Vyell Walker was then at the height of his powers, and *Lillywhite's Guide to Cricketers* described him as 'the best all-round cricketer in the world'. His record justified such a description. He was an outstanding captain with a thorough knowledge of the game, and he was calm and encouraging to his players. He bowled his lobs round the wicket because he knocked his knuckles on the stumps when he bowled over the wicket. He varied his pace considerably and had a dynamic follow through which made him an exceptional fielder to his own bowling. He first played for the Gentlemen against the Players in 1856 when he was 19 years old, but his greatest achievement came in 1859. Playing for England against Surrey at The Oval, he scored 108 and took all ten wickets in an innings, 10 for 74, so becoming the first cricketer ever to take all ten wickets and hit a century in the same match.

The Middlesex side beat Kent at Canterbury in the return match in 1859 with Vyell Walker again taking the chief bowling honours. This time he shared them with Wells, whom Rutter identifies as Joe Wells, the Kent professional and father of the novelist H. G. Wells, but it is more probable that the bowler in question was the professional George Wells, who had played, and bowled, in the first match at Southgate.

In 1860, Middlesex county cricket remained dormant although the standard of cricket at Southgate remained high, and all the great players of the age appeared there. The old Southgate club played until 1877 and, in its 22 years existence, won 133 of the 192 matches in which it competed, losing only 27.

The Middlesex matches were intermittent. A County side had played Surrey and MCC in the 1850s, but fixtures lapsed for want of organisation, and in 1861, the only game undertaken by the County was against MCC at Lord's for the benefit of Royston. John Walker led the side, although William Nicholson kept wicket. Nicholson was a politician who played five matches for Middlesex, but his greatest gesture to cricket was in giving financial support to Lord's in 1866, so saving it from the builders.

Middlesex beat MCC by 198 runs. Vyell Walker and Charles Lawrence bowled unchanged for the County. Lawrence was a professional, born in Middlesex, but this was his only match for the County. He went to Australia with Stephenson's side a few months later and remained there as a coach. Arthur Daniel hit 87, sharing a fourth wicket stand of 131 with Lawrence, who made 78, but the highlight of the Middlesex innings was Arthur Walker's 75 not out which included a hit onto the roof of the tennis court off the bowling of Rogers. Arthur Walker's career was to be brief, for he suffered a badly broken leg while playing football in the winter of 1862, and this virtually ended his cricket career.

MCC gained revenge with a narrow victory the following year when Middlesex also lost to Surrey at The Oval by 12 runs. Middlesex were set to make 383 to win, a phenomenal score in those days, and their second innings was opened by Russell and Isaac Walker. They put on 109, and Isaac went on to score 102, the first indication we have of a century by a Middlesex player in a county match, albeit before the formation of the Club.

I. D. Walker was the youngest and for many, the most talented, of the brothers. He was at Harrow, but the death of his mother had prevented him from going on to Cambridge. He was sound in defence, played straight and was a powerful hitter of the ball. W. G. Grace considered him 'one of the finest amateur batsmen I ever played with or against', and Bettesworth, the Walkers' biographer, said that 'he played such beautiful cricket that connoisseurs were charmed by it'. He shared one idiosyncracy with his brother Russell in that he was reluctant to wear pads. Russell had worn pads and gloves at Harrow, for one could not win a place in the side without them, but having made the side, he discarded them, for there was also a ruling that once in the team one was not left out. I.D. wore pads only when confronted by the fastest of bowlers like George Freeman of Yorkshire.

MCC and Surrey were the only opponents in 1863, but the days of tentative fixtures were nearing an end. Conscious of the developments taking place in the world of cricket, John Walker felt that it was time that Middlesex cricket should be placed on a sound basis and a County Club be formed. There were enormous difficulties, not least of which was the acquisition of a ground, but John Walker roused enthusiasm and mainly through his efforts, the County Club became an actuality.

A saviour of Lord's and an early Middlesex administrator—William Nicholson.

On the afternoon of Tuesday, 17 November 1863, John and Vyell Walker, Charles Gordon, closely associated with the famous Clapton Club, Charles Hillyard and William Nicholson met with Norris, the owner of a ground in Copenhagen Fields, near the Cattle Market in Islington. The professionals Fred and James Lillywhite were also on the ground in Islington, no doubt to tender advice if required.

On the Thursday of the following week, the same party met again at the Norris Ground, and Charles Hillyard, appointed Honorary Secretary *pro tem*, was asked to send a notice to sporting papers and others expressing the sentiment that, as 'a feeling has long existed that a Middlesex County Club should be established', a meeting would be held on Tuesday, 15 December 1863 at the London Tavern in Bishopsgate.

The Hon Robert Grimston was unanimously called to the chair at that meeting which decided that:

First. That no County Club be formed for Middlesex until at least 100 persons have promised to join it.

Secondly. That a further meeting be called as soon as the requisite number of names have been forwarded to Mr Hillyard.

A provisional committee was set up and met at the London Tavern a week later. Hillyard had received 50 names and the other members of the committee present added other names which brought the total to 103. Hillyard was asked to write to Norris and also to send a circular letter to the chief newspapers and influential people of the county:

'Middlesex County Cricket Club
Sir, – Middlesex being the only cricketing county in England that has no County Club, and a general desire having been expressed that such a Club should be established, a meeting was held at the London Tavern on December 15, and a Provisional Committee was formed for the purpose of considering the matter and endeavouring to ascertain the amount of support with which such a movement would be likely to be received.

The Provisional Committee are happy to be able to report that upwards of one hundred gentlemen have already signified their intention of joining the Club; and they hereby give notice that a GENERAL MEETING will be held at the London Tavern on Tuesday, the second day of February, 1864, at half-past four o'clock, when all those interested in the proposed movement, and especially the officers and secretaries of the Metropolitan Clubs, are earnestly requested to attend.

To render such an undertaking successful, it is necessary that it should receive general support throughout the County. Should you be inclined to give your aid and co-operation, you are requested, if unable to attend the meeting, to communicate with any of the Provisional Committee, or with Mr Hillyard, the Honorary Secretary, at the London Tavern, Bishopsgate Street, E.C.

The optimistic tone of this letter was in defiance of the tone of the meeting on 15 December when the enthusiasts asserted that the Club would be 'launched on a sea of public fervour, where, let us hope, despite all ill feeling displayed against it in certain quarters, it will successfully weather every storm and float triumphantly on the waves of prosperous popularity'.

It was emphasised that the club would not be set up in opposition to Surrey, that they would fix matches which clashed with no other clubs, and that, in any case, their venture had the blessing of the Surrey Club. This was true for Burrup, the Surrey Secretary, attended the meeting on 2 February 1864, and gave vocal support to the new club.

The provisional committee received a reply to their letter to Thomas Norris on 12 January. The proprietor of the Lamb Inn, New Cattle Market, Islington, offered to keep the ground in order and do all that was necessary for £250 per annum, or, for £150, he would let the ground to the Club who would then have to maintain it themselves. A third proposition, and the one which was accepted for financial reasons, was that the Club should pay £100 for which they would have exclusive use of the centre of the ground for matches and the whole of the upper part for practice while Norris was at liberty to play one or two public matches during the season when convenient to the County Club.

Two days before the General Meeting at the beginning of February, the Club received an offer from the Alexandra Park Company's general manager, John C. Deane, that they could have use of the cricket ground at Alexandra Park. This was turned down because it was felt that centring the County Club at Alexandra Park would make it too parochial. When one considers that the stated object of the new club was 'to get together the best players they could, both amateur and professional, from all parts of the county, and to make the Club as advantageous to men residing in distant parts of the county as to those in the metropolitan districts' this comes as something of a surprise.

The meeting on Tuesday, 2 February 1864, was well attended. The provisional committee was most warmly thanked, rules were drawn up and a committee elected. All items were carried unanimously in a state of euphoria. It was noted that Mr Hull of Uxbridge was present, and he was implored to bring other Uxbridgeans with him to a ground than which there was none better north of the Thames. Mr Beck proposed, and Mr V. E. Walker seconded: 'That this Club be now declared established under the name of Middlesex County Cricket Club'. The motion was carried unanimously. There was loud cheering.

Middlesex County Cricket Club had come into being.

IN SEARCH OF A HOME

THE YEAR OF 1864 WAS A SIGNIFICANT ONE in the history of the world. It was the year when the First Socialist International was formed, when the Federal Army entered Atlanta and General Sherman captured Savannah. It was the year in which Dickens began to publish *Our Mutual Friend*. It was also the year in which the Geneva Convention originated and in which, on 10 June, over-arm bowling was legalised. It was the first year of John Wisden's *Cricketers' Almanack,* and it was the year when, four days before his 16th birthday, W. G. Grace appeared in big cricket for the first time, scoring 170 and 56 not out for the South Wales Club against the Gentlemen of Sussex.

It was the year from which many would date the first County Championship, although the competition was, as yet, not organised and was more in the minds of the press than in the hands of administrators. The method for deciding the Champion County was simple: the number of matches lost being deducted from the number of matches won. Surrey were deemed to be the first Champions. They won four and drew two of their six county matches. Middlesex beat Hampshire twice and Sussex at home while losing to Sussex in the return match.

Eight matches were arranged for the inaugural season, beginning with the game between 14 colts and 11 gentlemen. Isaac Walker was top scorer in this first match on the Islington ground and, by coincidence, he was to be top scorer in the last match that was to be played there four years later.

A challenge from Hampshire to play home and away fixtures was accepted, but Frank Glover's challenge to meet Lancashire was declined. Middlesex trod softly in their first season with games against Buckinghamshire, Incogniti and Marlborough College as well as against MCC and Sussex, but it should be remembered that, although it was hoped to gather together the best cricketers in the County, the initial purpose of the Club was to provide practice facilities for members. The professional bowlers who were engaged, Frank Silcock, Catling, Ian Hill, George Hearne and Caldecourt, were to aid members in practice, not to strengthen the playing side of the County Club.

It was quickly apparent that the ground at Islington, although highly satisfactory in many ways, was in desperate need of a pavilion and, inevitably, it was John Walker who undertook the task of having a pavilion erected at a cost not to exceed £200.

The Islington ground has long since disappeared, a victim of the ever-advancing builder, but Thomas Case left us a vivid description of Middlesex's first home:

> It was an irregularly shaped triangle, wedged in between the market and the Great Northern Railway. At the main entrance, in the south-west corner, stood the inevitable public-house, from which, walking along the south wall, you came to the pavilion, which was in the middle of the south side, with its back to the market and its front to the side of the wicket. As you walked from the pavilion to the wicket, the railway going northwards ran on the right, but gradually cutting off more and more of the space, until at last in the far distance the ground terminated in a very acute angle, which nobody ever visited. From the pavilion to the wicket was downhill, so that the ground was on a slope, as at Lord's. Notwithstanding its somewhat unprepossessing appearance it was really a good ground, and with a better light than either Lord's or The Oval. Something like a brick foundation at times ominously showed itself at the surface, but what turf there was was good and well kept, the wicket was even, and there was a life in the ground which favoured quick scoring and fast bowling.

The second match to take place on the ground was the first eleven against the next sixteen, but the first occasion when the County put a side into the field was at Newport Pagnell on 2 and 3 June. Buckinghamshire were the opponents, and Middlesex had the better of a draw. There is some vagary about this match which did not have first-class status and in which George Hearne played for the county of his birth against the county which employed him.

The Middlesex umpire for several years was Robert Thoms, a keen follower of the game in general and of Middlesex cricket in particular. He recalled the strange beginning to the match at Newport Pagnall:

> My brother umpire was Harry Royston. On arriving on the ground – an open common – we found that there was no frame or any other article to mark out the creases with. In this dilemma I asked one of the attendants to go and fetch a piece of wood seven feet long from some carpenter

or another. Off he went, and back he came with a *coffin lid*. However, with that and the aid of the tape we marked out the dimensions, got over the difficulty, and put matters shipshape.

Robert Thoms. A keen follower of the game and of Middlesex in particular. He was the County's first umpire. He stood as umpire at every match played on the Cattle Market Ground at Islington and was one of the umpires in the first Test match played in England, 1880.

The first-class career of the new Middlesex County Cricket Club began three days later at the Cattle Market Ground when Sussex, who were to become the traditional bank holiday opponents, were beaten by an innings. As Sussex had drawn with the mighty Surrey side a week earlier and were to beat Kent by an innings a fortnight later, this was a splendid victory on the part of Middlesex.

Middlesex scored consistently to reach 261, and Sussex were 91 for six at the end of the first day. Sussex lost the services of Stubberfield, for he became unwell at dinner time on the first day, and he was replaced by G. F. Browne. One uses the term 'dinner', for the break was generally taken at two or three pm, and the gentlemen often left the ground to eat somewhat more heartily than is the custom today.

The Middlesex side was led by Vyell Walker, who shared the captaincy with his elder brother John for the first two seasons and then led the side on his own until 1872. In the opinion of umpire Thoms, he was 'the most prominent of captains'. He had a 'consummate judgment in changing his bowlers and shifting his fields, and that with a suavity of manner that made everybody feel well pleased with himself'. Thoms placed him above Grace, Harris, Hawke, Parr, Hornby, Murdoch and Woods as a captain, and Thoms saw all of them in action many times.

Vyell Edward Walker was a most dynamic cricketer and produced one of the outstanding performances in Middlesex cricket history in that first County game at Islington (see scorecard overleaf). When he bowled Thomas to end the Sussex first innings he was overwhelmed by the congratulations of his side who believed that he had taken all ten wickets. Indeed, some carried this belief with them for many years ahead, but Vyell Walker was deprived of the feat by a technicality. Payne had been beaten by a ball which had rebounded from Pooley's pads and broken the wicket with the batsman out of his ground. As Payne had touched the ball on its way to the keeper, he was deemed to be run out rather than stumped and so V. E. Walker finished with nine for 62. A month later, playing for the Gentlemen of Middlesex against the Gentlemen of Kent at Maidstone, he took ten for 37 and five for 50 and was top scorer in the match with 46. He was a truly remarkable cricketer. He spun his lobs from leg quite viciously, varied his pace considerably and was tigerish in the field.

MIDDLESEX *v* SUSSEX

Played at the New Middlesex Ground, Islington, 6 and 7 June 1864

MIDDLESEX WON BY AN INNINGS AND 52 RUNS

MIDDLESEX	FIRST INNINGS	
E. W. Tritton	c Ellis b Fillery	10
T. Case	b Fillery	30
G. Wells	c Payne b James Lillywhite	1
T. Hearne	c John Lillywhite b James Lillywhite	50
B. B. Cooper	run out	50
R. D. Walker	c James Lillywhite b Southerton	23
J. J. Sewell	b James Lillywhite	35
V. E. Walker	b James Lillywhite	14
E. Pooley	c James Lillywhite b Fillery	21
W. Catling	c sub (Wells) b Ellis	13
G. Hearne	not out	1
	b 6, lb 6, nb 1	13
Total		261

BOWLING	O	M	R	W
James Lillywhite	59	18	123	4
Fillery	34	12	58	3
Smith	5	2	9	0
Ellis	16.2	0	44	1
Southerton	3	0	15	1

Fall: 1-20, 2-25, 3-59, 4-116, 5-158, 6-194, 7-216, 8-235, 9-251

SUSSEX	FIRST INNINGS			SECOND INNINGS	
C. H. Smith	c Cooper b V. Walker	11	(3)	b V. Walker	11
John Lillywhite	c Cooper b V. Walker	3	(6)	b T. Hearne	0
C. Payne	run out	28	(4)	b T. Hearne	17
C. H. Ellis	st Pooley b V. Walker	4	(5)	b V. Walker	5
T. A. Raynes	c Cooper b V. Walker	13	(9)	b T. Hearne	15
Jas Lillywhite jun	c Tritton b V. Walker	19	(8)	b T. Hearne	14
G. F. Browne	st Pooley b V. Walker	11	(7)	c R. Walker b V. Walker	0
R. Fillery	c Pooley b V. Walker	8	(10)	not out	16
J. Southerton	b V. Walker	0	(11)	c Pooley b T. Hearne	0
James Dean jun	not out	6	(1)	c G. Hearne b V. Walker	14
F. F. Thomas	b V. Walker	2	(2)	st Pooley b V. Walker	0
	b 1, lb 4, w 1	6		b 3, lb 3	6
		111			98

BOWLING	O	M	R	W	O	M	R	W
T. Hearne	41	25	42	0	36	18	44	5
V. E. Walker	40	18	63	9	35	13	48	5

1st inns: 1-12, 2-17, 3-22, 4-44, 5-78, 6-91, 7-100, 8-102, 9-110
2nd inns: 1-0, 2-18, 3-31, 4-38, 5-39, 6-42, 7-56, 8-68, 9-97

Umpires: James Dean and R. Thoms.

Russell was the only other of the Walker brothers to play in that famous first inter-county match at Islington. There were four other amateurs in the side, a surprisingly low number for a County who were to field predominantly amateur sides for most of their matches in the earlier part of their history.

Opening batsman Edward William Tritton was a very talented athlete at both Eton and Oxford. He played in a non-first-class game for Surrey in 1864, his first year at Oxford, and his six matches for Middlesex were all during his years at university. He came down in 1867 after which he disappeared from first-class cricket. His opening partner, Thomas Case, was another Oxford man who appeared a dozen times for Middlesex between 1864 and 1868. He was kept out of the Varsity match of 1866 because of a hand injury sustained at Southgate two days before the match with Cambridge. A batsman of very high quality, he was one of Middlesex's first centurions.

The County met MCC at Lord's on 25 and 26 July 1864, and were bowled out for 20 and 154. The MCC won by five wickets and came to the Islington ground at the beginning of August confident of winning the return match, but Grundy and Wootton, the bowlers who had done the damage at Lord's, found the Cattle Market pitch less to their liking. They quickly got rid of R. D. Walker, Frederick and Pooley, but Tom Hearne hit 125 and Tom Case hit 116. Middlesex scored 411 and won by an innings and 232 runs.

Case gave up first-class cricket at the age of 24 in order to concentrate on an academic career. He became Professor of Moral Philosophy at Oxford and was President of Corpus Christi College. He occasionally wrote on cricket, and his comments and descriptions are a valuable source with regard to the early history of the Middlesex Club.

John Joseph Sewell's nine matches for the County were spread over four seasons, but it is difficult to see what qualification he had to play for Middlesex. He was born in

Cirencester and at Marlborough he was recognised as one of the most brilliant batsmen of his day. He appeared for Wiltshire and for Norfolk, and his life would suggest that he was ever a wanderer. In 1866, against Surrey at The Oval, he played an exhilarating innings of 166, the first innings of 150 or more in the County's history, but the following year he emigrated to South Africa where he died in 1897. His son Cyril came to England with the South African side in 1894 and remained to become secretary and captain of Gloucestershire shortly before the First World War.

The remaining amateur, Bransby Beauchamp Cooper, was also to leave England and settle abroad. Born in India, he was educated at Rugby where he was an outstanding cricketer. He played for Middlesex from 1863 to 1867 before moving to Kent for whom he played for two seasons. An exciting right-handed batsman and occasional wicket-keeper, he scored consistently for Middlesex without ever matching his achievements at representative level. He and W. G. Grace were primarily responsible for the Gentlemen beating the Players at Lord's in 1865, the amateurs' first triumph for 12 years, and in 1869, at The Oval, Cooper hit 103 for the Gentlemen of the South against the Players of the South as he and Grace put on 283 for the first wicket in three hours forty minutes. This established a first-wicket record which was to stand for 23 years.

Cooper moved to the United States in 1870 and played some cricket there before going on to Australia where he represented Victoria for several seasons. He appeared for Australia in the first Test match in March 1877, so that Middlesex may claim him, somewhat tenuously, as their first Test cricketer.

Of the professionals, George Wells, although born in Whitechapel, played mostly for Sussex. In 1864, he played for Middlesex in the game at Islington and for Sussex in the match at Hove so that he was on the winning side both times. One of the smallest men in cricket, he was nicknamed 'Tiny' and was a useful batsman and a bowler of medium pace round-arm and slow under-arm.

The second of the professionals, William Catling, was not of the top flight and was engaged by Middlesex in the first two years of their existence.

Edward Pooley should have played for England against Australia in the first Test match, but he had been detained by the authorities in New Zealand. His struggle with life was never as successful as his struggle to become a first-class cricketer. Born in 1838, he lied about his age for fear that Surrey would consider him to be too old. He played for Surrey Colts in 1861 and was engaged as a bowler at The Oval the following year, for, as yet, the world had no sense of his prowess as a wicket-keeper. His regular connection with the Surrey Club did not begin until 1865 and a year later he established a reputation as one of the greatest wicket-keepers that the game has known. He had already hinted at his capabilities in seven matches for Middlesex in which he had taken seven catches and made seven stumpings. He was to remain a member of the Surrey XI, unsurpassed at taking slow bowling, until 1883. His end was sad. His human fallibilities condemned him to poverty and the shelter of the workhouse.

The 'father' of Middlesex professionals, Tom Hearne. (Courtesy of Allsport)

The Hearne brothers, George and Tom, were born in Chalfont St Peter. Tom was the elder by three years, but he was to play for Middlesex until 1875 when he was 49. A medium-pace bowler, a fine batsman and a good fielder, he was one of the best all-rounders of his day. It was he who first reached a century for Middlesex, and his career was terminated only when he suffered a stroke of paralysis. He made a remarkable recovery, however, and for more than 20 years, until 1897, he was head of the ground staff at Lord's, inculcating into his charges the qualities that made him the epitome of all that was good in the Victorian professional cricketer – honesty, industry, loyalty and dedication to the game. He was a regular member of the United All England XI before the formation of the Middlesex County Club so that he came to the County as a mature and experienced cricketer, and he was to be the backbone of the side for a decade. His quality and his fame were assured by an innings of 122 not out for the Players against the Gentlemen at Lord's in 1866.

George Hearne had begun his association with Middlesex with the Walkers at Southgate, and, ever mindful of the financial necessities of life, he acted as groundsman at Islington because he felt that the job of Club bowler left him in 'want of employment and remuneration during the winter season'. This concern for his financial security caused him to leave Middlesex at the end of the 1868 season to become groundsman at the Private Banks Ground at Catford Bridge.

His move to Kent was a great loss to Middlesex, for the Walkers had long had their eyes on his son, 'Young George', a very talented cricketer. He had been born in Ealing so was qualified to play for the County, but Lord Harris invited him to play for Kent Colts after his father had moved to Dartford. When Vyell Walker later asked the youngster to play for Middlesex Lord Harris replied that, as he had played for Kent Colts, George Gibbons Hearne was now a Kent player, a view not consistent with his lordship's later legislations, particularly as there was no documentary evidence of any professional engagement.

Five professionals was the most that Middlesex fielded in any game in that first, highly successful season. The nucleus of the Club was essentially amateur, and this was by necessity as well as by choice, for, however well Middlesex had performed on the field, the Club's financial affairs gave cause for some unease.

There was a healthy balance of £113 17s 6d plus arrears of subscriptions to be collected, but Norris was not happy. He had lost money on the season and wanted £150. The pavilion had cost £278 and a fund was organised to pay off the debt and the interest. Norris then raised the rent for 1865 by £50.

Tempered by these economic considerations, the Club chose not to increase its number of county matches in its second season although the opposition selected was stronger. Challenges were accepted from Lancashire and Surrey, and two matches were also arranged with Hampshire. The first, at Islington, was won by an innings, but the return match was not played as the date clashed with the Eton and Harrow match which 'everyone was anxious to see'. Middlesex could not raise a side, and, with some justification, Hampshire complained of a cancellation 'on such frivolous grounds'.

There was defeat at Old Trafford in the first meeting with the Red Rose county even though Middlesex, most unusually, fielded six professionals. Among them was George Howitt, a very good left-arm fast bowler for whom his native county, Nottinghamshire, were able to find no regular place. Howitt, however, made no mark in the game against Lancashire, his first for Middlesex, for again the honours went to Vyell Walker, even in defeat.

He did not bowl on the first day when Lancashire were out for 243. Middlesex were 83 for two at the close with Russell Walker on 37. Next day he took his score to 84, but there was a late middle-order collapse and only a spirited last wicket stand between Howitt and J. H. Morley, who was wicket-keeper in this, his one and only match for Middlesex, brought the first-innings scores level.

In their second innings, Lancashire were bowled out for 178, the incomparable Vyell Edward Walker taking all ten wickets for 104 runs in 44.2 overs, five of which were maidens. His record was to stand until 1888 when George Burton, a round-arm slow bowler, took all ten Surrey wickets at The Oval.

The match against Surrey at The Oval in 1865 produced its heroes too. It was played five days after the game at Old Trafford, and Middlesex won by 158 runs. It was, according to Haygarth, 'a glorious and unexpected victory for Middlesex (the new county) over the crack county'. I. D. Walker hit a ball from Stephenson out of The Oval, and Charles Francis Buller made a brilliant 105 not out in the second innings.

Buller was another fine all-round athlete. Educated at Harrow, he was recognised as one of the finest, and certainly one of the most stylish and handsome, batsmen of his generation. He followed a military career, but he was to appear at irregular intervals for a decade.

Arthur Daniel was another fine amateur batsman who had been at both Harrow and Cambridge, but his career ended in 1869 and four years later, at the age of 31, he was dead of consumption.

The victory over Surrey at The Oval and the draw in the return match at Islington, in which, in spite of a century from Jupp, Middlesex held the upper hand, had brought the new County Club to the forefront. They entered a bolder programme of eight matches in 1866 with confidence high. There were still mumbles of discontent from, and about, Norris, but the financial position had improved. Viscount Enfield had become President of the Club and Vyell Walker had become Club captain as well as joint Secretary with Hillyard. Matches were arranged with Cambridgeshire, Nottinghamshire, Lancashire and Surrey, and the only defeat suffered came in the first match of the season when George Tarrant and Thomas Hayward bowled Cambridgeshire to an innings victory at Islington.

A fortnight later Middlesex humbled the mighty Notts side at Trent Bridge. Middlesex won the toss and batted first, but they lost three for 46. Russell Walker then played an accomplished innings of 90, Vyell hit 58, and Middlesex reached 221. Tom Hearne and Russell Walker bowled unchanged as Notts were dismissed for 88 and 66, Hearne finishing with 12 for 76 and Russell Walker eight for 73.

Although behind on the first innings, Middlesex, thanks to Hearne, fresh from his triumph for the Players, rallied to beat Lancashire at Old Trafford, and just over a week later completed the double over the northern county.

Surrey were the next visitors to the Cattle Market Ground. They were not enjoying the best of seasons, but few could have expected the total annihilation that they suffered at Islington. They chose to bat first, and with Howitt taking seven for 38, they were bowled out for 108. By the end of the first day, with Tom Hearne and Vyell Walker together, Middlesex were 122 ahead with five wickets standing. The partnership was extended to 161 the next day, Hearne hitting 146 with six fours, and Vyell Walker being run out for 79. Middlesex reached 402 and went on to win by an innings and

172 runs. Howitt took three more wickets in the Surrey second innings when Russell Walker had five for 38. Howitt's part in the match was remarkable in that when he took seven wickets in the first innings he caught the other three batsmen off the bowling of Tom Hearne.

Tom Hearne was to be involved in a curious incident in the next match, the drawn encounter with Nottinghamshire at Islington. He was about to bowl when a pigeon flew close to him overhead. Instead of bowling he threw the ball at the pigeon and brought it down. He had the trophy stuffed and kept as a memento in his home in Ealing.

A week later, Middlesex went to Cambridge, and with Vyell and Russell Walker to the fore, they won with ease, but this was not a pleasant match and proved to be the last encounter between the two counties until they met in the 60-over competition more than a century later. Cambridge-shire ceased to be first-class after 1871 although they had once been one of the powers of the land. Again we should turn to Case for his memories of the unhappy game at Fenner's.

Middlesex batted first and, recovering from the loss of both openers, Case and Calvert, for one and nought, made 248. The great Robert Carpenter was injured while fielding for the home side and took no further part in the match, and Newman was brought on as substitute. George Tarrant, who had already been severely punished by R. D. and V. E. Walker, refused to bat, and Case was witness to his actions:

> I very well remember seeing that spoilt child of fortune, who had been gifted with a miraculously fast delivery, but also with an entire absence of manners, lying down superciliously watching the match which he had deliber-ately done his best to ruin. Of such conduct it would be difficult to find a parallel in the annals of cricket.

Tarrant apologised a year later and Henry Perkins, the Cambridgeshire Secretary and later Secretary of MCC, appealed to Middlesex to revive the fixture, but the innings victory by Middlesex at Fenner's in 1866 marked the end of contests between the two counties for over 100 years.

Middlesex went from Cambridge to The Oval where, in the last match of the season, Surrey were beaten by an innings and 70 runs on 20, 21 and 22 August. This was the occasion of John Joseph Sewell's greatest innings, and the victory confirmed Middlesex as the Champion County. Some may baulk at the title, asserting that the County Championship was not yet in existence, but that Middlesex were recognised as the premier county is undeniable, and, at the invitation of MCC, they were invited to play England at Lord's in 1867.

Middlesex were severely trounced in this match, but this was the least of their problems. The game marked the end of Sewell's matches for the County, for, having no reasonable claim to qualification, he was barred thereafter. The triumphs of the previous season were not repeated and of the five county matches played, four were lost. V. E. Walker, who had averaged an outstanding 52.37 in 1866 saw his average halved, and the bowling was generally weak.

In any moment of triumph there can be found the seeds of decline, and so it was with Middlesex. The geographical position of the County, its proximity to London, meant that a high proportion of talented amateurs was always available, but, by the nature of their upbringing and the social customs of the day, gentlemen were almost exclusively brilliant batsmen. The job of bowling was entrusted to professionals upon whom Middlesex relied to a very small extent. This tended to give Middlesex the characteristics of being generally weak in bowling, of being a colourful and attractive side, and of being totally unpredictable.

Not only were things now not going so well on the field, there were also financial and other problems off it. By 1867, a professionals' pavilion had been built. V. E. Walker had paid for it, but he wished it to be considered as the property of the Club. His generous offer was welcomed by the committee, for the 'Championship' year of 1866 had resulted in a loss of £63 7s 5d, and there were more murmurs of complaint from Norris.

For the time being, however, events on the field again lifted spirits. The 1868 season began with defeats at the hands of Sussex, Kent and Yorkshire before Kent were beaten in the return match at Islington. The first match against Kent had been at Gravesend and marked the debut for Middlesex of Edward Rutter. A contemporary of B. B. Cooper's at Rugby, Rutter was a slow left-arm bowler who was to serve the Middlesex County Club in various capacities for over 50 years. He was also a noted rugby player and was a member of the first committee of the Rugby Union entrusted with the task of drawing up the rules of the game.

Rutter had made his contact with Middlesex and the Walkers when he played at Southgate for the Free Foresters, of whom he was to be Secretary for many years. That was in

July 1868, and, having been born in Hillingdon and having impressed the Walkers with his bowling, he was pressed into service for the County in their next match, at Gravesend, a few days later. Rutter recalled his debut in *Cricket Memories*:

> Though pleased at being invited, I naturally felt a good deal of anxiety as to doing myself justice. The ground, too, was hard and more suited to fast bowlers. We had a strong side, but through some misunderstanding V. E. Walker, our captain, at the last moment stood out of the team, as Charlie Buller turned up unexpectedly. It was, I think, a great mistake for, though Buller was one of the most dashing bats in England, and made 40 on this occasion in his first innings, it did not in my opinion compensate for the loss of our skipper's wonderful judgment in the field. I soon realised what a different game cricket was when played under conditions . . .
>
> I took five wickets in the first and six in the second, quite a satisfactory debut for me in the county team. But we lost the match by 43 runs, owing, I fully believe, to the absence of our captain and his great generalship.

Rutter was in the side when Kent were beaten at Islington, and he was in the side at The Oval two days later when C. E. Green played his first game for Middlesex.

One of the great characters and benefactors of the game, a future President of MCC, Green was a very fine batsman and a fast round-arm bowler. He won his blue in all four years at Cambridge, coming down in 1868, but although his county cricket at first-class level, save one game for Sussex, was played for Middlesex, he is best remembered as the leading spirit behind Essex's rise to first-class status after the formation of the Club in 1876.

Green played an important part in the match at The Oval, 'the best public ground then in England – a light soil, drying quickly, good wickets, good light and plenty of space', which ranks as one of the most dramatic in history. Mainly due to a stand of 49 between I. D. Walker and Green, Middlesex made 112 in their first innings. They batted without Richard Bisset Halliwell, the wicket-keeper, who arrived late. Richardson kept wicket until Halliwell arrived. For some reason, Halliwell played this match, as he did many others under an alias, and was known as Mr H. Brown.

Rutter and Howitt bowled Middlesex to a useful first innings lead of 19 runs, and, after an uncertain start to their second innings, they built on the lead well with Richardson in excellent form. The first Middlesex innings had been ended by a hat-trick from Street, and at their second attempt, the Middlesex tail again failed to increase the score with any significance, so that Surrey were left with 187 to win.

SURREY *v* MIDDLESEX

Played at Kennington Oval, 30 and 31 July 1868

MATCH TIED

MIDDLESEX	**FIRST INNINGS**			**SECOND INNINGS**	
G. H. Jupp	c Southerton b Street	18		c Griffith b Southerton	12
T. A. Mantle	c Street b Southerton	1		c Griffith b Southerton	26
T. Hearne	c Pooley b Street	0	(8)	c Pooley b Griffith	29
I. D. Walker	c Street b Bristow	37	(5)	c Griffith b Southerton	13
H. A. Richardson	b Street	0	(7)	b Griffith	56
C. E. Green	c Southerton b Street	44		b Southerton	0
W. H. Benthall	c Griffith b Bristow	3	(10)	c Jupp b Griffith	9
★V. E. Walker	c Griffith b Street	9	(9)	not out	19
E. Rutter	not out	0	(3)	lbw b Southerton	0
G. Howitt	c Sewell b Street	0	(11)	st Pooley b Southerton	0
R. B. Halliwell	absent	—	(4)	b Southerton	0
		0		b 2, lb 1	3
Total		112			167

BOWLING	**O**	**M**	**R**	**W**		**O**	**M**	**R**	**W**
Street	28.2	2	51	6		29	11	47	0
Southerton	19	6	33	1		34.2	7	82	7
Bristow	9	1	28	2		6	2	8	0
Griffith						13	4	27	3

1st inns: 1-7, 2-12, 3-33, 4-33, 5-82, 6-88, 7-111, 8-112, 9-112
2nd inns:1-30, 2-30, 3-30, 4-45, 5-45, 6-62, 7-138, 8-138, 9-167

SURREY	**FIRST INNINGS**			**SECOND INNINGS**	
T. Humphrey	c Benthall b Howitt	7		c Hearne b Rutter	52
H. Jupp	c Richardson b Rutter	6		c Howitt b Rutter	40
T. Sewell jun	c V. Walker b Rutter	0	(10)	not out	8
E. Pooley	hit wkt b Rutter	2	(3)	b Howitt	17
H. H. Stephenson	c V. Walker b Rutter	1	(4)	c V. Walker b Rutter	29
C. Griffith	b Howitt	31		b Howitt	2
J. Bristow	b Rutter	9		lbw b Rutter	19
★C. Calvert	b Howitt	7	(5)	c I. Walker b Rutter	4
J. Southerton	not out	13	(8)	c V. Walker b Rutter	2
J. Street	b Howitt	2	(9)	b Howitt	4
F. Roberts	b Howitt	7		b Hearne	0
	b 6, lb 1, w 1	8		b 6, lb 3	9
Total		93			186

BOWLING	O	M	R	W		O	M	R	W
Rutter	25	3	69	5		36	7	68	6
Howitt	24.3	14	16	5		43	16	67	3
Hearne						21.3	9	23	1
V. E. Walker						5	0	13	0
Mantle						8	3	6	0

1st inns: 1-13, 2-13, 3-16, 4-17, 5-18, 6-63, 7-63, 8-71, 9-83
2nd inns: 1-90, 2-111, 3-121, 4-128, 5-144, 6-173, 7-174, 8-185, 9-186
Umpires: Julius Caesar and W. Inwood.
*Captain.

As Rutter reports, 'it was a hard fight all through', and when the ninth wicket fell the scores were level. Rutter had been bowling splendidly and had taken six wickets, but, seeing the last man was young and inexperienced, Vyell Walker took off Rutter and brought on Hearne. According to Bettesworth, Howitt, who had just finished an over, was put on immediately at Rutter's end, as was permissible under the laws of the time, and Hearne was brought on at the end from which Howitt had been bowling. Bettesworth also speaks of a brilliant piece of fielding by Green at long stop which saved what would have been the winning run. Rutter's account is slightly different, but the outcome is the same:

It was a tie, and Roberts, a colt, quite young and playing for the first time, was to receive the first ball of an over from me. The excitement was intense, and the young batsman was confidently and rightly assumed to be in a state of nervous tension. V. E. Walker now showed his masterly judgment. Successfully as I had been bowling, he concluded that a young man in a fright would be less intimidated by a slow ball and more likely to make a run off it, whether by a correct or fluky stroke, than when facing a fastish good-length ball. So he put on Tom Hearne. There was no fear of his bowling a loose ball, but it would be one that the batsman must either play or lose his wicket. It was an intensely exciting moment. The fieldsmen were all drawn up to save the one – the crowd standing round in breathless silence awaiting the result. Tom Hearne was equal to the occasion, poor Roberts was not, and his stumps went flying at the first ball. No one can realise the strain of cricket unless he has gone through such an experience. The excitement on the ground was tremendous – it was better than a win.

This excitement was followed by victory at Hove and over Yorkshire at Islington. This was a creditable victory and owed much to Howitt who took 11 wickets in the match. Tom Emmett made his first appearance in London, taking seven for 43 in Middlesex's first innings. Then Middlesex and Surrey combined to beat England by one wicket at The Oval in a match for Caesar's benefit before the season ended with victory over Surrey in the return match at Islington.

The Middlesex innings of 139 was highlighted by the hitting of the eccentric Halliwell, on this occasion playing under the alias of Mr More. Rutter had noted Halliwell's hitting powers in the match against Kent at the Cattle Market Ground:

> While I was in with Halliwell, a hard hitter, he effected a tremendous slog to square leg for which we ran eight without overthrows – an instance of how a boundary alters the game and makes the effort of the batsman nowadays so much less.

Halliwell repeated his prodigious hitting against Surrey, and *John Lillywhite's Cricketers' Companion* commented that his batting was as sensational as ever:

> After playing several overs ably, he let go the painter at everything, he drove Griffith to the off, then cracked him into the corner, then to the Pavilion; next he sent the first ball to the Railway fence, and the last to square leg. He then got Southerton right over the Pavilion, into the Cattle Market, and the following ball forward for three. This severe hitting spoilt Griffith's analysis, so he retired in favour of Street, but the onslaught continued. Mr M. sent the last ball of his first over to the lower gate – a rare leg hit – for six, and there was much shouting – he had a solitary single in his 38.

Appropriately, perhaps, Halliwell stumped T. Sewell jnr off Howitt to end the match. Howitt finished with 12 for 53, Surrey being bowled out for 89 and 35, and that was the last game of county cricket that was staged at the Cattle Market Ground at Islington.

John Walker had made his last appearance in first-class cricket, for Southgate against Oxford University, earlier in the year, and his health and his energy were failing. More significantly, there had been further trouble with Norris who had staged races on Whit Monday and a fete the following day on the Islington Ground. He was contrite, but he was not to be trusted, and on 26 January 1869, at The Old Furnwal Hotel, Holborn, a meeting was held at which it was resolved that the Club should 'discontinue to play at Islington or hold meetings or practise there'.

Middlesex were now homeless. Robert Fitzgerald, the Honorary Secretary of MCC, who had, in fact, played once for Middlesex in 1864, offered the Club the use of Lord's. He was an energetic and influential man who realised that the programme of matches at Lord's in the 1860s and early 1870s was a mediocre one which attracted little interest. He sought to enliven the programme by having Middlesex play their county matches at the famous ground, but the County Club showed little interest. They wanted free admission for members, and as they could not function as a practice club at Lord's, they did not consider the idea seriously.

Charles Gordon, joint vice-president of the Club with John Walker, offered the new ground he was founding near his residence in Adelaide Road, which runs north of Primrose Hill and Regent's Park, but this was neither ready nor fit for county cricket, and the offer was rejected.

In fact, Middlesex played only two matches in 1869, both against Surrey, the 'home' fixture being staged at Lord's. Middlesex won the first by 43 runs, Howitt and Hearne taking nine wickets each. The return match at The Oval saw R. D. Walker hit 92 and then join with Howitt in nearly bringing off a sensational victory as Surrey lost eight wickets in scoring the 37 runs that they needed.

The position of the Middlesex Club had now reached a critical stage. Charles Gordon had resigned his membership, possibly in protest at the refusal of the County to use his ground. There was a deficit of £204 10s, and it was proposed that the pavilion and furniture at Islington should be sold to liquidate this debt. In fact, the pavilion was sold to Richmond Cricket Club for £153, but Middlesex had to move and re-erect it at a cost of £83. This left the Club with £20 10s 11d in the bank and with a debt of £152 15s 6d to V. E. Walker, who was asked to negotiate with the Amateur Athletic Club for the use of their ground at West Brompton, but at a rent that was not to exceed £100 a year.

The ground at Lillie Bridge, West Brompton, was rented, but, in 1870, the pitch was not good enough for important matches, and the two matches with Surrey, one of which was lost and the other won, were both played at The Oval. The match in August was originally scheduled for Lillie Bridge, but it had to be transferred to The Oval. *Lillywhite's Companion* stated that although the turf at West Brompton was not in a condition for playing, 'it decidedly promises well for the future', but, for the time being, the future looked bleak. V. E. Walker had broken one finger and dislocated another in playing for MCC against Nottinghamshire at Lord's two days before the first Middlesex match, and, although he continued to field throughout the Notts first innings, he was unable to appear for the County during the season. He was luckier than George Summers, the Nottinghamshire batsman, who was hit on the head by a ball from Platts in the game against MCC and died a few days later. The wicket at Lord's was not good at this time, and this was one reason for the Middlesex resistance to Fitzgerald's overtures, but the move to Lillie Bridge had not been a success, albeit that no county game had yet been played there.

A committee meeting was held at the Inns of Court Hotel on 28 December 1870, at which it was learned that several members had resigned and that others intended to do so. It was apparent to all that many more members were required if the Club was to continue satisfactorily. R. D. Walker proposed and J. H. Morley seconded: 'That a General Meeting be called for the purpose of considering the advisability of continuing the Club'.

That historic Special General Meeting was held at the Inns of Court Hotel, Holborn, on 18 January 1871. It was attended by only 13 members. There was general despair at the number of subscriptions, some of long standing, that remained unpaid. V. E. Walker spoke of the ground at West Brompton of which, although it was newly laid down and although the summer had been dry, few members had availed themselves. He said, with some passion and a hint of despondency, that 'a great deal more interest must be taken by the county in general'. It was felt that there was so much cricket at Lord's and The Oval that Middlesex were being squeezed out. There was a sense of apathy in the county which was becoming overwhelming, and the proposition was put to the meeting as to the desirability and practicality of Middlesex County Cricket Club continuing its existence. The vote was taken. Six voted that the Club should be wound up; seven voted that it should continue. The Hearnes, Hendren, Compton, Edrich, Titmus, Murray, Brearley, Gatting and the rest owe their county careers with Middlesex to seven men who, with vision and courage, decreed in January 1871, by a majority of one, that the County Cricket Club should remain in existence.

The vote was democratic and was accepted by all. J. H. Morley stated that he had been for the abolition of the Club, but that he would do all in his power to see now that it thrived. It was decided that two grounds should be viewed, the one at Lillie Bridge, the other at Tufnell Park, to fix the County Ground. V. E. Walker stood down as Secretary and P. M. Thornton replaced him, but it was to be Vyell Walker's energy in the coming months which helped the Club to survive and ultimately to prosper.

Nine days after the momentous general meeting, V. E. Walker chaired a committee meeting at the Inns of Court Hotel. There had been a suggestion that Middlesex County Cricket Club should amalgamate with the Amateur Athletic Club at Lillie Bridge, but it was felt that cricket and athletics did not go well together. J. G. Chambers' ground at West Brompton still remained the better site for the County Ground, however. V. E. Walker was concerned that there was not as much grass on the ground as they had hoped, and he was uncertain as to the quality, 'stuff had been thrown down and that it was believed to be sour', but Burrup, the Surrey secretary, assured Walker that The Oval was in a similar condition. Page's ground at Tufnell Park was considered, for the owner had offered it a very low rent, but, although large and of great potential, it was imperfect in that there was no pavilion, poor accommodation and the pitch had not been properly tended. Middlesex remained at Lillee Bridge.

They played their first, and, as it transpired, their only County game there, on 18, 19 and 20 May 1871, when they drew with Surrey. The highlight of the match was an innings of 94 not out by Bernard Pauncefote, a stylish middle-order batsman from Oxford University, who went to China and later Ceylon on business and was lost to cricket after 1872.

The return match at The Oval was won by six wickets when I. D. Walker and C. E. Green put on 105 for the third wicket and scored very briskly.

The only other first-class game was against MCC at Lord's in mid-June. W. G. Grace and John Smith began the match with a stand of 161, the first hundred coming in 57 minutes, but MCC were all out for 338 by late afternoon. Middlesex lost I. D. Walker at five which, at 5.45 on the first day, the

Walter Hadow's 217 in five and a half hours against MCC at Lord's in June 1871, was the first double century hit for the County.

Monday, brought Walter Henry Hadow to the wicket. He was 41 not out at the end of the day when Middlesex, having also lost Wilkinson, were 81 for two. Hadow was finally out at 5.45 on the Tuesday, his innings, interrupted several times by rain, lasting $5\frac{1}{2}$ hours and giving him 217 runs, with four fives and 16 fours.

Not only was Hadow's double-century the first for Middlesex, but it was also only the second made in an important match at Lord's, the first, by Ward, having come 51 years earlier. Hadow had been a sensational schoolboy cricketer at Harrow where he hit a century when he was 13 and 181 not out, at that time the highest score for the school, against the Household Brigade before his 17th birthday. He was not quite so successful at Oxford, but he was to average more than 22 in his matches for Middlesex, for whom his three brothers also appeared. Walter Hadow was tall, batted with his legs wide apart, hit cleanly and attractively, making particular use of his strong wrists, and was renowned for his cutting. He dropped out of the Middlesex side during the latter part of the 1870s.

Middlesex went on to beat MCC by an innings so giving them two wins and a draw for the season. Rutter and Howitt had bowled well, but if the cricket of the County was good, the Club itself was still far from healthy.

At a meeting at the University Club in Jermyn Street in December 1871, the committee agreed that Lillie Bridge was not suitable as a county ground, for 'it was in an isolated position and consequently not having any neighbourhood'. The ground was good for cricket, but nobody would come to watch the game there. An offer from Alexandra Park was considered, but again it was dismissed as being too parochial in its north London setting, and the Club decided that their third home would be Prince's ground, near Hans Place, where Lennox Gardens now stand.

The ground was owned by two brothers, and Rutter describes it:

> It was a large open space in the midst of a fast-growing district, at the back of Harrods and very accessible. The owners had developed it skilfully, and laid down excellent wickets. On one side of the ground a club had established itself, where society forgathered and practised roller-skating, which was in vogue just then. It was very select, and no outsiders were admitted to that part; a great rendezvous for tea, and altogether a fashionable lounge. The cricket, however, was carefully looked after, the ground well kept, and the public had every convenience.

The restrictions on movement due to the exclusivity of the private club at Prince's led to Middlesex making an important decision, namely that they would no longer be a practice club and that therefore the subscription would be reduced to £1.

The five seasons spent at Prince's cannot be considered as among the most successful in Middlesex history. The first match Middlesex played there was against Yorkshire on 23, 24 and 25 May, 1872 when the northern county won by two wickets. The last was against Nottinghamshire on 10, 11 and 12 July 1876. The match was drawn. In the interim, Middlesex played 16 matches at Prince's, winning only the games against Surrey and Yorkshire in 1873, and against Surrey in 1876. The opponents for the first two seasons were Yorkshire, Surrey and Oxford University while Notts were added in the last three seasons.

The move to Prince's marked the end of Howitt's career. Sciatica of the left hip twice deprived Middlesex of his services in 1872, and his bowling showed something of a decline in the next two seasons. He did not play at all in 1875, reappeared in one game the next season, but the sting had gone from his bowling.

Rutter, too, retired from the side after 1875, but he maintained his prowess to the end. In 1874, he bowled the great Richard Daft of Notts with a ball at which the batsman played no shot, and, in his penultimate match, against Yorkshire at Prince's, he took seven for 61 and three for 72, but he felt that eight years was enough for county cricket and left the game that year, although he continued to serve Middlesex in other capacities.

Another change was that Isaac Donnithorne Walker succeeded his brother Vyell as captain. I.D. was probably the best batsman of the Walker brothers and gave Middlesex and Harrow Wanderers, whom he founded, notable service. He was particularly strong on the off-side and was famous for his 'Harrow-drive', a shot now extinct, at least in the first-class game. He would shape as if to play an orthodox drive, but, daringly, he would send the ball skimming over cover's head to the boundary. The hit was too much in the air to satisfy the stylist, but it was mightily effective. He was by nature a punishing player, but he could defend when necessary, and at Trent Bridge, in 1874, he batted nearly four hours for 37 as Middlesex struggled against Notts. Walter Hadow, with his brisk medium pace, took four for nine and eight for 35 in that match and finished on the losing side.

Russell Donnithorne Walker was almost I.D.'s equal as a batsman and certainly his equal in generosity of spirit and in what some would call eccentricity. He astonished the Yorkshiremen who came to Prince's for the first county game by his appearance, which Rutter described as 'négligé, for he wore a queer-shaped felt hat with a ribbon round it and wore neither pads nor gloves. I.D. followed this custom, as we have noted, but neither brother, although they batted on fiery wickets against very fast bowling, ever sustained serious injury.

The attendances at Prince's were good. Rutter claimed that on occasions there were some 3,000 spectators, a sizeable crowd in those days, but still Fitzgerald tried to persuade Middlesex to come to Lord's. He approached the County for a second time in February 1874, and, at first, V. E. Walker seemed intersted by the idea, but the general feeling of the membership was that they would be receiving little for their money if they went to Lord's and that they should remain loyal to the Prince brothers without whose liberalism there would have been no club. The Princes had also shown a willingness to be accommodating and to effect any alterations that Middlesex desired. V. E. Walker expressed the opinion that 'arrangements in vogue at Lord's would not attend a county club like advantage' while the view was also forwarded that gates at Lord's were not and would not be as good as those at Prince's. Generally there was a desire to remain settled. The County Club had had enough of movement.

These opinions were endorsed at the Annual General Meeting in December of the same year where doubts were raised as to the financial viability of county cricket at Lord's. The most important event at this meeting, however, was proposal by V. E. Walker, seconded by P. M. Thornton, that Mr A. J. Webbe should be elected a member of the Club. There was no opposition to the proposal, and so began an association that was to last for 66 years.

Webbe made his debut for Middlesex against Oxford University at Prince's, 17, 18 and 19 June 1875. He was 20 years old and was in his first year at Oxford where he was to gain his blue in all four years. The first match of the season at Prince's had seen C. I. Thornton, one of the greatest hitters in the history of the game, make his debut for Middlesex. A cousin of the Middlesex secretary, Charles Inglis Thornton was already an established cricketer with Kent and Cambridge University before he joined Middlesex. Indeed, he was reputed to have hit every ball of a four-ball over from V. E. Walker out of the ground in a match at Canterbury. For Thornton, adventurous by nature, cricket was a game, never a serious business.

These two gave the Middlesex batting a very necessary fillip. In his third match, against Notts at Prince's, Webbe carried his bat for 97 in an innings of 201 and with Montague Turner making nine dismissals behind the stumps, Middlesex were in sight of victory when rain washed out the last day. Thornton had stolen Webbe's thunder in his debut match with 62 in 49 minutes off the Oxford bowling.

The improvements on the field were not mirrored in events off it. A dispute had arisen with Prince over expenses at matches and he had astounded Secretary Thornton by refusing credit for the half expenses of a match, £37 15s 3d, although this had been agreed in advance. There was a growing friction as the 1876 season began.

The second match in the programme brought the victory over Surrey and a century for Cuthbert John Ottaway. A month later, he took another century off the Notts bowling at Prince's in what was to be his last innings for Middlesex. One of the most gifted amateur batsmen of his day, he retired from the game when called to the bar.

His centuries were the first hit for Middlesex since Walter Hadow's double century at Lord's five years earlier, but there were three other centurions, I. D. Walker and Arthur Burghes, his only first-class hundred, against Oxford, and R. D. Walker, who hit 104 against Surrey at The Oval.

Once more the match between Surrey and Middlesex produced a memorable encounter. Surrey took a first innings lead of 77, but Russell Walker, ably assisted by H. R. Webbe, the younger brother of Alexander, took Middlesex to 322 in their second innings. This left Surrey needing 246 to win. When the ninth wicket fell the score was 240. The scoreboard at The Oval in those days gave the runs by tens, and when the last pair, Barratt and Street, were together the game was held up for a few minutes while enquiries were made as to how many runs were required to win. The scorers replied that Surrey needed two more runs. At that point, Barratt, who had played a fine innings of 67 was caught by Burghes at cover off the bowling of Henderson. The Middlesex team, 'in high feather', rushed to the pavilion believing that they had won, but it was later revealed that the scorers had made an error in their addition and Middlesex and Surrey had once again tied.

A sadder event in that last season at Prince's occurred a month before that game in what was, in effect, Middlesex's last game at Knightsbridge. Needing 55 to win, Notts had made 10 for one when Tom Box, regarded as the best wicket-keeper in England in the earlier part of the century and latterly ground-keeper at Prince's, died of a heart attack while putting up the score. The game was immediately abandoned, and Middlesex played no more at Prince's.

Henry Perkins had succeeded Fitzgerald as Secretary of MCC and yet another approach was made to Middlesex to move to Lord's. An Extraordinary General Meeting took place at the University and Junior Atheneum Club in Jermyn Street at which was raised Perkins' proposal that Middlesex

should play four 'home' matches at Lord's in 1877, that they should retain all the gate money, would pay all expenses and that members would be admitted into the pavilion free. Rutter was in the chair and says that I. D. Walker's was the only dissident voice, his opposition being on the grounds of finance, although he admitted the advantage of a change of ground. Secretary Thornton's minutes reveal that: 'A long and desultory conversation took place.' Would that all secretaries were so honest!

The main concern was that Lord's was a bad ground for slow bowling, but it was felt better to be at Lord's than at Prince's where dressing-room arrangements were 'hardly fit for gentlemen'. Rutter believed that: 'The brothers Prince were getting rather restive, and the certainty that the ground would shortly be built over made the offer of the MCC most desirable'. Thornton felt that Lord's offered a better chance of permanence; the wandering years were taking their toll. It was decided to accept Perkins' offer.

A fortnight later another General Meeting was convened. Perkins had stated that he had no power to bind the MCC beyond a year, 'but that provided the rules of Lord's ground were observed, there could be no doubt that the MCC would joyfully retain the Middlesex Cricket Club at Lord's'. Middlesex sought a permanent home. The offer was an uncertain one, but Thornton stated that he had confidence in Perkins. He trusted him. Middlesex moved to Lord's, their fourth and last home.

The Middlesex XI which met Nottinghamshire at Trent Bridge in August 1876. Back: Howitt (umpire). Back row: Flanagan, Burghes, Mr C. J. Lucas, Mr M. Turner, Mr R. Henderson, Mr C. F. Buller. Seated: Mr W. H. Hadow, Mr A. J. Webbe, Mr I. D. Walker, Mr J.W. Dale and Mr H. R. Webbe.

THE END OF AN ERA

THORNTON HAD THREATENED TO RESIGN if Middlesex did not move to Lord's, for he could see no future for the Club otherwise. These were years of great change in cricket. In 1873, there had been an attempt to bring some order into the chaos that ruled regarding qualifications, and it was agreed that at the start of a season a cricketer should determine whether he was to play for the county of his birth or the county of his residence, but he would no longer be able to play for both in one season. The County Championship itself, although not formally accepted until the counties themselves agreed a method of deciding it for the 1890 season onwards, was featured in *Lillywhite, Cricket, Wisden* and, later, the writings of W. G. Grace. The few matches that were played were contested keenly, but Middlesex did not meet the great Gloucestershire side of W. G. Grace until 1879, for example, so that it was difficult to arrive at a true assessment of the worth of each county.

As Rutter had predicted, the large and lovely ground belonging to the Princes became prey to the property developers. Had it not done, it could well have outshone Lord's in the century ahead, for it was more spacious and boasted a better programme of matches. *Lillywhite's Almanack* welcomed the Middlesex move to Lord's as an event of which the famous ground was desperately in need:

> For some time there has been a complaint that there was not so much first-class cricket at Lord's as the revenue and position of the club warranted, and beyond all doubt, with the exception of the two fashionable meetings of the season, there had been for some time to the outside world an air of monotony and apathy about the cricket at Lord's. The addition of the Middlesex fixtures filled a decided blank in the Marylebone programme, and there was certainly more life in the appearance of matters at headquarters than in the previous year.

Middlesex began their career at Lord's with a match against Yorkshire two months after the first Test Match had been played in Australia. Yorkshire were, in fact, without their players who had played on that tour, for they had not returned to England until 2 June. The match with Yorkshire cannot claim to be Middlesex's first at Lord's for they had long since met both Essex and Surrey there, but it was the beginning of their new career as residents at headquarters.

Yorkshire won the game by 35 runs, even though Middlesex led by 21 on the first innings. To C. E. Green, who hit 65, went the honour of the first fifty at the new home. H. R. Webbe followed him with 58 in the second innings. Surrey, Oxford University and Nottinghamshire were also successful at Lord's, so leaving Middlesex with a barren first year at their new ground. There were good individual performances, but still no sign of a fast bowler.

As was the custom for many years to come, Middlesex's home matches were clustered into the first part of the season, and it was not until they ventured away that they began to reveal better form. At The Oval, fielding 11 amateurs, they were beaten by six wickets in spite of a magnificent 95 for I. D. Walker who had an outstanding season with the bat. This was followed by a draw at Sheffield where the Hon Alfred Lyttelton played for Middlesex for the first time.

The appearance of Alfred Lyttelton in the Middlesex ranks began a tradition which was to last for most of the next hundred years, that is the tradition of soccer-playing cricketers who have graced the Middlesex side. Alfred Lyttelton had played for Old Etonians in the FA Cup Final of 1876 and he played for England against Scotland at The Oval in the year of his Middlesex debut. He was also the best amateur tennis player of his day and excelled at racquets. He was 20 years old when he first played for Middlesex, but he had already made his mark as the Cambridge wicket-keeper and with a sparkling century for MCC against Lancashire earlier in the season.

From Sheffield, Middlesex went to Trent Bridge where Lyttelton and A. J. Webbe both hit centuries, their first for the County. This was the closest Middlesex came to victory all season, for they made 400 and bowled Notts out for 192. Following on, the home side were 198 for nine on a last day fractured by rain. It was a sad occasion for Middlesex, for it represented the last appearance of Vyell Edward Walker. He was 40 and had played 52 matches for the County.

He was to continue to serve cricket and Middlesex, becoming President of MCC in 1891 and was President of Middlesex from 1898 until his death in 1906. He had, in fact, occupied every important post in the Club. The energy and enthusiasm of his eldest brother John had created the County Club, and V.E. himself drove it through the most difficult of periods to a place of calm and prosperity. Few men have been so loved and revered by their fellows.

It was he who organised the England tour to Australia in 1878–79, and the original intention was for I. D. Walker to captain that side, but an illness to Arthur Walker prevented him from going and Lord Harris led the team. One Test Match was played, which Australia won by ten wickets, and the England side included A. J. Webbe. It was to be his one and only Test Match, but he can take credit as being the first Middlesex cricketer to play for England, although A. P. Lucas, later to play for Middlesex, was also in the side.

The Vanity Fair *cartoon of Hon. Alfred Lyttelton who first played for Middlesex in 1877. He was a brilliant wicket-keeper and a gloriously free-hitting batsman.*

As one star fades, another rises, and the season after V. E. Walker left the side saw the arrival of Stanley Winckworth Scott, the Hon Edward Lyttelton and the first of the Studds, John Edward Kynaston.

Scott's debut came in the first match of the 1878 season when Surrey were beaten to give Middlesex their first victory in their new home. Edward Lyttelton's first game was at Lord's on 20, 21 and 22 June, when Middlesex met the Australians.

The Australians were touring England for the first time and had captured the public imagination, so that 5,788 paid for admission to Lord's on the first day of the game and 6,191 on the second. Middlesex fielded 11 amateurs and Isaac Walker asked the Australians to bat when he won the toss. It had been a wretchedly wet start to the season so that there was probably some justification for his action. In the event, he was rewarded, for Hadow and Robert Henderson, a slow bowler from Harrow whose penultimate game for the County this was, sent back the Bannermans and Horan with only 13 scored. The Australians were eventually out for 165, and when A. J. Webbe and Alfred Lyttelton took Middlesex past the hundred with only two men out the County looked set for a big score. Unfortunately, the fast medium pace of Tom Garrett proved too much for the remaining batsmen. The last eight wickets fell for 15 runs and Middlesex were out for 122 just before the close of the first day.

The Australians again began uneasily, but were revived by Spofforth and Gregory. They reached 240 for seven at which point James Robertson bowled Bailey and Boyle with successive balls, saw the next blocked and bowled Allan with the fourth. Robertson was a quick bowler who had made his first-class debut the year before for an England XI when already 27. He, with Scott and Salmon, a good wicket-keeper, were the first positive products of the Middlesex Colts side which P. M. Thornton selected.

Needing 284 to win, Middlesex had little hope of victory, and that hope seemingly evaporated when the first five wickets went down for 13 runs. Edward Lyttelton then came in. He and I. D. Walker added 58 before Walker was out for 23, and Middlesex ended the day at 79 for six, defeat imminent.

Only 774 paid for admission on the last day, but they were witness to a great innings. Edward Lyttelton had been 37 not out overnight, but he took his score to 113 before being caught off Allan. His innings lasted under two hours and included 14 fours. It could not bring Middlesex victory, but it was reckoned as the finest innings of the summer. Australia's win by 98 runs was the first of a long series of disappointments for Middlesex in their matches against the old enemy.

Spofforth, the demon Australian fast bowler, presented Edward Lyttelton with a walking stick in honour of his great innings.

Like his brother Alfred, Edward Lyttelton was a great all-round sportsman and played soccer for England against Scotland in 1878, which was indeed his *annus mirabilis*. He was captain of Cambridge University and led them to victory over Oxford, MCC and, by an innings, the Australians. A month before they met Middlesex the Australians had beaten a strong MCC side in a day, bowling them out for 33 and 19, so that Edward Lyttelton's innings had a right to be called a masterpiece. *Wisden* waxed lyrical about it:

> On the Saturday, in weather so hot that the glass stood at 105 in the sun, Edward Lyttelton hit so brilliantly that he made 10 runs in an over (four balls at that time) from Allan and 12 in over from Spofforth, 31 runs in 14 minutes, and 57 out of 69 in 41 minutes, before Spofforth bowled H. R. Webbe for 17. E. Lyttelton went on hitting in superb style until last out to a catch at slip for 113, his 76 runs that morning having been made in 74 minutes.'

The writer errs on facts, for Spofforth was, in fact, wicketless, but the spirit is true. Edward Lyttelton was 'splendid in style', cutting late and square and driving on the off in 'the true Etonian manner'. Sadly, he was to play only 12 more games for Middlesex, retiring from first-class cricket in 1882, and the historic hundred against the Australians was to be the only century of his career.

Two commendable victories over Yorkshire, at Lord's and Sheffield, two drawn games with Nottinghamshire, in the first of which, at Lord's, Hadow hit 140, and a draw at The Oval completed Middlesex's programme, so leaving them with three wins and three draws in county matches. This was enough for the magazine *Cricket* to hail Middlesex as Champions although *Wisden* and *Lillywhite* deemed the title undecided, and Grace awarded the laurels to Nottinghamshire. There is some justification for this, for

Nottinghamshire's programme, like Yorkshire's, was far fuller than that of Middlesex. Followers of the County might well like to claim the title, however, for it was to be a quarter of a century before Middlesex were again able to celebrate.

Middlesex remained conservative in their approach to fixtures. The challenge from Gloucestershire, established under W. G. Grace as one of the great counties, but with their power just beginning to wane, was accepted from 1879 onwards, but Lancashire, Kent, Derbyshire and Somerset were all asked to wait a little longer. The fixture list was gradually increased, but one fact which made Middlesex hesitate to extend their list was that, being a predominantly amateur side, they could never be certain of the availability of players. In 1880, for example, 25 players were used in nine matches, and only four men played in every match. The previous season had seen 14 bowlers used, but only five had bowled in more than two matches. The two most notable of those five were A. F. J. Ford and C. T. Studd.

One of three cricketing brothers, F. G. J. Ford was renowned as one of the greatest hitters and most entertaining batsmen the game has known.

Augustus Frank Justice Ford was the first of three brothers to play for Middlesex. He made his debut against Surrey at the beginning of 1879 and took 11 for 72 in the match, and he finished the season with 38 wickets. A medium-pace round-arm bowler, he was in his second year at Cambridge. He was later to hit a century for Middlesex against Surrey, but he faded from the game after 1882.

His elder brother William Justice Ford also made his Middlesex debut in 1879, playing in the last two matches of the season and hitting 74 against Gloucestershire at Clifton where A. J. Webbe hit 122. The legends surrounding W. J. Ford are amazing, and he has passed into cricket folklore, yet he played only seven times for Middlesex and in only 25 first-class games in all. In these matches, and some minor ones, he earned the reputation of being one of the greatest hitters that the game has ever known, and most historians would place him second only to C. I Thornton.

He hit the ball out of the ground nearly everywhere he played, and his longest measured hit was said to be 143 yards, 2 feet. Legend has it that once, in a game at Marlborough, he was 92 not out when the last batsman joined him and that, anxious to reach his century, he hit the next ball so hard that he and his partner were able to run ten before it was recovered. Yet alongside these exciting events must be placed his first-class record. For Middlesex, against Kent at Maidstone in 1885, he hit 44 in 17 minutes and 75 out of 90 in 45 minutes, this second innings being the highest of a career which brought him just 711 runs, average 17.77.

He taught in England and New Zealand and became a noted writer on the game. His history of Middlesex, published in 1900, remains a fine work of reference on the Club's early days.

The Studd brothers present a different case. John Edward Kynaston Studd, later the founder of London Polytechnic and a Lord Mayor of London, we have already noted. He played 11 times for Middlesex, but ended his association with the County and with cricket when he left Cambridge in 1884.

George Brown Studd was a very useful batsman who played four Test Matches in Australia in 1882–83 and served Middlesex well on occasions until he left England to do missionary work, first in India and China, and later in Los Angeles. It was his calling as a missionary that deprived first-class cricket of the immense talent of Charles Thomas Studd.

He made his debut for Middlesex against Yorkshire at Huddersfield on 8 and 9 August 1879, a few months before he went up to Cambridge where he was awarded his blue in all four years in residence. He made a 'pair' on his Middlesex debut, but took three for 52 and four for 16 with his fast medium-pace right-arm bowling. He began the following season with 65 not out in the drawn match against Surrey at Lord's, and his star began to shine brightly although he was still short of his 20th birthday.

In 1882, he made his Test debut for England against Australia, for by then he was established as the finest all-round cricketer in England. The season saw him top the first-class batting averages with 1,249 runs, average 32.86, and he took 131 wickets; 280 of his runs were scored for Middlesex for whom he took 58 wickets. He was the first Middlesex player to achieve the 'double', and the first cricketer after W. G. Grace to have accomplished the feat. He repeated the deed in 1883, and this time he scored 461 of his runs and took 56 of his wickets for Middlesex.

He came down from Cambridge after a career that was described as 'one long blaze of cricketing glory', but suddenly, the heir apparent to Grace, the most exciting talent in England, was gone. In 1884, he played in five of Middlesex's 11 matches and also appeared for MCC and the Gentlemen of England, but at the end of June he left the first-class cricket field for good.

Nine years earlier, while at Eton, he had attended a revivalist meeting held by the Americans Moody and Sankey. Influenced by his father, the evangelists and above all his own beliefs, he dedicated the rest of his life to spreading the Gospel. He sailed for China in February 1885. He was two months past his 24th birthday. The fortune he inherited from his father he gave to charity, for his commitment to Christianity was total. He worked in China, in England and America, and, in 1913, hearing of the state of the multitudes in the Belgian Congo, at that time the darkest part of what was then a dark continent, he set out for that part of Africa. He endured dangers, illness and hardship, but he worked in the Congo for the rest of his life, dying there in 1931.

Alongside the serious and exemplary conduct of the major part of his life, cricket was no frivolity. He applied himself rigorously to the game, and he reached the pinnacle of achievement because he dedicated himself to the task.

C. T. Studd was a great batsman, upright in style,

The Studd brothers.
C. T. Studd was the finest
all-rounder in the world after
W. G. Grace, but his life
was given to missionary work.

particularly strong on the off. Tall and straight in delivery, he brought the ball down from a good height which gave pace to his bowling. What he might have achieved had he given himself to cricket and to Middlesex for a longer period, we can only conjecture, but the County should be proud of the fact that for 34 matches over a period of five years, they had the assistance of a very great cricketer and a very great man.

Not all the gifted amateurs were lost to Middlesex through other needs and attractions. George Frederick Vernon joined the County in their first year at Lord's and played for them more than a hundred times over a period of 17 years. He also played once for England on the tour of Australia, 1882–83, when C. T. Studd was also in the side. He was not one of the great batsmen of his day, for there was a suspicion that he did not play straight, but he had a marvellous eye for the ball and was a tremendous natural hitter.

An equally powerful hitter, but a far better batsman than Vernon, was Timothy Carew O'Brien, who made his debut for Middlesex in 1881 while at St Charles College, Notting Hill, three years before going up to Oxford. He was destined to be one of the great Middlesex players and servants and was in the side for the best part of 17 years as well as serving on the committee.

Another to make his debut in the same year as O'Brien was George Burton, who was engaged as a professional in 1881 when he was already 30 years old. He was a coachsmith by trade and continued with his work in conjunction with playing for Middlesex, often putting in some six or seven hours at the trade before taking the field for the County. He later joined the MCC ground staff and became Middlesex scorer and coach at Mill Hill School.

Middlesex had been so woefully short of professional bowling that George Burton's slow right-arm was a great acquisition. He was steady rather than spectacular, and he played for the County until 1890, taking more than 500 wickets at under 17 runs each. His lowest haul was his 36 in his first season, but even that began sensationally.

His debut was in the first match of the 1881 season against Surrey at Lord's, and he had Jupp caught by A. F. J. Ford off the second ball that he bowled. Although handicapped by the absence of a good wicket-keeper in this game, he took five for 20 in the second innings and Middlesex won by ten wickets.

Had Burton had more able support throughout his career, Middlesex would have fared better than they did. I. D. Walker himself always seemed reluctant to bowl, and to the end of his days he despaired of finding a bowler in Middlesex.

The batting was exciting, and was further supplemented when A. P. Lucas moved from Surrey after the 1882 season. Lucas was a classical batsman whose defence was admired by all. Born in Westminster, he was qualified for Middlesex by birth. His first game for Middlesex was against Gloucestershire at Lord's at the end of May 1883. Middlesex trailed by 48 runs on the first innings, but when they batted again, Lucas opened with I. D. Walker, shared a stand of 69 and was finally bowled by W. G. Grace for 97. He batted for $3\frac{1}{2}$ hours and hit a six and eight fours. Middlesex won by 85 runs.

Lucas played only ten more matches for Middlesex in the next five years, and his 97 in his opening game proved to be his highest score for them. At the persuasion of C. E. Green, he moved on to Essex, who had just come into existence, and played for them until 1907, captaining the side for three seasons.

Perhaps the Middlesex batting of the early 1880s was erratic by nature, but it was fiercely entertaining in character. There was an infectious corporate personality of exhilarating abandonment about Middlesex batting which, happily, has endured as a characteristic of the Club for most of the ensuing century, exploding occasionally into periods of grandeur, manifested in the likes of Hearne and Hendren, Smith and Human, Compton and Edrich, and Gatting and Butcher.

Typical of the batting of the early 1880s was that of Charles Leslie, another to play for England on Bligh's tour of Australia in 1882–83. C. F. H. Leslie hit a hundred for Oxford University against Middlesex in 1881 and the following year hit 141 for the County against Notts at Trent Bridge. He and I. D. Walker put on 131 for the second wicket, Leslie's runs being scored in under four hours.

The bubbling excitement of the Middlesex batting had to have its eruptions, and one of the most memorable came at Clifton in mid-August 1883. The Middlesex–Gloucestershire matches had quickly become established as highly competitive and entertaining fixtures, and this one was no exception. Middlesex had won at Lord's earlier in the season so that Grace and his men were intent on revenge, but I. D. Walker won the toss and the Gloucestershire bowlers were put to the sword in a merciless display of hitting.

Webbe went early, but Alfred Lyttelton joined I. D. Walker in a stand of 324, which *Cricket* described as 'the longest stand ever made by two batsmen in a first-class match'. Walker batted for under $3\frac{1}{2}$ hours and hit two sixes and 17 fours. Lyttelton hit a six and 21 fours. They scored their runs together at a rate of approximately two a minute. Bettesworth reports on the stand:

> Until after lunch, when the score was over a hundred, the two amateurs played a sound game without taking any risks, but presently they began to let themselves go, and eventually were hitting against each other, with the apparent object of seeing who could hit the greater number of balls over the ropes. Nothing in this long partnership was more noticeable than the way in which

Mr Lyttelton made the sixteen runs which brought his score to a hundred. When he stood at 84 he had to face Mr W. G. Grace, but instead of taking extreme precautions, as is generally done in these days when a man is nearing his hundred, he hit every ball of the over to the boundary with tremendous force. At one time during the afternoon 170 runs were put on in an hour. Such a complete mastery was obtained over the bowling that the strategy of the Gloucestershire captain was at last confined to spreading his men out in the long-field in the hope that one of them would be able to cover himself with glory by making a catch. At length, when the partnership had lasted for three hours and twenty minutes, and had produced 324 runs – a record at the time – Mr Walker was caught at mid-off for 145, an innings which included two 6's and seventeen 4's. Mr Lyttelton survived him only a short time.

For Alfred Lyttelton, the best amateur wicket-keeper of his day, it was the highest score of an illustrious career. For I. D. Walker, nearing his 40th birthday, there were to be no more first-class centuries.

C. T. Studd followed this memorable stand with an innings of 91, and Middlesex reached 537 on the second morning. W. G. Grace finished with figures of one for 154 – rarely can he have been so savaged. Gloucestershire were bowled out for 189 and forced to follow on. They were 221 when their ninth second innings wicket fell, but the last two batsmen held out for the final ten minutes of the match to force a draw.

The following season, 1884, T. C. O'Brien scored centuries in both matches against Gloucestershire, his first for Middlesex, and topped the batting averages, but the season was overshadowed by I. D. Walker's announcement that it was to be his last. There was no falling away of his powers. He took ten for 72 in the first match against Gloucestershire, at Lord's, carried his bat through the innings against Surrey at Lord's, scoring 47 out of 126, made 80 against Notts at Trent Bridge, averaged over 25 for the season and, in his farewell to first-class cricket, hit 50 and 27 at Cheltenham. Never again was a member of the Walker family to take the field for Middlesex.

It was a regret and a shock to his fellows that I.D. had decided to leave the game, but he had taken the decision in advance, reasoning that although he could bat nearly as well as ever, he felt that he was less able in the field than he had once been. Perhaps he was right to leave the game while his powers were so little diminished.

Middlesex players of many generations subscribed for a cup which was presented to him to mark his retirement from the game and his contribution to the Club.

He was to die in 1898, two days before the Eton and Harrow match at Lord's, and his death was mourned by all. The flags at Lord's were flown at half-mast, and the occasion was a sad one. Russell Donnithorne Walker was to be the last survivor of the great brotherhood. He was to die in 1922 while President of the Club, having seen the dreams of John, Vyell, Isaac, Arthur, Alfred, Frederic and himself totally realised.

The brothers shared a profound knowledge of the game, and they were all excellent captains. I.D. was probably less tolerant than Vyell had been, but he fostered a joy in the game which has lasted until today.

At an Extraordinary General Meeting in 1881 it was announced that the financial success of the Club made it possible to pay off the long-standing debt to V. E. Walker, the Club's sole creditor. With typical generosity, V.E. would accept only half the sum that was due to him. Middlesex County Cricket Club now owed nothing to the Walkers, except their very existence, and that is a debt which future generations must continue to pay in their attitude and application to the game.

Isaac Donnithorne Walker's successor as County Captain was A. J. Webbe. For the first time in the history of the Club, the side would not be led by a Walker. The first part of the history of Middlesex County Cricket Club was at an end.

THE BEGINNINGS OF A GOLDEN AGE

ALEXANDER JOSIAH WEBBE CAPTAINED MIDDLESEX from 1885 until 1898, when he shared the leadership. No man has led the County for longer, nor has any one served the County for longer, for he was in turn Honorary Secretary and President of the Club and active in its affairs until his death in 1941 at the age of 86.

He learned his cricket at Harrow and first played for Middlesex when he was up at Oxford. He stood at the wicket with legs wide apart. He had the best possible temperament, for he was patient in defence, strong in stamina and powerful in attack. In many respects, his stance at the crease anticipated that of Jessop, for Webbe too was a croucher.

He was an immensely popular man and in his four years at Oxford led the side for two seasons. His leadership of Middlesex followed in the tradition of the Walkers for whom he had the greatest affection, but he was a distinctive personality with his own ideas. Warner said of him that the captains of Middlesex who followed Webbe could always go to him for encouragement and sympathy:

> No county captain ever had a more helpful and understanding supporter. We may count ourselves a very lucky band. Webbe was the soul of Middlesex cricket. He was a fine leader, kindness itself, with a rare charm of manner, and no one ever had a more loyal and truer friend. To 'lame dogs' and in the troubles which from time to time befall cricketers he was a veritable champion.

From all that his friends and companions were to say of him, it seems that Webbe was a man whose life was composed of

> . . . little, nameless, unremembered, acts
> Of kindness and of love.

He was, in every respect, a good man.

His ascendancy to the Middlesex captaincy could not have had a more depressing beginning. In dismal weather at The Oval, Middlesex were bowled out for 25 and 77 and were beaten by an innings and 64 runs. Defeats at the hands of Yorkshire, Surrey and Gloucestershire at Lord's, in spite of Scott's 135 not out and a first innings lead of 58, followed.

The kindest and gentlest of men, a great captain and a life-long servant of the Club, A. J. Webbe.

The first of two victories came at Lord's in July when G. B. Studd hit 104 and Webbe, batting down the order, 67, and Kent were beaten by ten wickets.

Arthur Shrewsbury hit 224 not out as Notts beat Middlesex at Lord's in the next encounter. By coincidence, the only other century against Middlesex that year was W. G. Grace's 221 not out at Clifton. The second Middlesex victory came in the match against Yorkshire at Sheffield, 17, 18 and 19 August, when, having been led by 32 on the first innings, the metropolitan county won by 49 runs. The significant thing about the match was that it marked the first-class debut of A. E. Stoddart.

Stoddart was already an international rugby player of note, and, in 1885, at the age of 21, he joined Hampstead Cricket Club. It is generally accepted that he had shown little interest in cricket until that time, but he had, in fact, played at St John's Wood School (Olivers School in Acacia Road) and for Blenheim Cricket Club. His impact on cricket at the Hampstead Club was immediate as *Cricket* reported:

> Some weeks ago mention was made of a very fine innings of 185 not out, by Mr A. E. Stoddart, for Hampstead against the Granville Club of Lee. I notice that during the five weeks which have passed since that match (played on the 4th July) Mr Stoddart, who I take to be the well-known Rugby International footballer, has completed as many as four 'centuries' for the Hampstead Club

July 18 *v*. Hendon	113
July 21 *v* MCC and G.	108
Aug. 4 *v* Blackheath	108
Aug. 8 *v* Old Carthusians	120

> As, in addition, Mr Stoddart is a particularly good bowler as well as a brilliant field, I should fancy the executive of the Middlesex County Cricket Club, for which I believe he is qualified, would do well to seriously entertain the advisability of giving him a good trial.

Middlesex had taken action as this was being written. Stoddart, born in South Shields, was qualified for Middlesex by residence. On his debut, opening the innings, he scored three and 21. The match against Notts at Trent Bridge followed immediately on the game at Bramall Lane. Again going in first, Stoddart hit 79 and 15.

Whatever the disappointments of the first season under Webbe's captaincy, when so many of the experienced players were available for only a handful of matches, the arrival of Stoddart was to prove a landmark in Middlesex history, for he was destined to be an England captain and a public idol. His name was immortalised the following season, when he appeared in all the Middlesex matches, and when he hit 485 in six hours, ten minutes, playing for Hampstead against Stoics on 4 August. This was, at the time, the highest innings of which any one could find record, and it was not surpassed until A. E. J. Collins hit 628 not out in a junior house match at Clifton College 13 years later.

In fact, Stoddart followed his 485 with 207 against
Blackheath three days later and 98 for Middlesex against
Gloucestershire at Gloucester two days after that, giving him
790 runs in five days.

For the earlier part of Stoddart's historic season, Middlesex
were captained by Vernon. A. J. Webbe, and Middlesex, had
suffered a sad loss when Herbert Ross Webbe, a year younger
than A.J., had collapsed and died while conducting prayers in
Paddington. J. G. Walker, a Scottish international rugby
player, opened with Stoddart in Webbe's absence, providing
a pairing which, with its rugby associations, may be unique.

Webbe returned to the side for the match with Notts at
Lord's in June, and at Gravesend in August, Webbe and
Stoddart put on 205 for the first wicket against Kent. Both
men hit centuries and Stoddart's 116 was his first in first-class
cricket.

*A. E. Stoddart, an
exceptional talent whose
highest innings was the last he
played in first-class cricket.*

A week after Webbe's return to the side, Middlesex played one of the most memorable games in the Club's history. It was against the Australians at Lord's, and it was at a time when matches against the tourists were affairs taken very seriously. Middlesex batted first and lost Webbe and Stoddart cheaply, but S. W. Scott, J. G. Walker and Spillman, who kept wicket for Middlesex that season, revived their side with stands of 42 and 84 so that the County reached 259. George Spillman's 87 was the highest score of his career.

S. P. Jones and H. J. H. Scott began the Australians' reply with a partnership of 155, and with George Giffen also in fine form, the score was 272 before the second wicket fell. There followed some magnificent bowling by George Burton who finished with eight for 136 as the tourists were all out for 354.

Stoddart was out at 22, but Webbe and S. W. Scott put on 107. Vernon apart, the remaining batsmen failed against Palmer, and the Australians were left with a target of 123.

Burton quickly had H. J. H. Scott stumped, and later had Jones caught by Webbe, but the tourists reached 73 with only two wickets down. In retrospect, it can be argued that Webbe erred in delaying bringing West into the attack. Robertson had opened the bowling with Burton and sent down 19 overs for 40 runs without taking a wicket before being replaced. West's introduction changed matters.

John West was a medium-pace bowler and one of the three professionals in the side. He later became a first-class umpire. He dismissed Bruce, Evans and Garrett, and with Burton bowling unchanged to take six for 56, the Australians found themselves still three short of victory when the last man Pope joined Blackham. The runs were scrambled, and the tourists scraped home.

Wisden's main concern was that Captain Hyde, a regular attender at Lord's, had died suddenly during the match.

Before the season was out, the youngest of the seven Ford brothers, three of whom played for Middlesex, had made his debut: Francis Gilbertson Justice. He was the first of an exciting new generation of batsmen who were to come into the side in the next few years, but in the immediate future it was A. J. Webbe himself who was to dominate.

In one week in August 1887, he played two mighty innings. On 5 August, at Canterbury, he carried his bat through the Middlesex innings of 412 to score 192 not out. In the second innings of the next match, against Yorkshire at Sheffield on 12 August, he again carried his bat, this time for an innings of 243 out of 527. It was the only double-century of his career. He batted for 370 minutes and hit 41 fours. He enjoyed the best year of his career, hitting 1,244 runs, average 47.84, in all matches. For Middlesex, he scored 732 runs at an average of more than 52 and was also top of the bowling averages with his fast-medium pace.

Bowling was still the Middlesex problem. Eight centuries were scored against the County, and Oxford University scored 555 at Chiswick Park to win by an innings, while Arthur Shrewsbury made 267 as Notts hit 596 at Trent Bridge.

Webbe's form slumped in 1888, but O'Brien played consistently well when he was available. Stoddart was in Australia playing rugby and was sorely missed, but, above all, the bowling was again the weakness, with one exception, George Burton.

He carried the attack on his shoulders, taking 79 wickets. He began with ten against Yorkshire at Lord's and had nine when Lancashire visited headquarters. In the next match, he had 11 against Notts, whom Middlesex beat by an innings, their first victory over the great county of the mid-19th century for 22 years. In a low-scoring match on a dreadful wicket against the Australians Burton took six for 39 and two for 12, but the pinnacle was reached in the successive away matches with Surrey and Yorkshire.

At The Oval, on 19, 20 and 21 July, Burton stamped his name into the cricket record books. Middlesex won the toss and batted. J. G. Walker and Scott put on 80 for the second wicket, but they were bowled out for 161. Surrey closed the day on 12 for one, Boddy Abel having been caught by Vernon off Burton for nought. There was no play on the second day so that when play began on the last morning, the Saturday, only 11 wickets had fallen. So well did Burton bowl that it looked for a time as if Surrey would not save the follow-on, but Key rallied them and they took a first innings lead of two.

Burton, however, was invincible, he took all ten wickets, four of them caught at short slip by Robertson, for 59 runs in 52.3 overs, 25 of the maidens. His performance bettered Vyell Walker's record and was to stand for 12 years.

With Lohmann taking seven wickets, Surrey bowled out Middlesex for 53 in their second innings, but they themselves lost seven wickets in scoring the 52 they needed for victory. Burton took three for 19.

The next County match was against Yorkshire at Sheffield. The home side were bowled out for 112 and 122. Burton's figures were eight for 48 and eight for 66. His match figures of 16 for 114 were equalled for Middlesex ten years later, but they have never been bettered, and Burton still shares the County record.

He was never to reach these heights again, although he performed adequately in his remaining two seasons with the Club. He played only one match, his last, in 1893. Appropriately it was against Yorkshire. He caught Wainwright and scored six not out and 0, but in his 15 overs he failed to take a wicket.

Burton came late to the game, and he bowled for much of his career with very little assistance and, importantly, he did not have the help of a regular wicket-keeper of high rank. This was a fact that troubled those administering the Club, and the gap left by the departure of Alfred Lyttelton was not to be filled adequately until the arrival of MacGregor.

Burton's success was a triumph for honest endeavour and accuracy, yet even as he was enjoying his finest moments, his successor was appearing on the scene.

A. J. Webbe had seen a young man coaching and bowling on the Evelyn School Ground in Buckinghamshire. He had been born and bred in Chalfont St Giles in Buckinghamshire and he was just 21 years old. He had relations who had played for Middlesex in the Islington days, and there was cricket in his bones as there was in those of all his family. His name was John Thomas Hearne, and he was to become Middlesex's longest servant and, in the eyes of many, the greatest bowler ever to play for the County.

Webbe invited him to play in a colts match at the beginning of the 1888 season and then to play against the Australians at Lord's on 14, 15 and 16 June. On a sticky wicket Middlesex were bowled out for 68 and 62. Hearne failed to score in either innings, being run out in the first and bowled by Ferris, who, with Turner, bowled unchanged, in the second. He came on as first change bowler when McDonnell and Harry Trott were hitting freely and almost immediately had Trott lbw. He later had Worrall caught by Burton and finished with two from 11 overs. He did not bowl in the second innings, and the Australians won by eight wickets.

Webbe had not played in the match against the Australians because of an injured hand, but he was impressed with

Hearne and asked him to play in the next County match, against Surrey. One of the masters at Evelyn School, however, pointed out that J.T. had no qualification for Middlesex so the offer had to be declined. Although he continued to work at the school, Hearne went to live with his brother in London so fulfilling the necessary residential qualification which made him eligible to play for Middlesex from 1890 onwards.

Meanwhile momentous events were taking place in cricket. In 1889, the over was increased from four to five balls, and declaration on the last day of a match was authorised for the first time. Middlesex included John Thomas Rawlin, a fast-medium bowler who had played for his native Yorkshire, for four matches. He was not impressive, but he was to form a lethal partnership with J. T. Hearne in the years to come. The beginning of a golden age in Middlesex cricket was being foreshadowed. Loyal followers of the club might suggest that it began on 22 June 1889.

Stoddart was back. Gloucestershire and Lancashire had been beaten. The knee had been bowed to Notts and Surrey. Yorkshire arrived at Lord's for the match which began on Thursday, 20 June. It was not one of their better seasons, but they were always formidable opposition.

Lord Hawke won the toss and Yorkshire batted. *Cricket* reported:

> Though the wicket had at the outset recovered from the recent rains the Yorkshiremen, who went in first, only made a moderate start, four of the best batsmen having been dismissed by the luncheon hour on Thursday for a total of 101. On resuming Lord Hawke hit freely to the tune of 44 runs in half-an-hour, and Moorhouse and Hall, who had been batting from the first with all his wonted care, raised the total to 200. The last five batsmen, however, gave Hall little assistance, and the innings closed for 259, by no means a large total on a pitch all in favour of the bat.

The innings, in fact, lasted for $4\frac{1}{4}$ hours, and in the $1\frac{1}{2}$ hours left on the first day, Middlesex made 116 for the loss of Stoddart and Webbe.

Scott and Nepean went quickly on the Friday morning, but O'Brien and Walker added 80 for the fifth wicket, then O'Brien:

. . . found in Mr Vernon a partner even more to his taste, the two amateurs adding 112 runs in fifty-six minutes. Mr O'Brien's 92 was a fine exhibition of dashing cricket. He was only in two hours, and his score was made up of 14 fours, 6 threes, 5 twos, and 8 singles. Mr Vernon's hitting was even more effective, and his 82, in which there was only one chance when he had made 51, were got in an hour and forty-five minutes.

One hundred and nine runs in arrears, Yorkshire began their second innings dreadfully, losing Ulyett and Lee with only eight scored, but:

On Peel joining at four o'clock, a great change took place in the game. The two professionals were proof against all the changes of the Middlesex bowling for three hours, and by the end of the second day had raised the score to 222, or 113 runs on, and thus entirely altered the aspect of the match. Peel, who had given only one chance, a hard return to Burton, when he had got 35, was then not out 149, and Hall not out 59. Lovely weather favoured the last day's play and some remarkable cricket was the result. Peel and Hall only added 15 to their extremely long partnership, which had realised 214 runs, when an extremely fine catch at mid-off sent back Peel. His innings of 158 was certainly the best he has ever played, and we should say one of the finest ever played by a left-handed batsman at Lord's.

Yorkshire finally reached 388, and Middlesex were left $3\frac{1}{2}$ hours in which to score so that:

. . . the possibilities seemed either a drawn game or a victory for Yorkshire.

It seemed, too, at first as if the former was the aim of the Middlesex team, as at half past five the score was only 129 with four of the best batsmen out. Mr O'Brien here joined Mr Nepean with ninety minutes left for play, and at once commenced to force the pace of the run-getting. He scored so freely from all the Yorkshire bowlers that before long it began to dawn on the spectators that a victory for Middlesex was not such an unlikely event as was at first thought. Matters, however, were not improved when Mr Nepean, who had played another very useful innings of 62, was caught at 182, to be followed 15 runs later by Mr

Hadow, who was cleverly taken at the wicket. At twelve minutes past six Mr Vernon joined Mr O'Brien and with only four wickets to fall and still 83 runs to get in 48 minutes the whole question of a win for Middlesex depended on these two amateurs. No pair better fitted for such a task, however, could be found, and they scored so freely from all the Yorkshire bowlers that in 38 minutes the runs were knocked off, and Middlesex had won an extraordinary match amidst the greatest excitement by four wickets. In the three days 1,295 runs were made. This is the highest aggregate ever recorded in an important match. Mr O'Brien scored 192 for once out, and his hitting at the finish was equal to the very best ever seen at Lord's.

O'Brien was born in Dublin, educated at Downside and had qualified for Middlesex when he was resident in Notting Hill as we have noted. W. J. Ford said of the close of the Yorkshire match that so critical was the finish 'that Vernon dared not play quietly to ensure O'Brien's hundred, as every possible run was required to defeat time; however, O'Brien just put the coping-stone on his marvellous innings.' Vernon, in fact, won the match with a single, but O'Brien was the hero of the hour. His hundred had come in 80 minutes with 14 fours. *The Times* reported:

> There was a demonstration in front of the pavilion at the end of the game and cheer after cheer was given for Mr O'Brien. His hitting all round the wicket was of great brilliancy, his precision and skill in timing the ball being most remarkable.

Thirty-five years later, in his *Recollections and Reminiscences,* Lord Hawke wrote of that famous encounter which was scheduled to finish at seven, with no tea interval:

> To go out for a win meant risking defeat, but apparently that never entered their heads. There was one stroke of luck when Vernon played on without removing the bail. Though desperately keen to save the match, I thoroughly appreciated the batting. Only the epithet 'superb' could describe the power and judgment of O'Brien's hitting. I put on every bowler and they each tried all they knew, but we might have been Lilliputians flogged by two giants, so

MIDDLESEX *v* YORKSHIRE

Played at Lord's, 20, 21 and 22 June 1889

MIDDLESEX WON BY 4 WICKETS

YORKSHIRE	FIRST INNINGS		SECOND INNINGS	
G. Ulyett	c Vernon b Bacmeister	20	c Hadow b Burton	0
L. Hall	not out	85	c Nepean b Webbe	86
F. Lee	b Hadow	32	c West b Burton	4
R. Peel	c Scott b Hadow	3	c Webbe b Bacmeister	158
E. Wainwright	b Bacmeister	17	c Vernon b Stoddart	29
*Lord Hawke	c O'Brien b Nepean	44	b Stoddart	20
R. Moorhouse	run out	28	b Stoddart	21
S. Wade	c Stoddart b Burton	18	st West b Nepean	20
L. Whitehead	b Stoddart	0	b Stoddart	16
†D. Hunter	lbw b Burton	3	not out	9
W. Middlebrook	c West b Burton	0	c West b Nepean	5
	b 5, lb 4	9	b 15, lb 5	20
Total		259		388

BOWLING	O	M	R	W		O	M	R	W
Burton	48.3	26	50	3		43	18	70	2
Bacmeister	30	12	62	2		27	14	53	1
Nepean	13	0	44	1		19.2	1	69	2
Stoddart	14	4	43	1		33	17	79	4
Hadow	13	2	40	2		27	13	38	0
Webbe	9	5	11	0		22	13	29	1
West						8	1	21	0
O'Brien						2	0	9	0

1st inns: 1-26, 2-75, 3-81, 4-101, 5-156, 6-214, 7-247, 8-252, 9-259
2nd inns: 1-0, 2-8, 3-237, 4-293, 5-313, 6-323, 7-256, 8-366, 9-379

MIDDLESEX	FIRST INNINGS		SECOND INNINGS	
A. E. Stoddart	c Middlebrook b Ulyett	46	b Ulyett	18
*A. J. Webbe	c Hall b Middlebrook	13	c Hall b Ulyett	5
S. W. Scott	c Moorhouse b Ulyett	33	lbw b Peel	36
E. A. Nepean	c Middlebrook b Ulyett	31	c Lee b Middlebrook	62
J. G. Walker	st Hunter b Wainwright	30	c Hunter b Ulyett	25
T. C. O'Brien	lbw b Wade	92	not out	100
E. M. Hadow	c Hall b Wainwright	0	c Hunter b Middlebrook	1
G. F. Vernon	c Lee b Middlebrook	86	not out	30
†J. E. West	c Lee b Middlebrook	2		
G. Burton	not out	15		
L. H. Bacmeister	c and b Whitehead	15		
	b 1, lb 2, w 2	5	b 1, lb 1, w 1	3
Total		368	(6 wickets)	280

BOWLING	O	M	R	W	O	M	R	W
Peel	36	9	91	0	32	12	69	I
Middlebrook	25	I	70	3	22	6	57	2
Wainwright	13	3	45	2	18	5	55	0
Ulyett	21	5	67	3	21	2	69	3
Whitehead	15.3	8	22	I	7	2	27	0
Wade	27	9	68	I				

1st inns: 1-30, 2-68, 3-121, 4-130, 5-210, 6-210, 7-322, 8-335, 9-336
2nd inns: 1-20, 2-35, 3-73, 4-129, 5-182, 6-197

*Captain; †Wicket-keeper.

consummate was the mastery shown over our attack, not only by O'Brien, but also by Vernon, who ably played up to him. At last it came, not merely to the runs being made within time, which, bar accidents, grew to certainty, but whether Tim would get his century into the bargain. Both were accomplished seven minutes ahead of the clock, and I believe the opponents were as admiring as the victors were pleased.

Lord Hawke had the greatest admiration for O'Brien, later Sir Timothy O'Brien, Bart. For Hawke, the Irishman 'never pottered nor was in doubt how to play a ball'. Perhaps it was a manifestation of his fiery temperament that made O'Brien jump out at the ball, for he lived life to the full for every one of his 87 years. When he died, in December 1949, he was the oldest English Test cricketer.

It was good that he lived to see the Compton and Edrich era, for he had lamented to Lord Hawke when watching a match at Lord's in 1923: 'In my day we waited for the full pitch and half-volley, but when they were served up to us we sent them to the boundary, thanking God for them. Whereas, nowadays, these balls are treated with profoundest respect by modern batsmen.'

O'Brien's last first-class match was in 1914 when, approaching his 53rd birthday, he hit 90 and 111 for Mr L. Robinson's Eleven against Oxford University.

The only other Middlesex centurion in 1889 was F. G. J. Ford who, on a damp wicket at Cheltenham which had restricted Grace to a laboured century and hampered all other batsmen, hit 108 in 110 minutes, a sample of things to come.

The hopes for the future were dampened by the wet

summer of 1890, but there were significant additions to the Middlesex ranks. In the first match of the season against Kent at Lord's, Middlesex fielded Burton and another professional bowler, James Phillips, who was the first in a line of overseas players to appear for the county.

Phillips was a medium-pace bowler who was a ground bowler at Lord's. He was also a bowler to the Melbourne Club, Victoria, and he played for the state where he had been born from 1885 to 1896. When more and more cricketers from the empire came to play in England in the next 15 years qualification restrictions were to be imposed which would prevent a man from representing both an English county and his state or province in one and the same year, but Phillips was able to enjoy the best of both worlds. He was to be free of the resentment which other players were to suffer in a few years' time.

He took over 200 wickets for Middlesex and was a useful, rather than a star, acquisition, but he is better remembered as the umpire who did so much to eradicate illegal bowling at the end of the century. More importantly in Middlesex history, Phillips was to play a vital role in advising Albert Trott to come to England.

Phillips took seven for 48 in his second match, but that was against Somerset who had not been granted first-class status at the time, and it was the third match of the season that provided what Middlesex cricket had so long desired, a bowler of the very highest quality.

In June 1890, J. T. Hearne was mowing the grass at Evelyn School when he received a telegram asking him to play for Middlesex that day. He himself told what happened next:

I turned over my pitch-mowing job to someone else, dashed to the station, and from a newspaper found that Middlesex were playing Notts. When I arrived at Lord's just before lunch-time I saw 99 for no wicket on the scoreboard. Not until reaching the dressing-room did I learn that my side were batting. If Notts had been at the wickets I should not have played in that match. I remember Mr Webbe leaning out of the pavilion window as I passed down the little alley to the players' room and saying, 'It is quite all right but I nearly left you out.'

When Notts batted near the end of the day I bowled J. A. Dixon with a real beauty, and as we left the field the great Arthur Shrewsbury said to me, 'Well bowled, young 'un. If you bowl like that you will get someone else out tomorrow' – and I did – six for 62. That is how I began my connection with Middlesex and, barring a couple of matches missed through a strained arm, I went on playing for the county without a break until I retired from county cricket in 1914.

One of Hearne's victims was Shrewsbury himself, and in the next match, he bowled W. G. Grace for four and had E.M. caught for 16. There were match figures of eight for 91 against the Australians, and when, later in the year, he was joined by Rawlin, the Middlesex attack at last had teeth.

The model professional, a man for all seasons, J. T. Hearne.

The following year Hearne swept all before him. Against Yorkshire at Lord's, he took 14 wickets for 65 runs, but Middlesex still lost. When Lancashire visited Lord's a week later he was devastating. Middlesex made 96, but, with the visitors' score at 26 for one, Hearne dismissed Sugg, Crossfield and Paul with the first, third and fifth balls of one over and then accounted for Yates with the first ball of his next to give him four wickets in six balls. His final analysis was eight for 22. All of his wickets were clean bowled.

There were 11 wickets against Kent, ten in the return matches with Yorkshire and Lancashire, nine for 32 in a rain-ruined game at Trent Bridge, and a final total for Middlesex in 16 county matches of 118 wickets at 10.39 runs each. He was the first bowler to take 100 wickets in a season for Middlesex, who played 16 matches, and he was top of the first-class averages.

Rawlin gave fine support with 65 wickets, and Middlesex were third in the table. This was a fine performance when one considers that Webbe was absent for much of the time with an injury that F. G. J. Ford was not available and that there was no regular wicket-keeper. O'Brien was the leading batsman, but Stoddart also batted admirably, carrying his bat for a magnificent 215 at Old Trafford.

In simple terms J. T. Hearne was a right-arm medium-pace bowler who moved the ball in from the off, yet such a clinical statement tells nothing of the man or the beauty of the action. R. L. Hodgson, who wrote under the pseudonym of 'A Country Vicar', said of him:

> With a run up to the wicket which was the embodiment of grace, perfect action, a high delivery, right-hand, medium-pace, and a sharp break from the off, J. T. Hearne was a model to gaze at, admire, and try to imitate. He could not, I think, turn the ball very much on a hard, true wicket, but under any conditions his absolute control of length worried the best of batsmen. He was a master of his art. Behind those quiet eyes a fertile brain, with infinite resource, was always working. He had every wile and strategem at his command, and he was essentially a trier.

Hodgson put him above Lohmann and S. F. Barnes, bowlers of a similar type, for 'both as match-winner and match-saver – for bowling men out and for keeping down the runs' Hearne was inferior to no man.

Perhaps A. E. Knight, a fellow professional, captured the essence of Hearne the cricketer most accurately when he wrote of him that 'a certain strength and dignity characterise his whole work. His triumph is the triumph of simplicity, perfectly executed.'

As it transpired, Hearne's 118 wickets for Middlesex in 1891 were the beginning of a record run, for he was to reach a hundred wickets for the County for eight consecutive seasons, his 145 in 1893 being his biggest haul. That was the season in which he first reached 200 wickets in all first-class cricket. He was to reach the pinnacle of achievement in 1896 with 257 wickets, 118 for Middlesex. He went to the hundred mark on 12 June. Charlie Parker of Gloucestershire reached the same mark on the same day in 1931, but no bowler has ever taken a hundred wickets earlier, and one can confidently predict now that the record will never be beaten.

It was in 1896 that Hearne took the first of his three hat-tricks for Middlesex. The first hat-trick for the County had been taken by Tom Hearne at Islington in 1868.

Rawlin had his days, too, as did the batsmen. Stanley Scott, having played for the County with consistency since 1878, enjoyed a purple streak in June 1892, and his run of success included an innings of 224 against Gloucestershire. It almost marked the end for Scott, for pressures of business forced him to give up the game a year later.

In mid-July 1892, Gregor MacGregor made his Middlesex debut. He was just 23, but he was already a Test cricketer and a Scottish international rugby player. He had gone up to Cambridge in 1888 and was immediately recognised as a wicket-keeper of exceptional talent. He stood up to the wicket to the fastest of bowling and, in his prime, he had no superior, certainly among amateur keepers. His arrival brought to Middlesex cricket the class wicket-keeper that had been needed since the retirement of Alfred Lyttelton.

MacGregor was to be a future captain of Middlesex, but for the moment the attention focused on another future captain of the County, A. E. Stoddart.

In 1893, he became the first Middlesex batsman to score a century in each innings of a county match. He accomplished the feat against Notts at Lord's on 5, 6 and 7 June. Opening with Webbe, he scored briskly and 50 was on the board in 20 minutes. By lunchtime Stoddart was 101 not out. Only Francis Ford and MacGregor offered him substantial assistance later in the innings, and Middlesex were all out for 327 in 215 minutes. Stoddart carried his bat for 195.

When Middlesex batted again with a lead of 26 Stoddart batted 195 minutes before being caught by Flowers off Mee for 124. Middlesex won by 57 runs shortly before time.

W. J. Ford described Stoddart's first innings as 'dazzling' and his second as equally as good. Stoddart was very much the hero of the time. He scored more than 1,100 runs for his County, more than 2,000 during the season, was the leading batsman of the year and, captaining England at Lord's in the absence of W. G. Grace, he became the first captain in Test History to declare an innings closed. At the end of the season Middlesex presented him with a silver bowl 'in appreciation of his splendid cricket for the County'.

One of his outstanding achievements came in the match with Surrey at Lord's. Middlesex won by eight wickets at The Oval so that Surrey were particularly anxious to win the return match at Lord's. There has always been an intense rivalry between the two sides, for they are, in effect, the two counties who vie for the position of representing the capital.

Middlesex trailed by 179 on the first innings and had to follow on, but Stoddart and O'Brien put them back into the match with a wonderful opening stand of 228. Playing in the match was Cyril Foley, who had made his debut for the County in the opening match of the season against Somerset at Lord's. Foley believed that he was asked to play for Middlesex because he had just previously 'managed to make some runs for the MCC against Briggs and Mold on a difficult wicket'. He was a very useful right-handed batsman, but his career in cricket was always at the mercy of his military career. He spent seven years in Africa, took part in the Jameson Raid, the Boer War and the First World War, and even became involved in an expedition which anticipated *Raiders of the Lost Ark*.

Foley's memories of the Surrey match shed a light on the rather bizarre events of the time. Talking of the mighty stand between Stoddart and O'Brien, he says:

> Just after they had put us in front Walter Read, as a last resource, went on with lobs from the Nursery End. He kept on the leg side in the hopes of getting O'Brien caught on the leg boundary, but the latter, quite aware of this, and realizing that lobs did not break an inch, turned completely round and drove them with terrific force up against the pavilion rails, a thing I have never seen done

before or since. Wood, the wicket-keeper, had perforce to take refuge in the slips and the crowd roared with laughter.

After successfully hitting four fours in this manner O'Brien, in attempting a fifth, hit the ground instead of the ball (which struck him on the leg) and raised a cloud of dust. The *off* bail was then observed to be lying on the ground. A perfect pandemonium ensued. Wood declared that O'Brien had trodden on his wicket. O'Brien inquired how Wood could possibly have seen anything when he was running away and suggested that he, Wood, had knocked the bail off himself before taking to flight. Read declared in a loud voice that he had clean bowled O'Brien.

The controversy raged for a considerable time before it occurred to anyone that there were umpires present. At last Read appealed for a decision. The umpire could not give one as he said that Read had blocked his view, and appealed to his colleague at square leg. As O'Brien was between the latter and the wicket he could not give one either. O'Brien as usual had the last word. 'Anyhow, I'm not going out,' he said.

Thanks to a glorious 74 out of 91 in 55 minutes by Francis Ford, Middlesex reached 377 and then Hearne and Rawlin bowled out Surrey for 119 to give Middlesex a splendid victory by 79 runs. Stoddart and O'Brien's 228 had come in 150 minutes. Stoddart was the first to go. He had hit 11 fours in his 125 and outscored the ebullient O'Brien who took three hours over his 113 and hit 18 fours. 'A large crowd assembled outside the pavilion after the match to cheer Middlesex's unexpected victory.' Always a fiery character, O'Brien was later to miss matches against Surrey because they objected to his attitude.

More than 18,000 people, excluding members, saw the match against Surrey, and another large crowd attended the game against Sussex a month later. The match coincided with the wedding of the future King George V and Queen Mary, and many who had cheered the procession came to watch the cricket. Again there was controversy. This time it involved Foley himself:

A Sussex bowler named Guttridge bowled me a ball which narrowly missed my wicket, struck Butt, the wicket-keeper, on the pads and rebounded into the wicket. Butt replaced one bail and I the other. As I was preparing to receive the next ball, Henty, the umpire, said: 'You're out.' Although I had no right to query his decision, I was so flabbergasted that I said: 'What for?' To my astonishment he said: 'For handling the bail.' I walked out like a man in a dream.

There were reports that some of the crowd invaded the pitch in protest, but, as *Cricket* related:

Having persuaded the umpire to retract his decision, Murdoch requested Foley to continue, which he did, a pleasant courtesy which reflected great credit on the Sussex captain.

Henty, the umpire, was not so lucky. He was suspended for two years.

Under the new points system which was adopted for 1893, Middlesex finished third in the Championship, and they were to finish in the same place the following year. This was Rawlin's best season with 90 wickets for the County and 104 in all. It was also the season which saw Pelham Warner make his debut for Middlesex.

Born in the West Indies, educated at Rugby and Oxford, 'Plum' Warner hit 163 for Middlesex second eleven and was invited to play in the matches against Somerset at Taunton and Gloucestershire at Clifton. He scored six, four, 14 not out and 29 not out so that his beginning was by no means sensational. Indeed, Warner was not a great batsman. He was a good county player, but his passion for the game, and for Lord's and MCC in particular, was unbounded. The gods of cricket smiled on him more consistently than they have done on many men. He once suggested that he had only suffered a bad decision once in his whole career, which most would find very fortunate. He was constantly plagued by ill-health, but he lived a long life, and the end of his playing career was touched by romance. Opinions on him will never agree, for he was always on the side of the angels and, when his playing career had ended, he seemed to be granted a licence not offered to all in that he was selector, manager, journalist and critic all in one. Above all, however, was his unquenchable passion for the game, and from that passion Middlesex were to derive great benefit.

Webbe was missing for some of the 1894 season. He was batting in the nets at Hove and was hit in the face by a ball which came through a hole in the side of the net. He returned fully fit the following season, but Middlesex fell away a little. Hearne and Rawlin apart, their bowlers seemed to provide likeable fodder for the opposition. Grace, MacLaren, Sammy Woods, Ranjitsinhji and Hayward were among those who took 11 centuries off the Middlesex bowling. The batting was a different proposition. Stoddart hit 928 runs for the County alone, and Sir Timothy O'Brien hit the only double-century of his career, 202 against Sussex at Hove.

The match was played on 12, 14 and 15 June. Webbe won the toss and decided to bat first. He, Stoddart and MacGregor scored briskly, but Rawlin was out for nought, and when O'Brien joined R. S. Lucas the score was 146 for four. In 195 minutes they added 338 for the fifth wicket. It is the longest standing batting record in Middlesex cricket. Middlesex finished the day on 498 for six. O'Brien, who batted for four hours and hit 27 fours, added another 20 to his score on the second morning. Lucas, who scored 185, the only first-class century of his career, batted for 230 minutes and hit 23 fours.

Robert Lucas, from Teddington, was a hockey international, but he had shown his prowess as a batsman for Middlesex with an innings of 97 against the might of Surrey in 1894. Opposed by Richardson and Lockwood, he and Phillips, 67 not out, had put on 149 for the ninth wicket at The Oval.

Middlesex specialised in rearguard actions at this time. Webbe and Hearne added 138 for the ninth wicket against Kent at Lord's in August 1895, and as Rawlin was absent injured, it was, in fact, the last wicket.

If Webbe was now moving into a period of decline, for he often dropped down the order at this time, sometimes as low as No 9 or 10, A. E. Stoddart was at his peak. He was considered by many to be second only to W. G. Grace as a cricketer, and even if, in 1896, he did not do as well in the Test Matches as many would have liked, he scored 1,100 runs for the County and hit centuries against Kent, Somerset, Lancashire and Yorkshire.

Tall and handsome with a splendid physique, Stoddart had returned from Australia in triumph after leading England to victory there in 1894–95, and, indeed, his major successes were in Australia. He was, in the last years of the century, a public idol. In Arlott's words, he was 'the choice of music hall songsters and the light versifiers as the image of cricket'. Aggressive and adventurous by nature, he was essentially a Victorian amateur who never quite realised the dreams that the English public had of him. He was, perhaps, so talented in so many directions that he tired of things more quickly than others and never wanted anything enough.

He and Herbert Hayman, another Hampstead cricketer, began the 1896 season with an opening partnership of 218 against Yorkshire at Lord's, but Brown and Tunnicliffe had two century partnerships and Yorkshire won by ten wickets. Hayman was one of several opening partners for Stoddart that season. R. S. Lucas, Warner, whose batting began to improve, O'Brien and James Douglas were the others. Stoddart and Douglas put on 178 in the second match with Yorkshire, which was drawn. The same pair put on 158 against Notts and 166 against Kent within the text ten days. Douglas was to prove a most able opening partner for Warner and was to serve Middlesex cricket well as a committee man.

Middlesex, 1896.
Standing: Mr E. H. Bray, Phillips, Rawlin.
Seated: J. T. Hearne, Mr A. E. Stoddart, Mr A. J. Webbe (capt), Mr T. C. O'Brien, Mr R. S. Lucas.
Front: Mr P. F. Warner, Mr R. W. Nicholls and Mr H. R. Bromley-Davenport.

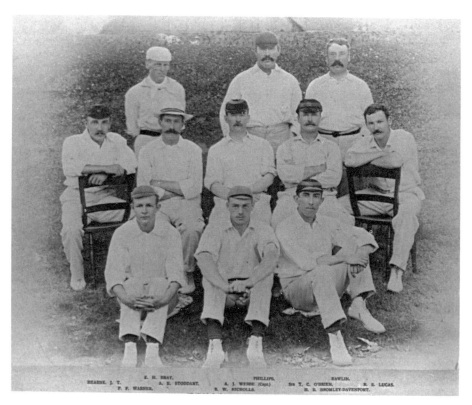

Injuries to MacGregor and Hayman severely affected Middlesex in 1896, but this was J. T. Hearne's great year and although he again had little support, the County climbed back to third in the Championship. Elsewhere, however, events had taken place which were to have a great influence on the future of Middlesex.

Stoddart's team in Australia in 1894–95 had encountered a most exciting young cricketer by the name of Albert Trott. He made a sensational Test debut at Adelaide, hitting 38 not out and 72 not out and taking eight for 43 in the second innings. He hit 85 not out in the next Test, did not bowl, was less successful in the third and last and finished with a batting average of 102.50. His form disappointed the following season, but he was young and no one doubted that he would be in the side to come to England in 1896 which was to be led by his brother. He was not chosen, and his omission will ever remain one of the cricketing mysteries.

By nature, Albert Trott was not a man to suffer injustice without reaction. He sought the advice of Phillips, the Middlesex bowler whom Stoddart had taken to Australia as umpire. Jim Phillips told him to seek his cricketing fortune in England, so Albert Trott sailed with the official Australian side led by brother Harry, settled in London, obtained a position on the MCC ground staff at Lord's and began a residential qualification for Middlesex.

He was followed from Australia by James O'Halloran and William Roche, and, in 1898, Sydney Pardon wrote in *Wisden* that the presence of Roche, O'Halloran and Trott on the MCC ground staff with the object of them qualifying for Middlesex had aroused 'some ill feeling and dissatisfaction among the other counties'.

This was not the first time that the prospect of an overseas player appearing for Middlesex had caused concern. Spofforth, the Australian fast bowler, settled in England as a director of the Star Tea Company and assisted Derbyshire from 1889 to 1891. As Derbyshire did not have first-class status at the time, this caused no adverse comment, but when, in 1891, he bought a house in Hampstead and it was suggested that he was qualifying for Middlesex, *Cricket* declared the opinion that this would not be in the best interests of the game. As it transpired, Spofforth restricted his cricket to the Hampstead Club who, with Hayman, Dr Thornton, MacGregor and Stoddart in their ranks as well, were a formidable side.

That Albert Trott was needed by Middlesex became apparent in the 1897 season when Hearne bowled tirelessly with even less support than he had had in previous years. Middlesex did not win a match until they beat Sussex at Lord's by seven wickets on 14 August. MacGregor was run out for 141, the highest score of his career, while Douglas also hit a century. The batting shone brightly for most of the season. Warner hit 176 against Notts at Lord's in June, his first century for the County, but he was overshadowed by the emergence of Francis Ford.

Ford, the youngest of seven brothers and the third to play for Middlesex, had been with Stoddart's side in Australia, 1894–95, and had shone at Cambridge where he was a contemporary with MacGregor and Foley, but his three great years for Middlesex were from 1897 to 1899, after which he was forced to retire through ill-health. He topped the first-class batting averages in 1897 and was an immense attraction at Lord's. He stood 6ft 2½in, had long thin legs and was nicknamed 'The Stork'. A left-handed batsman of elegant style, Ford revelled against fast bowling. His cover driving had a lazy charm and his reach turned good length balls into half-volleys. Warner said of him: 'He was a great box office draw in his day, as a cinema magnate might put it; certainly, at his best, he was a star of the first magnitude.'

He was a fearless hitter and, in June 1897, in a match against the Philadelphians which coincided with Victoria's Jubilee, he hit 112 in 70 minutes to win the game, and among the opposing bowlers was J. B. King, a fast bowler of the highest quality.

Ford was always at his best in a crisis, for at such times he seemed to bat with an 'aristocratic audacity'. At Headingley, in 1898, for example, on a wicket that was so difficult that 31 was the highest score of the match, he came to the wicket in the second innings and began to lash the ball in all directions, finishing the game by hitting Haigh high into the crowd.

By this time, Albert Trott had arrived in the side. In his matches for MCC in 1896 and 1897, Trott had already excited expectations, for, in the second season, he had taken 48 wickets at very low cost. His career for Middlesex did not begin auspiciously. He played in the opening match of the season against Cambridge University, took the wickets of Worthington and Stogdon, and then so badly damaged a hand that he could not play again for more than a month.

Middlesex did not win in his absence, and he was severely

mauled by Brockwell and Abel when he played his first county match at The Oval at the end of June. He hit a brisk 45 and the match was drawn. Defeat at Old Trafford followed, but then came an amazing run until the end of the season. Of the last 12 matches, ten were won and two were drawn. Middlesex finished second in the table behind Yorkshire. It was the highest position that they had attained since the County Championship had been organised on proper lines.

Ford hit four centuries, Douglas and Stoddart two, Hayman and C. M. Wells, a house master at Eton, one. Hearne took 125 wickets for Middlesex in the Championship, 222 at 14.05 in all matches, and he was the leading bowler in the country for the second time in three years. He and Albert Trott totally dominated the Middlesex bowling, for, in his first season for the County, although missing four matches, the Australian had taken 102 wickets. Eleven or 12 wickets in a match became commonplace, and in August alone Trott took 74 wickets. On a wicket which gave any assistance, he and Hearne were unplayable, and they bowled out Yorkshire, the eventual Champions, for 45 in the second innings. Trott had seven for 13 in 14.1 overs.

Webbe had led the side in 1898 with some reluctance. His vice-captain, A. E. Stoddart, who led the touring side to Australia in 1897–98, had not had the success that he had enjoyed in 1894–95, but he returned in May seemingly as good as ever. Webbe played in only six of the 18 county matches, and Stoddart as well as Francis Ford and MacGregor led the side on occasions.

Stoddart, according to *Wisden*, was 'the same delightful batsman as ever, playing a game that in its combination of grace and power could hardly be beaten.' But the shadows were already drawing in.

Webbe resigned as captain at the end of 1898 season. He had led the side for 13 years, and he was approaching his 44th birthday. He had continued in the style which the Walkers had initiated, and it was said of Webbe that to know him was to love him. A gentle man of charming manners, a witty raconteur and a generous spirit, Webbe allowed his kind heart to govern his head at times, but the world and Middlesex cricket were enriched by his presence.

He was to appear once more for Middlesex when the county was short in July 1900. He played against Worcestershire, at Worcester, and hit ten and 59 not out which helped save the game.

It was confidently predicted that Stoddart would succeed Webbe as captain. He had led England and, at 35, remained one of the finest batsmen in the world. But Stoddart, to the dismay of all, declined. He had grown tired of first-class cricket, believed that Middlesex had some fine young batsmen and a good attack and had no need of him, and he resolved to concentrate on golf and cricket for Hampstead. He played once for the County in 1899 and scored nought. In May 1900, he reappeared against Sussex at Lord's and made one. As a compliment to the faithful Hearne, he promised to play in J.T.'s benefit match a fortnight later.

He made 12 in the first innings and Middlesex were out for 172. Somerset, the opponents in this Whitsuntide match, took a first innings lead of 69. David Frith, Stoddart's biographer, described what happened on the following day:

> The day was fine but cool. The wicket was firm and fast. And on that wicket for over four hours Stoddart entertained ten thousand people. He raised 151 with Hayman, and after Beldam had been sleeping partner for a few overs, Nicholls helped add 152.
>
> Stoddart's cutting and straight-batted driving were sumptuous, but even to the short rising deliveries he drew back calmly and did as he wished with the ball. Woods broke down; Braund was no-balled before releasing the ball (a run was added); and the Somerset fielding became ragged as Stoddart hit mercilessly. As he passed 200 his condition was beginning to flag, and finally, seeking his 37th boundary, he advanced to Lewis and through sheer exhaustion was left stranded as Newton broke the wicket.
>
> He was heard to say later that his innings of 221 (his thirteenth first-class century at Lord's) would be 'a consolation for my old age'. Old age, of course, never came.

That innings of 221 was the highest score of Stoddart's career. It was also his last innings for Middlesex.

In April 1915, sick, distressed by his financial position, made restless by an unfortunate marriage and generally burdened by the weight of a world which he could no longer comprehend, he shot himself through the head. It was a tragic postscript to the first golden age of Middlesex cricket, the saddest possible end for one who had brought much brilliance to it.

CHAMPIONS

WEBBE'S REIGN HAD SPANNED THE OPENING of the present pavilion at Lord's, the official adoption of the County Championship and, in 1897, the introduction of the county cap. Within two years of his retirement he was to succeed Thornton as Secretary of the Club and he was later to become President. He served the Club in various capacities until his death in 1941, and he helped foster a tradition which Warner aptly described as 'a peculiarly happy atmosphere about Middlesex cricket' in that 'those who have played their part and retired from active participation in the game still seem to retain the keenest interest in everything that appertains to the club'.

Webbe was succeeded by Gregor MacGregor with Francis Ford, in what was to be his last season, as vice-captain. MacGregor's first season in charge was to be a momentous one, and, ultimately, disappointing. The season began sensationally with the Whitsuntide match against Somerset, whose games with Middlesex were to provide some of the most extraordinary cricket of the beginning of this century. C. P. Foley was playing in the match and recalled it some years later:

> I was staying in the country with the late Jack Menzies and it rained so continuously all the Whit-Monday that no play was possible. I did not even come up to London. In the train on Tuesday, Menzies, who knew nothing about cricket, told me he had dreamt in the night that a side had been dismissed for 10 runs and had clearly seen the figures 10. 10. one below the other as they would appear on the score-board. When I got to Lord's I found that play could not begin before 12.30. Somerset went in and in 20 minutes the score-board showed 8 for 8. It was then I remembered what Menzies had told me. I rushed up to Stoddart between the overs and offered to bet him £1 (which he refused) that Somerset would make exactly 10, which would be the lowest score on record for a first-class match. But here the coincidence fades out, for they made 35. We made 86 and then, extraordinary to relate, the score-board in Somerset's second innings read 5 for 5.
>
> I thought Menzies' dream was coming on in the second act, and again offered to bet a sovereign with Stoddart,

but I had told him of the dream meanwhile and, luckily for me, he was frightened and refused. Somerset made 44 and the match was all over at 4.45 Fancy finishing a first-class match in four and a quarter hours.'

Foley was top scorer on the Middlesex side with 20, and J. T. Hearne's 15 not out was crucial. It was the bowlers, of course, who revelled in the conditions. Tyler of Somerset took eight for 42, and the Middlesex pair of Hearne and Trott had figures of five for 14 and three for 30, and four for 18 and seven for 13 respectively.

This match had witnessed William Roche's debut for Middlesex, but his slow right-arm off-break bowling was not needed. 'Micky' Roche's career with Middlesex was to be brief, but it contained some spectacular performances. In the second match of the season, against Gloucestershire at Lord's, he was put on to bowl for the first time in the second innings and took six for 28, clean bowling the last four batsmen. Middlesex won by seven wickets. They were now ready for Yorkshire, the next visitors to Lord's.

Trott and Hearne bowled the reigning Champions out for 203. Warner then played a composed innings of 150, and Albert Trott, after a careful start, savaged the Yorkshire bowling and hit 164. W. J. Ford remarked ruefully that 'with a little more care at the beginning of his innings he would have made many more long scores'. Middlesex reached 488 to lead by 285, but Brown and Tunnicliffe began a fight back with a stand of 152. Thereafter it was Trott and Roche who dominated the match. Trott took four for 130 to add to his five for 98 in the first innings, and Roche had five for 93 as Middlesex snatched victory by an innings and two runs.

Twelve wickets for Trott against Sussex gave a memorable win in the next game. Brann and Fry began the match with a stand of 135, and Ranjitsinhji hit 120. Sussex made 387, but Francis Ford hit a glorious 160 and Trott lashed the ball far and wide for 123, and Middlesex, leading by 79 on the first innings, went on to win by four wickets.

The fifth visitors to Lord's were Kent, and Middlesex struggled painfully against Mason and Bradley to subside to the depths of 55 for nine. Roche then joined Richard Nicholls in a stand of 230 which, at the time, was the highest stand that had ever been made for the last wicket in first-class cricket and is still a Middlesex record. As a world record it was to last ten years before Woolley and Fielder bettered it, and it has only twice been surpassed since, by Kippax and Hooker at Melbourne, 1928–29, and by Sarwate and Banerjee at The Oval in 1946.

Nicholls, another Rugby product, made 154, the only century of his career, and Roche hit 74 not out. Trott and Hearne took eight wickets apiece, and Middlesex won by 118 runs. Thirteen wickets from Trott brought a ten-wicket victory over Leicestershire to extend Middlesex's run at the beginning of the season to six wins in succession, but then came disaster. The side lost its way and suffered three defeats and a draw before Rawlin hit the only century of his career and Middlesex beat Surrey. This match saw Bosanquet, who had played one game the previous season take his first wicket for Middlesex when he bowled Bobby Abel.

The form until the end of the season was good although it could not quite match the glories of the opening period. Against Nottinghamshire, at Trent Bridge, after Warner, Douglas and Moon had gone cheaply, Cyril Wells hit 244 so beating Webbe's record of the highest score for the County.

Wells was an all-round sportsman. He captained England at Rugby and played a few games for Surrey before assisting Middlesex, the county of his birth. He was a most remarkable man. A classical scholar with a double first from Cambridge, a wonderful judge of wine and possessor of one of the finest stamp collections in the world, he was a housemaster at Eton where one of his young charges at the beginning of the century was George Oswald Allen to whom he gave the greatest encouragement. Wells was featured in a *Vanity Fair* cartoon as one of the men of the day which indeed he was, but he could only assist Middlesex in the school holidays, and last played in 1909.

Good as Wells' performance was, the outstanding player of the season was Albert Trott. He created a world record by scoring 1,000 runs and taking 200 wickets in the season. In all, he took 239 wickets, including 150 for Middlesex, and he was the leading bowler in England.

Trott, according to Foley, was 'as hard as nails' in the way in which, in bitterly cold weather, he fielded without a sweater. By the end of the 1899 season, the Australian had become one of the most popular cricketers ever to appear at Lord's. Arguably, he was the first in the line that stretched through Hendren to Compton and the heroes of the present, the men who have sent a shiver of excitement through the crowd as they took the field.

C. M. Wells, schoolmaster, scholar and cricketing eccentric. In 1899 he hit 244 for Middlesex against Nottinghamshire at Trent Bridge, the highest score made for the County at that time.

In May 1899, he hit a ball from Fred Tate so that it struck one of the two MCC arms that crown the highest pinnacles of the pavilion. Foley, who was batting at the other end in this match for MCC, insisted that it was a bigger hit than the one which came two months later and won Trott eternal fame. Playing for MCC against the Australians, he hit a ball from Noble over the pavilion. Many believe that this mighty achievement was the seed of his decline, for ever after he was trying to repeat that shot.

As a bowler, he could be devastating. He possessed infinite variety. His arm was low, but he imparted considerable spin and was able to generate considerable pace. Warner considered his yorker frighteningly effective so quickly was it bowled. Above all he was a character, rich in fun, fond of a drink. One of his early brushes with authority was when he gave his name to a newspaper column which criticised the arrangements for a match at Lord's as being scandalous because the beer gave out at lunch time. Called before Francis Lacey, the MCC Secretary, he answered honestly that he had not seen the piece and was told to be more careful of his 'ghost' in future as, in any case, the report was not true.

'Alberto' was loved at Lord's, and even those who believed that he should not have been playing for Middlesex enjoyed his cricket and his attitude, yet his career was shorter and his achievement, in the end, less than they should have been. Perhaps Gregor MacGregor found the core when he said: 'If you had a head instead of a turnip, Alberto, you'd be the best bowler in the world.' The comment could equally well have applied to his batting or to the conduct of his life, yet for two years at least he was the greatest all-rounder in the world and few men have given their fellows as much pleasure.

Had Middlesex sustained their opening run in 1899 a little longer, they would have been Champions. As it was they finished second to Surrey.

The next three seasons saw the dominance of Yorkshire.

Middlesex failed to reproduce the form in 1900 which they had shown the previous year, yet there were several heartening features. Warner suddenly blossomed into a batsman of a considerably greater accomplishment that his earlier career had promised. C. B. Fry wrote of him:

> His style is almost classically correct, without being so moulded as to suppress individuality. Perhaps the most noticeable point in his play is the absolute straightness of his bat, but his orthodoxy is of the kind that appears natural, such is the ease that much practice gives.

Fry was correct in his judgement, for Warner came to success through application and total dedication to the game rather than through any natural gifts with which he had been endowed. He hit 1,335 runs for Middlesex in 1900 with five centuries, giving the innings the most solid of foundations.

Albert Trott. Lord's has never seen a more popular cricketer.

Trott, too, was in magnificent form, again passing two hundred wickets, again completing the 'double' in all matches, though his batting for Middlesex showed signs of decay, and establishing a County record with 154 wickets which was to stand for 55 years. Against Somerset, always a County against whom he thrived, at Taunton, he bowled 14.2 overs, five of which were maidens and took all ten wickets for 42 runs in the first innings, so beating Burton's county record. Fry was in no doubt as to his ability as a bowler at this time:

On the whole he may be regarded as the most original, inventive, and enterprising performer with the ball at present engaged in first-class cricket. He is not a length bowler, yet he keeps a length; he sets no more store by break, yet he can make the ball go both ways; he is not a slow; yet he bowls slow; nor fast, yet none is faster. His methods and means are as various as the wickets on which he bowls and the batsmen to whom he finds himself opposed. Perhaps he may best be described as a pace bowler, for he relies, except on bad wickets, chiefly upon never-ceasing variations of speed to deceive batsmen and get them out.

Trott was also a brilliant fielder and the idol of Lord's.

J. T. Hearne, although not perhaps the force of yore, took 95 wickets for the County, and there was some interesting, though expensive, bowling from Bosanquet.

Bosanquet had just come down from Oxford and, against Leicestershire at Lord's on 19, 20 and 21 July, he emulated Stoddart by scoring a century in each innings, 136 and 137. His first innings was made in 110 minutes, and he so monopolised the scoring that his 100 came out of 120. But Bosanquet was to remember that match for another reason as he was to relate later:

> Somewhere about the year 1897, I was playing a game with a tennis ball, known as 'Twisti-Twosti'. The object was to bounce the ball on a table so that your opponent sitting opposite could not catch it. After a little experimenting I managed to pitch the ball which broke in a certain direction; then with more or less the same delivery make the next ball go in the opposite direction! I practised the same thing with a soft ball at 'Stump-cricket'. From this I progressed to the cricket ball.
>
> I devoted a great deal of time to practising the googly at the nets, occasionally in unimportant matches. The first public recognition we obtained was in July 1900, for Middlesex v Leicestershire at Lord's. An unfortunate individual (Coe, the left-hander) had made 98 when he was stumped off a fine specimen which bounced four times. This small beginning marked the start of what came to be termed a revolution in bowling.

This revolution was still in the fermenting at the beginning of the century, but Bosanquet was developing into a very useful cricketer.

He and Warner passed a thousand runs for the County in 1901, but the bowling was further hampered by Hearne's apparent continuing decline, Wells' inability to play regularly, Bosanquet's expensiveness and, most of all, by the injury which Trott sustained in the match against Essex at Leyton. He split his hand in stopping a hard return and could not play for three vital weeks. Middlesex lost the encounter with Essex when he could bat in neither innings, nor bowl in the second, and managed to beat only Gloucestershire during his absence. They finished second in the table, having suffered their only other defeat, to Yorkshire, earlier in the season.

One of the interesting acquisitions in 1901 was Reginald Schwarz, who appeared in two matches. Born in Kent, he was to go to South Africa and play Test cricket for that country. He did not bowl for Middlesex in 1901 and took one for 117 in 1902, but later, studying the methods of Bosanquet, he changed from a medium-pace to a googly bowler. More truthfully, Schwarz was an off-break bowler with a leg-break action. He rarely bowled the leg-break itself.

The hopes that had been raised by Middlesex's climb to second place in 1901 were dampened in the following year by the most wretched summer for nearly a quarter of a century. The game with Lancashire was abandoned without a ball being bowled; several others were ruined. The side slumped to 12th. MacGregor was able to play in only ten of the 18 matches, Warner in 13, Nicholls in 11. There was much difficulty in getting a fully representative side together earlier in the year, and Middlesex did not win a game until, thanks to Trott, they beat Kent by five runs on 26 July.

Five weeks before, J. T. Hearne had taken four wickets in five balls, including the hat-trick, when, after two barren days, Middlesex bowled Essex out for 64 at Lord's, but, for the main part, it was a season of uninterrupted gloom.

C. B. Fry hit his fifth century in succession against Middlesex for whom George Beldam, the only man to play in every game, hit 155 not out, the highest score of his career, in the match against Surrey at Lord's in mid-July.

Beldam had made his debut two years earlier, and he also played for Grace's London County side at the beginning of the century. He was a careful and patient amateur batsman who is best remembered for his pioneering work in cricket photography. In 1907, he produced the plates for 'Great Batsmen, Their Methods at a Glance', a quite remarkable work for its time.

The Middlesex side of these years began to earn the reputation for being what a Yorkshireman later called a league of nations side. More memorably, Cardus was to assert in the 1930s that whereas qualification for other counties was by birth and residence, qualification for Middlesex was brought about by some mystical ceremony on Paddington Station. Warner himself admitted that the side had a somewhat cosmopolitan look:

> Beldam was of French descent, being descended, he assured us, from La Belle Dame de Picardy; our friend Ahsan-ul-Hak was an Afridi; W. P. Robertson was born in Peru, and Trott in Australia; Dalmeny, who played for us two or three times, was a Scotchman; Rawlin came from Yorkshire; J. T. Hearne was born in Bucks; Bosanquet was a Huguenot; Schwarz's father was a Silesian; and I was born in the West Indies.

Ahsan-ul-Hak, from the Punjab, played his three games for the County in 1902. Lord Dalmeny and Schwarz did not play in 1903 when the only newcomer of note was, late in the season, Ernest Beldam, a cousin of George's. Yet, somehow, the side was able to perform in a way which it had never done before.

MacGregor was again absent at the beginning of the season, and Warner led the side in the opening matches. He led from the front. In the first game of the season, against Gloucestershire, at Lord's, he and Leonard Moon put on 248 for the first wicket. Warner hit 149 and Moon 122. Moon was an aggressive batsman, a Cambridge blue who, commissioned in the Devon Regiment, died of his wounds in Salonika in 1916.

Warner and Moon put on their runs in under $2\frac{1}{2}$ hours, and by lunch, with Warner 93 and Moon 95, 190 were on the board. With the departure of Moon, Middlesex collapsed and lost eight wickets as 91 runs were scored. Trott and Griffin then added 94 in 50 minutes, and Trott continued his annihilation of the Gloucestershire bowling when, in conjunction with Hearne, he put on 69 in 25 minutes for the last wicket. Trott was out for 103, and Middlesex had reached 502 on the first day with half an hour still to play. Gloucestershire lost no wickets that evening, but they were beaten in two days, Trott taking six wickets and Hearne seven.

The Whitsuntide match against Somerset saw Warner hit 135. Again runs came at a phenomenal pace. Middlesex reached 441 and Somerset were 96 for one at the end of the first day, but Trott took five wickets on the second, and Middlesex, watched by large crowds on the first two days, swept to victory by 112 runs.

Yorkshire, whom Middlesex had not beaten since 1899 and who had been Champions for the past three seasons, were the next visitors to Lord's. At lunch, they were 149 for four. By early afternoon they were all out for 157. J. T. Hearne had recaptured all his old glory and taken six for 39. Consistent batting and more fine bowling by Hearne gave Middlesex victory by nine wickets early on the third day. It was, said *Wisden*, Middlesex's most notable performance of the season.

The weather in 1903 was even more wretched than it had been the previous year. Only $1\frac{1}{2}$ hours play on the third day was possible in the game with Notts and no play at all was possible against Essex. The match against Sussex at Hove was also ruined by rain. Middlesex were idle for three weeks so that their magnificent start to the season and the ardour and excitement which it had engendered were temporarily dampened.

When their fixtures resumed with the match against Surrey at Lord's on 13, 14 and 15 July, Middlesex enjoyed the one bout of fine weather. On a fast wicket Middlesex took control of the game on the second day. George Beldam, who had just done well for the Gentlemen against the Players, and Bosanquet put on 134 in 70 minutes in the second innings, having added 82 in the first. Trott took six for 66 in the first Surrey innings, Bosanquet six for 46 in the second, and Middlesex romped to victory by 221 runs.

Bosanquet took ten wickets at Tunbridge Wells and played two good innings, but Kent had the better of the draw. A low-scoring match at Old Trafford was also drawn, mainly because of the rain, but Essex were well beaten at Leyton.

Although Warner was absent with a chill, Middlesex were strengthened by the availability of James Douglas and the ebullient Cyril Wells, whose hard-hitting and off-break bowling were to prove invaluable in the next few weeks. MacGregor had returned to the side for the game against Surrey so that Middlesex were now at full strength.

Beginning with the match at Leyton, Middlesex won

Champion County, 1903.
Back row: Rawlin,
Mr J. H. Hunt, Trott,
Mr E. A. Beldham,
J. T. Hearne.
Seated:
Mr B. J. T. Bosanquet,
Mr P. F. Warner,
Mr G. MacGregor,
Mr C. M. Wells,
Mr G. W. Beldham.
On ground: Mr J. Douglas
and Mr L. J. Moon.

three matches in ten days. The victories at Taunton and Bristol were remarkable achievements, the outcome of a side playing with verve, spirit and self-belief. The match at Taunton was played under conditions favourable to batsmen. Somerset made 253. Middlesex replied with 312. In their second innings the home county batted solidly throughout to reach 371, and Middlesex were left $3\frac{1}{2}$ hours in which to make 313 runs. They reached their target with a quarter of an hour to spare, a wonderful achievement. Bosanquet hit 74 out of 106 in 65 minutes and runs came at a hundred an hour. Cyril Wells played two fine innings, and it was he who cracked the winning boundary with Hunt at the wicket with him and only J. T. Hearne to come. J. H. Hunt, a Wykehamist, took five for 60 in the first innings, the best performance of his career, and four for 102 in the second. He was killed on the Western Front in 1916. He bowled medium pace. Beldam, Moon, Trott and Warner also turned in good performances, but, as *Wisden* remarked, this 'brilliant victory was the outcome of collective rather than individual excellence.'

At Bristol, Middlesex trailed by 81 on the first innings, and, on the second evening, with four men out, they had a lead of only 70. James Douglas played with intelligence and total dominance on the last morning. He hit 204, the only double-century of his career, in $5\frac{1}{4}$ hours. He shared stands of 132 for the fifth wicket with MacGregor and 187 for the sixth with Wells. MacGregor declared when Douglas was out, leaving Gloucestershire $2\frac{1}{2}$ hours in which to score 374. More realistically, he was giving his bowlers that amount of time in which to bowl out their opponents. They needed only two hours. Bosanquet, six for 64, and Wells, four for 33, bowled unchanged, and Middlesex won by 272 runs.

Middlesex now stood out as the only unbeaten County in the country. In 12 matches, one of which had been abandoned, they had had seven wins and four draws. Their fortunes were at their highest point. The Championship beckoned, and they went to Headingley full of confidence. They received a rude shock. In what was described as the greatest county match of the season, Yorkshire won by 230 runs. Hirst and Rhodes bowled Middlesex out for 79 on a wicket which gave them only a little assistance, and Hirst, Rhodes and Jackson demolished them in the second innings.

Confidence was badly shaken, for it seemed that, in spite of all that had been achieved, Middlesex might still be deprived of the title. A very keen fight for first place now looked likely, with Sussex and Yorkshire strongly in contention, but weather again took a hand.

A drawn match at Trent Bridge in which there was no play on the third day was due to be followed by matches against Lancashire, Sussex and Kent at Lord's. Sadly, rain made play possible on only two out of the nine days, and no play at all was possible in the match with Kent. The abandonments were an advantage to Middlesex, but the last game against Surrey at The Oval still had to be won, or, at least, defeat had to be avoided if Middlesex were to win the title.

They batted with unusual caution on the Monday, taking nearly five hours in which to make 230. Warner and Moon had gone early, but George Beldam batted with great fortitude for four hours and 40 minutes for 112. Four wickets went for 55, but Beldam had good support from Wells and cousin Ernest, and with Trott and MacGregor hitting lustily, Middlesex totalled 281.

There was rain on the Monday evening, and on the Tuesday, Surrey were routed by Trott and Hearne. In consecutive overs, Trott three times took two wickets, the spell bringing him six for two in 17 balls. Hearne finished with four for 26, Trott six for 19, and Surrey were out for 58. Following on they reached 100 for 3, but Wells took five for 26 and Middlesex won by an innings and 94 runs. They had won the *official* Championship for the first time in their history.

There were some who considered that the County had been fortunate in the weather and that they were a lucky side not deserving of the title. A fortnight later those critics were silenced when Middlesex, with Warner getting a hundred, outplayed the Rest of England XI in a drawn match at The Oval.

Gregor MacGregor who led Middlesex to their first official County Championship in 1903. He was a hard-hitting batsman and a brilliant wicket-keeper.

The reasons for the Middlesex triumph were apparent. They had a well balanced side of all round efficiency, and collective excellence was the dominating characteristic of their cricket. There was no outstanding batsman like a Stoddart, but, as *Wisden* commented:

> The batting strength was remarkable and would of course have been still more apparent in a normal summer. The bowling was abundant and well varied and from first to last the fielding was maintained at a pitch of quite exceptional smartness. Indeed, to their fine fielding more than anything else the eleven owed their triumph.

This was the pinnacle of Middlesex's first golden age, for the next few years were to mark a period of decline. Trott, in spite of several excellent performances in the Championship season, had shown signs of falling away, and his batting had lost its efficiency to a marked degree. He was to play nine single-figure innings in succession in 1904 when, after an indifferent start, the County rallied to finish fourth.

Hearne maintained good form although nearing the veteran stage. His 12 Test Matches, which featured a hat-trick against Australia, were in the past, but there was an Indian summer yet to come. Warner, Bosanquet and George Beldam remained consistent scorers, and Bosanquet's leg-break and googly bowling had now been honed to a quality where it brought him 132 wickets in 1904 which, with his 1,405 runs, brought him his only 'double'.

Briefly, he was to puzzle the Australians at Test level, and they still refer to that off-break with the leg-break action, the ball which, for a time, revolutionised cricket and still gives occasional joy, as the 'Bosie' after its inventor. Benny Green has described him as the perfect example of the Edwardian gentleman, an athlete 'whose life was one long sunlit saunter from pavilion to conservatory'.

Bosanquet brought the ball down from a great height, for he stood six feet tall, and, if he were occasionally variable in length and accuracy, he was ever a threat capable of demoralising any side.

In May 1905, against Sussex at Lord's, he established a record which was equalled by George Hirst the following season, but which has never been bettered.

In the first innings, he hit 103 in $1\frac{1}{4}$ hours as Middlesex made 369. He then took three for 75 as Sussex were bowled out for 259, and he followed this with 100 not out in 75 minutes, the second time in his career that he had scored two centuries in a match. Bowling unchanged with Hunt throughout the second innings, he took eight for 53 so completing one of the most remarkable all-round performances in the history of the game.

He was not alone in producing individual performances of brilliance, and the 1904 season ended with two outstanding batting achievements by James Douglas. At Taunton, he and George Beldam out on 191 in 110 minutes for the second wicket. Beldam hit 141 and Douglas 114, reaching his hundred before lunch. Ten days later, at Trent Bridge, Warner and James Douglas put on 306 for the first wicket. It stood as a Middlesex record for 43 years.

In 1907, after two season in the doldrums, Middlesex showed improvement and rose to fifth, but when all else in that season is forgotten one individual performance will be remembered. It was produced by Albert Trott on the occasion of his benefit match against Somerset at Lord's. Although he was to play for Middlesex for the best part of three more seasons, it was, in effect, his swan-song.

The inventor of the googly and for a brief period a very fine all-rounder— B. J. T. Bosanquet.

Rain seriously interfered with play on the Whit Monday and runs were never easy to come by. It took Tarrant half an hour to open his account, and, similarly, in the Somerset first innings, Braund was half an hour without scoring. The whole of the first day was taken up by the Middlesex innings, and, with Braund and Johnson adding 119, Somerset came to near parity before being halted by the bowling of Tarrant.

Batting for the second time, Middlesex owed much to Trott, Murrell and Dr Edward Litteljohn, and Somerset were left to make 264 to win. It was at this point that Trott took over. He caught Johnson off Tarrant and, with successive deliveries, dismissed Lewis, Poyntz, Woods and Robson. He was reported to be unlucky not to have accounted for Lee first ball as well.

Later, with Somerset on 97, he took his second hat-trick of the innings when he accounted for Mordaunt, Wickham and Bailey. No other bowler in county cricket has ever done the hat-trick twice in the same innings, although his four wickets in four balls was to be equalled two months later.

Trott joked that he had bowled himself into the workhouse, but as his feat had been accomplished on the third day, it was unlikely that it affected the gate receipts. Reporting in *The Times*, however, Philip Trevor gave some support for Trott's humorous assertion:

> Somerset began batting with Mr Palairet and Braund, and there was nothing in the early play to suggest that collapse which followed. Braund played sound cricket, and Mr Palairet made a number of excellent scoring strokes in his best style. The score was taken easily enough to 56, and then Mr Palairet was caught at cover point. Mr Beldam and Mignon had been replaced as bowlers by Trott and Tarrant. Mr Johnson came in, made a few hits, and was the finely caught by Trott off Tarrant's bowling, the second wicket falling with the total at 74. Lewis succeeded him, and this was the beginning of the end.

Poyntz and Woods evidently were deceived by the flight of the ball, Woods while trying to chop. Lee, Trevor maintains, hit at the ball and missed, and all in the pavilion, as well as MacGregor, who let the ball go for four byes, believed that Trott had hit the wicket again. 'It was a wonderful over, and one is scarcely likely to see one like it bowled again in a first-class match.'

In the second hat-trick, Mordaunt and Bailey were taken at mid-off, and Trott himself caught Lee off Tarrant at short slip. The two hat-tricks came within half an hour.

Trevor could not explain the reason for these amazing events, although the light was not good:

MIDDLESEX *v* SOMERSET

Played at Lord's, 20, 21 and 22 May 1907

MIDDLESEX WON BY 166 RUNS

MIDDLESEX	FIRST INNINGS		SECOND INNINGS	
P. F. Warner	b Mordaunt	46	b Lewis	11
F. A. Tarrant	c Lee b Lewis	52	c Palairet b Mordaunt	28
G. W. Beldam	lbw b Mordaunt	12	lbw b Lewis	0
B. J. T. Bosanquet	c Johnson b Mordaunt	32	b Bailey	29
E. S. Litteljohn	c Braund b Lewis	44	b Mordaunt	52
A. E. Trott	b Lewis	1	c Wickham b Robson	35
H. A. Milton	b Lewis	3	b Mordaunt	0
*†G. MacGregor	c Woods b Bailey	39	c Poyntz b Robson	39
H. R. Murrell	b Robson	33	c and b Braund	9
J. T. Hearne	not out	3	not out	4
E. Mignon	b Bailey	1	c Wickham b Braund	0
	b 15, lb 4, nb 1	20	b 3, lb 2, nb 1	6
Total		286		213

BOWLING	O	M	R	W	O	M	R	W
Lewis	32	14	88	4	7	2	17	2
Bailey	16	5	33	2	16	3	58	1
Braund	13	1	33	0	13.4	1	55	2
Mordaunt	30	6	97	3	15	1	47	3
Robson	7	1	15	1	6	2	30	2

SOMERSET	FIRST INNINGS		SECOND INNINGS	
*L. C. H. Palairet	c MacGregor b Mignon	6	c Bosanquet b Tarrant	35
L. C. Braund	c MacGregor b Bosanquet	59	not out	28
P. R. Johnson	b Tarrant	57	c Trott b Tarrant	14
A. E. Lewis	c Tarrant b Mignon	31	lbw b Trott	1
E. S. M. Poyntz	lbw b Tarrant	9	b Trott	0
S. M. J. Woods	c Bosanquet b Tarrant	17	b Trott	0
E. Robson	not out	20	b Trott	0
F. M. Lee	b Hearne	18	c Trott b Tarrant	7
O. C. Mordaunt	c Beldam b Tarrant	1	c Mignon b Trott	4
†Rev A. P. Wickham	c Trott b Tarrant	0	b Trott	0
A. E. Bailey	c Litteljohn b Tarrant	3	c Mignon b Trott	0
	lb 14, w 1	15	b 4, lb 4	8
Total		236		97

BOWLING	O	M	R	W		O	M	R	W
Beldam	4	1	15	0		3	1	10	0
Mignon	24	6	88	2		5	1	24	0
Trott	5	1	10	0		8	2	20	7
Hearne	8	1	22	1					
Bosanquet	8	0	39	1					
Tarrant	15	4	47	6		14	4	35	3

Umpires: F. W. Marlow and S. Brown

In the second innings Trott performed two hat-tricks in his benefit match.
*Captain; †Wicket-keeper.

But that defective light was even the primary cause of Trott's success was not the case. Two or three of the victims he deceived in the flight of the ball, and the uncomfortable necessity of batting under unpleasantly dramatic conditions was no doubt responsible for the the rather poor efforts which some others of his victims made.

In one respect his success on the field had a touch of irony in it. The game was all over by lunchtime. Had it lasted well into the afternoon, as at one time seemed probable, there would certainly have been a large attendance of the public, and Trott would have been the financial gainer thereby.

Poor Alberto! By this time he had put on much weight and he was no longer able to bowl that yorker of bewildering pace. His appetite for fun and for life had caused him to decline quickly so that his general form was a pale carbon copy of what it had been in those two great years at the turn of the century. At the end of his playing days in 1910, he became an umpire, but perhaps he loved his fellow professionals too much to want to give them out. Ill-health forced him to give up umpiring; then, in July 1914, came the greatest tragedy. He was suffering from dropsy, but he discharged himself from hospital and returned to his lodgings in Willesden Green. There was no hope of recovery, and he found the monotony of life in hospital and the pain of life without cricket intolerable. He believed that the only solution was to shoot himself. To his landlady he left his wardrobe and the four pounds that were his wealth.

He should be remembered not only as a very great all-round cricketer, albeit for too short a period, but as one of the greatest givers of fun that the game has known. When he died something of the spirit of a golden age died with him.

CHAPTER SIX

WARNER

MACGREGOR RESIGNED FROM THE CAPTAINCY at the end of the 1907 season. He had led Middlesex to their first universally recognised title and had done an admirable job. As well as being a sympathetic and intelligent captain, he had maintained his form as an outstanding wicket-keeper to the end of his career. He was at the centre of one controversial incident in his last season when MacLaren refused to play on in the Middlesex – Lancashire game in mid-July. There was very little play on the first day, but the weather was fine on the second. The pitch, however, was deemed unfit for play, a decision which caused the crowd to become very restless and demonstrate their anger. Some walked on the pitch and were cleared by police. The following day MacLaren, the Lancashire captain, issued a statement to the press to the effect that the game would not continue because the spectators had ruined the pitch by trampling upon it. MacGregor did not sign the statement, and it was aparent that he was not in agreement with MacLaren. There were subsequent exchanges between MCC and Lancashire, and it is interesting to note that Pelham Warner, in the *Westminster Gazette*, wrote:

> If county cricket be such a serious and solemn thing that a match is to be abandoned because a rebellious spectator has walked across the pitch, then some of us may be driven to think that the cryptic phrase may for once be bluntly applied, 'It's not cricket.'

Warner was the natural successor to MacGregor as captain. He had already played a significant part in Middlesex's Championship triumph by leading the side so successfully in the first part of the season when MacGregor had not been available. The team that he inherited was changing in shape, and Warner was directly responsible for some of the changes that had been brought about.

It was he who was instrumental in bringing Frank Tarrant to England. Tarrant had first played for Victoria in 1898–99 when he was 18 years old. When Warner was in Australia in 1902–03 he heard that Tarrant was anxious to make a career in England, and it was Warner who instigated the negotiations that brought Tarrant to England to serve a two-year residential qualification period for Middlesex. Ironically, he was related to George Tarrant, whose sulking had brought to an end the matches between Middlesex and Cambridge some 40 years earlier.

Tarrant, on the MCC ground staff, appeared for Middlesex second eleven in August 1903, and was 47 not out against Essex second eleven at Lord's when rain ended the match. He impressed in second eleven matches the following year and, on the occasion of his first-class debut for Middlesex, against the South Africans at Lord's, June 1904, he hit 31 and 11, but failed to take a wicket. In 1905, he was a regular in the side from the middle of June onwards. He hit 162 not out against

The greatest all-round cricketer of the Edwardian period, Frank Tarrant sacrificed a Test career to play for Middlesex.

Essex at Leyton and bowled moderately well, but he did little to suggest the greatness that was to come.

Tarrant had been employed as a ground bowler at Melbourne where he earned 30s (£1.50) a week. Ambitious to make his livelihood at cricket, he had no option but to come to England to realise that ambition. He arrived unknown and unheralded, but he became the subject of much criticism as the first major row over importations erupted. Tarrant, however, was an intelligent man and a diligent professional, and he rode the storm well. He offended no one, violated no traditions, and on the field itself, although he had, in fact, debarred himself from Test cricket, he became an all-rounder who would have an automatic place in a world eleven.

In 1907, he became the first Middlesex cricketer to achieve the 'double' for the County alone, and he repeated the feat in the next five seasons until the outbreak of war. His six 'doubles' for the County constitute a record which is never likely to be beaten.

He performed the hat-trick four times for Middlesex, another record, and the first of his hat-tricks, against Gloucestershire at Bristol in 1907, became four wickets in four balls to equal Trott's feat of a few weeks earlier.

His actions caused a change in the laws governing registration, for he had returned to Australia and appeared for Victoria in the English close season. This caused an outcry, and an amendment was made to the existing laws on qualification which became:

> A cricketer may not play for more than one county within the calendar year; the penalty for the infringement of this rule to be disqualification for two years. A British Colony, Dependency, or State shall, for the purpose of this rule, be regarded as a county.

Tarrant, like Trott, silenced his critics because of his zest for the game. He played always as if he were enjoying every moment of what he was doing, and his dignity and self-discipline allied to his outstanding skill won him respect. In contrast to his enthusiastic nature, his batting was initially over-cautious which was one reason for Warner seeing him as a suitable opener, but he developed some strong on-side play to balance his excellent cutting and his range of shots developed after a season in county cricket. He batted right-handed, but his bowling was left-arm slow-medium. He was accurate and incisive and on a wicket that gave him any assistance he was deadly. As an all-round cricketer in the immediate pre-war period only Hirst of Yorkshire was his equal, and there are many, *Wisden* included for a season, who placed him above Hirst. It is doubtful whether any county has had a more meaningful overseas acquisition. One can think of only Hadlee and Rice, the Nottinghamshire pair, who have achieved as much.

Another to arrive at Lord's at much the same time as Tarrant was 'Joe' Murrell. Harry Robert Murrell, to give him his proper name, had played for Kent from 1899 to 1905, had impressed with his safe fielding and sure catching, but had had limited opportunities to display his prowess as a wicket-keeper because of the consistently fine form of Huish. Having been born in Hounslow, he had a birth qualification for Middlesex and joined them in 1906. He kept wicket in eight matches in his first season and spasmodically over the next two seasons, but Warner valued him highly and by 1909 he was the number one wicket-keeper, a most worthy successor to MacGregor.

These were vintage years for the discovery of talent in Middlesex. In 1905, Tarrant's first year in the side, the names of the Hendren brothers, Elias and Denis, appear in the second eleven score book. Denis's career with the County was brief and he later appeared for Durham before becoming a first-class umpire. Elias 'Patsy' Hendren was to become one of the great heroes of Middlesex cricket, a national institution, a man of delight.

'Patsy' played for Turnham Green Cricket Club from the age of 12 onwards, impressing with his fielding, his determination and his courage. He was training as a fitter in an engineering shop when he played for Eighteen of Turnham Green and District against J. T. Hearne's England Eleven. Richardson, Trott, Brockwell and George Beldam were among those in Hearne's side. Hendren played a straight bat to the very fast bowling of Richardson and fielded like a demon. After the game Beldam invited him to Lord's and to meet Mr MacGregor. The career of one of the most loved men in the history of the game had begun.

He was given an extended run in the side in 1908, Warner's first year as captain, and the following season he was regular. Like Denis Compton more than a quarter of a century later, Hendren began low in the batting order. The first match of the 1909 season saw him No 10 against Gloucestershire at

Lord's and he hit 19 not out to dominate a last wicket stand of 18 with Mignon which won his side the game. There was something else notable about that match. It marked the first appearance for Middlesex of J. W. Hearne, 'Young Jack', a distant relation of J.T., whose name was to be linked perpetually with that of Hendren.

In the seven seasons in which Warner led the side before the First World War, Middlesex did not finish lower than sixth in the Championship. They were third in 1910 and 1911 and runners-up in 1914. It had originally been intended that MacGregor should continue to lead the side in 1908, but pressure of business prevented him from appearing in any matches. His career was, in fact, over. George Beldam was also absent, but the consistency of Warner and the great leap forward by Tarrant compensated for these losses and Middlesex remained a strong batting side.

Warner and Tarrant began the season with a stand of 203 in 170 minutes against Hampshire at Lord's, and Middlesex made 502 for nine declared. Twelve days later, against Somerset, again at Lord's, the County established what was then a record by making 596. On this occasion Warner and Tarrant went cheaply, but Moon and Bosanquet, whose appearances were becoming less and less frequent and whose bowling had virtually passed into extinction, put on 227 in two hours. Dr E. Litteljohn and C. C. Page then added 149, Charles Page making the highest score of his career, 164 not out, in 110 minutes. He and Mignon added 93 for the last wicket in 40 minutes, and the Middlesex total of 596 occupied only 325 minutes on the second day, even though there was a 20-minute interruption for rain.

A Cambridge blue and an amateur soccer international, Charles Page played very infrequently and not at all after 1909, even though he was then only 25 years old.

For Warner's consistency and captaincy no praise can be too high. He had an unflagging enthusiasm for the game. His friend Harry Altham gave one of the best assessments of him when he wrote:

His rise was not meteoric, nor his ascendancy ever preeminent; his method was not spectacular, nor his performances in representative cricket really sensational. Yet no one can fairly deny to him the title of 'great'. On every sort of wicket, against every sort of bowling, he would be found scoring heavily, but nowhere quite so consistently as on his home wicket at Lord's. Far from robust or muscular in frame, he was blessed with that great cricketing gift, a rare physical co-ordination, and his batting, if not graceful in the ordinary sense of that term, was extremely attractive in its balance, neatness and precision. With strokes all round the wicket, he was especially strong on the on-side, and to bowl straight off-breaks to him was a highly expensive waste of time. On sticky wickets his back play was soundness itself, and he was always on the look-out for the quick-footed drive; on fast wickets he was a beautiful cutter, and, indeed, an off-side player on classic lines.

But, quite apart from his technical proficiency, he was very great in temperament, in the fighting spirit that welcomed a crisis, in the optimism that could carry both himself and his men through the dark days, and in his profound knowledge of the game. It was these qualities that made him a great captain.

Perhaps one would hesitate at the use of the word 'great' applied to Warner in the overall context of world batsmen, but of his value and service to Middlesex and to cricket there can be no doubt.

His value was never more apparent than in his second season as captain when, in spite of being troubled by ill-health, he hit three centuries. Tarrant, who finished just above him in the batting averages, hit two, and no one else reached three figures.

This was a time of intelligent rebuilding, and the batting, with many of the old faces gone, was weaker than it had been for several seasons. As well as 'Young Jack' Hearne, F. T. Mann made his debut this season. He played three matches in July, began with nought against Lancashire and ended with 56 against Somerset.

The bowling relied heavily on Tarrant and, to a lesser extent, on the ungainly pace bowling of Edward Mignon. How much the side owed to Tarrant, especially when Warner was not available, could be seen from the extraordinary events at Bristol on 26 August. Tarrant took seven for 18 as Gloucestershire were bowled out for 33, which is the second lowest score for which Middlesex have ever dismissed a side. The lowest was also by Gloucestershire, but it came 15 years later. Middlesex were bowled out for 145, Tarrant carrying his bat through the innings for 55. In their second

'Plum' Warner. A lifetime dedicated to cricket, Middlesex and MCC.

innings Gloucestershire made 81, Tarrant, who bowled unchanged throughout the match, taking six for 49. The game was over in a day, which was an embarrassment to the home county who had arranged for the Duke of Beaufort to make a special presentation to E. M. Grace during the lunch interval on the second day.

Tarrant, and Middlesex, received a tremendous boost in 1910 with the amazing return to form of J. T. Hearne and the emergence as an all-rounder of the highest quality in J. W. Hearne. 'Old Jack' took 116 wickets for the County at 12.30 runs apiece and was the leading bowler in the country. It was a stupendous achievement for one who was now 43 years old and was bowling on wickets which presented a harder job to the bowler than they had done in his youth. He passed the hundred mark for the County again the following season and performed the hat-trick for the fourth and last time.

J. W. Hearne began the season quietly, but Warner had faith in him, and Hearne responded with an innings of 155 against Somerset which he followed by taking five Somerset wickets for 28 in the second innings to give his side victory. By now, he and Hendren were generally batting No 3 and 4 in the order, but Hendren's talents were developing more slowly, although he was two years Hearne's senior.

Hearne's leg-break and googly bowling could be a decisive weapon in any match. At Lord's, in August 1910, he took seven Essex wickets in 25 balls without conceding a run. The match ended in a sensational win for Middlesex whose eighth wicket fell when they were still 100 short of their target. Stan Saville, on vacation from Cambridge, stayed with Warner who hit a century and the runs were scored.

The following year J. W. Hearne hit four hundreds for the County, including an innings of 234 not out against Somerset at Lord's. He also took 87 wickets for the County, did the hat-trick against Essex at Lord's (his only other hat-trick was also against Essex) and completed his first 'double' in all first-class matches. He was just 20 years old. He was named as one of *Wisden's* Five Cricketers of the Year, and he was chosen, at Warner's insistence against the opposition of others on the Middlesex committee who thought him too young, to go to Australia with the MCC side which Warner himself was to lead. In the event, Warner played in only the opening match of the tour due to illness and Douglas, the Essex captain who was born in Middlesex, led the side. Hearne's bowling was little used in the Tests, but he hit a century in his second international appearance.

An immensely popular player with a quiet manner and a gentle sense of humour, Jack Hearne earned the reputation of not enjoying the best of health. He was considered frail, but his son asserts that he was generally in the very best of health (he lived until he was 74) and that he was unlucky in that he was only ill at one or two vital occasions.

Always immaculate in his dress and appearance, Hearne was a stylist. He combined a sound defence, a perfectly straight bat and an ability to drive hard with a delicate placing of the ball so that in the aesthetic pleasure that he gave he anticipated Robertson and Eric Russell.

He was not alone in developing rapidly. The medical brothers, Edward and Arthur Litteljohn, had considerable success as batsmen. Edward hit three of his five first-class hundreds in 1911, but the pair were all too rarely available. The names of G. E. V.Crutchley and R. H. Twining, both of whom later became Presidents of the Club, appear for the first time in the Middlesex side, and Murrell's wicket-keeping won general acclaim. More significantly, at the beginning of June 1911, 'Patsy' Hendren hit 134 not out against Sussex at Lord's. It was his maiden first-class hundred, full of resolute hitting. More than a quarter of a century and more than five hundred appearances later, he was to leave Middlesex cricket with a record 119 centuries to his credit, 48 more than his nearest rival and close friend Jack Hearne.

The dreadfully wet summer of 1912 did not help Hendren's progress, and Middlesex were further handicapped by Warner's continued illness, which restricted him to eight appearances, and by J. W. Hearne's moderate form. He seemed exhausted by the demands that had been made upon him at a very early age. To balance this, F. T. Mann played more regularly and Nigel Haig made his first appearance, although he was used primarily as a batsman, his one wicket costing 101 runs. The season also noted the arrival of Harry Lee who had, in fact, played twice in 1910.

Lee had been engaged as an off-break bowler, but he was to be recognised as a rugged and determined batsman shortly before the outbreak of war. He was born in Marylebone, worked in his father's greengrocer's shop, collecting and delivering early in the morning, and had two cricketing brothers, John and Frank, who, after very brief careers with Middlesex, played for Somerset for several seasons.

In spite of Warner's return to fitness and form and J. W. Hearne's first 'double' for the County, testifying to his complete rehabilitation, Middlesex failed to make a strong challenge for the title in 1913. The batting was very strong. Hendren reached a thousand runs for the County for the first time, F. T. Mann recorded a maiden century and Tarrant was what he had been since 1907, a model of consistency and determined application. Murrell, too, as well as keeping magnificently, played some useful innings. In the innings victory over Nottinghamshire at Lord's in June, he and Mordaunt Doll shared an unbeaten eighth-wicket stand of 182 in two hours. It remains a record. Doll, an amateur from Charterhouse, hit 102, the only century of his career, and pulled a ball over the grand stand score-box into a garden in Elm Tree Road during a furious display of hitting.

But what the County desperately lacked was a bowler. Tarrant and J. W. Hearne bowled wonderfully well, but old J.T., though as accurate as ever, was finding it harder to get men out. Mignon had virtually disappeared, and Haig's bowling was still in embryo form. The old Middlesex problem had reasserted itself, yet, in 1914, with no notable additions to the staff, the County came close to winning the Championship. That they came so close was due almost entirely to Tarrant and J. W. Hearne. For the County alone, Hearne scored 2,021 runs and took 114 wickets, while Tarrant had 131 wickets and hit 1,743 runs. No side has ever been so well served by two all-rounders of the very highest class. Tarrant bowled 1,068.2 overs, Hearne 777.5. The next highest was old J.T., 533. Nobody else sent down 150, and all this was on top of long and productive innings.

Middlesex CCC, 1912–13. Standing: J. T. Hearne, Murrell, Hendren, Tarrant, P. Clarke, J. W. Hearne. Seated: Mr N. E. Haig, Mr F. T. Mann, Mr E. L. Kidd, Mr W. P. Robertson and Mr E. S. Litteljohn.

They played a significant part in the initial Championship win over Sussex, but the next game, against Essex at Leyton, was one of the most remarkable in the Club's history. An overnight storm had soaked the ground and when play began late Johnny Douglas asked Middlesex to bat first, but the sun did not shine and the wicket played easily. Tarrant opened with Hon Rupert Anson, for Warner was absent due to the death of his mother-in-law. In 195 minutes, the opening pair put on 235 before Anson was caught off Douglas for 97, the highest score of his career. Tarrant was now joined by J. W. Hearne and in two hours they shared a stand of 229 which was ended only by the declaration. On the second morning both batsmen made a hundred before lunch. Tarrant's 250 was scored in five hours, 20 minutes, and he hit 24 fours. It was the highest innings played by a Middlesex batsman at that time.

Facing a score of 464 for one declared, Essex were bowled out for 173 and 235. Hearne took seven for 54 and seven for 92 to complete a remarkable match which ended with Middlesex winning by an innings and 56 runs, having lost only one wicket.

Tarrant hit 200 and Hearne 104 in the next match, against Worcestershire at Lord's. They shared a stand of 216, and Middlesex again won by an innings. A month later, against Lancashire, again at Lord's, they put on 380 for the second wicket in $4\frac{1}{2}$ hours, a County record. Tarrant hit 198 and Hearne 204. Their century partnerships became almost commonplace, and Middlesex went to Maidstone on 23 July unbeaten.

They gave an uncharacteristically wretched display in every department of the game and Kent won by an innings. The outbreak of war on 4 August cast general gloom. Warner temporarily gave up cricket as did F. T. Mann and W. P. Robertson. The zest had gone out of all. Only Hendren flourished in August, and the match with Yorkshire at Sheffield was nearly cancelled when Middlesex believed that they could not raise a team. Harry Lee moved up to open and hit a fine hundred against Notts and Warner returned to play against Surrey, the eventual Champions, and Middlesex had the better of the draw.

On 27 and 28 August 1914, Middlesex beat Kent at Lord's in two days by 298 runs. J. T. Hearne took seven for 65 in the first innings and two for three in the second. It was his last County Game, although he did reappear for Middlesex against Scotland in 1923 when, aged 56, he took six for 64. He was elected a committee member in 1920, an honour never previously accorded to a professional.

Only three men have taken more wickets in a career. Only Titmus has taken more wickets for Middlesex. As a senior professional, he exerted a very strong influence on Middlesex cricket and on the behaviour of the younger players. On tour, the amateurs stayed at one hotel, the professionals at another. Harry Lee remembered his early days under J.T. who was in charge:

> There was a set hour for us to be at meals or in bed. When we came to sit down, the juniors stood back until the seniors had chosen their places. Then J.T. would take his seat at the head of the table, and carve the joint, handing round the plates in proper order of seniority, and giving himself the carver's portion last of all.

The First World War also brought an end to Frank Tarrant's career with Middlesex. He coached and played in India, returned to Australia and was close to Test selection in the 1920s when in his 40s. He dealt in race-horses in India and Australia and died a wealthy man, the friend of princes.

Unquestionably, he is the greatest all-rounder never to play Test cricket, and his record would suggest that he is the greatest all-rounder to have played for Middlesex. Above all, he was an enthusiastic and dedicated professional, an untiring servant of the club and an intelligent and kindly man.

Warner became a captain in the army and was attached to the Foreign Office. Crutchley was wounded and spent nearly four years in a prison camp, and Harry Lee too was wounded and a prisoner of war. Twining, Doll, Hebden, H. W. Studd and F. T. Mann were among others wounded while C. A. Saville, like Moon and Ash, never returned. The First World War took its toll of Middlesex cricket as it did of the whole nation, and when first-class cricket was resumed in 1919 the ranks were depleted by age as well as by illness.

Warner had been most unwell and was very doubtful as to whether or not he would be able to play again – in any case he was now in his 46th year. He hit 101 in the match against the Australian Imperial Forces in May 1919, the first post-war century, but he was twice attacked by cramp and, in the end, was forced to retire, being carried into the pavilion.

Hendren gave evidence of having matured into a fine batsman. Lee, in spite of injuries sustained during the war, proved an admirable opener, hitting four centuries while Hearne, although suffering from an injured finger which greatly reduced his effectiveness as a bowler, batted with his usual elegance.

The outstanding feature of the year was a record fourth-wicket stand of 325 in 175 minutes between Hearne and Hendren against Hampshire at Lord's. Hearne hit 218 not out and Hendren made 201. It was their first great and exciting stand together.

Middlesex won this game by an innings and later beat Lancashire at Old Trafford, but these were their only two victories. It was a miserable season with the silly experiment of restricting county matches to two days. Middlesex won only two games, the worst record in their history until that time, but they lost only three of their 14 matches.

The reason for the lack of success was obvious. With Tarrant and J. T. 'Tireless' Hearne gone and J. W. only half fit to bowl, the attack was virtually non-existent. Haig had shown improvement, and there was some capable medium pace bowling from Dr Churchill Gunasekera of Ceylon, but there was hardly anything that would frighten the opposition.

There were, however, two interesting newcomers, G. T. S. Stevens and Jack Durston. Greville Stevens was still at University College School, but he had so impressed the cognoscenti with his enterprising batting and leg-break and googly bowling that he had been called up for the Gentlemen and was very much seen as a Middlesex and England star of the future. His 198 runs and 24 wickets in 1919 did nothing to dispel that view. Durston, a pace bowler, had much more limited success, his five wickets costing 74.20 runs each. He had joined the Lord's ground staff in 1914 and was also a professional footballer with Brentford. Durston could move the ball considerably, but he was always handicapped in that a physical quirk prevented him from getting his arm absolutely straight.

Both men were to play important parts in events twelve months later, but before the 1920 season began none spoke of Middlesex as anything but a struggling county with a very weak attack.

Pelham Warner had announced that this was to be his last season. Thankfully, the authorities declared that the three-day county game was to be reinstated. People had just begun to shrug off the war, however deep the scars and bitter the memories, in an attempt to take up life again. There was no touring side, and the public returned joyfully to the county game, not realising, perhaps, that the slaughter of Europe had brought an end to cricket's greatest golden age as it had done to so much else.

The season began with two trial matches and defeat at the hands of a strong Oxford University side for whom Stevens, now in his first year at university, batted well. The first encouragement came when Warwickshire were beaten by an innings at Lord's. The game was over by lunch time on the third day. Warner and Lee made 165 for the first wicket before Warner was forced to retire with cramp. Hearne hit 96, and then 'Patsy' Hendren played an innings of sheer delight. He hit three sixes and 12 fours in 158 out of 279 in two hours, 25 minutes. His third fifty came in 20 minutes and he hit successive deliveries from Quaife onto the pavilion roof and into the ladies' enclosure. Gunasekara took five wickets in the first innings; Leslie Prentice, an amateur off-break bowler who played only a dozen games for the County, a career-best six in the second.

Middlesex v Sussex at Lord's, May 1920. The County established a record when each of the first four batsmen hit a century. Left to right: P. F Warner (139), H. W. Lee (119), J. W. Hearne (116 not out) and N. E. Haig (131).

The victory over Warwickshire drew little comment. It was a fine win, but the midland county were known to be very weak. The innings victory over Sussex in the Whitsuntide Bank Holiday match, however, made people sit up. Prentice again bowled well, and Harry Lee took five for 21 with his rather harmless-looking off-breaks so that Sussex were all out by four o'clock on the first day, the Saturday.

Warner and Lee replied with an opening stand of 241. It ended when Lee was caught off Gilligan for 119, his second century in succession. Warner reached 139 and was out at 284. Haig, playing his first innings of the season, joined Hearne, and they added 227 in 110 minutes. Haig hit 20 fours in his 131. Hendren clouted a quick 17 before falling to Tate. Warner declared at 543 for four, with Hearne 116 not out. It was the first time in the history of the game that the first four batsmen on a side had each scored a century. Lee continued his rich vein of form with six for 47. The match was over in two days.

Lancashire, at Old Trafford, gave a sharper focus to reality and claimed the extra half-hour in an effort to force victory, but they finished 37 short of their target and the match was drawn. At Trent Bridge, Notts confirmed that something nearer to normality had returned when, in spite of Hearne's ten wickets and courageous batting, they won by 151 runs.

Two matches at Lord's followed. Hendren hit 183 not out and Durston took nine wickets as Hampshire were beaten by nine wickets. Durston was quick and initially wild, but he had benefited from coaching and advice, and he now allied control and steadiness to his pace. In the coming weeks he was to reap a rich harvest.

Yorkshire had the better of a draw and looked winners until Hearne and Hendren put on 124 in two hours. Frank Mann hit lustily, two of his three sixes coming off Macaulay, the first over the sight-creen at the Nursery End, and defeat was honourably avoided. At Southampton, in the return match with Hampshire, Harry Lee hit the first double-century of his career, Durston again took nine wickets and victory came by nine wickets. Frank Mann gave further evidence of his great hitting powers.

Lancashire and Somerset were beaten to bring three wins in a row. Hendren, Hearne, Lee, an invaluable all-rounder while Stevens was unavailable, Haig and Durston were all in magnificent form, but the run of success was stopped when Essex drew at Lord's and won at Leyton.

The match at Leyton was a memorable one. Essex were bowled out for 133, and, with Lee and Warner in harness for the third wicket, Middlesex looked to be heading for a substantial lead. But Warner had to attend a selection committee meeting at Lord's which was to choose the side to tour Australia in the winter and retired when he was on 22. In fairness, it should be stated that Johnny Douglas had to leave the match and go to Lord's after bowling only four overs, but Warner, cut off in mid-innings, was a great loss, and the Middlesex lead was restricted to 79, Lee carrying his bat for 80.

It seemed to matter little, however, for Jack Hearne took eight for 49 as Essex crumbled to 196 all out in their second innings. Middlesex needed only 118 to win, a simple task, but J. W. H. T. Douglas produced one of those mighty, physical performances for which he was renowned, and Middlesex were soon struggling at 33 for six. Warner batted with his usual skill and resolution in such a position, but he could find no one to stay with him until, at 67 for eight, Murrell joined him to hit a valiant 23 and see the score to 102.

Durston defended stubbornly, and the score mounted, but, at 113, with four runs separating the sides, Douglas bowled Warner with a magnificent break-back. The two skippers left the field with their arms around each other. Only eight minutes of this rousing match remained when Warner was out.

The points system in operation in 1920 allowed five points for a win, three for a lead on the first innings, and games in which there was no decision on the first innings were ignored. Positions were decided on the percentage of points obtained out of the maximum possible. When Middlesex went to Hove on 31 July they stood sixth in the table.

Stevens had returned from Oxford for the Essex matches so that it could not be said that he had brought good fortune with him. He played a decisive part in the victory at Hove, however. Lee hit another century, but it was Stevens' bouncing leg-spin that won the match in which he had figures of 13 for 60. He bowled with the carefree exuberance of youth and gave the team the fillip, the extra dimension that it needed at a vital time.

If Stevens was the hero at Hove, Hearne was the match-winner at Canterbury where he produced a brilliant display of leg-break bowling at a crucial moment when all seemed lost. Middlesex did not bat well against Woolley and

Freeman, not then the force he was to become later, and only Hendren, 77 not out, and the aggressive Nigel Haig with 57 rescued them from oblivion and took them to 212. Haig's part in the match was by no means over. In a spell of 37 balls he took seven for 14, using the soft pitch to good advantage and troubling the best of batsmen. He bowled Middlesex back into the game after Hardinge and James Seymour had put on 139 for the second wicket. Haig bowled a brisk medium pace, generally with little variety, but with considerable movement.

Kent's first-innings lead was kept to five, but, with Freeman bowling well, Middlesex again struggled and were out for 127. Kent's task of scoring 123 seemed as simple as Middlesex's task had been at Leyton. They moved into the fifties before a wicket fell, and when rain ended play early on the second afternoon Kent were only 29 runs short of victory with four wickets in hand. That Middlesex had brought the game to this state was due to Hearne, who had accounted for Hubble and Hedges, bowled Bickmore for 51 and, most importantly, bowled Woolley first ball.

On the last morning, Troughton drove a little too ambitiously at Hearne and was caught and bowled. Wood was comprehensively bowled by Hearne, and Humphreys, almost Kent's last hope, was brilliantly run out by Hendren from cover, the last man to whom a risky single should have been taken. Hearne bowled Freeman second ball, and Middlesex had won by five runs. Even the self-disciplined Warner exploded with excitement. Hearne had taken eight for 26.

Hearne followed this with 178 and nine wickets at The Oval where Surrey were beaten by an innings and 33 runs, more than 23,000 people watching the first day's play.

Middlesex had moved to fifth in the table. Hendren hit 232, Durston took nine wickets and Notts were beaten by nine wickets, and then came another pulsating match, against Yorkshire.

At Bradford, on a sticky wicket with a slow outfield, Wilfred Rhodes thrived and Middlesex made 105. Hearne bowled as effectively for the metropolitan county, and Yorkshire were 69 for seven, but Burton and Dolphin batted with panache and gave their side a lead of 64, substantial in the context of the match. Lee, Hendren and to a lesser extent Warner ground Middlesex back into contention, but the real flurry came from Haig who hit a violent 86 so that Yorkshire wre left to make 198 to win. They were handicapped by the absence of Kilner as Middlesex had been by the indisposition of Skeet. Sutcliffe, at slip, and Holmes, behind the wicket, fell to Durston. After lunch the same bowler bowled both Rhodes and Burton, and with Hearne and Haig performing well, Yorkshire slipped to 140 for eight. The game was in Middlesex's grasp, but for once they relaxed too soon and nearly paid the price. Waddington and Wilson took Yorkshire to within five runs of victory and then Stevens bowled Waddington with a quick googly.

Middlesex were now third behind Kent and Surrey. Back at Lord's Somerset were brushed aside, and at Edgbaston, with the marvellous Hearne hitting 215 not out in under five hours and Mann a lusty 91, Warwickshire were beaten by nine wickets. The win over Somerset had taken Middlesex into first place, and for the first time there was thought that the Championship could be won.

Two gloriously aggressive innings by Hendren were the corner-stone of the decisive win over Kent at Lord's. Amazingly, this was Middlesex's eighth win in succession, but still they could not claim the title. Lancashire had won at Leyton, and in their last match they played Worcestershire at Old Trafford. No side in contention for the Championship could have wished for a better fixture with which to conclude. *Wisden* was unrelenting in its condemnation of the pear county who had been 'in too much of a hurry to get back to first-class cricket' and 'only in name could Worcestershire be described as a first-class county', for the eleven as a rule was completely outplayed. The match at Old Trafford was no exception, and Lancashire won by nine wickets.

The crowd at Old Trafford believed that this victory had given their side the title, and the team were cordially congratulated before a large gathering of members. The match at Lord's, however, was still in progress.

Middlesex had a much more difficult task. Their final encounter was against their old rivals from across the capital, Surrey. No romantic novelist could have planned a more dramatic ending to the season, and to Warner's career, and one should leave the description of the match to Warner, the culmination of 'My Cricketing Life':

> Saturday, August 28th, dawned fine and bright, if a little cold, to the relief of many an anxious Middlesex partisan up betimes to see the state of the weather. And what a

mighty throng crowded into Lord's! By tube, by bus, by rail from the country, by cab, and on foot they poured into the ground, and when Fender and I came out of the pavilion to toss there must have been 20,000 spectators. But every moment the turnstiles wre clicking, and by quarter past three there were over 30,000 people. The pavilion and Members' Stands were full almost to suffocation, the Mound was crammed, and the ring extended twenty yards in places inside the ropes. The gates were shut at 3.15, and after tea people were sitting two deep on the grass *in front of the pavilion,* a sight neither I, nor anyone else, has ever seen.

From the first ball the air was charged with electricity; everyone seemed to feel that something out of the common was going to happen, and that one and all were about to witness a match that would never be forgotten. Truly a fine setting for the contest that was to ensue. I won the toss, and naturally elected to bat on the excellent wicket that had been prepared. We started badly. Three, including Hearne and Lee, who fell to a marvellous catch by Hitch at short leg, who took a fast moving hit with his right hand, were out for 35 runs, when I joined Hendren.

Runs were terribly hard to get, the bowling being accuracy itself, the fielding superb, especially in the part of Hobbs, who cramped all the runs on the off-side, Hitch, Howell at mid-on who ran so fast that I christened him Spion Kop, and Sandham at deep third man. Not even Hendren, or Mann, or Haig could do anything else but score very slowly, and six wickets were down for 149.

Stevens now came in, and once again proved what a good man he is at a crisis. He was missed in the slips from an easy chance when he had made 12, the one blemish on Surrey's otherwise superb fielding, but he batted very well indeed, and was scoring freely when Fender bowled him. Still at the end of the day we could only show a total of 258 for eight wickets, admittedly very slow going on a good wicket. But, I repeat, the Surrey bowling was splendid, and was manoeuvred with marked ability by the Surrey captain. Many critics left the ground thinking that we had already lost all chance of winning the match, and many blamed me for my slow play in getting only 70 runs not out between five minutes past one and six-thirty, allowing, of course, for the usual intervals. I can only, like the West Indian, reply that 'I was doing my best for de

honour of my country', and I simply found it impossible
to score faster.

Murrell was more optimistic, and remarked that '250
runs always take some making. There are two long days'
cricket before us, and if you had got out we might have
been out for 150 or less.'

Monday was another fine day. We were all out for 268,
Rushby hitting the top of my off stump with a good-
length ball that came with his arm after I had added but 9
more runs. Surrey headed us by 78 runs, scoring 341 for 9
wickets, when the innings was declared closed. Our
bowling was not quite up to the mark. Durston was good,
but neither of our googly bowlers were in form, and two
or three catches were missed which should have been held.
Sandham played a magnificent innings of 167 not out,
scoring all round the wicket, though his best stroke was
the square and late cuts, Ducat got 49 very well, and
Fender made 30 in a very few minutes.

We had an anxious three quarters of an hour batting,
but Skeet and Lee played with grim determination, and
resisted all the 'bottled lighting' which Hitch put into his
deliveries, and the wiles of the clever Fender. There was a
big crowd as on the Saturday, and the general opinion at
the close of play was that Middlesex could not win.

Tuesday, August 31st, found our dressing room full of
letters and telegrams, and bunches of white heather sent
by supporters who had not given up hope. Skeet and Lee
early gained a supremacy over the Surrey bowling. They
started confidently, and after a time, runs came fast, and at
lunch, 1.30, 199 runs had been made, and both were
undefeated.

At 208 Lee was bowled, and at 249 Skeet was caught in
the slips, both men falling to Hitch. Lee had scored 108
and Skeet 106; and it was their great batting that first put
us in a position which gave us a chance of victory. Skeet
has the courage of the Rugby footballer, a cool head,
considerable powers of defence, and playing constantly in
first-class cricket improved his stroke play. Lee plays his
cricket in the same happy spirit as Hendren, for he loves it
all, and if the purists in style object that he crouches in the
most ungainly manner at the crease, my reply is that he
gets up to play the ball. He is certainly a very fine batsman,
and he will be unlucky indeed if he does not play for
England one of these days.

MIDDLESEX *v* SURREY

Played at Lord's, 28, 30 and 31 Aust 1920

MIDDLESEX WON BY 55 RUNS

MIDDLESEX	FIRST INNINGS				SECOND INNINGS		
C. H. L. Skeet	c Ducat b Rushby	2			c Fender b Hitch		106
H. W. Lee	c Hitch b Fender	12			b Hitch		108
J. W. Hearne	c and b Hitch	15			lbw b Rushby		26
E. H. Hendren	b Reay	41			c Sandham b Rushby		5
*P. F. Warner	b Rushby	79	(9)		not out		14
F. T. Mann	c and b Fender	12	(5)		c Peach b Fender		22
N. Haig	b Reay	18	(6)		b Rushby		1
G. T. S. Stevens	b Fender	53	(7)		not out		21
H. K. Longman	b Fender	0					
†H. R. Murrell	c Ducat b Hitch	9	(8)		b Reay		0
T. J. Durston	not out	0					
	b 12, lb 12, nb 3	27			b 8, lb 4, w 1		13
Total		268			(for 7 wkts, dec)		316

BOWLING	O	M	R	W		O	M	R	W
Hitch	32.1	10	66	2		20	5	71	2
Rushby	23	9	48	2		22	7	73	3
Fender	28	4	76	4		16.5	2	70	1
Reay	26	17	31	2		18	1	61	1
Ducat	3	1	10	0		3	1	12	0
Shepherd	6	3	10	0		4	0	16	0

1st inns: 1-4, 2-23, 3-35, 4-88, 5-109, 6-149, 7-239, 8-245, 9-268
2nd inns: 1-208, 2-249, 3-254, 4-261, 5-265, 6-290, 7-291

SURREY	FIRST INNINGS		SECOND INNINGS	
J. B. Hobbs	c Mann b Hearne	24	c Lee b Haig	10
A. Sandham	not out	167	c and b Hearne	68
M. Howell	c Murrell b Durston	7	st Murrell b Stevens	25
T. Shepherd	c Murrell b Durston	0	c Hendren b Stevens	26
H. A. Peach	hit wkt b Stevens	18	b Stevens	11
A. Ducat	st Murrell b Lee	49	lbw b Hearne	7
*P. G. H. Fender	c Haig b Durston	30	b Durston	1
W. Hitch	b Durston	1	b Stevens	6
G. M. Reay	c Haig b Lee	6	b Hearne	5
†H. Strudwick	b Hearne	9	b Stevens	10
T. Rushby	not out	6	not out	7
	b 17, lb 5, nb 2	24	b 11, lb 1	12
Total	(for 9 wkts, dec)	341		188

BOWLING	O	M	R	W		O	M	R	W
Durston	30	9	97	4		14	1	42	1
Haig	10	4	25	0		8	0	19	1
Stevens	16	0	72	1		13.4	0	61	5
Hearne	24	8	57	2		11	0	37	3
Lee	15	2	66	2		4	0	17	0

1st inns: 1-59, 2-78, 3-82, 4-128, 5-227, 6-275, 7-277, 8-312, 9-335
2nd inns: 1-22, 2-62, 3-120, 4-122, 5-143, 6-155, 7-166, 8-168, 9-176

Umpires: J. Blake and G. P. Harrison.
Middlesex's victory won them the Championship.
*Captain; †Wicket-keeper.

At luncheon time I altered the order, and ordered up the 'Sturm Struppen', as I used to call Hendren, Mann, Haig, and Murrell, but though Mann made a few powerful blows, the others got out at once, and at 3.32 there were seven of us out for 291 runs. I now joined Stevens, and to my dying day I shall never forget the tumultous welcome the crowd gave me on going out to play my last innings for Middlesex at Lord's.

I was cheered all the way to the wickets, cheering in which the Surrey eleven joined and there was a big lump in my throat, and I would scarcely see, when I took block. In seven and a half minutes Stevens and myself scored 25 runs, running like rabbits between the wickets, and taking all sorts of risks even with such a fieldsman as Hobbs. At 3.40 I closed the innings. I was proud to be in with young Stevens at the finish – he, the rising star, and I, whose sun was fast setting; and I was glad indeed to be undefeated in my last innings in first-class cricket on my beloved Lord's.

Surrey were thus left with 244 runs to make in three hours. Would they get them? or should we get them out? Someone suggested I had been a little rash, to which I replied, 'It's a case of World-Power or Downfall, and I hope I shan't share the fate of the ex-Kaiser! Eighty runs an hour is not a very great rate of scoring, but it is just enough to compel Surrey to play a free game; and I rely on our googly bowlers to do something big.'

We went out to field determined to make the effort of our lives, and with the knowledge that Lancashire had beaten Worcestershire at Old Trafford, we meant to win, if possible, but in any case, to die fighting. Victory was everything to us, and to attain that was worth risking a great deal.

Champion County, 1920. Standing: Lee, H. K. Longman, Durston, N. Haig, C. T. S. Stevens, C. H. L. Skeet. Seated: Hearne, F. T. Mann, P. F. Warner (captain), Murrell, Hendren.

It was exactly a minute to four o'clock when Durston from the nursery end bowled the first ball to Hobbs, Haig being the other bowler. After two or three overs, the bowlers changed ends, and at 22 Hobbs was had at second slip, the ball bounding off Hendren's hands to Lee.

Howell played very well, but he was beautifully stumped at 62, and Shepherd joined Sandham. Shepherd is a young cricketer of high promise, and he and his partner scored quickly. 70, 80, 90, 100, 110 went up, but at 120 Shepherd fell to a beautiful catch by Hendren, who had to judge a big high drive, backing the while with the screen not ten yards behind him.

The time was now 5.27, so that Surrey had, at this point, 124 runs to make with little more than an hour and a half to go. Stevens had been given a rest after bowling for twenty-five minutes, but a quarter of an hour later he was back again, at the nursery end, and it was off his bowling that Hendren made the catch.

Previous to this Hendren had been fielding at short leg, but I saw Fender signal from the balcony of the pavilion to the batsmen to force matters, so I promptly placed Hendren in the long field, as I thought that a catch was more likely to go in that direction than to short leg, and I wanted to make a certainty of it, and to leave nothing to chance. Fender's appearance was the signal for a prolonged burst of applause from the Surrey partisans, but after nearly cutting my right hand off at point with a terrific square cut he was clean bowled, hitting across a straight well-pitched-up ball, something between a yorker and a half volley of Durston's. 122-4-1.

Peach is the next batsman, and ten minutes later Hearne relieves Durston at the pavilion end. At 5.47 Stevens clean bowls Peach with a beautiful ball which pitches on the leg stump and hits the top of the off, and to which the batsman played forward. 143-5-11. But Sandham was still there, and with Ducat, Hitch and Reay – all heavy hitters – to come, it only wanted a dashing little innings of 80 or so from one of these men, and, with Sandham quite at his ease, Middlesex would be beaten.

At four minutes to six Sandham got out. Hearne bowled him a full pitch which he hit fairly hard straight back to the bowler, who clutched it eagerly. Sandham had played perfectly for 68, and I shall be surprised if he does not go in first for England within the next few years. 155-

6-68. Surrey now needed 85 to win, sixty-four minutes to go, and four wickets to fall. Many were afraid of Hitch, but a hitter of Hitch's type does not like googly bowling, and I was more afraid of Ducat.

Hitch was missed, by Hendren of all people, at deep square-leg, from a low hard hit, but one which Patsy would accept nine times out of ten. A groan goes up all round the ground, but five minutes later a fine length googly, this time from Stevens, which it would have taken a Ranji or a Fry to stop, clean bowls Hitch, and away he walks, amidst terrific Middlesex shouts this time. 168-8-6.

Time, six minutes past six! Reay attempts a rustic swipe at a leg-break of Hearne's and is bowled, and in comes Rushby, smiling and unmoved, the last hope, with Strudwick at the other end, of Surrey. But no man can tell the result of a cricket match until it is over, and number eleven has often brought off an unexpected coup.

A ball of Stevens's beats Rushby and the wicket-keeper, and goes for four byes, and Strudwick makes a two here, a single there, while Rushby shows no sign whatever of trepidation. It is now Strudwick's turn to face Stevens, and with the fourth ball of his fourteenth over that splendid young cricketer sends down another fine googly, and at twenty minutes past six Middlesex had won the championship.

As long as I live I shall hear the yell of delight and the thud of thousands of feet rushing across the ground. From every side they swarmed, and I was tackled just above the ankles – the right place to tackle, they used to tell us at Rugby – by a fine big fellow, and deposited far up the pavilion steps, borne by the joyous crowd. What my feelings were, no words of mine could describe.

CHAMPIONSHIP AND DECLINE: THE AGE OF HEARNE AND HENDREN

THE FEAT OF WINNING THE LAST NINE GAMES of the season to snatch the Championship is one that is unrivalled in the history of the game. The final, dramatic match against Surrey has no equal in Middlesex annals, save perhaps a Benson & Hedges Cup Final triumph more than 60 years later, and Warner's farewell has tended to overshadow much of the next 15 years although Frank Mann took the side to the title with almost equal bravura in 1921.

The success of Warner's team was founded on a glorious spirit. Greville Stevens, who was six years younger than anyone else in the match, was to say many years later: 'Under Plum we all tried beyond limitations. Without him we would never have gained the day.'

Stevens himself was to play a less important part in Middlesex cricket than one could have hoped for. He assisted the County until 1932, and he played in ten Test Matches, including England's triumph over Australia at The Oval in 1926, but his appearances were infrequent. His ultimate record is of a promise that was never quite fulfilled because, after university, he never had the time to give to the game.

Challen Skeet, noted for his brilliant fielding, won his blue at Oxford in 1920 and played a few games for Middlesex in 1922 before being lost to first-class cricket when he joined the Civil Service in Sudan. His century in the second innings against Surrey which, with Lee's hundred, made victory possible was the only three-figure innings of his brief career.

Henry Longman, a former Surrey and Cambridge batsman whose place at No 9 (he was no bowler) would cause raised eyebrows, followed a military career and never played for Middlesex after that historic day in August 1920.

The professionals continued to give yeoman service, swallowed only by age, illness, injury and the ever-increasing ravages of Test cricket.

In 1920, Hendren hit 2,095 runs for Middlesex; Hearne hit 1,638 and took 123 wickets; Durston took 111 wickets and was now a pace bowler of control and aggression. In 1921, he was to form a highly successful opening bowling partnership with Nigel Haig.

Patsy Hendren.

In the winter that preceded that season, Hendren and Hearne went with the side led by Douglas to Australia. England lost every Test Match, and although Hendren batted quite well in the series, Hearne was taken ill and did not play after the first Test. Neither could he play for Middlesex until the end of May, but by then the County was already ahead in the Championship race with victories over Hampshire, Sussex and Notts.

Mann and Haig were proving themselves free scorers, and Haig this year did the 'double' for the first time, and played for England. He and Durston made their Test debuts at Lord's. In Durston's case, it was to be his only Test. Hendren also played, but he had a wretched time in the two Tests in which he appeared. The gloom of England's performance in that series tended to darken all else and has obscured the remarkable performance of Middlesex who, having won their last nine county matches of the previous season, won the first eight of 1921.

The first occasion that they failed to win was when Lancashire outplayed them at Lord's, but they still managed to draw. Four days later, at Old Trafford, they won the return match with ease. Then came a win at Southampton to make it ten wins in 11 matches, although it should be added that Warwick Armstrong's Australians had won comfortably at Lord's at the beginning of June.

The first defeat of the season came at The Oval, 16, 18 and 19 July, when Surrey won a magnificent match by 19 runs. Middlesex were set to make 370, and at 159 for six, they were in a hopeless position, but Stevens and Leonard Burtt put on 132 in 110 minutes before, most unfortunately, Stevens was run out. He had hit 78, and L. L. Burtt made 50. He was playing his second, and last, match for the County.

The only other defeat occurred at Canterbury when the Middlesex batting twice collapsed. Ample revenge was gained at Lord's three weeks later so that Middlesex again entered the last match of the season, against the arch rivals Surrey, with the Championship in their grasp. The stage was set for an even more thrilling climax on this occasion, for the only other side who could win the title were Surrey themselves. Middlesex needed only to avoid defeat to take the title.

For such an historical and exciting match, it has received scant coverage. Its romantic appeal could not compare with the fixture the previous season, but it was a magnificent attraction in its own right, a necessary balm to the public after the horrors suffered at the hands of the Australians. The match excited enormous interest. There were close to 16,000 paying customers on the first day, 17,663 on the second, and 14,311 on the third. *Wisden* takes up the story:

> Surrey won the toss, but their advantage was quickly discounted, Knight, Sandham and Ducat being out when only 56 runs had been scored. Knight was bowled by a deadly break-back. Shepherd and Jardine made ample amends for the disastrous start and, taking infinite pains, put on 144 runs together in two hours and twenty minutes before Jardine was bowled. When he left Surrey had done very well, but two more wickets fell for 10 runs, and the innings was finished off for 269. Shepherd took out his bat for perhaps the best of all the fine innings he played last summer. The importance of the occasion made him at times unusually cautious, but he hit with splendid power, and was rarely at fault. His 128 not out included a dozen 4's. Middlesex lost one wicket before the call of time, and on Monday morning they broke down so badly that soon after the luncheon interval they were all out for 132. Surrey's bowling was excellent, Reay being at his best, and Strudwick in getting rid of Hendren brought off a

wonderful catch on the leg side. Going in with a lead of
137, Surrey were in a most flattering position, and when
their score stood at 115 with only two men out they
looked to have the game in their hands. A startling
collapse followed the dismissal of Shepherd, however, the
last seven wickets going down for 69 runs. D. J. Knight
was for once last season in the form of 1919. His innings of
74 was perfect. Haig brought about Surrey's collapse. He
bowled very finely, and caught and bowled Shepherd in a
wonderful way, running up the pitch and taking the ball
low down with his left hand. Middlesex had rather more
than a quarter of an hour's batting before stumps were
drawn, and, taking no risks, Twining and Lee hit up 19
without being separated. The third day's cricket was
unforgettable. A sterner fight no one could wish to see.
The great point in favour of Middlesex was that they were
free from anxiety as to the clock. There was always ample
time in which to get the runs. Lee was out at 48, and then
came the batting that won the match. Hearne joined
Twining at five minutes past twelve, and not until twenty
minutes past five did the second wicket fall, 277 runs being
added in four hours and ten minutes of actual play. The
only mistake, so far as could be seen, was a chance offered
by Twining when he had made 59 to Knight in the slips.
Apart from this the batting of both men was flawless.
Surrey fielded untiringly, trying the hardest until at five
minutes past six Hendren made the winning hit.'

Twining hit 135 and Hearne 106. Haig and Durston each
took seven wickets in the match. One of the strengths of
Middlesex during the season, apart from the continued
success of Lee, Hearne and Hendren as batsmen, was the
emergence of several young amateurs of quality.

For Richard Twining, whose only other century for
Middlesex was to come some years later, the innings against
Surrey was the innings of his life-time. A product of Eton and
Oxford, he had been badly wounded in the knee at Gallipoli,
and it was believed that he would not play again. He was on
crutches as late as 1919 and was slightly lame for the rest of his
life. He was yet another whose business commitments
restricted his Middlesex appearances, for he played in only 32
matches in 18 years. He was to serve the Club nobly as an
administrator, being both Treasurer and President. By tragic
irony, he lost his son in the Second World War.

The Hon Clarence Bruce, for 20 years on the International Olympic Executive, played more frequently and was always a useful hard-hitting middle-order batsman. He retired from cricket when he became Baron Aberdare in 1929.

Gerald Edward Victor Crutchley had been noted before the First World War as an unearther of good cricketers, and he was another who was to give excellent service as an administrator of the Club. He had had the misfortune to be taken ill when he was 99 not out for Oxford in the Varsity match of 1912, but he gave some good performances for Middlesex as batsman and medium pace leg-break bowler. His son Edward played twice for the County in 1947 with little success, and his daughter Rosalie is the noted actress.

Frank Mann was a very different leader from Warner, and with customary modesty he publicly declared that the success of the team was entirely due to his predecessor, that he had inherited a fine team and the only part he played in winning the Championship was by spinning the coin. He contributed far more than that, especially several innings of necessary violence. Harry Lee said of him, with good judgement: 'He was not, perhaps, among the great captains, but his good nature, modesty and sportsmanship added very much more to the game than he took from it.'

Years later, 'Gubby' Allen was to remember Mann as 'the most unselfish man you could ever wish to meet'. 'I went to complain to him about something one day on tour and found him in a dreadful attic in the hotel. The rest of us had large, comfortable rooms, but Frank had taken what was left so that the rest of us should be well looked after. He was a delightful man.' Like his son more than 20 years later, he was a successful and popular captain of England in South Africa.

Lee himself enjoyed another fine season in the second Championship year. He hit 243 not out against Notts at Lord's. He and Crutchley put on 231 in $2\frac{1}{4}$ hours for the first wicket, and with Mann hitting 53 off 20 balls, Middlesex made 612 for eight declared. This established a new record for the County, but it was to last only two years.

One of the most interesting features of the season was Mann's decision to invite 'Gubby' Allen to play in two matches in August. Allen, a protégé of Warner's, was in his last year at Eton and was the outstanding Public Schools fast bowler of the year, but it was still a brave, and unusual, decision of Mann's to play him at such a crucial stage in the Championship race.

Frank Mann—an ever-encouraging skipper. (Courtesy of Allsport)

Allen, in fact, had been born in Australia but had come to England when he was six; the family home was in Buckinghamshire. Warner had gone to live in the same village as the Allens and had become very friendly with them. Buckinghamshire wanted 'Gubby' Allen's services and were a little upset when Middlesex claimed him on the grounds of a residential qualification, for the Allens also had a flat in London. 'Warner was a marvellous judge of a cricketer. He was able to assess a man's strengths and weaknesses after one over, and he was good with people.' He wanted Allen for Middlesex, and he got him.

Allen had been much helped at Eton by the arrival of George Hirst as coach. Hirst was one of the early quick swing bowlers, and Allen could swing the ball. 'I could swing the ball from the age of twelve or thirteen,' he recalls, 'but I did not know why. One day it went one way, the next day the other. George Hirst explained to me what I was doing. He was a lovely man, a tremendous help.'

Middlesex won both matches, against Somerset and Warwickshire, with ease. Allen took a wicket in each match, his first coming when he bowled Robson, the veteran Somerset all-rounder.

On vacation from Cambridge the following summer, he played in ten matches, took 12 wickets and topped the bowling averages, but, although he was to captain England and later to play a most important part in the administration of the game, he was to appear most irregularly for Middlesex in all the years that he was to be associated with them.

Frank Mann led the side until the end of 1928. Middlesex were runners-up in 1924, but for the rest of Mann's reign they were a middle-of-the-table side.

For most of this time Mann was supported by Haig, although he could not bowl in 1923 because of injury, and by the professionals, Hendren, Hearne, Lee, Durston and Murrell. A most useful acquisition in the early 1920s was the amateur left-handed opening batsman, Hugh Lloyd Dales, generally known as 'Horace', but, unquestionably, these were the great years of Jack Hearne and 'Patsy' Hendren. Hendren hit 277 not out against Kent at Lord's in 1922, the highest score made by a Middlesex batsman at that time, and Hearne hit two double-hundreds and, with 94 wickets, came close to completing the 'double' in matches for Middlesex.

Jack Hearne was essentially a back-foot player. He had one special shot when he hit the ball square of cover. He also spun the ball prodigiously, although not always accurately. As a man, he was loved and respected. 'Gubby' Allen says of him, 'Of all Middlesex players when I first came into the side, he gave me more help than anyone else.'

'Young' Jack Hearne. Elegance, dedication, loyalty and greatness.

Yet, off the field, 1922 was a sad season for Middlesex, for, on 29 March, the Club President, Russell Donnithorne Walker, died. He was succeeded by A. J. Webbe. R. D. Walker was 80 years old when he died and he had enjoyed a good life, but his death brought to an end the connection between the famous brotherhood and the County Club.

It was a pity that he did not live to witness the match against Hampshire at Southampton in June the following year. Rain on the last day deprived Middlesex of a chance of victory, but before that they had hit the highest score in their history.

Hampshire made 342. Middlesex responded with Dales and Lee putting on 174 for the first wicket, and Hearne and Hendren put on 375 for the third. This stood as a world record for eleven years and was a Middlesex record until 1948. The Middlesex score-card read as follows:

H. L. Dales	c Shirley b Kennedy	103
Lee, H. W.	b Boyes	107
Hearne, J. W.	c and b Shirley	232
Hendren, E. H.	not out	177
Beton, S.	not out	3
	b 13, lb 5, w 1, nb 1	20
	(for 3 wkts dec)	642

The runs came in 173 overs. Sydney Beton was making his debut. This was only the second time that the first four batsmen on a side had all made centuries, the previous one being against Sussex three years earlier as already noted.

That Hearne and Hendren should have shared the world record stand was appropriate, for they, above all others, were carrying Middlesex on their shoulders. For the second season in succession, Hendren was the leading batsman in the country and, for the first time, in all matches he topped three thousand runs. Hearne had his right hand broken by a ball from Gilligan in the match at Hove on 6 August, and he could not play again for the rest of the season, yet he achieved his fifth, and last, 'double' in all matches and scored 1,222 runs and took 103 wickets for Middlesex alone.

In the wet summer of 1924 which followed, the pair again dominated, but they now received fuller support from the occasional amateurs. Dales hit three hundreds. Stevens regained something of the all-round form of his youth, and Allen's pace bowling brought about one remarkable victory, that at Weston-super-Mare, when his 7 for 32 helped dismiss Somerset for 82 before lunch on the first day.

With the early fixtures all at Lord's, the team began well. They demolished Yorkshire, but this was described as 'a travesty of what a match between Yorkshire and Middlesex should be, owing to Middlesex taking the field without Hearne and Hendren and Yorkshire without Sutcliffe, Holmes, Roy Kilner and Macaulay – all playing in the Test trial'. Yorkshire were bowled out for 192 on a good wicket, and Middlesex, scoring at a furious rate, made 465 for eight declared. Dales and Stevens hit hundreds, but it was Mann's 79, which included four sixes off Rhodes, two on to the roof of the pavilion, which captured the imagination.

The first defeat was in the Whitsuntide match with Sussex when the batting collapsed before Tate and Gilligan. Middlesex were all out for 41 in their second innings.

There was also defeat by Somerset at Lord's when Robertson-Glasgow took nine for 38, the best analysis ever returned against the County, but Kent, Essex and Hampshire were all beaten in quick succession in away fixtures.

The return match with Yorkshire at Sheffield began sensationally, for, having been put in, Middlesex, through Dales and Stevens, hit 64 in the first half-hour. Hendren was run out on 99, and Bruce made 88, and Middlesex just snatched first innings points.

This match was not without its repercussions. Yorkshire's defeat at Lord's had been their first for over a year, and it had rankled. At the time, some found it amusing. A member in the pavilion is said to have been woken by one of Mann's sixes, fallen asleep again and been woken again by another six thudding behind him. Abe Waddington at mid-off laughed when Rhodes was hit for sixes, and the bowler enquired 'What the bloody hell are you laughing at?' Rhodes later remonstrated that he should never have been taken off after Mann's barrage, for he was 'just teasing him'. By the time the teams met at Bramall Lane, however, the humour had disappeared. Frustrated by their inability to bowl Middlesex out, the Yorkshire side resorted to constant appeals, backed by a vociferous and hostile crowd. Middlesex left Sheffield determined that they would not meet Yorkshire the following season. Umpires Butt and Reeves reported Yorkshire in general and Waddington in particular. There was enquiry and censure, but negotiations between the two committees resulted in the sides agreeing to meet in 1925.

Frank Mann must take much credit for resolving this argument. He was a generous, warm and tactful man. His captaincy was founded on encouragement, and he earned respect and response. No man could have set a better example. He had been wounded three times in the war, and on the last occasion, in 1917, had had most of one foot shot to pieces. He was sent to Norfolk to convalesce, and many thought that he would have difficulty in walking after the war, but he spent his time in Norfolk getting himself down to a scratch golfer. His rugby career was over. He had been an England trialist, and deprived of a cap by injury, but although never as nimble as he had been before 1914, he stationed himself at mid-off and not much got past him.

Sensation was the key word in Middlesex cricket in this year, for the next match, at Trent Bridge, still sends shudders through Nottinghamshire supporters when it is recalled. Carr and John Gunn hit centuries which took Notts to a seemingly unassailable 462, and Middlesex, out for 253, were forced to follow on. At 108 for five in their second innings, Middlesex looked well beaten, particularly as Bruce had had to retire hurt temporarily with an injured hand. Bolstering the Middlesex side, however, was John Lindsay Guise, on vacation from Oxford. He hit a most courageous hundred and took the score to 283 before he was eighth out. Bruce then returned and, batting one-handed, hit seven fours in a wonderfully brave innings of 58. Durston battled well for 28, and Middlesex were out for 358. This left Notts to make 150 to win, and with George Gunn and Whysall opening with a stand of 72 in 50 minutes, a home win looked a formality. Haig then bowled Gunn, and 'Gubby' Allen accounted for Whysall. Allen bowled at a terrifying pace. He took six wickets in 33 balls, finished with six for 31, and Middlesex won by 27 runs. Allen was not really fast until he began to play for Middlesex. 'Joe Murrell stood back to me so I thought I had better bowl quickly.' George Mann, Denis Compton and many others consider that he had the best action of any fast bowler they have seen.

Yet there were to be more sensations. Another fine run of success took Middlesex to their last three matches with every chance of winning the Championship. Rain on the last afternoon at Lord's blighted their hopes against Kent, but with Yorkshire losing to Surrey, Middlesex travelled to Bristol knowing that victory over Gloucestershire would almost certainly assure them of the title.

Broad shoulders and stout heart. Jack Durston.

They could not have asked for a better start. Haig and Durston bowled unchanged and in $1\frac{1}{4}$ hours Gloucestershire were out for 31, the lowest score for which Middlesex have ever dismissed an opposing county.

The pitch, however, was difficult throughout, and the home side had, in Charlie Parker, one of the finest slow left-arm bowlers that the game has known, although he was to be grossly undervalued by Pelham Warner and selectors. He opened the bowling with Wally Hammond, and Middlesex were out in 21.1 overs, their lead restricted to 43. They would not have had that big lead had Guise not batted with a late flourish.

Parker's seven wickets included the hat-trick, Twining, Allen and Mann being the victims. How many captains, going in to save the hat-trick, have been stumped?

Middlesex still held the upper hand, and, on the Monday, Gloucestershire lost two wickets before they cleared the

GLOUCESTERSHIRE *v* MIDDLESEX

Played at Packer's Ground, Bristol, 23, 25 and 26 August 1924

GLOUCESTERSHIRE WON BY 61 RUNS

GLOUCESTERSHIRE	FIRST INNINGS		SECOND INNINGS	
A. G. Dipper	c Dales b Haig	6	c Durston b Haig	7
F. J. Seabrook	c Murrell b Haig	7	b Durston	4
W. R. Hammond	c Hearne b Haig	5	not out	174
B. H. Lyon	c Durston b Haig	4	c Hendren b Hearne	42
†H. Smith	b Durston	3	lbw b Hearne	2
F. G. Rogers	c Dales b Haig	0	b Hearne	0
B. S. Bloodsworth	not out	1	run out	9
*Lt-Col D. C. Robinson	b Durston	0	c Lee b Haig	24
P. Mills	c Murrell b Durston	0	b Allen	3
C. W. L. Parker	b Durston	0	c Dales b Haig	13
G. Dennett	b Haig	3	not out	5
	lb 1, nb 1	2	b 6, lb 1, nb 4	11
Total		31	(for 9 wkts dec)	294

BOWLING	O	M	R	W	O	M	R	W
Haig	12	7	11	6	33	2	95	3
Durston	11	4	18	4	16	3	61	1
Allen					9.2	1	26	1
Hearne					21	1	75	3
Lee					5	1	9	0
Murrell					4	0	17	0

MIDDLESEX	FIRST INNINGS		SECOND INNINGS	
H. L. Dales	c Dipper b Hammond	7	lbw b Mills	42
H. W. Lee	c Lyon b Parker	21	b Hammond	21
J. W. Hearne	c Rogers b Parker	6	c Hammond b Parker	6
E. H. Hendren	c Hammond b Parker	5	lbw b Parker	23
R. H. Twining	c Lyon b Parker	1	b Mills	8
G. O. Allen	c Dennett b Parker	0	c and b Parker	31
*F. T. Mann	st Smith b Parker	0	c Lyon b Parker	22
J. L. Guise	c Lyon b Hammond	22	c Dennett b Parker	0
N. Haig	b Mills	8	lbw b Parker	0
†H. R. Murrell	c Hammond b Parker	2	b Parker	22
T. J. Durston	not out	0	not out	3
	b 1, nb 1	2	b 2, lb 8, nb 2	12
Total		74		190

BOWLING	O	M	R	W	O	M	R	W
Hammond	9	2	27	2	13	8	22	1
Parker	10.1	3	30	7	31.1	5	101	7
Mills	2	0	15	1	15	4	45	2
Dennett					8	4	10	0

Umpires: H. W. Phillips and W. Reeves.

Middlesex's defeat deprived them of the Championship.

*Captain; †Wicket-keeper.

arrears. It was at this point, however, that Wally Hammond took over. At the time, he was relatively unknown. A squabble over qualification had delayed his entry into the Gloucestershire side and the double-hundreds and the eight successive summers leading the first-class averages lay a decade ahead, but he gave notice that afternoon that a great batsman had arrived. Haig suggested that an unnamed Middlesex fielder dropped him twice before he had made 50 and again at 70, while he was missed by another fielder when he was on 137. Allen reckons he was missed five times. *Wisden* verifies only the last chance. He batted for four hours and hit a six and 21 fours with all the majesty that those fortunate enough to see him will have imprinted on their memories for the rest of their lives.

The game had now swung violently in favour of Gloucestershire, for Middlesex needed 252 to win on a pitch that was badly cut up and had never been good. They made a splendid effort, and there even seemed a possibility that the miracle would be achieved, but then Parker did the hat-trick for the second time in the match and Gloucestershire won by 61 runs. It was to be 23 years before Middlesex gained revenge for that reverse.

The last match of the season was ruined by rain and Yorkshire won the title. Warner, in *The Cricketer*, stated that Middlesex were the better side, well balanced with some excellent fielding. He also hinted that relations between Middlesex and Yorkshire were rather strained, but they were certainly righted by the following season.

It was to be more than a decade before Middlesex again challenged so strongly for the Championship, and in the interim they were to slip to the lowest point in their fortunes. There were good moments and interesting moments, but for the rest of Mann's period as captain and for all of that of his successor, they were never more than a middle-of-the-table side at best.

The bowling was the major weakness. Hearne suffered a series of misfortunes. Allen was rarely available, and more and more fell on the ageing shoulders of Durston and Haig. The batting had moments of total glory.

At Trent Bridge, on 23 June 1925, they achieved possibly the greatest victory in the history of Middlesex cricket and one of the greatest in the history of the County Championship.

Notts, out for 167, took a first innings lead of 40 which was soon extended to a lead of such magnitude as to put the game out of Middlesex's reach. Carr hit 123 and Payton 126 not out so that when Carr declared on the Monday evening he set Middlesex the task of scoring 502 to win.

Cambridge University had scored 507 in the fourth innings to beat MCC in 1896, and the Players had made 502 to beat the Gentlemen in 1900, but the highest score a County had made to win a Championship match was closer to four hundred than to five, and that on only two occasions, both by Lancashire.

Middlesex had an hour's batting on the Monday evening and lost Stevens, Lee and Hearne to close at 60 for three. North left early the next morning, at 66, but Hendren and Bruce added 154 in 95 minutes. Bruce was out at 220, having hit a six and 14 fours. In the afternoon, Hendren and Mann took Middlesex to an historic victory with an unbeaten stand of 271 which remains a seventh-wicket record for the County. Hendren, playing an almost faultless innings, hit 20 fours. It was his third double-century in a fortnight. Mann hit 14 fours, and the stand occupied $3\frac{1}{4}$ hours. The Middlesex second innings, the highest made by a county side to win a Championship match, is worthy of note:

G. T. S. Stevens	lbw b Flint	28
Lee, H. W.	b Flint	19
Hearne, J. W.	c Matthews b Barratt	5
Hendren, E. H.	not out	206
North, E. J.	c Flint b Matthews	3
Hon C. N. Bruce	c Payton b Staples	103
E. L. Kidd	b Matthews	7
*F. T. Mann	not out	101
	b 14, lb 7, w 5, nb 4	30
	(for 6 wkts)	502

Of the amateurs to make an appearance, one was H. J. Enthoven and another, the year before he went to Oxford, was Lord Dunglass. He played once for Middlesex in 1924 and once in 1925, and he was better known later as Sir Alec Douglas-Home, Prime Minister from 1963 to 1964.

More significantly from a Middlesex point of view, a Cambridge all-rounder, Walter Robins, made his County debut in 1925 and quickly established himself as a brilliant fielder. At that time Robins was not the great leg-break and googly bowler he was to become later. He only developed that art under the tutelage of Aubrey Faulkner who ran a highly successful indoor school. Unfortunately, Hearne, after showing his very best form, scoring more than a thousand runs and taking 52 wickets in 15 matches, was taken ill and missed the last six weeks of the season.

'Joe' Murrell decided to make 1926 his last season, and he later became county scorer. A keen student of the game, Murrell was an invaluable aid to his captains, Warner and Mann, who readily sought his advice. He was a wicket-keeper of the highest standard, never valued as highly as he should have been, nor honoured, because he was contemporary with 'Tiger' Smith and Herbert Strudwick. He was particularly strong on the leg side and, in his younger days, a very good hitter of the ball when required. Taller than the average keeper, he was essentially a team man, and his loyalty and devotion were among the Middlesex treasures of the early 1920s. Few men have been better loved by their fellows. George Mann recalls that his father 'leant on Joe' and that, in the days when gentlemen and players were distinguished by initials and accommodation, 'he would have been at home in either dressing-room'. As scorer in the years after the Second World War, his influence on the attitude of younger players was immense. All wanted to travel with Joe or have a chat with him. His own adoration was bridge, a passion he shared with 'Gubby' Allen, and Murrell's wife reported to Allen

Frank Mann leads Middlesex on to the field, 1926.

that her husband's last words before he died were 'I think if it rains tomorrow, I'll play bridge with Mr Allen.' He was succeeded by Fred Price, another keeper strong on the leg side.

Price quickly proved his worth in a side where the fielding in general was beginning to creak and where Hendren alone maintained consistently brilliant form. In 1927, he was engaged in another record stand, this time with Durston for the tenth wicket, and, having seen his friend Hearne snatch the Middlesex record with a score of 285 not out against Essex at Leyton in 1929, he bettered it with the first triple hundred ever made for Middlesex, 301 not out against Worcestershire at Dudley in July 1933. He batted for nearly seven hours and hit 29 boundaries. He was 44 years old at the time and had already indicated that it was time to retire. Ten days later, he hit 222 not out against Essex at Leyton. This was the 21st of his innings of 200 or more, and only Hammond and Bradman have bettered that record.

Hendren was blessed with great physical strength, agility and stamina. He played all the shots, but excelled in the hook, which he performed with such contemptuous bravery as to become the idol of all in the Caribbean. Brilliant in the field, a fact which kept him his team place in the early days when his batting was failing, he so loved the game and people that he made it a joy for friend and foe alike.

Robertson-Glasgow compared him to the Fool in Lear, for where Shakespeare's clown tries to prevent his king from going mad, Hendren tried to prevent cricket from taking itself too seriously lest it forgot it was a game. He was a man of impish, elemental humour:

> But, besides that humour, that natural outlet of balanced faculties, he had dignity and judgment. He would burst that balloon, pomposity, and upend the façade of hypocrisy and show. He liked slapstick, but he knew when and at whom to throw the pie. His short, square build, busy movements, and low-geared run were made for comedy.

G. O. Allen recalls that one day at The Oval, 'Patsy' put down two catches at slip off him. 'As I was walking back to my mark I noticed him disappearing to long-leg. I shouted to Robbie, who was the captain, "Where's he going?" and Robbie said, "He's off. He says he's never going to field slip to you again, and I can't stop him."'

For Middlesex, his feats were prodigious. Twenty times he scored more than a thousand runs in a season, and on seven of those occasions he passed two thousand. His 2,669 in 1923 remained a record in spite of the events of 1947, and he hit 2,623 in 1928. This was Frank Mann's last year as captain.

Mann's decision to stand down was regretted by all. He was immensely popular on and off the field, loved and respected by the professionals. His record as a hard-hitting batsman cannot be judged from his figures alone, for he was ever-ready to sacrifice his wicket in the interests of the side. He led by example.

Mann's successor was Nigel Haig, who had turned 40 when he took up the post. He took over at a most difficult time. Several exciting amateurs were making their mark, but few were able to give their time fully to the game so that in Mann's last season as captain, for example, 26 players were used, and the same number appeared in 1929. Hearne split his hand in the match against West Indies in 1928 so that he could not play again during the season, which left him with nine appearances, while, a year later, E. T. Killick, recognised as a batsman of England potential, and G. E. V. Crutchley could play in only two matches, and Allen in six.

To balance this were the exciting developments in the cricket of Walter Robins, who did the 'double' in all matches for the only time in his career in 1929, and of Ian Peebles, who reached a hundred wickets for the County in 1929 and 1931. Their advent, however, tended to produce a less varied attack, for it contained three leg-spinners with a fourth, Jim Sims, just starting his career.

Other professionals beginning their careers were George Hart and Joe Hulme, both brilliant fielders.

Remarkably, Haig took more than a hundred wickets in his first season as captain, and Durston gave honest support after missing the first few matches of the season, but this year marked the end of their decade as a pair of opening bowlers as good as any in the country. Age and the amount of work that they had to undertake over the years due to lack of support were telling against them. Durston had put on weight and lost the incisiveness that he once possessed in his opening overs. He had never been as quick as Larwood, Voce or Farnes were to be, but he had been brisk enough to keep batsmen wondering. Now he had dropped to a military medium, his natural talents wasted in the defensive role to which he was now cast.

*'Gubby' Allen—more than
60 years as cricketer,
administrator and inspiration.*

What he and Haig, and Middlesex, desperately needed was
the regular support of 'Gubby' Allen, but that was not to be,
for the young Allen was having to earn a living in the city.
However infrequently he appeared for Middlesex, Allen was
seen as an England fast bowler, and the first of his 25 Tests was
played in 1930. His matches for Middlesex were invariably
against the strongest opposition, and Haig was most anxious
that Allen should play against Lancashire at Lord's in June
1929, for the Red Rose county had been champions for the
past three seasons.

As E. W. Swanton, Allen's biographer, has pointed out,
the fast bowler stipulated that he would play, but that he
could not be at Lord's on time because he first had to work at
Debenham's. In fact, he did not take the field until ten to
twelve and was put on to bowl as first change. He bowled
from the pavilion end and soon accounted for Hallows, but

this was the only wicket to fall before lunch. Working up a terrific pace after lunch, he bowled Watson and Iddon, but Ernest Tyldesley reached an admirable hundred before he, too, was bowled by Allen. Lancashire were 215 for four at tea, but they collapsed before Allen's pace in the early evening and were all out for 241. Allen clean bowled eight men, had Hopwood caught behind and, remarkably, had McDonald stumped.

McDonald had been hit by Allen and next ball attempted to give the bowler 'the charge'. Allen saw him coming, so did wicket-keeper Price who moved up as the bowler bowled a slower, wider ball. McDonald was stumped.

Allen's final figures, a Middlesex record and the only time a bowler has taken ten wickets in a *county* game at Lord's, were: 25.3 overs, 10 maidens, 40 runs, 10 wickets

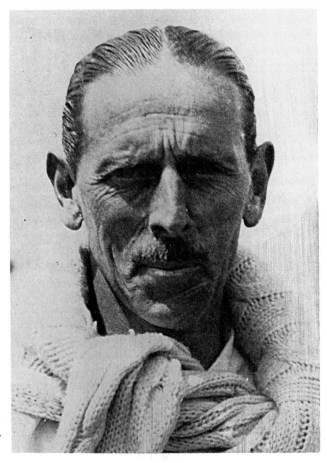

Nigel Haig led Middlesex bravely at a difficult time. He was a top-class all-rounder for several seasons.

This was not Allen's only triumph during the season. At The Oval, two months later, he and Harry Lee put on 319 for the second wicket, Lee making 225, Allen 155. The stand, and the Middlesex victory by eight wickets, was not without its humour. Allen takes up the story:

> At tea, we were two hundred for one, and Percy Fender said to us 'Two hundred at tea time on a wicket like this. It's disgraceful.' I said to him, 'Percy, it's not the score at tea. It's what it is at the close of play that matters.' We only had an hour and three-quarters after tea, but we hit another 225, and then I had a biff and got out in the last over. Pat Hendren had to come in because they hadn't appointed a night-watchman. He didn't say a word to me as we passed. He was furious, and he holed out first ball, and I don't think he and Nigel Haig spoke to each other for a fortnight.

Unfortunately, this heralded no resurgence in Middlesex's fortunes. In 1930, they finished bottom but one in the table, the worst performance in their history. Thirty-five players were used! Haig's assessment of the season is interesting, accurate in its findings, but also prophetic in its last sentence:

> A number of reasons contributed to this debacle. But the principal one was the lack of bowling of the three amateurs who had taken 100 wickets the previous season. Only Haig was a regular bowler, and he was but a shadow of what he had been the year before. Robins was only able to play in five matches and Peebles in nine. Actually this was the first and the worst of five lean years. It was the first time in the history of the club that difficulty was found in securing the services of amateurs, the side frequently having to take the field with seven, eight and even nine professionals.

Haig, a nephew of Lord Harris, had contemplated becoming a professional himself in the early stages of his career, and his uncle had remarked that a man could do worse, for it was an honourable profession, but means had been found to make the move unnecessary. Haig's observation, seemingly with some horror, that as many as nine professionals were in the Middlesex team at one time was indicative of a change in cricket as a whole, for, increasingly, it was becoming less of an amateur game.

The sense of fun that the amateur brought to the game was

still apparent, even when Middlesex were not doing so well. Against the 1930 Australians, Greville Stevens dropped Don Bradman in the gully twice in one over off 'Gubby' Allen. 'All he said to me at the end of the over,' recalls Allen, 'was "bowl at the bloody wicket". A few moments later he was put on to bowl and almost immediately bowled The Don, and he turned to me and said, "I told you so".'

How much the talented amateur came to be missed is witnessed by the fact that E. T. Killick, now entered upon a career in the church, played only once in 1931 and hit 206 against Warwickshire. In 13 years for Middlesex, he played in fewer than 50 matches, but he averaged over 35. He died in 1953 while playing cricket for the clergy of St Albans and district.

Careers were drawing to a close. In 1933 and 1934, Haig shared the captaincy with H. J. Enthoven, a stock-broker who had his moments as a batsman and also as a change bowler of medium pace. He did the hat-trick against the Australians in 1934, but this was an isolated incident for the County at a time when the bowling was woefully weak and most county batsmen enjoyed playing against Middlesex.

Durston's honest and durable playing career came to an end in 1933 as, to all effect, did Harry Lee's, for he played in only four matches in 1934.

In the era of Hearne and Hendren, the worth of Harry Lee has tended to be obscured, but here was one of the greatest servants a county club ever had. He was solid and dependable, never giving less than his best and capable of doing a bit of everything, batting, bowling and fielding. He tended to be dour, hunching low and watching the ball with studied exaggeration, but he made a lot of runs and others would not have flourished without him.

As we have noted, he was reported killed in action in the First World War, but, in fact, he had broken a thigh and was a prisoner of war. He returned with one leg shorter than the other and was told that he would never play cricket again, but he scuttled after the ball in the field for another 15 years without giving a hint that he had been wounded, and when he died, in 1981, he was 90.

To the end of his playing career he showed his worth. The county was anxious to blood young players and omitted him for most of the 1934 season, but he was recalled late in August and immediately hit 119 against Warwickshire. He later became a first-class umpire.

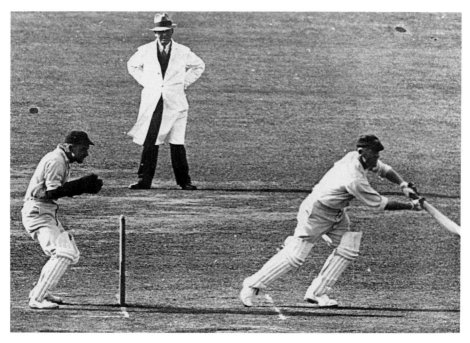

Harry Lee—solid and dependable for 23 years.

That Middlesex recognised his worth can be seen from the fact that, in June 1934, the committee received a letter from Mrs Lee stating that she had recently suffered a severe illness and that the doctor's fee amounted to £100. The committee had special regard for Harry's valuable service to the club and told her to send the account to Middlesex County Cricket Club. Nevertheless, later the same year, it was 'decided with regret that his (Lee's) services were no longer required', and the Secretary of MCC was requested to advise him accordingly. It should be noted that it was the Secretary of MCC who carried out this task, for, at this time, Middlesex was run very much as a subsidiary of the Marylebone Club.

These were changing times. Durston had been appointed coach and captained the second eleven, and, on 23 August 1934, an item in the minutes of a committee meeting read: 'Subject to the approval of Norfolk it was decided to approach W. J. Edrich in regard to the possibility of his becoming qualified to play for Middlesex.'

Here was a seed which was to have the finest of flowerings.

Middlesex had made an earlier excursion into the minor counties when they engaged 'Big Jim' Smith from Wiltshire. A fast right-arm bowler, he had a sensational first season in 1934 with 143 wickets for Middlesex and 174 in all matches.

Haig's retirement came in October 1934, but it had been expected from earlier in the year. The committee paid public tribute to him:

> He had a very large share in Middlesex attaining the position of Champion County in 1920 and 1921. After he became captain of the side, it was increasingly difficult to get together a regular eleven, owing to the number of matches played and the claims of business on many of the best amateurs. Mr Haig carried on most gallantly. His untiring energy both in bowling and fielding and good nerve when things have been going wrong, have been a great example to the eleven.

Certainly he led Middlesex at one of the most difficult periods in their history, but he had helped to encourage and foster young players who were to take the County close to supremacy in the next few years. Trouble dogged him to the end. His last match as captain was against Notts, and the bowling of Voce caused such adverse comment that Middlesex launched an enquiry and threatened not to play Nottinghamshire in the future.

Haig stated that Voce had bowled fairly for 20 minutes and then had carried out a 'direct and consistent attack on the batsman'. Muncer had been hit on the head and forced to retire hurt after a vicious attack, and there had been no expression of regret. Hendren said that the bowling had not been in the 'proper manner', that it was 'head high intimidation' and that he had no wish to play against Notts again if they were going to bowl like that. Hearne said that they bowled 'at you', and both umpires, Bestwick and Skelding, believed that it was not right to bowl three or four bouncers an over. Skelding described it as 'a cancer in the game'. This was August 1934.

Nottinghamshire offered their regrets, and the matter closed there.

There was a sense of urgency in the Middlesex camp. As well as reviewing Lee's financial position and offering assistance, the committee decided to pay for winter coaching at Jack Durston's indoor school for seven young professionals, Gray, Muncer, Harrington, Robertson, Sharp, Wilson and Young. Norfolk had agreed to release Edrich and Middlesex were to defray the costs of his living in London while he qualified. The County also hoped to play Jahangir Khan, the Indian all-rounder, father of Majid Khan, who was up at Cambridge and said to be qualified for Middlesex, but nothing came of this although the South African, H. G. Owen-Smith, was recognised as being qualified and played for three seasons.

A new agreement was drawn up between MCC and Middlesex over the use of the ground, and it is interesting to note that no official agreement between the two clubs existed until 1899.

There was a sense not only of urgency, but of a new dawn. The question remained as to who was to lead Middlesex into this period of revitalisation. H. J. Enthoven was 33, had captained Cambridge and shared the leadership of the county with Haig for the past two seasons, but his ability to commit himself totally to the game was always in doubt. The committee chose instead the 29-year-old all-rounder Walter Robins.

CHAPTER EIGHT

ROBINS

WALTER ROBINS WAS ONE OF CRICKET'S ECCENTRICS, and like all eccentrics he was not an easy man. It should be accepted from the start that he was capable of destroying a young man with a word or a gesture. He had no words of encouragement for a young player whom he did not feel was good enough, and some may interpret this as cruelty, but no captain in the history of the game has got more from his men, nor demanded that his side played brighter cricket. He insisted on aggressive, entertaining cricket, not for its own sake, but because he believed that that was the way to win matches. Middlesex were transformed. A side that had languished in the lower half of the table, playing cricket that often suggested drudgery, became one of the most enterprising and attractive of sides.

Robins himself was an outstanding cricketer, and soccer player (he later appeared for Notts Forest), at Highgate School. He did not live up to expectations in his first year at Cambridge, but he was a potential Test cricketer by the end of his period of residence. His play, like his captaincy, was audacious and original. He could turn his leg-breaks enormously, but he did not always have total command of length. There was a hint of the unorthodox in his batting, but his footwork has been compared to that of Fred Astaire. He was a magnificent fielder, especially at cover point, and his running between the wickets was scintillating. His athletic example and his positive and immediate decisions transformed the Middlesex side, roused it from its sense of gloomy despondency and made it play with the dynamism that its captain imposed on it, for, in truth, he left his imprint upon a generation of cricketers.

The team that he led in 1935 was essentially professional. The only amateurs to play with any regularity were Robins himself and J. H. Human. Owen-Smith, resident in London since 1934, played ten games while G. C. Newman played six. George Newman was an all-round athlete who had appeared for Oxford in the Varsity match in 1926 and 1927. His appearances for Middlesex from then until 1936 were limited, but he became a noted President of the Club from 1963 to 1976, his handling of the Annual General Meeting becoming a highly entertaining mixture of drama, political expertise and fun.

R. W. V. Robins—as a captain, he had no equal.

That John Human could not give himself more regularly to the game was a great sadness, for 1935 was, in reality, his one full season for the County. Tall and dashing, he was a happy cricketer who attacked the bowling from the moment he got to the wicket. No wonder Robins was so keen to have him in the side.

Robins's first season as captain was a dreadful one for batsmen. Leather jackets, the larvae of the crane fly (daddy long legs), ravaged Lord's, and the chemical firm that removed them also removed much of the grass so that batting at headquarters became a hazardous business. Only seven centuries were scored for Middlesex in the entire season, five by Hendren, two by Human, and the weakness of the side lay in the batting, for Smith, Sims, who passed a hundred wickets, and Robins gave the bowling some substance.

The real problem was to find a consistently reliable opening pair of batsmen. Price, whose wicket-keeping was most impressive, but, who, like Murrell, was to live for ever in the shadow of two great keepers, in this instant Ames and Duckworth, was often used as an opener and performed as

Fred Price pulls off another stumping. He claimed 977 victims during his career, and 312 of them were stumpings.

well as anybody. Muncer was tried early in 1935 and Hearne took over the position, with some reluctance, later. Hart was the most regular, but he never truly established himself. An excellent coach and a brilliant fielder, he was too self-effacing a batsman and never a good enough bowler to trouble the best batsmen. His fielding, however, earned him the right to be England's twelfth man at Lord's on more than one occasion.

Robins began with victories over Lancashire and Worcestershire, and, in spite of losing to Warwickshire, Middlesex maintained a challenge for the Championship by beating Somerset, Essex and Worcestershire in the return and taking first innings points in drawn matches, but rain and an indifferent run in mid-season meant that they finished third. This was an exciting leap after the mediocrity of recent years.

One of the most stimulating events of the season came in the rain-ruined match with Yorkshire, the Champion county this year and every year, save 1936, until the outbreak of war. On a treacherous wicket Middlesex collapsed to 32 for eight, at which point Jim Smith hit 57 in half an hour. He and Muncer put on 73, but Yorkshire took a comfortable first innings lead on the one day's play that was possible.

Smith had hit 53 in 41 minutes against Derbyshire the previous season, but from this point onwards a fever of excitement gripped the crowd whenever he went to the wicket. It is quite remarkable that a fast bowler who played five times for England and, by all accounts, should have played much more, is remembered not so much for his bowling as for his amazing powers of hitting. No cricketer in the years immediately before the Second World War caused so much excitement when he was at the crease.

Letters have come to the present writer full of affectionate memories for Smith in the 1930s. Peter Laverack, now living in Dorset, recalled:

> As a schoolboy in 1936, I went to Scarborough from nearby Malton, to see the county game Yorkshire *v* Middlesex. I arrived late, the score I seem to remember was Middlesex 70 for nine – and *Wisden* confirms that big Jim Smith hit 56 of the last 57 runs and three of his four sixes sent the ball out of the ground. Middlesex made 127 and in their second innings Smith was yorked by Bowes for nought!
>
> I have watched countless hours of first-class cricket. I was in London for some 30 years and after my playing days were over I virtually 'lived' at Lord's, but never did I see any sheer slogging comparable with that of big Jim Smith on Wednesday, 29 July 1936.

Coincidentally, another correspondent, Fred Jeavans from Newcastle, remembered going to the same match at Scarborough. Middlesex slumped from 12 for none to 12 for four in the space of two overs, Smailes taking three wickets in four balls. Smith's 56 came in 20 minutes with six fours as well as the four sixes. 'When he appeared in the second innings there was a murmur in the crowd and the field spread out – I can still see Hutton walking towards me with a broad smile on his face.' Anti-climax followed, but the hold that Smith exerted is remembered vividly more than half a century later.

In one of the finest essays on a cricketer that has been written, Terence Prittie analysed Smith's batting 'technique' and its appeal. He maintained that Smith, realising in his early days in first-class cricket that his footwork in batting was inadequate, decided to dispense with it altogether. He eliminated other mental problems by playing one stroke to all deliveries, simplicity itself:

> The bat goes up even before the bowler's arm comes over. It points at that moment, firmly and unwaveringly, towards deep third-man, and it begins its descent before the ball has left the bowler's hand. Thus it has the great cardinal virtue of arriving in time. The margin of error is, indeed, all on the other side, and I have frequently seen Smith complete his stroke before ever the ball has reached him. The result, too, is always diverting, because of the complete doubt surrounding the ball's destination up to the very last moment. Roughly speaking, one can only say that a straight full pitch will generally be sent somewhere in the direction of mid-wicket, a half-volley towards long-on, and a good length ball absolutely anywhere. Smith does not like short balls, and the bat's arc and reflex are such that they are usually hit straight up into the air.

He reached fifty in 11 minutes against Gloucestershire at Bristol in 1938. The only faster fifty has been by Inman of Leicestershire in 1965 and he was being fed full tosses to bring about a declaration. In 1935, he hit 52 in 14 minutes against Kent at Maidstone. It was commonly believed that if he hit a century, it would be the fastest of all time, but his one century, against Kent in 1939, came in 75 minutes and was not even the fastest of the season. The charm of Smith, of course, was that he remained eminently rustic to the very end of his career.

Haig drew attention to an innings of Smith's which was worthy of note. It was played in a charity match at Rayner's Lane in 1935. Smith went in No 9 against XV of Harrow and District and hit 173 in 53 minutes with 19 sixes and 12 fours. He also hit 11 singles. As Haig pointed out: 'His rate of scoring would have been considerably faster, but for the delay caused in searching for the ball, after it had been struck far out of the ground. In all some eight balls were lost.'

'Big Jim' Smith—fast bowler and volatile hitter.

Yet as Smith began to captivate the crowds, one of Lord's greatest of favourites was leaving the scene. Jack Hearne appeared regularly in 1935, played the first match of the 1936 season, *v* Warwickwhire at Lord's, and then no more. He had been cruelly treated by injuries. A broken wrist during the First World War had reduced the effectiveness of his bowling. He was a great leg-spin and googly bowler before 1914. He more generally bowled off-breaks after the war. He was a cricketer of refinement, a batsman who used delicacy more than blatant aggression, but to suggest that he was a stonewaller, a slow scorer, is a travesty of the facts. He was a man of good humour and good sense, and Middlesex had the good sense to employ his talents at a later date.

Jack Hearne left the field as a Middlesex player for the last time on Tuesday, 12 May 1936. Warwickshire had just beaten Middlesex by one wicket in spite of some splendid fast bowling by Jim Smith. Less than three weeks later, Denis Compton stepped out at Lord's to make his Middlesex debut. The occasion was the Whitsuntide match against Sussex. He was a week past his 18th birthday.

He had been in the twelve for the match against Kent at Maidstone the previous July, but Jack Young had the 11th place. Now he found himself in the side against Sussex, but he was down at No 11 in the order as 'Patsy' Hendren had been on his debut. Compton was a left-arm bowler, but Middlesex did not simply recognise his talent as a spinner. His first contribution for the County was to catch Jim Parks; his second was to have Harry Parks caught by 'Gubby' Allen off his bowling. On the Monday, before a full house, Middlesex, in reply to Sussex's 185, reached 162 for nine. First-innings points were all important so that a great responsibility was thrust on the young man in his first first-class innings. He played with cultured good sense. He and 'Gubby' Allen put on 36. Compton made 14.

As Compton came to the wicket Allen said to him, 'This chap Tate's a little bit quicker than he looks so play forward to him.' Compton played back to the first two balls he received and was nearly bowled. Allen turned to the umpire in despair. But then Compton played well until, playing forward to Jim Parks, grandfather of Hampshire's Bobby Parks, he was given out lbw. Allen was indignant and remembers turning to umpire Bestwick and saying, 'That was going well over the top, Bill. What a bloody awful decision.' When Middlesex went out to field, Bestwick beckoned to Allen who was just about to apologise for his remark. Before Allen could say anything, however, Bestwick said, 'I'm sorry about that decision, Mr Allen, but I had to get to the gents. It's a pity because I think that boy's going to be a good player.' Allen replied, 'He's going to be better than that, Bill.'

In the next match, against Notts, he batted at No 8. Against Northants, at Lord's, he batted No 7 and hit 87 in the second innings.

Northamptonshire were the opponents a fortnight later. Middlesex dismissed the home side for 298, but slipped to 85 for four themselves. Allen and Hulme gave Hendren support in two good stands, and at the close of the second day, Middlesex were 301 for five. Austin Matthews quickly took the wickets of Hendren, Hulme and Smith on the final morning, but Compton and Sims added 76 for the ninth wicket. When Ian Peebles joined Compton for the last wicket the score was 390 and Compton was on 44. Peebles defended while the young batsman offered a succession of drives, pulls and cuts. The last wicket added 74, of which 56 were scored by Compton to bring him the first of his 123 first-class hundreds.

He finished the season with more than a thousand runs in all first-class cricket, and Warner described him as the best young batsman to appear since Wally Hammond.

Middlesex's poor start to the season had put them behind in the Championship race, but they finished with four resounding victories and were second to Derbyshire. They were a fine all-round side, brilliant in the field. Robins' emphasis on positive cricket manifested itself in the fielding. Hulme, in particular, was magnificent, as befits one who was England's outside right and was the fastest man in Arsenal's outstanding side of the 1930s. So good a soccer player was Hulme that as a cricketer he has been underestimated, but he was a very able batsman who, for a period, was second only to Hendren in the Middlesex side, and he was also a useful medium-pace bowler.

Robins' dynamism was not felt to be what was required of an England captain in Australia. In the peace mission tour of 1936–37, Allen, who was never to be captain of Middlesex, was appointed captain of MCC. Robins was on the tour, as was Sims. Some felt that Compton should have been chosen, for he was such an exciting prospect, but, in any case, he was contracted to play football for the Arsenal. Had Bill Edrich made his debut in 1936, the original intention, it is likely that he, too, would have been in contention.

Joe Hulme. His fielding was a bright spot in a bleak period.

Edrich's papers had not been received from Norfolk by MCC until October 1934, six months later than they should have been, and this meant that he was not qualified for Middlesex until October 1936, instead of the April of the same year. In effect, he could not begin his career with the County until 1937.

He had already shown his worth in matches for MCC, and his debut for Middlesex, eagerly anticipated, came against Northants at Lord's on 8 May 1937. He bowled Timms, caught James and Cox at slip and had Clark caught behind. He opened the innings with Reg Butterworth, the Oxford blue destined to be killed in action three years later, and was out for 12.

It is strange how Northants seem to play such an important part in Middlesex history at this time. Although Northants attained first-class status in 1905, Middlesex would not grant them a fixture until 1930. There was no intention of giving them fixtures in 1936, but Northants pleaded that they would not be able to play the minimum number of matches required if Middlesex dropped them, and the metropolitan county relented. As one ardent Northants' supporter, John Watson, has pointed out: 'As they never recorded a win over Middlesex until 1950, you can imagine the rejoicing in the county at the time!'

Initially, Edrich was used as an opener, but he failed to find form and was pushed down to No 3. The move worked, for in the first week of June he hit 175 and 73 not out against Lancashire at Lord's. As with Compton, Edrich's first county hundred had a touch of the heroic. The score was two for two, but he batted for four hours and 20 minutes and gave a mighty display. In the second innings, Middlesex needed 174 to win on a rain-affected wicket. They began disastrously, losing six wickets for 35 runs. Edrich and Robins added 43, and Edrich and Sims 31. Jim Smith hit 33 out of 44 in 15 minutes, but Gray was run out in trying to give Edrich the strike, and Lancashire were left winners by 22 runs.

The innings, the situation, was perhaps typical of what one came to expect from Edrich for the rest of his career. It was full of guts and belligerence. Short and determined, he was always David beating Goliath.

The defeat by Lancashire was followed by a great win over Yorkshire, incredibly by an innings. Smith took ten for 119 in the match, Robins put the cap on a consistent batting performance with a brisk knock of 65 not out and Sims took five for 36 in the second innings, but if a man-of-the-match award had been given, it would have gone to Fred Price. He and Butterworth put Middlesex on the firmest of footings with an opening stand of 103, but before that Price had stamped his name indelibly in the record books by taking seven catches behind the stumps in Yorkshire's first innings. He was later presented with the ball. It is interesting to note that shortly before the season began he had spent a fortnight coaching in Selfridge's store.

Middlesex had been so pleased with Price's development as a wicket-keeper that they had released Wilson, his deputy, to join Gloucestershire.

When Middlesex beat Surrey at The Oval by three wickets at the beginning of August the Championship was a straight fight between Middlesex and Yorkshire. The victory over Surrey was a magnificent team effort. Owen-Smith had a spell of four for nought and Surrey were out for 170, but on a dusty wicket Middlesex were out for 151. Robins and Sims bowled splendidly, but Middlesex were left to make 229 to win. Price, Carris and Edrich went cheaply, and at the close of the second day they were 92 for six. Human and Owen-Smith took the score to 159 on the last morning, and Sims joined Human in the stand which brought victory.

Essex were annihilated in the next match, but rain hampered progress in the game with Warwickshire. Somerset and Kent were beaten convincingly, but Hardstaff saved Notts after Price, Hendren and Compton had hit centuries and Middlesex had scored 525 for nine declared. This ended Middlesex's hopes, and Surrey thrashed their great rivals' bowling in the final game. The match, however, belonged to 'Patsy' Hendren, whose last appearance it was at Lord's. He had written to the committee at the end of 1936 saying that 1937 would definitely be his last season. The committee were reluctant to release him, but they accepted that he had asked to retire in 1933 and that they had pressed him to stay on.

One can understand the committee's reluctance to allow Hendren to retire, even though he was 48, for he still numbered more than 1,400 runs in his final season and hit five centuries, the last of which came in his last county game.

Surrey had won the toss and, with Fishlock and Barling getting centuries, they made 509. Middlesex lost Hart for one and Price for two at which point 'Patsy' came to the wicket. He was given a tremendous ovation, greeted by a battery of photographers and cheered by the Surrey team. Overcome, he was nearly out first ball. He recovered his composure, and he and Bill Edrich put on 182 for the third wicket. Edrich was out for 96, but the old and the new had joined together in one last stand. Hendren went on to reach his century, and the crowd, led, it is stated, by the baritone Denis Noble, a Middlesex fanatic, stood and sang 'For He's a Jolly Good Fellow'. Hendren was out for 103, and in the second innings, inevitably, was lbw to Watts for nought.

It was not Hendren's last game for Middlesex, for Robins, excited by how close his side had run Yorkshire for the title, threw down a challenge to Brian Sellers to play a deciding charity match, and the Yorkshire captain accepted. Findlay, the MCC Secretary, was doubtful about the idea, but the game went ahead at The Oval in mid-September.

Yorkshire won by an innings and 115 runs, and the game was not a great success, at least according to Neville Cardus in the *Manchester Guardian*:

> There is something awe-inspiring about the result of the challenge match between Middlesex and Yorkshire. It makes Yorkshire look very terrrible and Middlesex very innocent and gallant. The idea of a challenge is a fresh one to most people; they expected (or at any rate hoped) that it would be a drawn-out struggle over four days with an antique air of heroic single combat. Memories of Sohrab and Rustum or Achilles and Hector perhaps revived in some members of the public. If so, they were disappointed. The match only took three days instead of four; it was not good weather for watching cricket and not particularly good cricket to watch; Yorkshire were solid (there ought to be a penalty for calling Yorkshire batting 'dour') and Middlesex were either frightened or badly off 'form'. Observers have an uneasy feeling that they have been cheated, as though the Big Bad Wolf had swallowed the three little pigs, or Charles, the Duke's wrestler, had thrown Orlando and broken his neck. The drama ought to have had a different ending. Even if Middlesex could not have won (and there seems no reason now why anyone should ever beat Yorkshire again) they might have been beaten in one of those dramatic finishes which are the stock-in-trade of schoolboy magazines. To prevent similar tragedies happening in the future Yorkshire ought to be kept well away from the top of the table. Perhaps the gods will see to this.

The gods did not. Yorkshire won the title again in 1938 and 1939, and although Middlesex were runners-up both years, they never came so close as they had done in 1937. As Robins had to admit: 'You were just too good for us.'

Hendren and Hearne were presented with inscribed tankards in recognition of their services, and Middlesex set about building a side that would overcome Yorkshire. In the rain-ruined match against Oxford University in The Parks in May 1937, they had given first games to S. M. Brown and J. D. Robertson, and it is interesting to record that Robertson batted at No 6 while Brown opened with E. W. Swanton, who was also making his first-class debut. Swanton later played against Cambridge and had one more game in 1938, but his career was to be shaped by the pen rather than the bat.

At the end of the season, Kent approached Middlesex in an attempt to acquire the registration of Syd Brown who had, in fact, been born in Eltham so had a birth qualification for Kent. Middlesex refused to release Brown and he held a regular place in the last two seasons before the outbreak of war without fulfilling the potential which his high scoring in the second eleven had promised. Robertson, on the other hand, who was initially offered a contract only for 1938, quickly established himself as the leading run-getter behind Edrich and Compton, and his style began to captivate.

At the same time that Robertson was offered his one-year contract, Harry Sharp was also given a contract, but he was told to look to another county. He had talks with Worcestershire, but in the light of future events Middlesex must remain well pleased that he did not move.

The lot of the professional cricketer at this time was not what it is today, and some may suggest that they were employed in a type of benevolent feudal system. In October 1937, it was decided that George Hart's services would not be required after 1939 and that he should be so informed. Six months later, at a committee meeting:

> It was reported that although G. Hart had for some years been regarded a Middlesex professional, the only agreement he had was one with MCC dated 1926, notice of the termination of which had been given in 1937.

Neither Hart nor Hulme was engaged after 1939, but they were given a joint benefit in their final year, the income from which, sadly, was greatly affected by the gathering clouds of war. Durston, too, found that his services as coach were no longer required, but lest one should feel that the club at this time acted in a somewhat despotic and unfeeling manner, it should be recorded that help was given when it was discovered that Stoddart's widow was in difficulties and Harry Lee was also aided and his rent was paid for six months.

The club itself was not without problems. In May 1938, Middlesex were informed by MCC that they would not stage their fixture against Notts at Lord's in 1939 as the ground was needed for the Eton and Harrow match. This set exhaustive enquiries in progress as to where else in Middlesex the game could be played. It was at first thought that Ealing could be the site, but when it was learned that it would take £200 to equip the ground suitably for a county match, the idea was dropped. Finchley was also suggested, but in the end the game was played at The Oval on 15, 17 and 18 July 1939, and was notable for the fact that Walter Keeton, the Notts opener, hit 312 not out. Only Hobbs and Holmes have played bigger innings against Middlesex.

By the end of 1937, Compton was a Test cricketer and Robins' Test career was over. He had led England against New Zealand in 1937 with a certain panache, but the advent of Doug Wright left him surplus to requirements as a leg-spinner and Hammond's decision to play as an amateur had virtually ended any debate over captaincy.

Edrich, who scored a thousand runs before the end of May in 1938, became a Test player the same year. Like Compton, he played in all the Tests against Australia, but he experienced a very lean time at the outset of his international career. Price also became a Test cricketer in 1938, his one appearance for England coming in the Headingley Test. He owed his selection to somewhat fortuitous circumstances, circumstances which most believed cost England the series.

Les Ames had back trouble and had dropped out of contention for a Test place early in the season. His replacement was the Yorkshireman Paul Gibb, but Gibb was one of the victims in the match at Lord's which was to cost England the series. The match was not a Test, but the fixture between Middlesex and Yorkshire. Yorkshire had won comfortably at Headingley a month earlier and were top of the table and unbeaten when they came to Lord's in July.

Robins won the toss and decided to send Yorkshire in on a rain-affected pitch. From the start, the ball flew dangerously from the fast bowlers. Few batsmen escaped receiving painful blows. Hutton was bowled by Edrich for 13, but he had a finger broken before he departed. Gibb scored four and was hit on the head so that he could take no further part in the match. In the second innings, Leyland retired hurt with a broken thumb after scoring one. All three would have been in the England side at Headingley. Yorkshire, in effect, batted three short in the second innings and Middlesex won by eight wickets. In a compassionate gesture, Robins allowed Wood, the substitute, to keep wicket in Gibb's absence. Price replaced Gibb in the England side, and Wood replaced Price for the final Test. Price had deserved his chance, but it had come a little too late.

Jim Smith reached his hundred wickets for the season in the match against Yorkshire. It was to be the last time he achieved the feat. He had put on weight, and while he sustained his accuracy, his speed and menace came in shorter spells.

The hero of the victory over Yorkshire was Bill Edrich. He opened with Robertson on a wicket that was only a little more subdued than it had been when Yorkshire batted. He showed all the grit and fighting tenacity that made him the great cricketer he was, and for three hours, 40 minutes, he defied Bowes, Smailes and Verity to score 53, by far the biggest score of the match.

The greatness of Edrich and Compton was apparent in that from a young age (they were 22 and 20 respectively in 1938) they were displaying a maturity and a knowledge of the game which was beyond their years. They were different in styles, Compton being the more immediately attractive, but their attitude to the game was the same, and it was the unrelenting application, the desire to win, and to win joyously, that forged them into the most unforgettable duet with which the game has been blessed.

At Chelmsford, a month before the victory over Yorkshire, it had been Compton who had displayed his genius in a dramatic victory over Essex. It was a game that had several twists of fortune. Essex made 300 and took a first-innings lead of 19. They were 44 for five in their second innings when Peter Smith came in and hit 101. Middlesex were left to make 241, which was not the easiest of tasks against Peter Smith's leg-breaks.

Edrich began aggressively, hooking Nichols for four with 'that controlled fierceness of his'. He and Brown put on 57 before Brown touched a Smith leg-break to slip. Price was 'pathetically unhappy' against Smith and was taken at silly point by Nichols above his head. Compton hit 16 of his first 18 runs in boundaries, off-driving Nichols, then cover-driving and hooking him off successive balls. Edrich straight drove Smith for four and then hooked him to reach his fifty. Middlesex were well on top, but Edrich played too soon at Smith and was caught and bowled. Hulme batted excitingly, but Compton sent him back when a second run looked safe and he was run out for 26. At lunch Middlesex were 172 for four, victory in their grasp.

First ball after lunch Hart gave a gentle catch to square-leg. Compton reached his fifty with a four to long-leg and Robins made a brave pull to the boundary before being caught behind off a rising ball. Muncer lifted Smith to mid-off, and Middlesex were 190 for seven, hope fading.

Smith hit his customary six and, equally traditionally, was dropped at long-on, but then he mishit to extra cover. Now it was Compton against Essex. He hit 'vehement boundaries' off successive deliveries from Nichols, the first to the sight-screen, the second to square-leg. Sims was lbw to a ball that kept low and when the last man, A. D. Baxter, joined Compton, 24 runs were needed for victory.

Middlesex CCC, 1938. Standing: Edrich, Muncer, Sims, Smith (J.), Gray, Compton (D.), Hulme. Seated: H. G. Owen-Smith, Hendren, R. W. V. Robins (captain), W. H. Webster, Price.

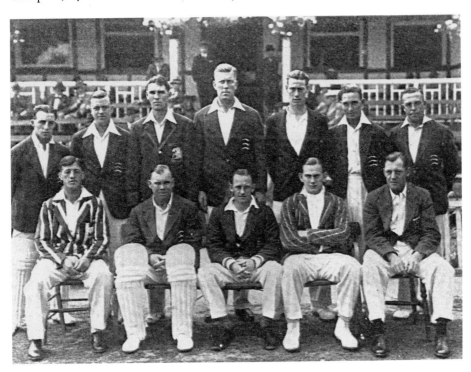

Baxter scored one run and the number of balls that he was allowed to face could be counted on one hand. Compton farmed the bowling before hitting Nichols for an 'insolent' four and driving the next ball through the covers for two and a magnificent victory.

The Middlesex title challenge faded in August, and at the beginning of January 1939, Robins resigned the captaincy due to pressures of business, his great ambition seemingly unfulfilled. There were those in the presss who thought him jumpy and nervy. Certainly he was excitable, but no man got more out of his men.

Ian Peebles was approached to see if he would play for the whole of 1939 and captain the side. He agreed. Peebles had been an outstanding leg-break and googly bowler in the early 1930s, one of the few to tax Bradman, but for a variety of reasons much of the art had deserted him by the time he took over as captain of Middlesex and he was little more than a change bowler in 1939. He was an intelligent and amiable man and quick to pay credit to his side for the continued success:

> Fred Price as wicket-keeper and head pro was the only player senior to me in the regular side, and the various amateurs who came in from time to time were naturally very old friends. Everyone was as keen as mustard, and we had no misfits. They all recognized that I was a new boy at the job and, to a man, did all they could to help me.

Jim Sims had a renaissance as a leg-spinner and was the leading bowler. Robertson and Brown gave glimpses of what was to come, and Laurie Gray was now opening the attack regularly. As batsman and fielder, George Mann made a most favourable impression when he came down from university. Again Middlesex were runners up to Yorkshire:

> Everyone was extremely kind about the season, the side and my first venture as a county captain, but I knew that there was an awful lot to be learnt. Even had I mastered the mechanics of my craft I was obviously not of the stuff of Warner and Robins, but the side seemed happy and quite willing to continue under existing arrangements. With Edrich, Compton, Robertson, Mann and Brown all young, and much good service still to be had from Smith and Sims, we had fine prospects ahead, and my greatest

Jim Sims—a true and faithful servant.

regret is that we never had the chance to develop our promise to the full.

The war, of course, ended many hopes greater than those of Middlesex. Peebles did not play to the season's end, for, with Swanton, he had already enlisted. The final match against Kent due to begin on Saturday 2 September was never played because of the international situation. In Hemingway's terms, we had witnessed the end of something.

JOY IN THE AIR

PEEBLES WAS WOUNDED DURING THE WAR and although he did play a few games in the years immediately after the war, his career effectively finished in 1939. That cricket survived and prospered at Lord's as an entertainment during the war years was almost entirely due to the efforts of Pelham Warner who became Middlesex President in succession to A. J. Webbe. In February, 1940, a year before his death, Webbe was too ill to attend the AGM. It was the first that he had missed since 1879, a testament to Warner's assertion as to how much old players have put back into the club. They have continued to do so.

The one-day matches arranged at Lord's were a huge success, and, in 1941, the game between Middlesex and Essex and Kent and Surrey drew the biggest crowd of the season. It is amusing to read, however, that Warner was questioned on the popularity and future of one-day games at the Middlesex AGM in 1942, and it was minuted that: 'While admitting the success of one-day matches since the outbreak of hostilities, Sir Pelham said he did not think they would be in vogue after the war.' Three years later, Warner and Middlesex were unwilling to support suggestions for a knock-out tournament, saying that it was 'not in the best interests of the game'.

Most of the Middlesex players were in the services, but they entertained at Lord's and elsewhere whenever duties permitted. One memorable Saturday afternoon in 1941, Bill Edrich was cheered all the way to the wicket because it had just been learned that he had been awarded the DFC for his part in a low-level bombing attack on Cologne. Another memorable event came three years later when players flattened themselves on the turf at the sound of an approaching flying-bomb. The 'doodle-bug' fell short of Lord's and after the explosion play was resumed. Jack Robertson hit the next ball into the Grand Stand for six.

Joe Hulme led the London Counties side which raised thousands of pounds for the war effort in its matches against club sides in the metropolitan area. Jim Smith played for Windhill in the Bradford League. His side took the Division 'A' title, and he took 45 wickets at 12.53 runs each.

There was a sadder side. Harry Lee, having lost a brother in each war, lost his son in a flying accident. The County paid for the funeral expenses. Paul Brooks, who had caused a sensation by bowling Bradman in the nets in 1938 and who had played for Middlesex in their last county match before the war, scoring 44 not out against Warwickshire, was fatally wounded in action in Italy. Ultimately, the peace came.

Fred Price was told his services were not required. J. C. Clay, the Glamorgan veteran, asked for the services of slow left-arm bowler Jack Young, who had played for Middlesex as long ago as 1933, but had never been given an extended run in the side. Middlesex replied that they were offering a contract to Young, but not to Len Muncer, and it was he who eventually joined Glamorgan, where he had considerable success. Jim Smith resigned, so his joyful hitting and fierce bowling had now passed into legend. Sims gained early release from REME, in which he was a Staff Sergeant, so that he could play in 1946. Leslie Compton could gain no early release, and it was he who had been seen as Price's successor behind the stumps. J. G. Dewes, a young left-hander, was signed on special registration, and C. R. Maxwell made himself available for the whole of the season.

The signing of Maxwell was seen as the major coup. In the years before the war, he had played for Nottinghamshire. An amateur, he was considered one of the best wicket-keepers in the country and a very useful batsman. Seven years is a long time, however, and on the resumption of first-class cricket it was apparent that Maxwell's talents as a wicket-keeper and as a batsman were not what they had been. He dropped out after four matches and later assisted Worcestershire. His immediate replacement was Horace King, another amateur, who had played occasionally before the war, but there was a wicket-keeping crisis.

Robins had accepted the captaincy again, and all seemed as it once was, yet Robins immediately effected a change, insisting that he and Maxwell, the only two amateurs use the same dressing room as the professionals, ending segregation. The 1946 season was simply a continuation of where things had ended in 1939. Yorkshire were first, Middlesex, having faltered on the run in, were second.

The season began in rain. The opening first-class county match, against Leicestershire, lost the first day to rain, but Middlesex beat the all-professional side in two days. Jim Sims' benefit match against Sussex at Whitsun was also ruined by rain. Amid the showers and thunderstorms there were some good individual performances, but, as yet, only a whisper of the sparkling team performances of 1937. Denis

Compton, Edrich, Robertson, Robins and Brown all reached a thousand runs for the County. In spite of a lean patch, Denis Compton made two thousand. Young took more than a hundred wickets, and Gray and Sims only just failed to reach three figures. The surprise was Edrich who, opening the bowling for most of the season with an energy and enthusiasm that transcended natural talent, took 68 wickets at 18.97.

Against Northamptonshire at Northampton, he hit 222 not out in $3\frac{1}{2}$ hours and then took the first six Northants wickets at a cost of 36 runs. He finished with seven for 69. In the penultimate county game of the season, he and Denis Compton put on 296 in four hours 35 minutes. It was heady stuff. The shape of things to come.

The wicket-keeping problem was solved when Fred Price's employers were contacted and they agreed to release him to restart his cricket career at the age of 44. One problem that would not go away was the search for a fast bowler to support Gray and to relieve Edrich of the burden that was being thrust upon him. Trapnell was one amateur tried, and Leslie Compton, now demobilised, was used as a medium-pace swing bowler rather than as a wicket-keeper, but, in truth, never with great success.

What was desperately needed was another 'Gubby' Allen, able to play regularly and 15 years younger. He appeared only twice in 1946, but, inevitably, it was against the stronger opposition. He turned out against Yorkshire a fortnight after his 44th birthday and, bowling 'very fast', he took four of the first five wickets, for eight runs. He finished with five for 26. Still unable to give himself regularly to the game, he nevertheless undertook to run the Club and Ground matches.

Middlesex lost the services of Arthur Childs-Clarke at the beginning of 1947. He had not played first-team cricket for 13 years, but, as captain of the second team, his influence on the young players – now first-team regulars – and his contribution to the success that was to follow should never be forgotten. He left to captain Northamptonshire for two seasons. Hever and Eaglestone were to leave later in the year and were to find glory with Glamorgan.

Eaglestone was in the Middlesex side for the opening match of the 1947 season. The opponents were Somerset. Edrich hit a century, but Middlesex were bowled out for 78 in their second innings and lost by one wicket. The hero of the match was Maurice Tremlett, who produced a spell of bowling on his first-class debut which had him hailed as the answer to England's prayer for a fast bowler. As it transpired, this charming man was to win more fame as a batsman than as a bowler.

Before we continue with the events of 1947, it would be as well to put those events in an historical context. At last, people began to realise that the war was over and, eventually, the sun began to shine. We still suffered a manpower crisis and mid-week soccer had been banned. There was still rationing, but there was, for the first time in eight years or more, a feeling 'now we are happy – now we are free'. There was austerity, of course, but there was also the first flush of pride in the new-born Welfare State. There was a greater sense of togetherness than one has witnessed at any time since, and if many goods were in very short supply, it gave to a simple act like the buying of a bar of chocolate a sense of adventure which a young person of today would find it difficult to appreciate.

In short, there was joy in the air, and, in retrospect, the contribution of Middlesex County Cricket Club, and two men in particular, was no small measure.

England had fared badly in Australia, and Hammond, the dominant figure in English cricket for 20 years, had retired. A brave new world was waiting.

The early season gave no true indication of what was to come. Robins was absent for the first four matches, and George Mann led the side. Robertson hit a century against Gloucestershire who were beaten by an innings in two days. Compton did not play in the next match because he was beginning his plunder of the South African bowlers, playing for MCC at Lord's. He was not missed. Thompson, a most able deputy, gave Edrich fine support, as did Eaglestone. Edrich himself, playing this year for the first time as an amateur, hit 225. As he had taken six for 28 in the victory over Gloucestershire he had announced that he was in the very best of all-round form. Warwickshire suffered the same fate as Gloucestershire but lasted a day longer.

Compton returned for the game against Worcestershire at Lord's, and now, for the first time, there was a sense of excitement. Yorkshire, whom history had cast in the role of perpetual arch-adversary, had started indifferently. Could Robins' dream at last be realised? It was too early to conjecture, but, against Worcestershire, Denis Compton hit his first century of the season.

Middlesex struggled against Perks and Howarth and collapsed, but Denis hit 88 not out after an early escape and Middlesex reached 207. With Edrich taking five for 61, Worcestershire were bowled out for 134. In weather which threatened rain quick runs were a necessity. Robertson and Brown set the pattern with an opening stand of 100. Then came Compton and Edrich. In 80 minutes they added 118. Compton hit his first century of the season in 114 minutes, Edrich took five for 69 in the second Worcestershire innings and Middlesex won by 234 runs.

The Middlesex plan of campaign was simplicity itself. Runs were scored as quickly as possible so that the attack, which had its limitations in penetration and balance, would have as much time as possible in which to bowl out the other side. Robertson and Brown were a magnificent opening pair. They attacked from the start without ever suggesting recklessness, and for Edrich and Compton they provided the soundest of platforms. Think of the bowlers who, having seen a hundred runs plundered in the first 80 minutes or so, take a wicket and see Edrich coming down the pavilion steps, next man in!

Robins returned to lead the side in the Whitsuntide match with Sussex. The sun shone. There were 17,000 people on the Saturday; 30,000 on the Monday. The game was over in two days.

This time Robertson and Brown went cheaply, but in under three hours Compton and Edrich added 223. Both made hundreds, and George Mann played a gloriously hard-hitting innings. Gray took seven wickets, Sims six, and the match was over shortly before 7.30 on the second day.

Against Hampshire, ten days later, Jack Robertson hit the first double-century of his career and an innings victory followed. Glamorgan proved stronger opposition. Edrich and Compton were on Test duty. Price took over as wicket-keeper to free Leslie Compton to concentrate on his batting and to bowl if necessary. It was not needed, but Middlesex had their hardest fight since the opening match of the season. On a sticky wicket, Jack Young took seven for 46, and Glamorgan were out for 99. Nevertheless, with Wilf Wooller in form as effective as Young's, the Middlesex first-innings lead was restricted to a meagre three. Haydn Davies and Dyson put on 88 for the first Glamorgan wicket in the second innings, and, on the Monday, the outlook for Middlesex was bleak. Gray met the crisis with a spell of bowling that was as honest in endeavour as it was effective in performance. He took seven for 69, but Middlesex still needed 201 to win on a wicket that gave encouragement to the bowler. Brown was hit in the face by a ball from Wooller and was carried off on a stretcher. At 102 for five, he returned and batted bravely, helping Thompson in a stand of 71. Alec Thompson was the hero. The least praised and probably least remembered of that 1947 side, he was a batsman eager to play his shots. No one would have found it easy to take the stage after Edrich and Compton, but when the responsibility was thrust upon him, as in this match, he accepted it. He scored 81 not out and Middlesex won by three wickets.

Still without Edrich and Compton, Middlesex entertained Notts at Lord's. A solid batting side, Notts made 317, but in an opening stand which lasted only $3\frac{1}{2}$ hours, Jack Robertson and Syd Brown put on 310, a new Middlesex record, though since twice beaten. Brown was first out for 155 which included a six and 16 fours. Robertson batted for another three quarters of an hour and made 183 with three sixes, a five and 14 fours. There has been no more exciting opening pair in the history of county cricket. Middlesex won by seven wickets and awaited the arrival of Yorkshire.

This time, in $3\frac{3}{4}$ hours, against an attack which included five bowlers who had bowled or were to bowl for England, on a wicket on which Yorkshire had been dismissed for 187, Robertson and Brown put on 222 for the first wicket. Brown made 130, Robertson 108, but rain disrupted the match too much for there to be a result.

There was a surprise setback at Colchester where Essex scored heavily and won by ten wickets in spite of Robertson and Brown beginning the innings with stands of 121 and 172.

This was Middlesex's second defeat in ten matches, and in a system which the public found far easier to understand than the pre-war percentage method, four points were given for first innings lead and twelve for a win. After ten matches, it was apparent that Yorkshire, with four wins, were no longer the main threat to Middlesex's Championship hopes. Middlesex led the table with 92 points, and Gloucestershire were in second place, only four points behind.

Whether or not Yorkshire were strong challengers for the title, they remained among the most formidable opposition in the world, particularly at Headingley. Middlesex met them at the end of June and were put in to bat on a damp wicket. Brown and Robertson made one and nought, and

Denis Compton was out for four, but Edrich, the eternal fighter, batted $2\frac{1}{2}$ hours for 70. Leslie Compton gave good support, but Middlesex made only 124. Edrich then dismissed Hutton and Watson for four runs, and Young and Denis Compton combined their left-arm spin to take four wickets each and bowl Yorkshire out for 85. The wicket was aiding the bowler to turn the ball viciously, and Wardle reaped a second innings harvest of seven wickets, but he could not dislodge Edrich, again given valuable assistance by the elder Compton. In under three hours, Edrich hit 102 in another masterly display. Five more wickets for Young, three for Denis Compton, and Middlesex had won a great victory by 87 runs.

Young had nine wickets on a doubtful pitch at Portsmouth, and Middlesex fought back to win. Then came the most remarkable game of a remarkable season.

By dint of having played two more matches, Gloucestershire had drawn level with Middlesex at the top of the table when the metropolitan county went to Leicestershire on 12 July. In the absence of both Robins and Mann, Bill Edrich led the side for the first time. Before a crowd of 10,000, the highest at Leicester since the Australians' visit in 1921, he won the toss and asked Leicestershire to bat. His decision was against convention, for the·wicket, if a little damp on top, offered no hazard to the batsman. Middlesex gained early reward, however. Prentice and Watson went quickly, and half the side were out for 114. Jackson and Riddington put on 107 in 75 minutes, and Leicestershire made 309.

Brown was struck in the eye and forced to retire, but Edrich and Robertson scored briskly to the close which came at 134. It was but a hint of what was to come on the Monday.

Edrich and Robertson took the score to 185, having shared a stand of 159, and then the avalanche of runs began. In 131 minutes, Edrich and Compton put on 277 runs. In the 140 minutes between lunch and tea, Middlesex scored 310. In all, 633 runs were scored on the second day.

In $4\frac{1}{4}$ hours, Edrich hit 257 with four sixes and 24 fours. Compton's innings contained 21 fours while Alec Thompson hit 15 boundaries.

Edrich's declaration left Leicestershire to make 328 to avoid an innings defeat. Les Berry, one of the greatest of campaigners and one who should certainly have played for England, led by example with an accomplished century. Prentice, Tompkin and Lester gave solid support, and

LEICESTERSHIRE *v* MIDDLESEX

Played at Grace Road, Leicestershire, 12, 14 and 15 July 1947

MIDDLESEX WON BY 10 WICKETS

LEICESTERSHIRE	FIRST INNINGS		SECOND INNINGS	
*L. G. Berry	lbw b Sims	53	lbw b Edrich	154
F. T. Prentice	c L. Compton b Edrich	1	c and b D. Compton	31
G. S. Watson	lbw b Gray	3	c Sims b D. Compton	4
M. Tompkin	lbw b Sims	33	c L. Compton b Edrich	76
G. Lester	b Sims	19	c L. Compton b Sims	40
V. E. Jackson	b Young	117	c Sims b Gray	7
A. Riddington	c Sims b Young	63	lbw b Sims	3
J. Howard	st Price b Sims	0	st Price b D. Compton	2
J. E. Walsh	c Brown b Sims	6	c Young b D. Compton	15
†P. Corrall	b Sims	5	c Gray b D. Compton	25
J. Sperry	not out	0	not out	2
	b 6, lb 3	9	b 21, lb 12, nb 1	34
Total		309		393

BOWLING	O	M	R	W	O	M	R	W
Edrich	13	2	37	1	15	3	37	2
Gray	22	6	65	1	21	4	64	1
Young	21.5	6	58	2	14	5	29	0
Sims	36	4	135	6	43	8	121	2
D. Compton	3	1	5	0	29.1	3	108	5

MIDDLESEX	FIRST INNINGS		SECOND INNINGS	
S. M. Brown	retired hurt	13		
J. D. Robertson	c Watson b Walsh	75		
*W. J. Edrich	c Riddington b Sperry	257	(1) not out	29
D. C. S. Compton	st Corrall b Walsh	151	(2) not out	33
A. Thompson	not out	89		
Hon L. R. White	lbw b Lester	6		
L. H. Compton	not out	29		
J. M. Sims				
†W. F. Price				
L. H. Gray				
	b 14, lb 3	17	lb 4	4
Total	(for 4 wkts dec)	637	(for no wkt)	66

BOWLING	O	M	R	W	O	M	R	W
Sperry	27	2	110	1	4	0	35	0
Riddington	18	0	75	0				
Walsh	35	1	159	2				
Lester	21	2	107	1				
Jackson	27	2	129	0	4	0	27	0

Umpires: G. P. Heaton and A. Mitchison.

*Captain; †Wicket-keeper.

Leicestershire went to lunch on the short, third day at 345 for four. As there were only 80 minutes' play remaining, a draw seemed the only possible result.

In early afternoon, Jim Sims took the wickets of Lester and Riddington in quick succession, and then Denis Compton, bowling a sustained spell of his 'chinamen' for the first time, bought the last three wickets. In 45 minutes after lunch, Middlesex had captured the last six Leicestershire wickets for 48 runs. It had been a mighty performance, but Middlesex had only 25 minutes in which to score 66 runs in order to win the match.

Edrich and Compton opened the batting. Jack Robertson and Leslie Compton sat padded up behind the sight-screen ready to run to the wicket should either of the openers be out. Leicestershire bowled tightly, and Berry set his field to save the runs, but there was no stopping Edrich and Compton. With the boundaries cut off, they relied mostly on running for almost everything. They reached the target in seven overs with four minutes to spare.

To be alive and eager in North London in 1947 meant following every moment that Middlesex made. The news of their doings was spread as if by jungle telegraph through Enfield, Southgate, Palmer's Green, Ealing, Uxbridge and Hounslow, and if one victory could convince the faithful that the County could, and would, win the Championship, it was the victory at Grace Road. It captured the imagination like no other county game had done since the days before the war. It was a match of heroic stature. It was *Boy's Own Paper* stuff.

Even the rude shock of losing at Taunton could not dispel the optimism. In any case, Alan Fairbairn, a left-handed batsman from Southgate, had scored 108 on his first-class debut to emphasise the quality of Middlesex's reserve strength in batting. He scored another century in his second match eight days later, but he was never able to give his time fully to the game, which is to be regretted.

The return of Edrich and Compton brought victory over Essex at Lord's. Robertson and Denis Compton hit centuries, but the main feature of the game was the bowling of Ian Bedford, a leg-spinner who was 17 years old, still at Woodhouse Grammar School, Finchley, and was the son of Bill Bedford, who had given noble service to Winchmore Hill for several years.

It is hard for followers of the game today to understand

how a side in contention for the Championship could give a
debut to an untried schoolboy and take the field with three
leg-spinners in their side, but these were more romantic
times. Ian Bedford had match figures of six for 134 and
bowled excellently.

He did not play at Northampton where Bill Edrich hit the

The terrible twins, Edrich and Compton. There was joy in the air when they played cricket.

highest score of his career. Robertson was out for nought and Brown for 17, but the 'twins' added 211, and Edrich and George Mann then added 155. Edrich's 267 not out was made in $5\frac{1}{4}$ hours and contained three sixes and 24 fours. Mann declared at 464 for five, and Northants then succumbed to the variety of Denis Compton's slow left-arm spin, ever experimental. He followed his 110 with six for 78. Middlesex won by eight wickets.

Fairbairn's second hundred, another six wickets for Bedford and an accomplished century by Robertson brought victory over Notts, and this was followed by a win at Hove where the weather, as well as Sussex, had to be beaten.

Gloucestershire, too, had been winning, however, and when Middlesex went to Canterbury on 6 August, the two counties were level on 176 points with Gloucestershire having played one game more.

The game at Canterbury provided some magnificent cricket. There were centuries for Compton, Edrich and Robertson, but the game was drawn and Middlesex came away pointless.

Gloucestershire took first innings points against Lancashire at Old Trafford, but they lost by ten wickets so that their lead was restricted to four points, and still they had played a game more.

Another outcome of the game at Canterbury was that Edrich had strained a shoulder and would be unable to bowl for the rest of the season. This was an injury of mixed fortune, for while Edrich's services as a bowler were lost to Middlesex, it was possible that he would not be chosen for England in the final Test against South Africa because they needed a pace bowler. Edrich was not the build for a fast bowler, but his endeavour, his aggression and his whole-heartedness made him as quick as anyone in 1947. He finished with 67 wickets at 22.58 runs each. He may well have emulated Jim Parks sen with 3,000 runs and 100 wickets if he had been able to bowl throughout August.

On Saturday 9 August, a day of brightest sunshine, 30,000 people were locked into The Oval to see the meeting of the greatest of southern rivals, Middlesex and Surrey. Robins won the toss, and Brown and Robertson put on 211. The stand was without blemish. Stuart Surridge bowled Brown when he had made 98. It was to be the lowest score of the day. Robertson followed soon after, and this brought Compton and Edrich together. In $2\frac{3}{4}$ hours, they put on 287 in front of a capacity crowd, bathed in sunshine and revelling in the riot of runs.

Robins declared at 537 for two, but Surrey faced the huge score cheerfully. McIntyre had taken off his pads to bowl three overs; now Leslie Compton opened the bowling while Brown kept wicket. After eight overs, big Leslie reverted to his position behind the stumps and caught Fishlock off Gray. Then he caught Barling off Sims and stumped Squires off brother Denis, who took six for 94 in the first innings and six for 80 in the second. Whatever the state of the economy and the manpower situation, there was a crowd of 20,000 on the Monday, and close to 5,000 on the Tuesday, although the game was over before lunch.

It was glorious stuff, but Gloucestershire won at Bradford and still led the Championship by four points.

With Gloucestershire engaged against the South Africans, Middlesex had a chance to take the lead in the title race when they met Kent at Lord's, but it was not to be. In spite of Robertson's century, Middlesex trailed by 72 on the first innings. Consistent Kent batting in the second innings led to a declaration, but it was hardly a sporting one. Middlesex were left four hours 20 minutes in which to score 397. That is a rate of nearly 92 an hour.

Robertson and Brown went quickly. Edrich was out for 31, but Mann and Compton added 161 in 98 minutes for the sixth wicket. There were no circles, no fielding restrictions, and most of the Kent fieldsmen were posted on the boundary, but Compton hit 19 fours in what was his 13th century of the season. When he fell to Wright for 168 the last five wickets went down in half an hour to Wright and Davies.

Middlesex lost by 75 runs, yet, 40 years on, Denis Compton would judge that the finest innings of his life, which will give some idea of its greatness. Edrich wrote later: 'His 168 was, I believe, the finest innings I have ever seen him play, brilliant, punishing, correct, offering no chances on a wicket heavily in favour of Doug Wright's wicked spinners.'

Compton says that he approached Robins when, after the early dismissal of Brown and Robertson, there was obviously little hope of a victory which had been very remote from the start and asked what he should do. Robins' reply was typically direct. 'Go for the bloody runs, of course!'

This defeat meant that when Middlesex travelled to Cheltenham for the most vital match of the season. Gloucestershire held a four-point lead in the Championship and both sides had played 21 games.

The match at Cheltenham awakened memories of the great contest with Surrey at Lord's in 1920, only this time it was the two leading contenders for the Championship who faced each other. The odds were slightly in favour of Gloucestershire. The wicket at Cheltenham, as were all in the county, gave assistance to the spinners, and in Cook and Goddard, Gloucestershire had two of the finest in the game. Tom Goddard was 47 years old, but he still believed that he should take a wicket with every off-break he bowled. As he took 238 wickets that year, there was some justification for his belief.

Gloucestershire lost nobody to the fifth Test Match at the Oval which, unfortunately, clashed with the game at Cheltenham. Middlesex lost Compton and Robertson, playing his first game for England as replacement for Edrich, who could neither bowl nor throw. Several newspapers suggested that Edrich's injury was diplomatic when it was announced that he would play for Middlesex, but he did not bowl again during the season, and you cannot pick a half-fit man for a Test Match.

Middlesex chose their side carefully. John Mann, younger brother of George, a forcing batsman and brilliant fielder, took one of the vacant places. He was an exciting cricketer, but, like so many talented Middlesex amateurs, was not able to devote sufficient time to the game. The replacement for Jack Robertson was Harry Sharp, a long and faithful servant who had appeared in only one previous Championship match and that twelve months earlier.

The ground was filled to capacity an hour before the start. The weather was magnificent, the setting beautiful and the atmosphere electric. Robins won the toss and had no hesitation in deciding to bat first.

Brown and Edrich opened the Middlesex innings. Gloucestershire had three seam bowlers, Middlesex one. Basil Allen chose to use his three seamers before he gave the ball to his two spinners. It was a decision that may have cost him the match.

Barnett, medium-pace off-cutters, and Lambert, fast-medium, opened the bowling. From the start the ball kicked and darted ominously. Brown and Edrich took risks in an effort to accumulate runs before the wicket deteriorated totally. They made exactly 50 before Brown was leg before to first change bowler Scott. It had been a priceless stand. In contrast to the 17 overs of seam which Allen used at the start of the match, Gray was to bowl only two overs in the whole of the game.

The introduction of spin brought Gloucestershire a second wicket, George Mann caught at slip, but 65 runs had been scored before Tom Goddard took that wicket. From that point Goddard was virtually unplayable. Robins, Thompson, John Mann and Leslie Compton perished in quick succession. Edrich remarked: 'There was no telling what he (Goddard) would so with the next ball, and the only thing was to wait till the direction off the pitch could be ascertained, and then, if possible, drop the wrists and let it go by.'

Goddard took five wickets in a row, and when Jim Sims joined Edrich the score was 101 for six. Sims, now senior professional, was one of the great characters of Middlesex cricket. He spoke always out of the side of his mouth, and was reputed to pass on messages on the field with the air of a faithful, but long suffering, retainer: 'Don't ask me, son, captain says so.' His greeting to Edrich, inevitably out of the side of the mouth, was: 'What's this fuss? This is elementary!' He then drove Goddard for four and a few balls later hooked him to the boundary. Sims was happier against slow bowlers. Against the quickies he was 'always a little apprehensive'.

Edrich's valiant, watchful, fighting innings came to an end when he drove at Cook and was caught at silly mid-off from a ball that jumped. Harry Sharp joined Sims, still in a jolly mood, at 112 for seven. Sims' message to Sharp was: 'I'll do them, Harry. Don't let them get you out.'

They didn't. Sims clouted Goddard a couple of times more before Goddard claimed him. Gray went quickly, but Jack Young swotted in all directions, and when Middlesex were all out in mid-afternoon they had made 180, the last three wickets having produced more than a third of the total.

Barnett, a most experienced campaigner, and Allen opened the Gloucestershire batting. They were grimly determined as Young and Sims took a little time to find the right length. At 37, Allen touched a ball from Sims that he should have left alone. Barnett and Neale fell in successive overs from Sims, but Crapp and Emmett played with great resource. They added 42 and just as it looked as if they might take command, Young held one back and had Crapp caught and bowled. A flurry of four wickets for seven runs put Middlesex right on top, but Tom Goddard took some revenge on Sims and Young with a couple of hard-hit fours, and Wilson, a former Middlesex player, gave sensible support so that the lead was kept to 27, and Middlesex were batting a second time ten minutes before the close of play.

From a Middlesex point of view, the worst possible thing happened. Edrich 'lost' a ball from Goddard and was lbw. In North London, when the news broke, there were some muttered imprecations directed at Robins for having sent Edrich in first on the Saturday evening – such is the reward for kingship. Sharp was sent in as night-watchman and, although his career ahead was to include ten centuries and three times a thousand runs in a season, he played the innings of his life on the Monday.

The ground was again bursting at the seams and the sun shone. Brown was bowled by Goddard and Robins, always the first up the ladder when a castle was to be stormed, joined Sharp. What followed was fighting cricket of the finest vintage. Sharp recalls his own method of playing Goddard:

> The ball was turning so much that I had worked out exactly what I would do with Tom Goddard's off-breaks. I knew that when it pitched in line with the stumps it would turn away down the leg side so I went with the tide and helped the ball on its way.

Robins played with controlled aggression. Sharp hit Goddard for eight leg-side fours. They added 70 before Monks took a magnificent running catch on the square-leg boundary. Sharp finally became another Goddard victim, but he had covered himself in glory in his first match of the season. Nor was his day over.

Goddard added eight wickets to his seven of the first innings, but Gloucestershire needed 169 to win on a wicket seething with demons.

Barnett and Allen began steadily. Gray, injured, was not on the field, but he would not have bowled. Young rubbed the ball in the dirt and exercised his spinning fingers. Sims was in his element. The fielding was dynamic. Sims had Allen caught at short-leg and Barnett was lbw, but Crapp and Neale played with a doggedness that kept Gloucestershire's hopes alive.

At 67 for three, Robins threw the ball to Sharp to try his off-breaks in contrast to the diet of slow left-arm and leg-spin. To Sharp, Robins said: 'Just keep it tight.' He was right, for as Sharp has admitted: 'You didn't have to rub the skin off your fingers to turn the ball on that wicket. It turned itself most of the time, so I just tried to drop it on a length. It worked. I had Neale taken at short-leg and then I had Emmett and Wilson caught behind. All three went down for a couple of runs. As soon as they got after me, Jim came back on and it was all over very soon.'

The interest and excitement engendered by this game cannot be over-estimated. At The Oval, during the Test Match, Denis Compton was fed regular reports on the state of the game at Cheltenham. It was believed that whoever won the game would win the Championship, and so it proved.

Leslie Compton hit a maiden first-class century and shared a stand of 181 in 93 minutes with Syd Brown in the victory at Derby. Denis Compton and George Mann added 303 in $3\frac{1}{4}$ hours as Surrey were beaten at Lord's. They were followed to Lord's by Northamptonshire. After Robertson and Brown had put on 147 for the first wicket, only Denis Compton could cope with the slow left-arm of Broderick and the leg-breaks of C. B. Clarke. Middlesex were out for 273. Young and Sims bowled the visitors out for 147. Then came the customary Middlesex panache, 303 at nearly five runs an over and a declaration. The pitch was crumbling. Gray bowled five overs and retired to the outfield. Sims joined Young in the attack. In 26 overs it was all over. Young took five for 36 and Sims three for 18. At 7.05 pm on Thursday, 28 August 1947, Middlesex became the Champion County.

The season was not quite done. In mid-September, at The Oval, Middlesex took on the Rest of England. They had tilted their strength at the country's might in 1920 and in 1921. The first time they had gained an honourable draw; the second time they had been humiliated. This time it was the Rest of England who were to be crushed. Edrich 180, Denis Compton 246, the second highest score he was ever to make for Middlesex, a total of 543 for nine declared, victory by nine wickets in a glorious feast of cricket, these were the ingredients of a marvellous game played in the late summer sun.

Advancing down the wicket to drive Tom Goddard,

GLOUCESTERSHIRE *v* MIDDLESEX

Played at Cheltenham College Ground, 16 and 18 August 1947

MIDDLESEX WON BY 68 RUNS

MIDDLESEX	FIRST INNINGS		SECOND INNINGS	
S. M. Brown	lbw b Scott	15	b Goddard	11
W. J. Edrich	c Allen b Cook	50	lbw b Goddard	5
F. G. Mann	c Crapp b Goddard	8	(5) st Wilson b Goddard	7
*R. W. V. Robins	c Scott b Goddard	2	c Monks b Goddard	45
A. Thompson	b Goddard	2	(6) lbw b Goddard	1
J. P. Mann	c Lambert b Goddard	7	(7) lbw b Cook	5
†L. H. Compton	lbw b Goddard	3	(8) c Barnett b Goddard	3
J. M. Sims	c Allen b Goddard	32	(9) c Neale b Goddard	5
H. P. H. Sharp	not out	14	(3) c Barnett b Goddard	46
L. H. Gray	lbw b Cook	0	(11) not out	0
J. A. Young	b Goddard	27	(10) c Wilson b Cook	0
	b 11, lb 7, nb 2	20	b 4, lb 9	13
Total		180		141

BOWLING	O	M	R	W		O	M	R	W
Barnett	4	0	15	0		3	1	6	0
Lambert	8	2	19	0		1	0	1	0
Scott	3	0	15	1					
Cook	21	9	41	2		18.5	8	35	2
Goddard	20.3	4	70	7		22	4	86	8

1st inns: 1-50, 2-65, 3-77, 4-92, 5-94, 6-101, 7-112, 8-140, 9-143
2nd inns: 1-5, 2-33, 3-103, 4-125, 5-128, 6-129, 7-135, 8-141, 9-141

GLOUCESTERSHIRE	FIRST INNINGS		SECOND INNINGS	
B. O. Allen (capt)	c Gray b Sims	20	c sub (Hever) b Sims	10
C. J. Barnett	c Young b Sims	19	lbw b Young	17
W. L. Neale	c Sharp b Sims	4	c sub (Hever) b Sharp	10
J. F. Crapp	c and b Young	10	c Robins b Young	40
G. M. Emmett	lbw b Young	33	c L. Compton b Sharp	0
C. R. Monks	lbw b Sims	4	c Brown b Young	4
A. E. Wilson	not out	17	c L. Compton b Sharp	0
G. Lambert	lbw b Young	5	b Young	1
C. J. Scott	b Sims	1	st L. Compton b Sims	8
T. W. Goddard	c and b Sims	26	c Edrich b Young	0
C. Cook	b Young	1	not out	0
	b 10, lb 1, nb 2	13	b 6, lb 4	10
Total		153		100

BOWLING	O	M	R	W	O	M	R	W
Gray	2	0	10	0				
Young	25.1	8	55	4	19	9	27	5
Sims	22	4	65	6	9.3	2	24	2
Robins	3	0	10	0				
Sharp					9	0	39	3

1st inns: 1-37, 2-44, 3-49, 4-91, 5-100, 6-100, 7-106, 8-107, 9-152
2nd inns: 1-22, 2-32, 3-67, 4-67, 5-69, 6-74, 7-91, 8-96, 9-100

Denis Compton had locked his feet together and fallen, but as he fell, he hit Goddard round the corner for four. Records tumbled – the most centuries in a season, the highest aggregate in a season. Records will always be remembered because they are written in the books for all to see, but what should never be forgotten is the manner of their making. When Compton and Edrich were batting there was excitement in the air. Men rushed from their offices to get to Lord's. Schoolboys played truant. Austerity was forgotten in clouds of happiness. It is difficult even now, 40 years on, to think of those days without the pulse racing a little faster, for they are, indeed, the 'blue remembered hills'.

More soberly, *The Cricketer* suggested that 'what is certain is that never in their long history have Middlesex had a more attractive and crowd compelling side than that of 1947.'

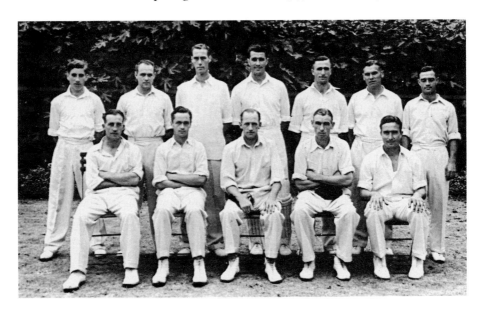

County Champions, 1947.
Standing: I. Bedford,
A. Thompson, L. Gray,
L. Compton,
J. D. Robertson,
S. M. Brown, J. Young.
Seated: W. J. Edrich,
F. G. Mann,
R. W. V. Robins, J. Sims,
D. Compton.

CHAPTER TEN

SETTING SUNS

WALTER ROBINS, A TEST SELECTOR, 41 years old and with
business commitments that could not allow him to play
regularly, resigned the captaincy in December 1947. One
reason that he did so was because a most capable successor had
presented himself in the person of George Mann. To follow
Robins was as difficult a task for George Mann as to follow
Warner had been for his father, yet he responded in a similar
way and with equal success.

The 1948 season was dominated by Bradman's Australians. Compton, Edrich, Young and Dewes all appeared in
the Test series. Without their assistance Middlesex still
performed admirably, if without quite the panache of the
previous season, and finished third, behind Glamorgan and
Surrey. That Middlesex did not win the title was due entirely
to the inability to gain first-innings points in several matches,
for they won as many matches as Glamorgan and Surrey, 13,
and lost fewer.

The wet summer of 1948 certainly did not aid Middlesex
in the tactics which they liked to employ, the making of runs
at high speed in an effort to give their attack the maximum
amount of time in which to bowl out the other side, yet the
early form suggested a repeat of 1947 when they won their
first four matches and went to the top of the table.

Laurie Gray's benefit match against Sussex brought in a
record £6,000 and the third victory. The fourth, at Lord's on
19, 20 and 21 May, was over Somerset.

Edrich and Compton came together with the score at 54
for two and in four hours they added 424 before Mann
declared with 50 minutes of the day remaining. This remains
the highest third wicket stand ever made in county cricket
and, at the time, was only 21 runs short of the world record
held by the New Zealanders Carson and Whitelaw. Mann
was criticised in the press for declaring before the Middlesex
pair had beaten the record, but Middlesex, under Mann as
under Robins, were an enterprising side who had victory as
their sole object from the start of a game.

His declaration came at 478 for two, and by the end of the
day, Gray had got rid of both of the Somerset openers, one of
them the dangerous Gimblett. Edrich finished with 168 and
Denis Compton with 252, which was the highest score that
he ever made for Middlesex.

Initially, perhaps, George Mann lacked Robins' genius for seizing the initiative in a situation, but Robins' talents had been born of long experience. Mann was less experimental than Robins, but he was an astute leader, a man of generous spirit exceedingly popular with all whom he led and one who followed Robins' doctrine of positive cricket. He was sound and orthodox and although there was criticism that he over-bowled Denis Compton and under-bowled Jim Sims, in his short reign he achieved much. There was always gladness when George Mann was captain, be it of Middlesex or of England.

Like his father, Mann is a modest person and places the reasons for continued success in the hands of others. 'Robbie was a dynamic leader. He had the belief that you should never stop trying to win a game until there was absolutely no more chance. Perhaps he went to extremes at times, but it was an attitude that, happily, was passed on to me and to all Middlesex captains who have followed him. I was inexperienced and not as good as those whom I had to tell what to do, but they made it easy for me, and we had fun.'

While it is easy to emphasise the qualities of the record-breaking Middlesex batting: the cultured stroke-play of Robertson, the eager purposefulness of Brown, the aggression of Thompson and Mann, the increasing dependability of Sharp and the genius of Compton and Edrich, it is equally easy not to give due praise to the bowling. Laurie Gray was the only pace bowler in the side as Edrich's bowling faded a little and declined in effectiveness. In every respect, Gray was a good club man. He had waited since 1934 to establish himself, and, like Durston before him, he was asked to carry a tremendous burden which he never shirked. Jack Young carried an even greater weight on his shoulders. A slow left-arm bowler, often pressed to open the bowling, sometimes with two or three overs of seam, he was unrelentingly accurate and could flight the ball cleverly.

Jim Sims was 45 in 1948 when he was presented with the ball for taking six for 65 against the Australians and when he hit his first century for 11 years. He was one of the great characters of cricket, a fact recognized by the Middlesex committee who re-engaged him for another three years at the end of 1948 to act not only as player, but as coach and later as manager of the young cricketers' side and as scorer. He was one of the world's great conversationalists with an unconscious verbal humour, always with a faint air of melancholy.

Ian Bedford, now having left school, played eight games in 1948, but with nothing like the success that he had enjoyed the previous year. The art of leg-break and googly bowling is a demanding one and imposes strains upon the muscles which are imposed by no other type of bowling. Bedford never carried into riper years the promise of his youth, although he was to reappear prominently and unexpectedly in Middlesex cricket in the years ahead.

The desperate need in the late 1940s was what it had been before the arrival and after the departure of Jim Smith: a quick bowler. Middlesex were acutely aware of this, but they were also aware that several leading players were growing old and that other problems wre presenting themselves.

The County held great hopes of Philip Whitcombe, a pace bowler who had won his blue all three years at Oxford, 1947–49, but the three successful games he had for Middlesex in 1948 turned out to be the extent of his county career. Middlesex had to look to the other university which gave blues.

Meanwhile Gray was sent for coaching at the Gover School in the winter of 1948–49 while there were ambitions for Routledge as a pace bowler which were never quite fulfilled. There were also hopes that an off-break bowler, Devereux, would be signed, but Devonshire refused to agree to his special registration and eventually he went to Worcestershire.

S.S. Rogers was released to join Somerset. Harry Sharp was given an extended contract and awarded his county cap by F. G. Mann. Sharp was to prove a great servant to the County. The way in which the County treated those who had served them well could be seen in the continuing weekly allowance paid to the widow of A. E. Stoddart.

Yet these were changing times in cricket, and Middlesex were sensitive to the shifting moods which were affecting the game and those who watched it. In the winter and spring of 1948–49, indoor practice was held at Chiswick, and the dependence which Middlesex had always had on MCC as their landlords was, for some, becoming frustrating.

Warner had tended to run Middlesex as an adjunct of MCC. The MCC Secretary sat in on all Middlesex meetings. The MCC clerical staff dealt with all Middlesex matters. In May 1949, a committee meeting was told that it would be impractical to employ a clerk at Lord's to work for Middlesex alone, and it was not until a year later that a full-time typist was employed by Middlesex for its own use. More significant was the question of players and who employed them, for the line of demarcation was often hazy.

In June 1949, severely weakened by Test calls, Middlesex included R. S. Cooper, 'Gubby' Allen, Horace Brearley, the father of the future Middlesex and England captain, and a 16-year-old, Fred Titmus, in the game against Somerset at Bath. Brearley's two games for Middlesex were both played that season. Rustom Cooper's county career consisted of eight matches spread over three years, but Titmus' career was to span five decades. Just as Allen had been responsible for Denis Compton's entry into the Middlesex side, so was he responsible for Titmus' debut; for Titmus, like Compton 23 years earlier, had impressed Allen in the nets.

Allen maintained incredibly good form in his rare appearances, even though he was just a month short of his 47th birthday when he played in the game at Bath. He hit 91, and he and Titmus put on 34 for the eighth wicket. Middlesex won by 36 runs. Allen took the first three Somerset wickets in the second innings, and his three games for Middlesex that season left him second in the batting averages and top of the bowling. Titmus bowled only two overs in the match and failed to take a wicket, but he had made his mark in more ways than one, and his 13 in the stand with Allen revived memories of Denis Compton's debut.

Titmus' first appearance for Middlesex had repercussions. At a committee meeting on 20 July it was reported that the Secretary of MCC had lodged a complaint regarding the playing of Titmus:

> An explanation to the Secretary, MCC, for playing F. Titmus, a Ground Boy on the MCC staff, in the Middlesex side against Somerset, was considered.
>
> Mr R. W. V. Robins apologised for their oversight in not obtaining the MCC Secretary's permission to play Titmus, who did not have an agreement with Middlesex.
>
> The Secretary, MCC, was asked to accept the Club's apologies and their assurance that measures would be taken to prevent any recurrence.

At a committee meeting in November 1949, it was decided to offer Titmus a three-year contract beginning on 1 January 1950. Thirty years later, he was to have played more games for the County than any other cricketer.

Titmus' solitary appearance in 1949 was in a season which, in many ways, marked the end of a golden period for Middlesex. The summer of 1948 had seen the County play their first ten Championship matches at Lord's and their next 11 away. The pattern was little altered in 1949 when nine of the first ten were at home and the next 11, which included the whole of July, were away. The use of Lord's for schools' matches and services' matches in the middle of the season created a lop-sided fixture list for Middlesex which was not to the liking of their followers, particularly as May was often a month of indifferent weather. It was an unhappy situation for a club where there was a restless surge for greater independence among some of the members. That surge had been appeased by the instigation of a Middlesex tie in 1949 and by the continued success of the County, but the rumbles remained.

The home advantage in the opening matches in 1949 proved to be of no great assistance in winning matches. Leslie Compton, batting with Mann as runner, held out for the last five minutes to save the game against Notts. Northants, Essex and Leicestershire were beaten, but the matches with Glamorgan, home and away, Lancashire, Sussex, Warwickshire and Yorkshire were all drawn.

The Whitsuntide match against Sussex was Denis Compton's benefit game. He won the toss, took a wicket in the first over he bowled and then entertained the Monday crowd with some magnificent batting. He took $2\frac{3}{4}$ hours to reach 103, but then he hit 79 in 44 minutes, hitting 20 fours in all. He was elated when his elder brother Leslie hit 59 not out at the close, for the Compton brothers had a warm and close relationship.

Denis's benefit raised £12,600, which was easily a Middlesex record at the time, but it was far less than had been expected. The Lord's Day Observance Society had singled out his benefit for special attack as it attracted great attention, and there was also much adverse and totally unwarranted publicity in the press where some earned their livings by suggesting that a great cricketer should not earn his.

Middlesex did not emerge as Championship contenders in 1949 until they began their spate of 11 away games, for they won the first four of them, against Gloucestershire, Somerset, Lancashire and Leicestershire. The most important victory, however, came at Worcester on 23, 25 and 26 July.

Worcestershire were leading the Championship table at

The golden boy of Middlesex and England cricket—Denis Compton. (Courtesy of Ken Kelly)

the time, and Middlesex were without Denis Compton and Bill Edrich, who were engaged in the Test Match at Old Trafford. Robertson had scored a hundred in the previous Test, at Lord's, but was dropped. In that Lord's Test, five Middlesex players had been in the England side.

Mann won the toss at Worcester, but Middlesex soon lost Brown. Robertson, however, was at his most magnificent and most majestic. In $6\frac{1}{2}$ hours, he hit two sixes and 39 fours, his footwork against the slow bowlers Jenkins and Howarth being a particular delight. He was involved in massive stands with Dewes, Mann, Allen and Robins, and he ended with the highest score ever made for Middlesex. His achievement of scoring more than 300 runs in a day was not accomplished again until Glenn Turner's triple hundred in 1982. Middlesex went on to win by an innings and 54 runs.

Middlesex v Worcestershire, at New Road, Worcester, 23 July 1949

Robertson, J. D. B.	not out	331
Brown, S. M.	b Palmer	3
J. G. Dewes	b Perks	45
*F. G. Mann	c Bird b Palmer	65
G. O. Allen	b Palmer	98
R. W. V. Robins	c Cooper b Bird	59
	b 14, lb 5, nb 3	22
	(for 5 wkts dec)	623

Sharp, H.†, Compton, L. H., Sims, J., Young, J. A. and Gray, L. did not bat.

In winning this match, Middlesex went to the top of the table. They consolidated their lead with the victory over Hampshire, but rather surprisingly lost when their batting collapsed at Hove. Syd Brown was left out for this match following his uneven form. He and Robertson had batted with an unforgettable splendour earlier in the year when, at Lord's, they had opened the match with Yorkshire with a stand of 198. The partnership was broken when Freddie Trueman had Brown caught by Hutton. It was Trueman's first wicket in the County Championship.

Brown was brought back after the catastrophe at Hove and hit 200 against Kent at Canterbury. This was the first of his two double-centuries for Middlesex. The second was to come two years later against Somerset.

If Brown was never of Test class, he was one of the very best of county batsmen, and he was a better player than several who played for England in the late 1940s and early 1950s. He was a chunky man, always looking for runs, always entertaining, perhaps a little vulnerable to the ball that dipped into him. To complement his exciting batting was his deep fielding which was of the very highest quality.

The decisive factor in Middlesex not winning the Championship outright in 1949 was two defeats at the hands of Surrey, the second in the penultimate Championship match. The last game was against Derbyshire at Lord's on 24, 25 and 26 August. Derbyshire made 228 and bowled Middlesex out for 139. John Warr then took five wickets, and Middlesex were left to make 193 to win. The Derbyshire pace attack reduced them to 36 for five, but Robins joined Compton in a stand of 90 in 70 minutes. Compton finished on 97 not out and Middlesex won by three wickets.

This victory left them at the top of the table, but a few days later Yorkshire won at Newport and claimed a share of the title. Typically, Mann believes that had he taken a bigger chance in just one match, Middlesex might have got the extra points needed to give them the title outright. This is a natural self-questioning, but Mann is being harsh on himself. The side always wanted to play with him and for him.

None should despair at the thought of having to share a Championship, particularly with Yorkshire, but the season had thrown up some problems, some of which were not to be resolved for many years.

The decline of Gray, who had lost his place towards the end of the season, had been compensated by the arrival of John Warr, a right-arm fast-medium bowler from Ealing who was then in his first year at Cambridge. Warr's eight matches at the season's end had brought him 30 wickets at moderate cost. He was a tearaway bowler with an action far removed from the classical, but he had energy, enthusiasm and fun in his cricket. Initially, his fielding was poor, but the fielding of Middlesex as a side in 1949 was way below the standard that it had been in previous years. Warr was to help

Joint Champions, 1949.
Back row: J. A. Young,
S. M. Brown, L. H. Gray,
J. J. Warr, L. H. Compton,
H. P. Sharp.
Seated: J. D. Robertson,
J. M. Sims,
R. W. V. Robins,
F. G. Mann, W. J. Edrich,
D. C. S. Compton.
Front: A. Thompson and
J. G. Dewes.

in the rejuvenation of Middlesex cricket at a later date, and he was chosen to tour Australia with Freddie Brown's side in 1950–51. This remains one of the strangest of selections in Test history, and why he was preferred to Les Jackson of Derbyshire, for example, will for ever remain a mystery. At the time of his selection, Warr was raw and had not served a long enough probation in the hard world of county cricket. He played in two Tests and took the wicket of Ian Johnson at a cost of 281 runs, figures which one journalist suggested flattered him. The irony is that, when bowling at his best some years later, Warr was never considered for England.

John Dewes, another Cambridge man, was also in Brown's side in Australia. A left-handed batsman, he was aggressively entertaining at university where he had a most impressive record, but in county cricket he often played with exaggerated caution, never fulfilling the hopes that all had had in him as early as 1945 when, along with the Hon L. R. White and Donald Carr, he played for England in the Victory Test match at Lord's. He played very little for Middlesex after 1950, although he had at one time been seen as a future captain.

This was the question which now plagued Middlesex. George Mann had done a magnificent job, both for England and Middlesex, but, early in 1949, he had indicated that he would not be available regularly in 1950. By August, the captaincy problem had become acute.

R. H. Twining had succeeded Frank Mann, who was ill, as President, and the captaincy issue was his first concern:

> The extremely important question of the captaincy of Middlesex in 1950 and future years was discussed at length. It was decided that until the availability of players likely to be considered for the captaincy was known, no decision should be made.

Significantly, at the same meeting, county caps were awarded to Warr and Dewes, and F. G. Mann, G. E. V. Crutchley and G. O. Allen were asked to investigate the future availability of amateurs to see who could be asked to lead the side.

The issue was still not resolved by November, when it was decided to delay the appointment of a new captain until George Mann returned from a trip to South Africa. In January, 1950, Mann agreed, reluctantly, to continue as

George Mann. An ebullient captain and an inspiring administrator.

captain because the County faced a crisis. A month later, the demands of business had become so great that Mann informed the club that he would definitely not be able to lead the side in 1950. In the circumstances, Walter Robins offered to take over.

As it transpired, Robins could play in only ten matches, and Middlesex had no fewer than seven captains in 1950: Robins, Allen, Mann, Dewes, Edrich, Compton and Sims. Such a situation was a recipe for disaster, and Middlesex paid the price accordingly. They were no longer a keen and energetic unit, and their decline was predictable.

On the credit side, several youngsters were brought into the side, Moss, Bennett and Titmus among them, but the press felt that none of them looked the part. Titmus was disappointing to some because he had been hailed as a batsman, but had had more success as a bowler. This was very harsh on a young lad of 17 who rarely batted higher than

No 7 and showed the greatest promise with his bowling. His first Championship wicket came when he bowled Rogers of Hampshire in the opening match at Lord's, and he finished the year with 45 wickets, an excellent performance in a side that was struggling badly and in which only Young and latterly Warr showed any incisiveness. Sims worked hard, but the edge had gone from his bowling. Bedford, the other leg-spinner, had seemingly lost control and confidence.

Don Bennett was highly regarded as an all-rounder. Born in Yorkshire, he had lived in Middlesex since 1940. In the early part of 1950, his family moved to Staffordshire, but Middlesex offered him a contract so that he could continue his studies at Ashford County Grammar School and retain his residential qualification for the County. He was still well short of his 17th birthday when he made his first-class debut.

Allen's career ended at Weston-super-Mare in August. It was only his 146th match for Middlesex, but his appearances had been spread over a period of 29 years. It would be well to ponder Allen's contribution to the game for a moment. Although refusing to bowl body-line, he was highly successful on that tour and he twice led England in series abroad. He has been President of both Middlesex and MCC and has served on the Middlesex committee since 1932. He was the youngest by nine years when elected to the MCC committee and he has served the old club as treasurer and as chairman of cricket. With Billy Griffith he helped form the Cricket Council which led to the establishment of the TCCB and NCA. He was chairman of the Test selectors from 1955 to 1961 and his wisdom and counsel are still an essential part of Middlesex cricket.

The season also marked the effective ends of the playing careers of Robins and Mann, whose life in the game had been happy but all too short. Like Allen, he was to give noble service in the administration of the game. Both Robins and Mann played occasionally after 1950, but never with any regularity.

It is doubtful if Middlesex, or any county, ever had a better captain than Walter Robins. We have already sung his praises, but as he passes from the stage, the last words should be with the man who had the unenviable task of succeeding him in 1939, Ian Peebles:

He started with a thoroughly good cricket education. He was devoted to the game, and knew cricket history so well that he had a fund of knowledge of the great players of the past, their strengths and their foibles. This contributed to a naturally shrewd tactical sense, and on the field he was alert and forceful, always seeking to keep the game alive, and always ready to take a chance in order to do so. He expected his players to be of the same mind and though patient (to a point) with inept triers, he was fire and brimstone to the slack, selfish or indifferent.

The departure of Robins, Allen and Mann had been anticipated. What had not been looked for was the incapacitation of both Edrich and Denis Compton and the falling off of Syd Brown. Edrich had a strained back which kept him out for a month, and he spent much of the summer in a plaster jacket. Certainly his powers of attack were never to be quite the same again.

For Denis Compton, a cloud had appeared on the horizon which was to darken the rest of his career, although there were many rays of sunshine still to come. During his double-century for Middlesex against the Rest of England in 1947, he had been forced to retire hurt with knee trouble shortly after reaching fifty. The knee trouble was the legacy of a football injury.

An exciting outside-left for Arsenal, and in wartime for England, Compton had damaged his right knee in a collision with the Charlton Athletic goalkeeper in the 1938–39 season. He had had a cartilage operation following this injury, but he was ever after plagued by the damage that had been inflicted and which grew worse with the wear and tear to which the knee was subjected by his sporting career. At the end of May 1950, he underwent another operation on the knee and missed cricket throughout June and July.

Reviewing the 1950 season, journalist Walter Flack said of Middlesex that they 'must now find a regular enthusiastic captain to weld the side together and they also desperately need at least two bowlers with the ability to take those quick wickets on which the fortune of a game so often depends'. The simplicity of the statement could not disguise the complexity of finding a remedy for such a situation.

The committee were acutely aware of the needs of the County and the growing restlessness of the members, some of whom set down a motion requesting that at least one non-MCC member should sit on the committee and that the County should strive for greater independence from the

Marylebone Club. Robins had resigned as captain, but no decision was reached as to his successor. As late as April 1951, it was hoped that Mann would return to lead the side, but this did not happen, and Edrich and Compton were appointed joint captains for 1951. One assumes that this course of action was taken in order to avoid offending one or other of the two players, but it created a situation which was doomed to fail.

The desperate need for new young players was recognised and for the first time attempts were made to develop youth cricket in the County. M. S. Glennie, the Southgate wicket-keeper and a Middlesex committee man, headed a sub-committee which was to deal with youth cricket. He was supported by H. P. Clark of Hornsey Schools, C. L. Scotten, the Middlesex Schools representative, and D. D. Crowley from Middlesex Grammar Schools. A recruitment drive was instigated and clubs throughout Middlesex were asked to bring to the notice of the County any emerging talent.

Much faith was placed in the fast bowling of Alan Moss, and he was not to disappoint. Born in Tottenham, Moss had come to the fore as one of the *Evening News* colts. The London evening paper gathered together some very promising young cricketers, arranged for them to be coached and played them as a team in several matches. Brian Taylor, the Essex wicket-keeper and future captain, was one of their products, Moss another. In 1951, his appearances were restricted because he was completing his national service. Indeed, the County had asked him before the season began to say when he would be available, and Moss replied that he had saved 40 days leave so that he could play for the County. In the event, he was able to play in 15 games and took 42 wickets to suggest that here at last was the fast bowler of whom Middlesex had dreamed for so long. Titmus was less fortunate and could play in only three matches.

This was a formative time for Titmus. He had been considered mainly as an aggressive batsman when on the Lord's ground staff, but had then become a dual-purpose bowler. He would begin with a few overs of medium pace and then switch to off-breaks. It was his slow bowling which was to bring him fame.

The best of Moss and Titmus lay ahead, yet the side made a remarkable improvement in 1951 and at the half-way stage looked as if they might come close to winning the title, but their final position of seventh was a clearer indication of their real talent. Denis Compton was still an automatic choice for the Test side and this, coupled with the need to rest his knee, limited his appearances in the County side. Nevertheless, he scored three Championship centuries in May when he came close to making a thousand runs in all cricket. His bowling was very effective, and had Young not begun to feel the effects of knee injury towards the end of the season, Middlesex might well have finished higher.

The England selectors were the only ones who did not seem to value Young, for he played no Test cricket after 1949, being replaced by men of far inferior talent and ability. Michael Melford, one of the wisest of journalists, was quick to recognise the contribution that the left-arm spinner made to Middlesex cricket:

> There were days when the bowling seemed to be almost entirely Young, perversely prevented by the laws of the game from bowling at both ends at once. Rarely in this wet summer were the wickets fast enough for Sims. Compton was not always available and the young fast-medium bowlers Moss and Bennett, promising though they were, could only be used sparingly. Young answered the call with prodigies of accuracy and endurance. He bowled nearly 300 overs more than anyone else in England and was once again by general agreement the best of his type in the land.

Jim Sims' playing days were drawing to a close, and the 1952 season was to be his last. He was to be appointed deputy head coach at a time when much was being done to restructure the County Club and put it on a firmer professional basis, for these were changing times in English cricket. There was concern that all was not well with the game. The euphoria of 1947 seemed an age away, and Middlesex were being watched by 100,000 fewer people in 1952 than they had been five years earlier. Their problems were minimal compared to several other counties.

Certainly Middlesex were making every effort to revitalise the club and the game. A new agreement was drawn up between MCC and the County in 1952 which, for the first time, allowed for a separate staff and a separate office for the administration of the County Club. In April of the same year, Walter Robins reported that he had been approached by J. W. Hearne, who asked whether he could be of any assistance in connection with the coaching of young players. Robins was enthusiastic about the idea and gave warm support to the plan to employ Hearne. There was a need to supervise the coaching of junior players, and it was first suggested that Jack Hearne should be paid £100 a year to supervise and carry out coaching in Middlesex practice nets on Tuesday and Thursday evenings and to attend second eleven and Club and Ground matches with a view to relating mistakes made in matches to the practice in the nets.

Later the committee gave unanimous support to the proposal that Hearne should be appointed County coach with Sims as his deputy. This meant that the leg-spinner with the round-shouldered delivery was to continue to serve the County to which he had given his life, and, indeed, he was to continue to serve them until the day he died. By then, in 1973, he was the County scorer, and he died in Canterbury, the night before Middlesex were due to play Kent.

The influence that he and Hearne had on the younger players was incalculable. Eric Russell remembers that the young men used to refer to them, behind their backs, as 'B and K' after the Russian leaders of the time, Bulganin and Kruschev, for they were hard task masters, but kindly men.

The young talent for which Middlesex were searching began to emerge. The second eleven report for 1951 gave notice of:

> Murray, J. T. a very promising young wicket-keeper and a good bat considering his age. With increased experience must definitely make the grade.

A young left-hander, Bob Gale, had been offered a three-year contract and his special registration had been approved by MCC. R. V. Bell was another of whom much was expected while, in his one game, Titmus had bowled excellently on a rain-affected pitch. Mike Murray, who was born in Westminster, had attracted attention when playing for the Combined Services and had been given a trial and revealed considerable promise as a right-handed batsman. It was decided to extend his trial period and leave it to him to decide whether or not he wished to turn professional. Later he was considered as a possible player/secretary at Worcestershire, but he decided to go into banking. His contribution to Middlesex was to be of major importance, for he became an outstanding Treasurer and then Chairman of the Club, leading it to a successful period of redevelopment in the 1980s.

After losing the first two matches of the 1952 season, Middlesex enjoined a successful run which took them to second place in the Championship. In July and August they fell away badly, however, but finished a creditable fifth.

Surprisingly, the fault was in the batting, which never reached its previous consistency. Robertson and Edrich both passed 2,000 runs, and, in the case of Jack Robertson, this was the seventh successive season since the end of the war in which he had reached the mark, a magnificent record which was unapproached by anyone else in the country. Immaculate in appearance, in style and in his timing, Robertson was to play until 1959, but already there were signs that he and others of the great side of 1947, which was not a young one, were drawing to the close of their careers. Gray had gone in 1951, Sims in 1952, and Brown, Young and Leslie Compton had all gone by the middle of the decade. Early in 1955, those three, along with Sharp and Thompson, were informed by George Mann who, like Robins before him, had become Hon. Secretary, that younger players would be preferred. Such a move was inevitable, for three of them were well past 40, and the other two nearing that age.

Jack Young was now sorely troubled by injury. By 1952, both of his knees gave him problems , and in June he broke a finger, but he still ended the season with 1,298 overs and 137 wickets in County Championship matches alone. What he could have achieved in a more balanced and penetrative attack one can only conjecture.

Edrich had changed to off-breaks and took 50 wickets in the season, but he was hardly the force he had been before his back problems. The one positive gain was the advance of Moss. Tall, strong and eager, he had a high, classical action and from the start he showed a willingness to learn, not become disheartened and to adapt to bowling at Lord's, a task which was not within the compass of all bowlers. He came close to a hundred wickets in 1952, his first full season, and provided the Middlesex attack with the spearhead of which it had been so badly in need for so long.

Middlesex also had the more regular services of Don Bennett, who had been invalided out of the RAF with defective hearing. Bennett worked hard with Jack Hearne to improve his batting, but his medium-pace bowling never became quite the potent force that had been anticipated.

As 'Joe' Murrell died and 'Patsy' Hendren took over as scorer, a wicket-keeper of whom Murrell would have been proud played his first games for Middlesex.

Towards the end of May, Leslie Compton was injured,

and his replacement at Leicester was the young keeper who had made such a good impression in the second eleven, John Murray. The first of more than a thousand catches he was to take for Middlesex was made when he held Smithson off Jack Young.

Denis Compton was captain in that game, which Middlesex lost, and scored a sparkling century, but he lost form in July and August and with it his place in the England side. Both he and Edrich were to return for the 'Ashes' triumph a year later, but neither was the dominant force, that he had been five years earlier. Age and injury had reduced their effectiveness in the field. Edrich was no longer a great slip fielder, and the days when Compton raced round the boundary, caught anything within reach, and much that was not, and threw with the speed of a bullet were in the past. Yet when one looks at Compton's record in all cricket in 1952: 1,880 runs, average 39.16, 77 wickets at 28.58 runs each, four centuries, 26 catches – one wonders how many others would have judged that a season of failure.

One thing was apparent. The sharing of the captaincy satisfied nobody. At the season's end, Compton tendered his resignation as captain. He said that he was not suited for the job and that it would be better if one man carried it out. Edrich was named as captain, Compton as vice-captain and Robertson as senior professional. Edrich was to lead the side until the end of the 1957 season and during his term of office Middlesex were to hover constantly between fifth and seventh position in the Championship.

One of the disappointments that Edrich inherited was the failure of Bill Knightley-Smith, a valued left-hand bat, to reappear for Middlesex after his promising first season which had brought him a county cap. A former captain of Highgate School, he was, perhaps, a little too rigidly orthodox in style. He later assisted Gloucestershire where he held an administrative post.

The desire to establish Middlesex on a more professional basis led to the founding of a new indoor cricket school at Alexandra Park, yet problems still existed in that promising players like John Murray were engaged on national service and could not benefit from the facilities at the school.

Murray had come from Notting Hill where he had played his cricket for Rugby Boys' Club. He had not kept wicket until the regular keeper broke a finger in the final of the Boys' Club competition, and he took over. He was already destined for the ground staff at Lord's as a batsman, and Archie Fowler was now asked to consider him as a wicket-keeper also. He had received no formal coaching as a keeper, and the first that he ever received was when Middlesex arranged for him to have two days' leave in April 1953, so that he could get instruction from Andy Wilson in Bristol. Wilson was the Gloucestershire wicket-keeper who had been Price's understudy at Lord's in the 1930s. The only other coaching that Murray received was some years later when, during a Middlesex and Surrey match, Jim Sims, the Middlesex scorer, asked Herbert Strudwick to come in early on the three days and give Murray some advice with his work on the leg side. In every sense, John Murray was a natural.

For the time being, however, Leslie Compton held the wicket-keeping position for Middlesex. Tall and a strong, a magnificent centre-half of the old school for Arsenal and England, Leslie Compton did not possess the build that one usually associates with wicket-keepers. He was never as neat at Price, nor as elegant as Murray, and he was a lesser keeper than both, but he was highly effective. A gentle giant of a man, he always looked as if he should score more runs than he did, but, more than most, his sporting career was blighted by the war. He was 35 before he was able to take a regular place in the Middlesex side.

If the old guard was passing from the scene, the new actors were already thrusting their way to the front of the stage. Alan Moss's excellent form continued, and he was selected for the MCC side to go to the West Indies in 1953–54. Had his career not coincided with those of Tyson, Trueman and Statham, Moss must surely have played in more than the nine Test Matches which were to be his quota. He would have been a regular new ball bowler in today's England side.

Don Bennett, though not often given the new ball, also showed signs of improvement. He batted consistently and was one of the most brilliant fielders in the country. In 1953, however, the exciting event was the emergence of Fred Titmus.

With his national service at an end, he was able to join the side from the start of the season, although this was inauspicious. In the tied match against Northamptonshire at Peterborough, he scored nought and one and failed to take a wicket. He was left out of the next two games, but was recalled for the match against Essex at Westcliff. Thereafter he was ever-present. He took 94 wickets in Championship matches alone, was awarded his county cap and was recognised as an off-break bowler of outstanding merit.

The Middlesex seasons began to follow a consistent pattern, an exciting start which took them up with the Championship leaders, followed by a decline in August when they slipped back to their mid-table position. The problem was that while the younger players were learning their trade and making rapid progress, some of the older players were fading fast. Harry Sharp, one of the club's greatest stalwarts, for example, hit 1,500 runs in 1953, but a year later he could manage only 316. Brown and Thompson had suffered declines which, if not quite so dramatic, were equally troubling. Robertson, too, although hitting nearly 1,500 runs, was reliant upon one purple patch in July for 500 of them.

Titmus continued to advance, and Moss, in spite of injury, had another fine season, but Bennett, although hitting a maiden century, tended to disappoint. In all, however, these were troubled times for county cricket. A zest had gone from the game and attitudes throughout the country leaned more towards defence than attack. This had never been the Middlesex way, and the committee was concerned that the County should maintain the policy of aggressive, attractive cricket which had been its trade-mark since the advent of Walter Robins.

Schemes were afoot, one in conjunction with the children's comic *The Eagle,* to encourage young people to come and watch first-class cricket, and G. O. Allen brought forward the idea of reduced entrance fees for those under 14. Hornsey and Hampstead Clubs were among those who supported efforts to encourage the young by giving donations.

The need to bring on young players was still of paramount importance. Gale was 'enthusiastic and keen', but his cricket was being played for the Army while on national service, and his Middlesex career did not start until 1956. An interesting recruit in 1953 had been Charles Robins, like his father a leg-break bowler and hard-hitting batsman. He had displayed precocious talent at Eton, but his bowling simply duplicated that of Bedford in an age when the leg-spinner was becoming increasingly unfashionable. Nevertheless, the young Robins had his days of success. Against Yorkshire at Sheffield in 1958, he took six for 40 and was only halted by some clouts from Burnet as the home side were bowled out for 101. He inherited his father's zest for the game, but it was to be used most significantly on the administrative side where his role in the reshaping of Middlesex was to be vital.

Alf Gover, at East Hill, was still being employed to help young bowlers like Bennett, Moss, Warr, Deller, Hurst and Tilley, while Hearne looked after Bick, Baldry, Delisle, Titmus and White at Alexandra Park.

The indoor school at Alexandra Park had run into problems. The lease of the school was to be terminated at Christmas, 1956, but G. C. Newman and R. H. Twining suggested that it should be surrendered at an earlier date so that the trustees could go ahead with the repairs and renovations for which they had permission. The surrender of the lease would also save Middlesex money in rent, but it was not possible for the club to be housed elsewhere. The only alternative was to construct a school.

A site was found at the Broadway, Muswell Hill. It covered an area of 38,000 square feet and was, in fact, a derelict cinema. It was estimated that the total cost of the purchase of this site and the erection of a building to house four nets, changing room, club room, professionals' room, a small flat for a permanent steward and a car park would cost between £15,000 and £20,000. It would also be possible to sell surplus land to set against some of this cost. Newman and Twining were of the opinion that 'the need for a Cricket School in North London has been established beyond debate'. The committee was not wholly in agreement as to North West London being the ideal place, and W. H. Webster and G. O. Allen felt that Lord's was the best place and enquiries should be made with the MCC.

Early in 1955, it was reported that the cost of the Muswell Hill project would be £25,000. This was considered to be high and the plan was dropped, although its value 30 years later, particularly such a prime site, would be hard to estimate. Nevertheless, the plan was thrown out, and it was Finchley that was to provide the indoor cricket school for the County. It has proved to be a happy choice.

As young players advanced and older ones moved nearer and nearer to retirement, the flames of Compton and Edrich still burned brightly, and both were in the England side in Australia which retained the 'Ashes'. Compton had undergone three operations on the knee, suffered periodical inflammations and was also troubled by lumbago, but he still batted with the sense of adventure that had made him the greatest attraction in the game. In the decade after the war, he received a daily fan mail which was beyond anything that has been received by a cricketer since.

In 1955 and 1956, however, he was hampered further by knee trouble and was forced to miss many matches. His only century for the County in 1955 was on Whit Monday when he hit 150 in Sharp and Thompson's benefit match with Sussex. There were 20,000 people at Lord's to watch it, and it was a reminder of past glories. But Middlesex had a new hero.

Fred Titmus became the first Middlesex cricketer for 26 years to achieve the 'double' when he scored 1,235 runs and took 191 wickets in all matches in 1955. For Middlesex, his 158 wickets created a record which is likely to remain unbeaten, so much has cricket changed in structure in the years since it was established. His performances set him out on his Test career.

That season provided Titmus with the first of his eight 'doubles'. Beginning in 1959, he completed the 'double' in four consecutive years in Middlesex matches alone. His batting was courageous and determined, founded on a sound technique. In an emergency, he opened the batting for England, and when Geoffrey Boycott made his debut in Test cricket against Australia in 1964, Fred Titmus was his opening partner. It is as a great off-spin bowler, however, that he will be chiefly remembered. He was never an enormous spinner of the ball, but no bowler had a greater variety of pace and flight. His mastery of the art of flight was one of the delights of the game, for to watch him in action was to be aware of a cricketing intelligence of the highest order. He could make the ball float, drift and dip, and he had a quicker ball that went with the arm which was lethal. He kept a perfect length, and if the pitch offered him any assistance, there were few who could survive against him.

With Moss, Young and Warr bowling admirably, the Middlesex vulnerability now was in batting. Robertson had something of a resurgence, and Dewes and Delisle gave an added dimension in late summer, but *Wisden* predicted that unless young batsmen could be found to take over from the veterans, 'Middlesex are likely to have many worries in the future.'

Bennett remained something of a disappointment. In his schooldays he had been seen as a future England all-rounder, but in being so categorised, he was done a disservice. Titmus

Fred Titmus, whose career for Middlesex spanned five decades.

says that he was never given sufficient opportunities with the new ball and that his batting never developed as well as it should have done because he went in too low down. In effect, he fell between two stools, and one who might well have been a Test cricketer ended as a good and loyal county player.

Ironically, it was an injury to Moss which gave Bennett an opportunity to shine. Moss bowled so well in the opening matches of the 1956 season that he was in the England side for the first Test. He tore a stomach muscle in that game and could not play again until the end of the season. Bennett stepped up to open the bowling with Warr, who had a splendid season, and did himself justice as a bowler for the first time.

That season saw the passing of most of the old guard, and many new faces appeared. Bob Hurst took over from Jack Young as the slow left-arm bowler. He had the ability to turn the ball sharply and was an effective bowler on good wickets, but he never seemed to have sufficient confidence in himself and retired in 1961. The younger batsmen, so urged by *Wisden*, ousted their elders. Parfitt, Hooker, Bick and Gale appeared in several matches while Eric Russell played in two.

Hooker was also a medium-pace bowler, and he enjoyed a

most lively Championship debut. The match was at Chesterfield at the end of May, and it was dominated by Bill Edrich, whose 208 not out in five hours was the last double-century of his career. He was at his pugnacious best and hit four sixes and 32 fours. His bombardment of the leg-side boundary recalled the halcyon days. He and Baldry added 139 in 119 minutes for the fourth wicket, and Ron Hooker joined him in a fifth wicket stand of 176 in 95 minutes which was ended only by the declaration. Hooker, after a nervous start, matched Edrich blow for blow and finished on 77. He then came on as second change and took the wickets of Smith and Kelly. Middlesex won by an innings, so completing a highly satisfactory debut for the young all-rounder. Like Parfitt, who had two years of national service in front of him, Hooker disappeared for a couple of seasons.

John Murray did not disappear. He missed the first Championship match of the 1956 season when Leslie Compton played, but from that point onwards he was the first choice Middlesex wicket-keeper for the next 19 years. He ended his first full season as the leading wicket-keeper in the country with 77 dismissals, 14 of which were stumped. The Titmus–Murray combination was to become a menace to every batsman on the county circuit.

What did not develop quite so rapidly as Middlesex might have wished was Murray's batting. J. W. Hearne had seen in him an immense batting talent, and he was to remain constantly frustrated and disappointed that Murray did not score more runs in first-class cricket. When Frank Worrell first saw Murray he wondered why he should ever fall below 2,000 runs a season, so good was his offside play. For not reaching these promised heights, Murray blames himself:

> They tried to make me an opening bat as well as a wicket-keeper, but I was never suited to that. I made a conscious decision to concentrate on my wicket-keeping and I never paid as much attention to my batting as I should have done. Perhaps I was wrong, but I loved keeping wicket and I had to work hard at it. I could get runs when we needed them, but at other times I got out too often to bad bowlers.

To criticise Murray as a batsman seems churlish in view of his subsequent record, yet he looked so splendid at the wicket. That splendour was something more than ornamentation as was realised in his second full season when, with

1,025 runs and 104 dismissals (82 caught, 22 stumped), he became only the second wicket-keeper in the history of the game to achieve a 'double'. Les Ames had done it three times, in 1928, 1929 and 1932, and it is not likely to be done again.

But while Murray's feat was celebrated there was a hint of sadness in the air, for both Compton and Edrich had announced their retirement from regular first-class cricket. In effect, Edrich was to play some 14 matches in 1958, but Compton played only three times, as an amateur.

Courageous, tenacious, optimistic, pugnacious, aggressive – there is no end to the list of words that could be used to describe Bill Edrich. On and off the field, he lived life to the full. When he finished with Middlesex he went back to captain Norfolk and scored runs and took wickets until he was well into his fifties. To be with him was to be infected by his enthusiasm, for the fun that was revealed in the cricket was the essential ingredient of the man.

Edrich left the first-class game because he felt that the natural gifts which had served him so well, notably his wonderful eye, were beginning to desert him; Compton bade farewell because the damaged knee which had plagued him for ten years had at last become too much of a liability. That he had played on for so long in a state of discomfort which would have made lesser men run for the safety of their beds was because he loved the game so much. His strength was that he communicated that love to all who saw him play.

His last game as a professional came in the final Championship match of the season, against Worcestershire at Lord's. It would have been inappropriate had he finished his official career on any ground but the one at which he had delighted so many people. On Saturday, 28 August 1957, after Gale and Walton had been dismissed, he joined Jack Robertson. They put on 225. Denis Compton batted three hours and hit a six and 17 fours in his 143. His career had been a romance so it could have ended in no other way.

He scored 48 in the second innings. Middlesex lost, and, to all intents and purposes, Denis Compton was gone. Yet even as the years separate us more and more from that glorious time when he and Edrich brought an unparalleled joy to the cricket fields of England, the memory of Denis Compton's batting remains as sharp and as vivid as ever. There was gladness when he was at the wicket, and every time you saw him it was as if you were seeing him for the first time. He made the world a most exciting place.

FRUSTRATION AND DESPAIR

WHEN WARR TOOK OVER THE CAPTAINCY IN 1958 he had in his side only one survivor from the team which had shared the Championship nine years earlier, Jack Robertson. Robertson gave valuable substance to a side which was, as yet, immature, but, in 1959, he lost his form and retired, so severing the last link with the immediate post-war period.

John Warr was a most able captain. A witty raconteur, an intelligent and successful business man, he was a shrewd assessor of men, both those under his command and those against whom he was playing. In his first year as captain, the side began well, but fell away badly. They were always in the first two until mid-June, but their inability to win matches told heavily against them. Their record was in complete contrast to what had been typical of them in the years since the war, for although they lost only four of their Championship matches, as many as 16 were drawn.

The reasons for this change lay in the batting which could find neither consistency nor confidence. It was hardly likely to with so many young players struggling to establish themselves. Bob Gale was now a regular opening batsman. At first, Jack Robertson was his partner, but in July, Robertson dropped down the order to give some needed substance to the middle of the innings and Gale and Eric Russell began a fruitful partnership.

They first came together at Leicester. Gale scored 52 and 73, and Russell hit 40 and 46 as they shared partnerships of 96 and 113. They indicated batting potential of the highest class, and, in the same match, Peter Parfitt hit 99, his top score of a season in which he was able to play 11 Chamionship matches when on leave from the RAF.

Parfitt had come to Middlesex solely on Bill Edrich's recommendation. Edrich had heard of his outstanding ability as a schoolboy, had gone to Norfolk to see him and had immediately suggested to Middlesex that he should be signed. Parfitt was considered to be Middlesex's most exciting batting prospect from the outset of his career. Something of a slow starter, he was a solid left-hander who was brave enough to be unorthodox once he was settled, for he was eager to attack the bowling. He also brought the

John Warr—joyful captain, humorist and preserver of the traditions of cricket.

bonus of being a magnificent fielder, one of the best catchers that the game has seen.

If Gale, Parfitt and Russell were new to the side, Murray, again the leading wicket-keeper in the country, Titmus, Bennett, Moss and Warr were richer in experience. As a bowler, Bennett again played a supporting role to Warr and Moss, who had excellent seasons, and were as good as any opening attack in the country. What the attack lacked perhaps was balance and variety, for Hurst played infrequently and achieved little, and Hooker's medium pace was rarely called into action.

Middlesex ended the 1950s full of unrealised potential. *Wisden* was less than enthusiastic about the side:

> For several years Middlesex have had an abundance of promising young players who, by now, should have developed. Unfortunately many of them remain no more than 'promising' and until they are able to make the most

of their natural talents Middlesex will remain a moderate side.

Gordon Ross still saw the County as being in a state of transition, but he agreed that:

> The batting was more in the nature of potential strength than hard reality. Whilst there were many signs of good days ahead, the batting suffered from inexperience of the first-class game; the young player, although batting well, was not quite sure how to put a score together, or how to look for singles when the bowling was tight.

Russell, Gale, Hooker, Titmus and Parfitt all scored a thousand runs in the Championship, Murray was only 14 runs short, and Ted Clark, straight from club cricket with Teddington, hit a hundred on his first-class debut against Cambridge University and played quite spendidly when he won a place in the Championship side. All those who hit a thousand runs hit centuries, for three of them maiden hundreds, and the batting was generally attractive. There were two maiden centuries at Gravesend in a memorable match at the end of May. One of the centurions was Ron Hooker, who endeared himself to the cricket correspondent of *The Observer* because he was trying to hit sixes when in sight of a maiden century. It is a match worth recording because it revealed that the spirit of Compton, Edrich and Robins was alive and well. Even *Wisden* was lyrical about the game:

> Middlesex won by 109 runs, taking 12 points to two by Kent. Not even the sternest critic of modern cricket would have faulted this match. It produced two maiden centuries, one of the fastest hundreds of the season, sixes in abundance, and an astonishing spree by Middlesex on the last day. Hooker's superb 137 included three 6s and twenty-six 4s, 122 in boundaries, and Kent won a thrilling tussle for first-innings points. Even these performances were eclipsed on the third day when in two hours before lunch Middlesex made 216 for two wickets. Gale raced to his century in eighty-seven minutes, and Russell, like his colleague Hooker, went ·on to complete his maiden hundred. Kent, set 294 to win in three hours, never recovered from a poor start but held out until five minutes from the end of extra time.

Warr and Titmus both passed a hundred wickets in

Championship matches alone, and Moss, although missing ten games through Test calls, took 73 Championship wickets. What then was the problem that condemned them to tenth place in the Championship? Ross was closer to the mark than *Wisden* in his assessment of the side. Too many batsmen were too eager to score too soon.

Eric Russell suggests that the best advice he received, and, in its way, a turning point, was when Warr said to him as they took the field one day: 'The trouble with you and the other young lads is that you want to hit a four every over. You are not looking for the singles and twos, the pushes into the covers. You'd score more runs if you did.' Like all of Warr's sound advice, it came at the right moment, and it had its effect. In 1960, Middlesex climbed to third in the Championship, the highest position that they had attained for 11 years, and had they not come pointless from the final match, against Worcestershire, they would have finished runners-up.

Middlesex were never out of the first four, and that they failed to maintain a stronger challenge for the title was due to the old failing. After a fine start and victories in the majority of matches at Lord's they lost their way in July and August. Colin Drybrough gave the side more variety in attack with his slow left-arm when he came on vacation from Oxford, but again the attack was almost entirely in the hands of Warr, Titmus and the magnificent Moss. Hampshire were bowled out for 82 in the opening match of the season, Glamorgan for 85 in the next, and few sides coped with the Middlesex attack with much confidence.

Eric Russell blossomed into an opening batsman of international stature. He represented the Players at Lord's and was chosen for the MCC side to visit New Zealand as was John Murray. Clark was laid low by a back injury, but his absence was compensated for by Sid Russell who hit a thousand runs in his first season. He was a rugged, almost brutal batsman with nothing of the elegance of his namesake, but he was effective before he moved on to Gloucestershire.

Good as the bowling was and however efficient the batting, it was the fielding which was Middlesex's main strength. As a man and as a leader, Warr was an enthusiast. He had taken a young side, full of promise, and drilled them into an effective unit. Murray was an inspiration behind the stumps, Parfitt brilliant close to the wicket, Hooker outstanding at short-leg, Eric Russell in the outfield and Gale

KENT _v_ MIDDLESEX

Played at Gravesend, 23, 25 and 26 May 1959

MIDDLESEX WON BY 109 RUNS

MIDDLESEX	FIRST INNINGS		SECOND INNINGS	
R. A. Gale	c Cowdrey b Page	26	c Halfyard b Page	106
W. E. Russell	b Pettiford	61	c Pretlove b Halfyard	120
J. D. Robertson	b Pettiford	0	run out	10
P. H. Parfitt	st Evans b Dixon	32	c Leary b Halfyard	6
R. W. Hooker	c Halfyard b Page	137	c Phebey b Page	4
R. A. White	c Pretlove b Dixon	0	(6) b Halfyard	20
F. J. Titmus	c Halfyard b Page	90	(7) c Pretlove b Page	11
R. V. C. Robins	not out	13	(8) not out	8
H. W. Tilly			(9) not out	9
★J. J. Warr				
†K. B. Day				
	b 1, lb 2, nb 1	4	lb 6	6
Total	(for 7 wkts dec)	363	(for 7 wkts dec)	300

BOWLING	O	M	R	W	O	M	R	W
Halfyard	28	10	100	0	25	3	112	3
Wilkinson	18	8	49	0	4	0	29	0
Pettiford	29	8	81	2				
Dixon	10	4	53	2	7	0	49	0
Page	22.1	5	76	3	21	4	104	3

1st inns: 1-83, 2-84, 3-89, 4-194, 5-198, 6-331, 7-363
2nd inns: 1-188, 2-216, 3-248, 4-252, 6-281, 7-284

KENT	FIRST INNINGS		SECOND INNINGS	
A. H. Phebey	c Day b Warr	32	b Tilly	13
R. C. Wilston	b Robins	6	b Warr	0
D. J. Halfyard	b Warr	12	(9) st Day b Titmus	0
S. E. Leary	c Robertson b Tilly	20	(3) lbw b Warr	7
★M. C. Cowdrey	c Day b Parfitt	83	(4) c White b Parfitt	50
J. F. Pretlove	b Warr	0	(8) not out	21
J. Pettiford	not out	95	(5) c Hooker b Titmus	21
A. L. Dixon	c White b Warr	83	(6) c Parfitt b Titmus	36
†T. G. Evans	b Warr	10	(7) b Tilly	6
R. W. Wilkinson	not out	3	c White b Titmus	10
J. C. T. Page			b Warr	5
	b 14, lb 11, w 1	26	b 12, lb 2, w 1	15
Total	(for 8 wkts dec)	370		184

BOWLING	O	M	R	W	O	M	R	W
Warr	37	16	62	5	20.5	5	47	3
Tilly	32	9	67	1	8	3	29	2
Robins	12	2	49	1	10	5	33	1
Russell	3	0	18	0				
Titmus	23	5	69	0	12	4	35	3
Hooker	11	1	49	0				
Parfitt	7	0	23	1	4	0	24	1
Gale	1	0	7	0	2	1	1	0

1st inns: 1-10, 2-28, 3-66, 4-124, 5-124, 6-191, 7-339, 8-356
2nd inns: 1-0, 2-11, 3-26, 4-100, 5-100, 6-106, 7-120, 8-131, 9-171

Umpires: R. S. Lay and D. J. Wood.
*Captain; †Wicket-keeper.

an excellent gully, while Warr led them with a thoughtful gaiety that made Middlesex an attractive side again. The sadness was that, at the age of 33, Warr felt he must concentrate on a business career and left first-class cricket, never to return, at the end of the 1960 season.

The progress that had been made under his guidance had been enormous. A very young side of immense possibilities had began to fulfill its promise. It was sad that he could not have stayed another two or three years until the side had matured fully. As it was, Middlesex faced another crisis regarding captaincy, and the problem was to take more than a decade to resolve, for the 1960s must represent a time of disappointment and frustration for the Middlesex Club.

The appointment of Warr's successor took the cricket world by complete surprise, and one can recall clearly the newspaper headline: 'Club Cricketer to Captain Middlesex'. This was only a half-truth, for, as we have noted, Philip Ian Bedford had played for the County while still at school. His leg-breaks and googlies had lost their potency, however, and he had disappeared from first-class cricket almost ten years before he was recalled as captain.

His return had been hinted at during Warr's last season, for it was believed that his bowling might give the attack the dimension that it had lacked, but none had anticipated that he would come back as captain. The demarcation between amateur and professional still existed, however, and Middlesex, once an amateur stronghold, was now bereft of gentlemen who could lead the side. Dewes and Delisle had left the game, and A. C. Walton, an attractive, hard-hitting batsman, did not play after 1959. Drybrough was still at university so that, with it almost obligatory to name an amateur as captain, Middlesex had few options.

In many ways, Ian Bedford was an inspired choice. He was a delightful man, immensely popular, even though his appointment must have been viewed with some scepticism. Titmus wrote of him that, because he had not played since 1950 and had never played regularly:

> He didn't have the intimate knowledge of the players in the game that is so helpful. But he was a popular captain and took his job seriously. He worried a great deal in private when things were not going well and in his second and last season he was injured for half the summer. So his captaincy, from his personal point of view, was not the happiest on record. On the field his team suffered from his modesty about his own bowling. I think he was anxious not to commit the error into which a bowler-captain can often fall, that of hogging the bowling. So he used himself too little. Off the field he was a tremendous social asset to the side.

Eric Russell endorses Titmus' view in that he found Bedford the kindest and gentlest of men and a valued companion, but that he and others almost had to plead with Bedford to bowl himself. In his first season as captain Bedford sent down only 303 overs in Championship matches while Titmus bowled four times that amount and Hooker, used as a stock bowler since Warr's departure, and Moss bowled over six hundred and eight hundred respectively.

In Bedford's first year things went well. The side began badly, but recovered well to hold third place again, and they were considered unlucky not to finish higher. The bowling was good, the batting spirited. Parfitt, Russell, Gale, Clark and Murray batted well; Hooker, Titmus and Bennett excelled as all-rounders. Causes never seemed lost. Facing Glamorgan's 298 at Lord's at the beginning of July, Middlesex were 137 for six. Murray then joined Bennett in a stand of 182 so that Bedford was able to declare 73 ahead. Moss then took eight for 49, and Middlesex won by nine wickets.

There was exciting promise of richer fulfilment. Parfitt had scored more than two thousand runs and was a left-hander of authority and power; Murray was England's wicket-keeper and, like Eric Russell, was incapable of a gesture that was not aesthetically pleasing; and Titmus was the most accomplished all-rounder in the country.

There had been some interesting debutants. John Price, a quick bowler from the Wembley Club, took 18 wickets in five matches. A slow left-arm bowler from Enfield Grammar School, Mike Smith, took 14 wickets, but also showed surprising promise with the bat.

In the absence of John Murray on Test duty, Michael Sturt of Brondesbury kept wicket. We should do well to dwell for a moment on the career of Mike Sturt. In 1961, as an amateur, he played eight times. The next year he kept wicket on six occasions. He was then not called upon for four years, but he played 11 times in 1967 and 1968. His readiness to fill in and to do the job so well was marked by the award of a county cap in 1967. It was now believed that his first-class career was over, but in 1976 he was again in the Middlesex side for six matches. His last two games came in 1978. In a period of 17 years, he played in only six seasons, yet he maintained an excellent standard behind the stumps and dismissed 71 batsmen. His continued fitness and ability to move into a key position with such aptitude testifies to his cricketing talent. He has been a most invaluable and influential administrator in recent years, a true club man who is now Chairman of the Cricket Committee.

A man incapable of an ineloquent gesture—John Murray keeping wicket to the bowling of Fred Titmus. Peter Parfitt is at slip and John Hampshire the batsman.

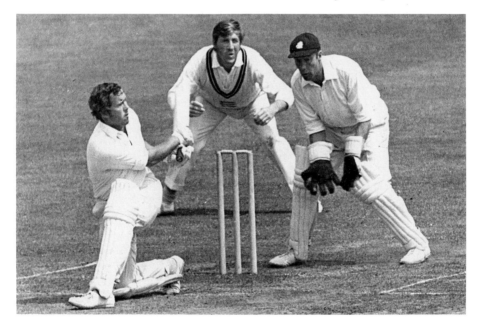

During the fourth Test Match, in July 1961, Murray's deputy in the Middlesex side was one who was to overshadow Sturt, the Cambridge university wicket-keeper, Mike Brearley. Brearley played against Derbyshire at Lord's and Hampshire at Portsmouth, scoring 12, 19, 6 and 5, and taking six catches.

The excitement engendered in Bedford's first year as captain disappeared in the second. The captain was injured and played in only 14 matches. Moss led the side in his absence and managed ably with limited resources although his own form suffered. Indeed, the bowling as a whole, Titmus apart, was below the standard of recent seasons. Murray had suffered from a leg injury and, for a time, lost his Test place while his batting fell away, but Eric Russell and Parfitt were among the country's leading batsmen. Gale was spoken of as a future Test player. He hit 200 against Glamorgan at Newport, the only double-century of his career.

Parfitt enjoyed a phenomenal season against the Pakistanis. He topped the Test averages with centuries at Headingley, Trent Bridge and Edgbaston, and he hit a century in each innings when Middlesex played the tourists. He was chosen to go to Australia with the MCC side as were Murray and Titmus. Inexplicably, Murray was to surrender his Test place to A. C. Smith on that tour and cruelly, and quite wrongly, was rarely again considered as England's number one wicket-keeper although, arguably, he was among the half-dozen greatest that the game has known.

Ian Bedford's second, and last, disjointed season as captain of Middlesex heralded a decade of enigma and gloom in the club's history. Probably through personal worries as to his own capabilities, the likeable Bedford resigned. Four years later, in September 1966, while playing for Finchley at Buckhurst Hill, he collapsed and died on his way to hospital. He was 36 years old. Those who had played under him were shocked and deeply saddened by the news.

Most felt that Alan Moss should succeed Bedford as captain. He had done well in the most difficult circumstances, and he was liked and respected by the players. He had also borne the burden of the attack with little support, but he was a professional, and traditions die hard. The distinction between amateur and professional was to be abolished in 1963, and the dividing line had already become blurred, but Colin Drybrough, the Oxford University and former

Highgate School captain, was named as Middlesex's next skipper.

He had made plenty of runs at Highgate and had scored quite heavily at Oxford, but, for Middlesex, he went in late and concentrated on his slow left-arm bowling which did develop as his experience of county cricket increased.

Drybrough could not have taken over at a more difficult time. Cricket was at the crossroads, and where once well over 20,000 people would have packed into Lord's for the Whitsun match against Sussex, a crowd of 3,000 was now a good one. The social climate had changed, and there was a dryness and a worry in the game as people pondered what to do next. Within two months of beginning his reign as captain, Drybrough had a most unhappy experience.

Middlesex were playing Kent at Tunbridge Wells and did well on the Saturday. Hooker and Titmus took four wickets apiece, and Kent were bowled out for 150. Middlesex finished the day on 121 for three, R. A. White, the left-hander who won his spurs this year, 43 not out, and Hooker 13 not out. These were the days before the Sunday League, and the team had stayed at a local hotel on the Friday night and had arranged to do the same on the Monday evening, but they returned to their London homes at the week-end. *Wisden* takes up the report:

> Three players arrived at the ground with plenty of time to spare. They were White and S. E. Russell, who had already been dismissed, and Clark, the twelfth man. White put on his pads and gloves and waited on the boundary, hoping his partner would be in time while the two umpires and the Kent players went to the middle. After a wait of a liberal two minutes, the umpires led the players off the field and it was officially stated the umpires had closed the Middlesex innings.
>
> It was decided that Kent should begin their second innings within ten minutes and Cowdrey agreed that Clark should keep wicket while, if necessary, White and S. E. Russell shared the bowling, Kent providing sufficient fielders to make up eleven in the field for Middlesex. Actually, Underwood, Catt, Prodger, Brown and Dye assisted their opponents, but within three overs the whole Middlesex side were present and fielding.

Kent recovered from their bad position and would have

won the match but for rain. For Middlesex, the incident was an embarrassment and a shame, though a traffic jam should take part of the blame. Ever since then the players have stayed locally the night before a game.

John Price joined the County on a regular basis and immediately impressed, working up a good pace from his long, winding run. He never perhaps quite mastered the art of exploiting the wicket at Lord's as Moss had done and never provided the consistent early break-through. He had come to the game very late for a quick bowler (he was 26 in 1963) and this was a handicap, yet he was soon to win a Test cap, and his career record is testimony to his hard work and the quality of his bowling. He was to play well into the 1970s, often with little support at the other end, for as he arrived so Moss departed at the end of the 1963 season.

Middlesex finished sixth in both seasons when Drybrough was captain. He had his weaknesses and his critics, and he failed to inspire a team where there was more talent than success, but Middlesex were to finish no higher in the ten seasons that followed his departure.

It was, perhaps characteristic of Drybrough's time with Middlesex that his most renowned achievement, the wickets of Scott, Crump, Larter and Bailey of Northants in five balls, the first three with successive deliveries, should come in a match in which Middlesex were beaten by ten wickets. This was in 1964, his last season. He ended with more than two hundred wickets for the County, and his loss as a bowler was felt.

In the first two seasons of the first of the limited-over competitions, the Gillette Cup, Middlesex were knocked out in the second round. In 1965, Titmus's first year as captain, they reached the semi-final, where they lost to Surrey by five wickets at The Oval. They did not win another tie until 1968 when they were again beaten semi-finalists.

It was the bowling which was the problem. Even though Bob Gale left cricket to pursue a career in the City mid-way through the 1965 season, the Middlesex batting was still strong. Russell, in particular, was splendid, and Parfitt and Clark had excellent seasons. Mike Smith had few chances, and his bowling had now almost evaporated, but Clive Radley, another Norfolk recruit, made a good impression and played in 17 games. Hooker bowled more than ever before. Bick won regular a place to bowl his off-breaks. Herman was tried as an opening bowler, and a young leg-spinner, Harry Latchman, who had been born in Jamaica but brought up in England, bowled with success in five matches.

Latchman's debut in the Championship had come in the match with Glamorgan at Lord's in mid-August, yet it is not for his three wickets that the game will be remembered, but for the unusual dismissal of the Glamorgan batsman Alan Rees in the second innings. Needing 286 to win, the visitors had been given a good start by Tony Lewis and Peter Walker, and Rees tried to maintain the momentum by moving down the wicket to attack Titmus. The off-spinner had devised a plan with John Murray whereby when a batsman was going down the wicket to him he would bowl a quicker ball down the leg side in the hope that Murray could bring off a stumping. It was a ploy that had worked on several occasions, but this time Rees dived to catch the ball as he was beaten by its speed and flight and, on appeal, he was given out 'handled ball'.

The match also witnessed a sparkling opening stand of 151 between Russell and Brearley on the first morning, and a century by Peter Parfitt. Brearley had captained Cambridge in his last two years and had come down from university in 1964 with a first-class degree in Classics and a good second in Moral Sciences as well as scoring more runs at Cambridge than anyone had ever done before. He had been selected for the MCC tour of South Africa, 1964–65, being seen as a future Test player and England captain. The tour had been a total disaster for him, and he had taken some time to find his touch in 1965 when he was used regularly as Russell's opening partner. Years of further study, some spent in the United States, took him out of county cricket until 1968, but he had led a strong MCC under-25 team in Pakistan in 1966–67, and had averaged 132.16 in first-class matches, with innings of 312 not out against North Zone and 223 in the second representative match. His best years with Middlesex, however, were still ten years in the future.

The Middlesex present was not so happy. In 1965, there was an inability to clinch matches that should have been won. Against Hampshire, at Lord's, for example, Ron Hooker took seven for 24, and John Murray held six catches, as the visitors were bowled out for 85. Parfitt hit a hundred, and Middlesex took a lead of 234. This should have been sufficient to ensure victory, but Hampshire finished the match 91 runs in front. Murray had two catches and a stumping in the second innings to equal Montague Turner's

Middlesex v Essex, Lord's, 1966. Barker (Essex) hooks Price for four. The Middlesex catchers look on anxiously—Radley, Parfitt, Titmus and Clifton.

record of nine dismissals in a match which had stood for 90 years.

The first year of Titmus's captaincy saw another record created when the skipper and Clive Radley shared a stand of 227 in three hours, 40 minutes for the sixth wicket. Both hit centuries; for Radley it was the first in first-class cricket.

Records and brilliant individual displays cannot compensate for mediocre team performances however. At Weston-super-Mare in July 1966, Hooker hit a magnificent century in 89 minutes on a crumbling wicket and Titmus performed the only hat-trick of his career, but neither man enjoyed a particularly good season. Price returned from injury to recapture form and his Test place, but the Middlesex attack was totally lacking in penetration in spite of some promise from Wes Stewart, a West Indian pace bowler who had come to Middlesex via Gloucestershire.

Middlesex cricket had lost its zest. The County no longer played in the attractive manner that had so long been its corporate personality. They were not helped by ever-changing legislation which attempted to infuse vitality into cricket by rules and regulations when a change of attitudes was needed. In 102 games in 1966, the first innings of each side was restricted to 65 overs, one of the more insane and destructive of innovations which happily had a short life.

The Middlesex fortunes reached their depth in 1967, although the County rose to seventh in the table and Russell and Harris, who had forced his way into the side with some bludgeoning displays, put on a record 310 for the first wicket against the Pakistani tourists. Like White and Latchman, Harris was later to move to Nottinghamshire. He was replaced as the Middlesex opener by Mike Smith, who had taken a considerable time to win a regular place in the side, but became an attractive and capable batsman when he did, and one most unlucky not to win Test honours.

There was an element of despair in the Middlesex cricket, and *Wisden* was uncompromising in its condemnation of the state of affairs:

> Though Middlesex climbed from twelfth in 1966 to seventh last year, there could be no general satisfaction at this elevation, for the county played much sub-standard and unattractive cricket, particularly at Lord's. In the quest for points Middlesex failed to fulfil the special responsibility they have, playing their home matches at the headquarters of the game. Such tiresome cricket seemed doubly regrettable, for the senior players were capable of scintillating play.
>
> Circumstances may have mitigated against an all-out drive for a win, but on the three days chosen to inaugurate Sunday cricket at Lord's, Middlesex batted with insufficient freedom to compel watchers to come again. The nadir was reached in the dreadful match against Hampshire at the beginning of July, though the teams made amends with an exciting finish at Portsmouth which resulted in the first tie in the Championship for eight years. However, the overall result of this unambitious outlook was that by the end of the season crowds diminished to the faithful few.

The Hampshire game at Lord's to which reference is made received universal condemnation. Only 12 minutes play was lost, and the match began with a fine hundred from Roy Marshall. After this hard labour set in. Hampshire declared at 421 for seven made in 145 overs. Middlesex were 371 for seven in 176 overs when the game ended. In response to protests as to why Middlesex had not sought to inject the match with some meaning and vitality, secretary Flower gave the official statement: 'Having been set to score 272 to avoid a follow-on, or 422 for first innings lead, and having lost four men for 123, Middlesex were not prepared to throw away wickets for the sake of gaining two points.'

It is easy to heap blame on Middlesex and Hampshire for this debacle, but, in truth, the whole of English cricket was sick. Frantic discussions were taking place in an effort to find some solution for the malady. The Sunday League, sponsored by John Player, came into existence in 1969, and the Benson & Hedges Cup followed three years later. Where once there had been only the Championship to play for, there were now four titles for which the 17 counties could compete.

Not only was the structure of the game being altered, but there was an injection of new blood into the county game. Overseas players had been representing English counties since the beginning of the century, and, as we saw with Trott and Tarrant, the issue had always caused heated debate. By 1967, however, it seemed that the cupboard was bare of home-born talent, and there was agitation that the qualification regulations concerning overseas players should be lifted. *The Cricketer* was one journal that argued in favour of overseas players being allowed into county cricket without a period of residential qualification:

> If the nurseries of England were stocked with talented players, there would be no need to import established players from abroad. Indeed, it might be a disservice to the game at home to do so, for young English cricketers might be discouraged or deprived of opportunity and experience. This is scarcely the situation today and the decision of the counties to make overseas players wait a year is a senseless compromise.

The agitation was successful. A move led by Notts, who had Sobers ready and waiting, allowed counties the immediate registration of overseas cricketers for the 1968 season.

The new regulation took many by surprise and several counties registered no overseas player for the 1968 season. Others failed to realise the significance of the change in legislation and signed players hastily and unwisely. Middlesex, among the most conservative of counties, signed nobody. Their traumas continued.

Fred Titmus was vice-captain of the England side in the

Caribbean in the winter of 1967–68. He played in the first two Tests, but shortly before the third he suffered a boating accident. His left foot became caught in the screw of a small boat and he lost four toes. Most believed that his career was over, but, with typical resilience, he was back for the first game of the season at Derby, and he was to miss only one Championship match, finishing with exactly 100 wickets.

Price and Latchman enjoyed fine seasons, too, but the year was a far from happy one. The batting was miserable, and 'until the middle of August spectators saw no improvement on the wretched cricket played during 1967'. Not a Championship match was won until Sussex were beaten in Hooker's benefit match at the beginning of June. There were two more wins that month and then a barren period. When the opposing side set targets Middlesex never reached them. The heart, seemingly, had gone from them.

The bonus point system had been introduced that year, and Middlesex, with 21 batting points, showed a lower return than anyone else. Their cricket was so tedious and their decline so rapid that it was obvious that poor form alone was not the reason for their problems. Titmus believed that his approach was responsible and shortly before the Gillette Cup semi-final match against Warwickshire he resigned the captaincy.

Titmus's failure as a captain remains a surprise. He had an astute knowledge of the game, was a cheerful, popular character with a ready wit and led with exemplary courage and determination. Perhaps, outgoing and happy as he was on the surface, his reading of a game was essentially a personal one which was not communicated fully and effectively to those with whom he played, some of whom had grown in the game with him.

Peter Parfitt succeeded him and led the side for the first time on 13 August when Middlesex lost the Gillette Cup semi-final, but he appeared to give the side new vigour, and the last four matches of the season were won to raise a note of optimism for the future.

That feeling of optimism was not sustained. Clark's brief career had virtually ended in 1966. Don Bennett played his last game in 1968 although his wisdom and expertise were to be used on the coaching side to great advantage. Hooker's last season was to be 1969. It was a pity that both he and Bennett missed the vintage years of one-day cricket that lay ahead, for it was a game in which they would have excelled.

The side had played with exuberance under Parfitt at the end of the 1968 season, but that exuberance was not maintained the following season. The first win in the Championship did not come until 8 July, and then, needing 223 to beat Northants, they reached 160 for one. Russell made 85 and Parfitt 71, but the rest collapsed, and Middlesex's victory in the end came by one wicket.

The batting throughout the season was fragile, and, as it transpired, this was one of only three Championship wins. Russell lost his form in his benefit season, Murray looked as if he should have achieved more than he did with the bat, and Smith and Parfitt were not at their best. Radley was head and shoulders above the rest, although there was some promise from Featherstone.

Norman Featherstone was one of two overseas players in the Middlesex side. he had been born in Rhodesia, and Middlesex had pressed to have him considered as a permanent resident of the United Kingdom, but he returned to South Africa to seek employment in the winter so that he had to serve a period of residential qualification before he was allowed to play for Middlesex. He was a delightful young man, a brilliant fielder, a useful off-break bowler and a most attractive batsman, but the impetuosity which was at first attributed to his youth never left him. He did not seem to relish the need for consistent application in the county game and left to join Glamorgan in 1979, a talent not totally fulfilled. The other overseas cricketer was Alan Connolly, who had been signed on special registration.

Connolly had bowled most impressively on the Australian tour of England in 1968. He was a fast-medium pace bowler who appeared to relish English conditions in the way that Terry Alderman was to do 13 years later, and it was considered a great scoop when Middlesex signed him.

He was a warm, likeable and friendly young man. In 1969, he took 74 wickets, which was far below what was expected, but was better than anyone else. He rarely made an early break-through and seemed to wilt when batsmen attacked him. He was not the first, nor the last, overseas player to find county cricket harder work than he had anticipated. His second season was a disaster. He was prone to experiment, expensive and went through the closing matches of the season almost wicketless. He did not return to complete his contract in 1971, retiring with a back injury.

Connolly's second season was not only a disaster for him, it was a disaster for Middlesex. Parfitt had never seemed to have the confidence of the committee, who took a long time to confirm him in the captaincy. The energy and enthusiasm of the senior players was sapped when it was discovered that the Australian importation was being paid more than they were. Such cases are not simply a question of finance, but of recognition for long and faithful service, or the non-recognition of it. All was not well with the County, for whom the changes in the game, socially, structurally and economically, appeared to be happening too quickly and could not be fully apprehended.

They had not yet grasped, for example, the value of an overseas player of outstanding quality, both as an attraction and as a cricketer who could help a county win a trophy. In the wake of Connolly, they signed Larry Gomes.

Gomes had toured England with the West Indian Schools side in 1970, and Middlesex attempted to sign him, but they were refused a work permit for the player. The government argued that work permits were only granted for eminent cricketers, which Gomes, with no first-class experience, was not. The matter was taken up with the Minister of Sport, but Gomes had to qualify by residence and made his debut in 1973 at the age of 19. He was a raw left-handed batsman and a medium-pace or off-break bowler scarcely worthy of a team place in his three seasons with Middlesex. He was a shy, reticent young man who would sit quietly and sip his orange juice after the game, remote from the social intercourse of the two teams. His time with Middlesex did much to turn him into a Test cricketer; it did little to help Middlesex in their attempt to get out of the depths into which they had fallen.

There seemed a total lack of urgency in the club, although there was concern. Connolly's failure threw the inevitable burden on Price and Titmus, for Keith Jones was a raw recruit and Herman had faded and was to move to Hampshire.

With such a limited attack, the batting needed to be brisk and authoritative, but that cannot happen when morale is low and the centre uncertain. Russell played with his old elegance. Smith scored heavily early in the season. Parfitt often jettisoned the cares that the captaincy and the situation had placed upon him to revive memories of better days, but Middlesex despite five wins, finished 16th in the Championship, and only rain at Bristol in September saved them from finishing bottom. Parfitt was replaced as captain.

In looking back on these years of frustration and despair,

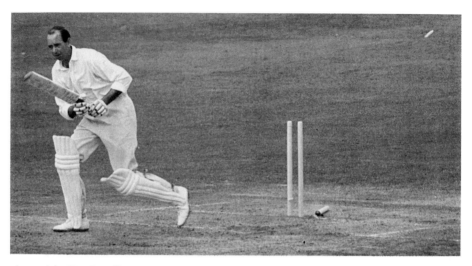

A rare sight. Eric Russell is bowled at Lord's. For nearly two decades he was among the most stylish and accomplished opening batsmen in England.

one still probes blindly for the reasons why a side which contained four players of world class won nothing.

Judgments, inevitably, are tempered by personal reminiscences and prejudices, yet it is hard to believe that there was ever a more accomplished wicket-keeper than John Murray. There was beauty in everything that he did. He would touch his cap with his white-backed gloves before settling on his haunches, and the hands would describe a graceful curve as he settled in position. The ball was taken, seemingly, always at the easiest height so that it could be tossed to slip in one liquid movement. That he should have scored more runs than he did before he left the game in 1975 we have already argued, but he still hit nearly 19,000 runs and 16 centuries. When he retired no wicket-keeper in history had had more dismissals.

Murray was badly treated by Test selectors. So was Eric Russell. He was cruelly unlucky. In Australia, in 1965–66, he began as the outstanding batsman in the England party. Attractive and polished, his smooth style, based on the principle of playing straight, won the admiration of all. He scored prolifically before the first Test, but there he split his right hand when fielding and had to bat No 11. Boycott, intended to go in at No 6, was moved up the order and was established by the time Russell was fit. Russell was still considered as good as any opener in England after this tour and won his place back with a century for Middlesex against the Pakistanis in 1967. He batted exquisitely before lunch on the first day, hitting three glorious off-side boundaries in one over before Intikhab bowled him for 43 on the stroke of lunch. That marked the end of his Test career, although his career with Middlesex lasted until 1972.

Eric Russell was immaculate as a batsman in every department. He was meticulous in dress, the trousers always neatly creased, the sleeves always turned up exactly just below the elbow, no hair out of place, no hint of untidiness. His art of batsmanship mirrored the style of dress. One could not watch Eric Russell at the crease without deriving pleasure from the man's every movement.

At first an exciting outfielder, he developed into a fine close catcher and formed an excellent combination with Peter Parfitt who was one of the finest fielders the game has known. As a batsman Parfitt had the same pugnacious determination that Edrich had possessed and that was to mark Gatting's style. His bat got broader the longer the innings continued, and he was ever ready to give the ball a belt.

To complete the quartet there was Titmus, whose days were far from over at the beginning of the 1970s and who was to share in a success that was denied to the others.

Why could these four not bring the triumph that they dearly wanted and the absence of which they have continued to regret? One obvious reason is that the side lacked balance. For a time there was no adequate pace attack. Moss, initially, and Price, later, never had adequate support. One can still recall Mike Smith, his slow left-arm days behind him, being asked to bowl a few overs of medium-pace long hops with the new ball because there was no one else to entrust it to on many occasions. At another time there was no supportive spin to Titmus, for the slow left-arm successor to Jack Young never came forward for any length of time.

Another reason is that the side lacked depth. There were inadequate reserves at crucial times, and at others no replacements pushing for places when top players lost form. Such a situation could breed a sense of complacency.

Lastly, there was the lack of leadership. Murray resigned the vice-captaincy which he held for a while. Drybrough, Titmus and Parfitt failed to get the best out of the side for a variety of reasons not all of their own making. Bedford lacked the confidence. The job of captaining Middlesex, a team with several capable players and strong personalities, was not a sinecure, and few relished it.

One man did. In fact, he was lured back to first-class cricket with the hint that he would get the post. His name was John Michael Brearley.

THE AGE OF BREARLEY

THERE WAS A GENERAL FEELING that Parfitt had been badly treated although the committee may be forgiven for believing that radical measures were needed. There were suggestions that Middlesex had turned back the clock, that they were trying to perpetuate a class distinction which had been eradicated when the demarcation between amateurs and professionals had been abolished in 1963. Certainly the halcyon days of Middlesex cricket had always been linked to the availability of an abundance of amateur talent and to conducting the game in a way which was generally considered to be an 'amateur' spirit. Certainly Middlesex could be accused of not realising, or not wishing to realise, the growing professional intensity in application, attitude and economic resources that cricket was demanding by the beginning of the 1970s. While Essex boasted Keith Boyce, Gloucestershire Mike Procter, Hampshire Greenidge and Richards, and Lancashire Clive Lloyd and Farokh Engineer, Middlesex offered their supporters a shy West Indian schoolboy with neither experience nor reputation.

The social differences between Parfitt and Brearley seemed apparent to all. Parfitt was a natural sportsman, a cheerful professional who had succeeded at the highest level and was renowned for his battling qualities and superlative close fielding. Brearley was an academic from City of London School and the University of Cambridge. His cricket at school and university had promised much, but since then he had done no more than dabble in the game. Whatever his success for Cambridge and for MCC under-25s in Pakistan, his record for Middlesex was undistinguished. He had not scored a thousand runs in a season for the County, nor a century in the Championship, and he was not to do either until 1973. He had begun as a wicket-keeper, but he had not kept for several years and when, on one occasion, he was put behind the stumps when Murray was unavailable, it came close to causing a revolution among second-eleven players.

All were aware of these points when he took over; few were aware of the qualities with which he was to grace the game in the next ten years. In the first place, although his background deemed him 'amateur' in the eyes of many, he turned out to be a captain of such professional efficiency and application that many would call him ruthless. In Test match terms, he was in the Johnny Douglas, Douglas Jardine mould, but he smiled and joked more often than either.

Secondly, the 'amateur' aspect of his character came to be one of his greatest strengths. John Arlott, not surprisingly, recognised this when Brearley became captain of England and said to him: 'The great thing about you, Mike, is that you're the only England captain who knows it doesn't *really* matter.' Few captains in the game have ever been able to ally an intelligent and professional approach to a sense of detachment which allowed them to accept that there were other things in the world more important than cricket.

Why a man of such scholastic attainment as Brearley should want to captain a county cricket team in their annual peregrinations was a fact which bewildered some. He could have had a high academic position and led a life of cloistered comfort. In practice and theory, however, Brearley's greatest interest has always been the human mind. He was excited by the prospect of pitting his wits against others. For him, cricket was a highly skilful and intelligent game of chess played with real people. The challenge appealed to him as do all those things in life which are tinged with the mystic.

The two men instrumental in persuading Mike Brearley to return to county cricket and to lead Middlesex were Charles Robins and Mike Murray. Robins had captained the second eleven for four years and had been of great assistance to Brearley before he went up to Cambridge. Robins was acutely aware of the need for good leadership in the club and for a general sense of reorganisation to bring Middlesex closer to the demands of the game as it was now being played. He was also aware that Midland counties were making overtures to Brearley who was interested in the art of captaincy. Murray had played club cricket against Brearley and, astute man that he is, did much to lead Brearley back to Middlesex when there was temptation from elsewhere. Brearley's own assessment of the situation and his reasoning is typically forthright:

> In the mid sixties I was torn between cricket and an academic life, but I decided I did not want to be a professional cricketer. In 1968, I took a job teaching philosophy in Newcastle, but I realised that I did not want to spend the rest of my life dealing with philosophy.
>
> I played for Middlesex in the summer vacation and I was lured back to cricket full time by the offer of the

captaincy. I certainly would not have returned otherwise. I was attracted by the idea of captaincy. I have got enjoyment from every aspect of the game when I have done well. I enjoyed the tour of India with Tony Greig's side, 1976–77, because we did well and there was a lovely feeling of team achievement, but it was the idea of captaincy that led me back to Middlesex. I like to be bossy. I hate to get bored. I want to be doing something all the time, and the tactics of the game fascinated me. I liked the idea of the inter-relation with people, and, above all, I like trying to get the best out of people.

The Middlesex side that I took over in 1971 simply did not have enough bowlers. Everything fell on the shoulders of Fred Titmus. There was occasional help from John Price, but Fred was really expected to bowl all the time. We never had more than two bowlers. There was no decent attack. There was also a division between the top players who had played several times for England and the rest. Younger players felt that their voice could never be heard.

We had a successful first season and were top of the table until August when I was injured, but the county was not geared up for signing players or attracting them. There were huge committees which meant that no one had the power to make an offer to a player when he became available. Moreover, Middlesex had not been playing attractive cricket so that people had not wished to play for us.

From the early seventies we began to play robust, forthright and adventurous cricket. There was resourcefulness and change. Players enjoyed playing for us and against us. It became possible for myself and one or two others to make offers to players, and the club as a whole became more attractive to other players.

There were difficulties as some of the older players reached the point where, for example, they were left out of the side in Sunday League matches, but that was an inevitable part of the changes that were going on in the club.

There was no instant success, but there was a rapid improvement in results and attitudes. Purposeful cricket had been promised, and that was what was forthcoming. For a time, with wins over Leicestershire, Sussex and Northants and no defeats, Middlesex were at the top of the table. They lost that position, but victory over Surrey at The Oval in mid-July put them back at the top. Now came the decline, and they finished sixth. In the John Player League they struggled, and Surrey beat them in the Gillette Cup.

These results would suggest nothing exceptional for most clubs, but, after a lean period, they gave renewed hope to Middlesex whose cricket had recaptured something of its former vigour and enterprise. Smith and Russell were a bright opening pair. Radley and Parfitt had excellent seasons, and Featherstone and Brearley himself were only a little way

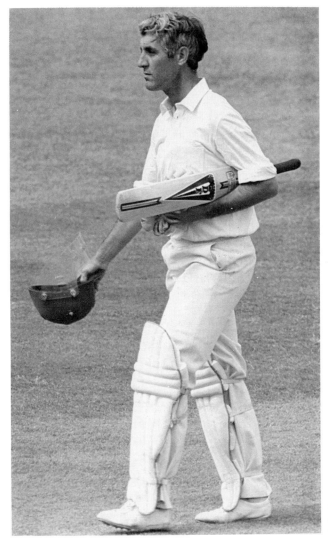

Architect of success—
Mike Brearley.
(Courtesy of Adrian Murrell)

behind. Keith Jones had an impressive season as Connolly's successor, but Jones' problem, like Price's, was that he had come so late into first-class cricket. Unlike Price, he was not to build on that first flush of success.

Another bowler to enjoy a good year was Harry Latchman. His leg-breaks were intelligently used by Brearley at a time when such bowling was facing extinction, but even Brearley was fighting a lost cause.

The following season, 1972, Latchman was used less and after one more year he was off to Nottinghamshire, the perpetrator of a bowling art for which cricket, obsessed by bonus points and limited-overs cricket, no longer had a use. His departure was hastened by the arrival of Phil Edmonds, the slow left-arm bowler for whom Middlesex had craved since the retirement of Jack Young.

Brearley's second year in command began with Middlesex in buoyant mood. They moved to fourth in the Championship, went well in the John Player League and qualified for the quarter-finals of the Benson & Hedges Cup, but then they faded dreadfully. Their main concern was a tendency for the batting to fall apart. They took a first-innings lead of 106 in the Championship match with Hampshire at Lord's, but were bowled out for 86 in their second innings and lost by five wickets. In the Gillette Cup match at Chalkwell Park, Westcliff, Middlesex were bowled out for 41 inside $1\frac{1}{2}$ hours. The wicket was suspect, but so was the Middlesex batting.

Parfitt, in his last season with the County, batted well enough to play in three Test Matches. Smith and Radley were both on the verge of international honours and topped a thousand runs for the County, but Russell, also in his last season, lost his form and Featherstone played in only half the matches.

Price bowled with consistent pace and hostility, but this was the last season in which he was regularly available. With Jones and Selvey, he formed an aggressive three-pronged pace attack. Edmonds formed an excellent spin combination with Titmus after the summer term at Cambridge so that a new Middlesex side was beginning to take shape.

A team in a transitional state is unlikely to be a contender for honours, although there was a period in 1973 when the John Player League looked to be within their grasp, mainly due to Marriott, a fast-medium left-arm bowler born in Jamaica, who took 28 wickets; and they lost the semi-final of the Gillette Cup to Sussex by only five runs. Such players as

Parfitt and Russell were not to be easily replaced, and when Price reappeared in August he emphasised just how much he had been missed. Not only did he take 26 wickets at low cost in eight Championship matches, but he seemed to inspire Selvey, who had impressed with his stamina and his ability to move the ball. He was never to become quite as quick a bowler as at first appeared, but he was to gain in control and incisiveness which, with his ability and willingness to bowl long spells, was to make him one of the most valuable bowlers in the country, but before that day arrived he was to experience a lean season.

Keith Jones was not to regain the penetrating form he had shown two years earlier, and 1973 was to be his penultimate season. Edmonds, already displaying moments of fire, bowled spectacularly after coming down from Cambridge and topped the bowling averages. He had an excellent model in Titmus, who had become the leading wicket-taker in Middlesex history, passing J. T. Hearne's record during the season.

Mike Smith batted consistently, hitting two centuries, scoring more than 1,500 runs and averaging nearly 50. John Murray hit two hundreds in successive matches, against Surrey at The Oval and Sussex at Hove, and Clive Radley was reliability itself, but the most comforting aspect of the batting was the improved form of Mike Brearley.

In the last county match at Lord's, against Yorkshire in mid-August, he hit 134 not out and shared a second-wicket stand of 90 with Smith and 199 with Radley, both of whom were out for 99. It was Brearley's first Championship hundred. He batted well in the return match with Yorkshire at Bradford, the last game of the season. His 83 meant that Yorkshire, troubled by a 'flu epidemic, had to score 208 to win. Cooper and Robinson came together at 192 for nine and edged the home side closer to their target, but, with the scores level, Selvey knocked back Robinson's middle stump. It was only the second tied match in Yorkshire's history.

As comforting as Brearley's improved form was the news from the second eleven and under-25 sides of young batsmen who showed great promise: Barlow, Butcher, Gould, Ross, and, for one game, Gatting. There was outstanding bowling, too, from an off-spinner, Emburey, and a seamer, Tim Lamb, who had done splendidly at Oxford where he finished ahead of Imran Khan in the averages.

Barlow and Butcher, and briefly Lamb, Ross and

Emburey found their way into the Championship side in 1974 when hopes ran higher than they had done for a quarter of a century. The season began with a gloriously heartening win over Hampshire. Radley hit a century, Gomes 85 and Selvey took nine wickets in the match. This victory heralded an impressive run in which, despite the occasional defeat, positive cricket brought emphatic wins over Warwickshire, Derbyshire, Yorkshire and Surrey, but the batting faltered towards the end and Championship hopes faded. Selvey lost his rhythm and his team place, and the bowling was almost entirely in the hands of Edmonds and Titmus, who provided the most balanced spin attack that Midlesex had ever possessed.

Six years after his Test career was believed to be over, Titmus was recalled to the England side for the tour of Australia and came out of the tour with credit.

The spin emphasis was rooted in the second eleven where John Emburey took 58 wickets. Under the careful guidance and instruction of Don Bennett, the second eleven won the Championship and the under-25 side the knock-out trophy for the third season in succession. Gould and Barlow were the leading batsmen, and it was to these two and to Roland

Clive Radley. The backbone of the Middlesex batting for 20 years and hero of three Cup Finals.
(Courtesy of Mark Leech)

Butcher that the County looked for the fifth batsman that was so desperately needed.

Smith and Radley had batted with their usual consistency, and Featherstone, used as an opener, had excited, perhaps, more than he had achieved. Brearley hit 173 not out against Glamorgan and 163 not out against Yorkshire in successive matches and seemed capable of batting effectively anywhere in the order, but, as so often in the past, pieces were missing from the Middlesex jigsaw which prevented them from being a trophy-winning side.

In 1975, the puzzle was still incomplete. Selvey recovered zest and control, Tim Lamb advanced, but the pace attack remained limited. Edmonds became a Test cricketer, Emburey played four matches with impressive results for his off-spin, but Titmus was less effective after a bright start. The attack still looked unlikely to force victories.

Norman Featherstone hit a not-out century in each innings at Canterbury where Middlesex won quite magnificently, and his stroke-play was still a joy, but for most of his career one felt that he played as if the sword of Damocles hung over him. There had been a time when he had had to be lured back from South Africa to continue playing for Middlesex; now there were doubts as to his future because Gatting had appeared over the horizon and Wayne Daniel was lurking in the wings. Featherstone's whole career with Middlesex was spent in a state of uncertainty. For the time being, however, no longer being asked to open, he hit more than a thousand runs, attractively, if inconsistently.

Smith, too, lacked consistency, but Radley was as dependable as ever, and Brearley blossomed.

Maintaining his ability to bat anywhere in the order, Brearley hit 1,656 first-class runs. Kanhai, Clive Lloyd, Barry Richards, Glenn Turner and Brian Davison stood ahead of him in the national averages, as did Boycott, the only Englishman in front of him. He hit four centuries, and suddenly, at the age of 33, he rekindled the hopes that there had been of him in his undergraduate days, and he was spoken of once more as a possible England batsman, although none could have imagined in 1975, the year of the first World Cup, that he would be leading England to the final in the second.

The fifth batsman was still the missing link. Gomes could not hold a regular place in the side. Gatting made his first-class debut against Worcestershire at the end of June, but he was barely 18 years old, and it was future glory rather than immediate returns that were expected of him. Graham Barlow, who had been on the fringe for six years, played in 16 games. A solid left-hander and a brilliant fielder, he batted with practical sense, but, although 25, he lacked experience at the highest level and he took some time to mature.

In the Championship, the weaknesses in attack and the lack of depth in batting could not be disguised, but in the one-day matches, with Titmus an immense asset as a restrictive bowler, success was tasted.

Quite miraculously, Middlesex qualified for the quarter-finals of the Benson & Hedges Cup competition. They were well beaten by Essex at Lord's, gained a comfortable win over Sussex and then lost to Kent at Lord's in astonishing fashion. The game was delayed until the Monday when Tim Lamb took two wickets in his fourth over and Phil Edmonds took four for seven in his first six overs so that Kent were 53 for eight. John Shepherd was then joined by Derek Underwood in a record stand of 81. Shepherd lashed at everything and hit 96. Underwood finished on 11 not out. Only these two reached double figures. Middlesex began as badly as Kent and were eight for three. Barlow and Featherstone put on 89, and Middlesex seemed to have the game won, for, in spite of Shepherd's innings, their target was a mere 138. Kent's West Indian had not completed his part in the match, however, for he dismissed Barlow, Featherstone and Murray in quick succession. With Titmus and Selvey together, Middlesex needed eight runs from the last over, but they managed only five.

In spite of this defeat, Middlesex were thrown a life-line when Essex beat Sussex. This meant that they could qualify if they beat Minor Counties (South) and bowl them out, for this would bring their striking rate above that of Sussex. The Minor Counties scored quite freely, but Barlow ran out Yeabsley in the last over to make the striking rate correct, and Vernon and Tim Lamb brought a nervous victory with two wickets and four balls to spare.

In comparison, the quarter-final win over Yorkshire seemed easy. Tim Lamb took four wickets in his last two overs to finish with five for 44, but, chasing 183, Middlesex made it hard going, and it was Radley's 30 not out which clinched the victory by five wickets in the last over.

Radley hit a hundred in the semi-final at Edgbaston where Warwickshire, needing six to win off the last over with three wickets in hand, scored two and lost two wickets as John Price bowled an inspired over. The final, Middlesex's first, was less compelling. Mike Smith hit 83, Phil Edmonds, who opened with him, hit the second ball of the match for six, but Leicestershire won with ease.

The Gillette Cup did not provide such close contests, and Middlesex moved to their second final of the season, a feat which had not been accomplished before. Alas, they were as comprehensively beaten by Lancashire as they had been by Leicestershire, and the cupboard remained bare.

The Gillette Cup final marked the end of John Murray's career. Total honesty, strength and grace had been among his most endearing qualities, and the deepest regret was that, like Russell and Parfitt, he had not been a member of a trophy-winning Middlesex side. He said later that he felt he went on too long, that he was playing from memory towards the end, but he was still enjoying it while Fred kept going. Their close partnership has continued on the administrative side. Murray's career ended in glory when he became the leading wicket-keeper, in terms of dismissals, in the history of the game. What was not so recognisable was the encouragement he gave to the younger players and the help he was to his captain.

The cupboard may still have been bare, but at least it had been opened and there had been a glimpse of what could be stored inside. Brearley was now an assured and authoritative captain. He knew what he wanted and was intent on getting it. The committee gave him full support. Gomes was with the West Indian side in 1976 when Featherstone played some of his best all-round cricket, so that Gomes was released after 1976.

One reason for retaining Featherstone was the anticipation that both Gatting and Gould would be needed for the Young England side. What was not realised was that Brearley and Selvey would make the Test side and that Barlow would play in the one-day international team.

Wayne Daniel would not be qualified for Middlesex until 1977 as he was touring England with the West Indian side. His fast bowling against England excited the appetite of Middlesex supporters, but, in the meantime, the County were still short of a pace bowler. Brearley learned that Somerset had released Jones and that the fast bowler was on the point of emigrating to New Zealand. At Brearley's insistence, Middlesex offered him a contract.

This signing was received with a sense of bewilderment in the press. Allan Arthur Jones had started his career with Sussex, but had moved to Somerset in 1970. His time with Somerset had been something of a tempestuous one. His attitude in the field had not always pleased his captain Brian Close, who had been driven to take drastic action. As Jones's services had been dispensed with by two counties, he had earned the reputation of being temperamental, hard to handle, lazy in the field and generally more trouble than he was worth. Perhaps it was that that attracted Brearley, who always liked a challenge. There was also the attraction that Jones was quick, and fast bowlers do not come in abundance.

Jones got off to a very good start. Smith and Brearley put on 133 for the first wicket in the opening Championship match against Kent at Lord's. Brearley and Radley added 146 for the second. Brearley made 153. Jones took eight wickets and Selvey, who had already taken eleven at Oxford, took six, and Middlesex won by 97 runs. Defeat at Edgbaston and draws with Northants and Surrey at Lord's did nothing to suggest that Middlesex were Championship material, but then, in a spell of good weather, they won four games in a row.

Jones and Selvey tore Essex apart, and Barlow hit 132 as Sussex were beaten by nine wickets at Hove, Jones and Selvey again prominent. Jones relished the two-day innings victory over Somerset at Bath, and at Gloucester only 11 hours playing time was necessary as Middlesex again won by an innings.

This match was to have an important bearing on the destiny of the Championship. Brearley was playing in the Test Match at Lord's and when Mike Smith won the toss he asked the home side to bat first. Play was not possible until less than an hour before tea and the pitch was damp. Selvey and Jones exploited the conditions magnificently. They bowled unchanged. Selvey took seven for 20, Jones three for 29, and Gloucestershire were out for 55. Edmonds, going in as night-watchman at number three, hit 78 in a sparkling manner and shared a stand of 122 with Barlow, who made 72. Smith declared as soon as the fourth bonus point, at 300 runs, was earned. Gloucestershire were demoralised and were confronted now by Titmus who tantalised them with his off-spin. He took seven for 52, and Middlesex were 28 points ahead at the top of the table.

Brearley carried his bat for 128 against Hampshire, but Middlesex were well beaten. This seemed only a temporary setback when, with Selvey in the Test side, Tim Lamb was given the new ball and took five for 32 as Sussex crumbled for 90. Gatting took three wickets and followed this with an innings of 94. Brearley hit 106 to indicate to the selectors their folly in leaving him out of the England side, and Middlesex won by an innings.

At Bradford and against Leicestershire at Lord's, Middlesex lost, and there was a tremble in their challenge for the title. At Bradford, they were left to make 237 to win. Radley had broken a finger on the first day and did not bat in the first innings, but when, in the second innings, the ninth wicket fell at 232 he came out to bat with his right arm in a sling in a valiant effort to win the match. He hit three before he was stumped off Cope so that Yorkshire won by one run.

Tim Lamb, going in number four as night-watchman, hit the highest score of his career, 77, against Notts at Lord's, but it was Roland Butcher with 63 not out who steered Middlesex to a four-wicket victory with two balls to spare.

Middlesex were now top of the table again, and they remained there after a nightmare defeat at Dartford. Middlesex reached maximum batting points, bowled Kent out for 151 and asked them to follow-on, 155 runs in arrears. The home side lost four wickets in levelling the scores, but tenacious batting took them to 348, leaving Middlesex to make 195. They collapsed before Johnson and Underwood, and Kent won by 57 runs after being behind for $2\frac{1}{2}$ days.

Titmus had been left out at Dartford, but he returned with a vengeance to take 12 wickets against Derbyshire. Featherstone, too, was enjoying the dry pitches. In the closing weeks of the season he took 30 wickets, spinning the ball sharply while flighting in a way that one had not associated with him in the past. He played a vital part in the victories over Essex and Glamorgan, where Radley returned to hit 113 not out and share an unbroken third wicket stand of 236 with Barlow, who made 140. The win over Essex, who were strong challengers, was crucial.

Lancashire survived a tense last day at Lord's so that the Championship could not be decided until the last game of the season, against Surrey at The Oval. Middlesex needed five points from the match to win the title. They had early problems as John Edrich hit the 99th century of his career. He was forced to retire hurt when he pulled a calf muscle going for the single which took him to three figures. Jones returned with a burst which gave Middlesex three bonus points for

County Champions, 1976.
Standing: H. P. Sharp,
scorer, M. O. C. Sturt,
A. A. Jones, P. H. Edmonds,
M. W. W. Selvey,
N. P. D. Ross,
R. O. Butcher.
Seated: C. T. Radley,
M. J. Smith, J. M. Brearley,
captain, F. J. Titmus,
N. G. Featherstone.
Insets: M. W. Gatting,
I. J. Gould, G. D. Barlow.
(Courtesy of Bill Smith)

bowling, and, at four o'clock on the second day, when it was learned that Gloucestershire had failed to take full bowling points against Derbyshire, Middlesex were Champions. They went on to beat Surrey in fine style.

It was essentially a team success. Titmus, in what he believed would be his last season, for he had retired and later became coach at The Oval, Edmonds, Jones and Selvey enjoyed great success, while Lamb, whose opportunities were limited, bowled splendidly as did Featherstone, top of the national averages.

Barlow had come out of his chrysalis. The solid left-hander had turned into a free-flowing stroke-maker. Middlesex had their fifth batsman. The jigsaw was complete.

Injuries and Test calls had been ridden well. The reserve strength had proved to be powerful. Butcher was an exciting prospect. Sturt, Ross and Gould had shared the wicket-keeping duties between them. Two cup finals in 1975 and the Championship a year later had placed the Club on a firm financial footing. They were at the top for the first time in 30 years. Now they had a new problem – how to stay there.

Not only had Middlesex won the Championship in 1976, they had been the only county to beat the West Indian tourists. Brearley was at the commencement of a run of success which has few parallels in the history of the game. The Packer Affair, and Greig's involvement in it, had projected Brearley into the England captaincy. He responded by leading his country to an emphatic victory in the 'Ashes' series. In 1977 Middlesex reached the quarter-finals of the Benson & Hedges Cup, finished third in the John Player League, shared first place in the Championship and won the Gillette Cup for the first time.

Brearley himself could play in only 11 Championship matches because of Test calls, yet he hit three centuries, scored 820 runs and finished 30 runs an innings ahead of Radley, who was second in the averages. Six of the County's nine wins came when he was captain.

There were disappointments and there were slips, especially at the beginning of August, but the side recovered and, somewhat fortuitously, had their match with Somerset postponed a week because of a backlog over the Gillette Cup semi-final. The game was transferred to Chelmsford, Middlesex's first venture outside the County boundaries since Walter Keeton had hit a triple century against them at The Oval in 1939 and their first home game away from Lord's since the match at Hornsey in 1959. They took seven points from the game at Chelmsford which were enough to give them a share in the title with Kent.

The season provided some controversial contests. At Lord's in July, Gloucestershire were bowled out for 80 and followed-on 263 behind. At the second attempt they batted with tremendous determination to reach 337. Phil Edmonds bowled 77 overs to take eight for 132. They were all out at 5.12, but Middlesex were allowed only 12 overs in which to make 75 to win when, as 38 minutes remained, they argued that they should have been allowed 13, one for each three minutes. They lost seven wickets and ended 12 short.

More astonishing was the game with Surrey at Lord's. There was no play on the first day and only five overs were possible on the second when Surrey lost Butcher for one. By 12.15 on the last day, on a rain-affected pitch, Surrey were bowled out for 49, and Brearley declared his innings closed after Emburey had faced one ball. Batting for a second time on a damp pitch, Surrey again succumbed to the cut and thrust of the Middlesex pace attack so that by tea they were out once more. Middlesex had captured 20 wickets and not scored a run with only 88 minutes remaining. In search of 138, Smith and Brearley set off at a spanking rate and 47 came

Middlesex at The Palace, 1976.

from the first seven overs. Smith was stumped for 51 with the score at 101, but Brearley and Radley brought victory with 11 balls to spare, Brearley hitting 66.

Wayne Daniel played a significant part in that memorable success, and the Middlesex attack was the most potent in the country. What the County had achieved in qualifying Daniel was a bowler who was not only among the fastest and most fearsome in the world in his early years, but a cricketer who was totally committed to the Middlesex cause.

Selvey had another splendid season, and Jones bowled well until a back injury put him out of action. He could not then regain his place because Emburey had been drafted into the side to form a lethal partnership with Edmonds. Few on the county circuit had a high opinion of Emburey when he played occasional games in the Championship before 1977. Brearley, always emphatic in his views, had insisted that Emburey was an off-spinner of the highest class, and he was soon proved right. The Middlesex attack was balanced and aggressive.

Another player in whom Brearley had supreme confidence, not at first shared by others, was Gatting, who played a full season, scored a thousand runs and, with Brearley's belief in him confirmed, was selected for England's winter tour.

Gatting's runs were most welcome as Barlow and Featherstone suffered in the damp summer, and Ian Gould, now the regular keeper, was very disappointing with the bat.

With Smith unobtrusive and dependable and Radley winning praise which was to bring him the first of his eight Test caps the following March, the batting was generally solid and could invariably produce the necessary flair. It was the confidence that one or two batsmen would play a necessarily substantial innings after others had failed that gave the side its strength. It was a decisive factor in the Gillette Cup triumph.

In the first round, Jones took three Kent wickets in five balls to leave the home side at 47 for five, but John Shepherd, ever a scourge of Middlesex, hit 101 and Kent reached 226. Smith and Brearley were out for 31, but the middle order all made good contributions and when bad light ended the first day Middlesex were 178 for five off 51 overs. The finish proved closer than expected with six runs needed off the last over, Selvey and Daniel together, and only Jones to come, but victory came with a ball to spare.

The second-round match with Warwickshire at Lord's also went into a second day. Brearley alone broke the restrictions imposed by tight bowling, but the Middlesex quintet, Gatting now the third seamer, provided an even tighter stranglehold on the Warwickshire batting, and Middlesex won by 31 runs.

By August the Lord's pitch had changed character and, put in to bat, Hampshire hit 247 for seven. Emburey, in particular, had suffered, but none of the Hampshire bowlers escaped punishment after Brearley had been out for three. Mike Smith and Clive Radley shared a record second-wicket partnership of 223. Smith scored 123 and Radley 94. Middlesex won the game with ease by seven wickets with 4.1 overs to spare.

The semi-final also produced a competition record and one which, hopefully, will never be beaten. The match was due to be played on Wednesday, 17 August. The teams attended the ground for six days and a 15-over game was played on the morning of Friday, 26 August. It was this state of affairs which caused the postponement of the Championship match and the rescheduling for Chelmsford, where the sides enjoyed finer weather. In the Gillette Cup game, Somerset batted frenetically and were out for 59 with two balls unused. Middlesex won by six wickets half way through the twelfth over.

The rain had made the preparation of the wicket for the final a very difficult task, and the outfield was still very wet

GILLETTE CUP FINAL
MIDDLESEX *v* GLAMORGAN

Played at Lord's, 3 September 1977

MIDDLESEX WON BY 5 WICKETS

GLAMORGAN

†A. Jones	lbw b Selvey	18
J. A. Hopkins	b Edmonds	47
C. L. King	c Barlow b Selvey	8
R. C. Ontong	c Gould b Gatting	0
M. J. Llewellyn	c Gatting b Featherstone	62
G. Richards	b Edmonds	3
†E. W. Jones	run out	11
M. A. Nash	c Gatting b Featherstone	3
A. E. Cordle	not out	8
T. W. Cartwright	st Gould b Featherstone	3
A. H. Wilkins		
	b 7, lb 5, w 2	14
Total (60 overs)	(for 9 wkts)	177

BOWLING	O	M	R	W
Daniel	11	0	41	0
Selvey	12	4	22	2
Gatting	7	1	28	1
Edmonds	12	3	23	2
Emburey	12	2	32	0
Featherstone	6	0	17	3

Fall: 1-21, 2-47, 3-50, 4-115, 5-129, 6-163, 7-163, 8-171, 9-177

MIDDLESEX

*J. M. Brearley	c E. W. Jones b Nash	0
M. J. Smith	lbw b Cartwright	22
C. T. Radley	not out	85
M. W. Gatting	c Hopkins b King	15
G. D. Barlow	lbw b Richards	27
N. G. Featherstone	b Nash	3
P. H. Edmonds	not out	9
†I. J. Gould		
J. E. Emburey		
M. W. W. Selvey		
W. W. Daniel		
	b 6, lb 11	17
Total (55.4 overs)	(for 5 wkts)	178

BOWLING	O	M	R	W
Nash	12	3	31	2
Cordle	8.4	1	29	0
Cartwright	12	2	32	1
King	5	1	19	1
Richards	12	2	23	1
Wilkins	6	0	27	0

Fall: 1-0, 2-45, 3-72, 4-146, 5-153
Umpires: D. J. Constant and T. W. Spencer.
*Captain; †Wicket-keeper.

when Glamorgan, put in to bat, began their innings. This was the first time in the history of the Gillette Cup Final that a captain was to put the other side in and win the match.

The pitch was unsuited to Daniel, deadening the pace, but Selvey bowled admirably and had Jones lbw after the veteran opener had begun a little too excitedly. King disappointed and hit to cover, and Ontong, once a Middlesex under-25 player, was caught behind off Gatting. The one innings of purpose came from Llewellyn. He lashed out at Gatting and hit Emburey, who had bowled with immaculate control, for one of the most magnificent sixes one has seen at Lord's, the ball landing on the guttering near the BBC commentary box at the top of the pavilion. One could reflect on the glory of that shot and wonder at the splendour of Albert Trott's famous blow off Noble at the end of the previous century.

Brearley handled his attack with a technical expertise that brought confidence and authority to his side. Featherstone was brought on as a sixth bowler, and his off-spin brought three cheap wickets. A target of 178 hardly seemed likely to stretch Middlesex.

It did not, but there was an early setback when Nash had Brearley caught behind with the first ball of the innings. In his second over Nash found the edge of Radley's bat, but Collis King dropped the simplest of chances at second slip. There was no second chance as Radley pushed, drove and nudged Middlesex to their first cup final victory at their third attempt. He was named man-of-the-match and Gatting took the fielding prize, although this was an area in which the whole Middlesex side had excelled. It was one of the great strengths of their cricket.

Gillette Cup holders, joint Champions, Middlesex were now the undisputed leading county, but success has its price. In 1978, they lost Brearley, Edmonds and Radley for six Test

Matches, 12 of the 21 Championship games, and Emburey was in the England side for the last Test against New Zealand. Their home fixtures at Lord's were crowded into the period before the middle of August when the wickets were damp and batsmen struggled. Brearley himself had a poor season, and the press questioned his right to be in the England side. His contribution was soon to be realised when he was no longer in the side. Mike Smith, for so long the hard-hitting opener with the disdainful, unobtrusive air, had a wretched summer, and the poor wickets made life difficult for reserve batsmen like Tomlins and Slack, who were feeling their way.

Gould, in spite of being hit on the head by a Croft bouncer and put out of action for two matches, batted with a flourish, but it was the bowlers who took the honours. Daniel was unsparing in his efforts. Jones returned after his bad back injury, but he was not the force that he had been in 1976. At the end of the 1979 season he left the County and joined Glamorgan, so becoming the first player since regulations were introduced to appear for four different counties. He has since become a first-class umpire and has established a fine reputation. His place in Middlesex history is, perhaps, a small one, limited in essence to one outstanding season, but his contribution in that season was a major factor in Middlesex winning the County Championship.

Above all other bowlers in 1978, however, stood Mike Selvey, fierce and hairy. He bowled more overs than Daniel and Jones combined and his endless stamina was allied to aggression and ability to move the ball that troubled the best. He was one of only four bowlers in the country to take a hundred wickets and his form in the closing weeks had much to do with the County's astonishing run, in which they won eight of their last ten games to finish third in the Championship behind Kent and an Essex side that was to become Middlesex's closest rivals in the next few years.

Essex it was who took the title and the Benson & Hedges Cup in 1979 while Middlesex, perplexed by bad weather and international calls, had only the compensation of a quarter-final appearance in the Benson & Hedges Cup, a semi-final place in the Gillette Cup and a fourth place in the John Player League. Their three Championship wins left them in 13th position, their lowest since Brearley took over.

Mike Smith reasserted himself with a thousand runs, a feat also accomplished by Barlow and Radley, but Gould fell away and Butcher, given more opportunity, lacked consistency.

*Unfailing energy and
enthusiasm—Mike Selvey.
(Courtesy of Adrian Murrell)*

Brearley and Edmonds were much missed with Test and
World Cup commitments while Gatting was a surprise and
controversial selection for the World Cup squad. In the event,
he did not play in a match. Selvey, Emburey and Daniel were
the main wicket-takers, but it was a most disjointed season,
dominated by rain and international cricket.

Having severed his connection with Surrey, for whom he
had played one match, Fred Titmus rather surprisingly
appeared in two games for Middlesex, but it was not thought
that he would play first-class cricket again. That was a
mistaken impression, for he was to appear in five matches in

267

1980 as part of a side who achieved almost total domination in English cricket.

Two players had left Middlesex after the 1979 season, Jones, as mentioned earlier, and 'Smokey' Featherstone. One is left with a wistful feeling of regret regarding Featherstone, for there appeared to be so much talent, so much attractive stroke-play that was never truly disciplined. There were also two new arrivals, Vincent van der Bijl, a fast-medium pace bowler from South Africa with a reputation for being a big hitter, and Paul Downton, reserve wicket-keeper to Alan Knott at Kent.

The signing of Downton caused a little controversy. His selection as reserve wicket-keeper for an England tour of Pakistan after a handful of first-class matches had created a stir, but with Knott still active, Downton was obviously looking for first-team cricket. John Murray rated him very highly indeed and was most anxious that Middlesex should engage him, particularly as Gould's batting had disappointed and the likeable left-hander seemed uncertain whether he could fill the role of both batsman and keeper. Downton himself was never in doubt that Middlesex was the side he most wanted to join. Gould left to join Sussex in 1981 and he played with such aplomb for his new county that he represented England in the World Cup and captained Sussex for a season.

Downton was not granted an automatic place in the side and did not play until the end of July, when he made his debut against Kent. As much as anything it was his batting which won him his place. Mike Smith had played four matches when it was realised sadly that his career was drawing to a close. Neither Slack nor Butcher had seemed to enjoy opening, and Downton was tried as Brearley's partner. He was an immediate success. He and Brearley put on 160 against Kent and 61 in the next match against Essex. Downton hit 64 and 67 and finished the season with 521 runs from nine matches.

There was early indication of Middlesex's good form with a successful run in the Benson & Hedges Cup which took them to the semi-final, where they lost to Northants by 11 runs. The combination of Daniel, van der Bijl, Selvey, Edmonds and Emburey was as formidable an attack as any county has ever fielded. Middlesex had expected Daniel to be in the West Indian party and van der Bijl had been signed as his replacement, but when Daniel was omitted in favour of

Croft and Marshall Middlesex had the bonus of being able to bowl the West Indian and the South African in harness.

Vincent van der Bijl was a gentle giant of a man. He would move in off his long run clutching the ball in his right hand as if he were reluctant to let it go. He brought the ball down from a full height and moved it sharply and late. He was a totally disciplined cricketer, and Brearley considered that his contribution to Middlesex cricket was immense. He 'saw the best in the rest of us rather than homing in so sharply on faults'. He became a great favourite at Lord's, and it is hard to believe that he spent only one season with the County, so great was his impact.

Like many big men he was a languid mover in the field, yet he was effective and although he did not appear to be running, he covered ground quickly. There was a feeling of courtesy in all his actions – even the massive, valuable smites at number nine.

Emburey had now emerged as one of the world's leading off-spinners and the amount of work he undertook and the number of wickets he captured were vital in a year when Edmonds had an operation on his knee and missed several matches. Maru came in as replacement for the injured Edmonds and proved himself a most capable left-arm spinner and brilliant fielder. He moved to Hampshire in 1984 because he was released by Middlesex, but his move was later regretted by the committee who still consider him to be a great loss. Another to choose a different county was De Freitas, a member of the MCC ground staff, whom Middlesex offered a contract. No longer having the privilege of the new ball, Selvey took fewer wickets at higher cost and Bill Merry and Simon Hughes, one of the season's most exciting discoveries, challenged him strongly. Yet Selvey's contribution can never be measured just by his figures. He was essentially a team man who bowled tirelessly at a time when others would have run for the shelter of third man.

Brearley had now relinquished the England captaincy and only Gatting and Emburey were called up for the Tests, although Roland Butcher was to play in the one-day international matches late in the season and to win a trip to the Caribbean.

It was Brearley who hit the first Championship century for Middlesex, 134 not out against Lancashire in the second match, but it was not until the third game, against Sussex at Lord's, that the first victory was earned. Radley was run out on 97 and Barlow hit 128 not out, and it is interesting to note that Middlesex's Championship successes in recent years have coincided with consistently aggressive contributions from the left-handed Barlow.

At the end of May, Essex led the Championship, but Middlesex gained a vital win over Surrey in the match at Lord's on 4, 5 and 6 June. Radley and Gatting hit centuries and Emburey took eight wickets as Middlesex won by an innings and went top of the table. The win was of great importance because Surrey, with Clarke and Jackman in top form, were challenging strongly for the title.

The return match at The Oval, ruined by rain, was drawn, but when Middlesex crushed Essex, the defending Champions, at Southend, the Championship seemed to be heading to Lord's. There was a sense of total efficiency about the Middlesex side and although their lead over Surrey was cut to four points by the beginning of July, they responded with an outstanding win over Hampshire at Lord's.

There was no play on the Wednesday, and Brearley asked Hampshire to bat when he won the toss. They batted sedately on an easy pitch, but van der Bijl took three wickets in an over and Pocock declared at 215 for eight. Brearley was hit on the head and retired, but Middlesex scored briskly and declared 128 runs behind. Tim Tremlett, then an opener, hit 74 not out, and Pocock set Middlesex to score 296 in 220 minutes, a formidable task. At 54 for three they looked doomed. Roland Butcher joined Clive Radley and, with a ferocious attack on the bowling, they added 177. Radley was out for 75, but in an innings which lasted 144 minutes and included nine sixes and eight fours Butcher scored 153 not out – for a few days the highest score of his career. A thrilling and amazing victory came with eight overs to spare.

Butcher has never been a consistent batsman, but his contribution to Middlesex cricket is incalculable. More than any man, he can play three or four innings a season which will win a match, and such a batsman can be decisive in winning the Championship. He followed his innings against Hampshire with an exhilarating knock at Scarborough. His 179 came in under three hours and contained eight sixes and 21 fours. Middlesex won by eight wickets, and they and Surrey moved ahead of the rest of the pack. Middlesex, who included Titmus in this match, held a lead of 15 points.

There was a rain-enforced draw with Kent and rain threatened the match with Essex, but Selvey, with the new ball, routed them in van der Bijl's absence. Following a Barlow century, Essex proved stubborn, however. Rain hindered Middlesex's progress, and at 282 for six, Essex looked safe, but Hughes and Daniel took the last four wickets for eight runs with only 3.2 overs remaining. Had Essex scored four more runs, the game would have been drawn, for there would have been no time for Middlesex to bat.

Suddenly, with the Championship almost won, Middlesex lost in successive matches to Leicestershire and Gloucestershire, for whom Procter made an inspired century. With some trepidation the side entertained a Notts side who were enjoying a good season. There was little to reassure Middlesex supporters in the opening stages of the match. Only Radley could cope with Rice, and Middlesex were 86 for six when van der Bijl joined Barlow. Barlow hit 97, stumped going for a big hit, and van der Bijl hit 76, his highest score for the County. They added 152. On the Monday, 19 Nottinghamshire wickets fell, 12 of them to John Emburey, and the game was over early on the third morning. In the meantime, Surrey were being trounced by Derbyshire and Middlesex had a lead of 25 points.

Surrey pulled back three points when both sides won their next matches. Van der Bijl had a splendid game at Uxbridge, taking ten wickets at this pleasant venue, home of the oldest club in the county.

Still Surrey clawed back the lead, winning handsomely as Middlesex were held at Hove, Wessels hitting 254 after Sussex had been asked to follow on, but time was running out. Middlesex knew that victory at Cardiff would bring them the title.

Nothing went right at the start. Gatting and Emburey were involved in the Centenary Test, play was not possible until 5.15 on the Saturday and Brearley lost the toss. Middlesex were put in and ended the day a miserable 41 for three. On the Monday, in difficult conditions, van der Bijl swung lustily for 40, and Middlesex made 163. Then he and Hughes took four wickets apiece and Glamorgan were out for 140. Middlesex were five points away from the title. Time was now their enemy, for only $6\frac{1}{2}$ hours of the match remained. Brearley led by example. He hit a magnificent 124 not out and declared at lunch with 211 on the board for the loss of Downton. Hughes made an early breakthrough and Glamorgan were 42 for three, but they batted with resolution. The seamers had borne the brunt of the bowling,

GILLETTE CUP FINAL
MIDDLESEX *v* SURREY

Played at Lord's, 6 September 1980

MIDDLESEX WON BY 7 WICKETS

SURREY

A. R. Butcher	b Selvey	29
G. S. Clinton	c Radley b Selvey	13
*R. D. V. Knight	c and b Emburey	11
D. M. Smith	c van der Bijl b Daniel	50
G. R. J. Roope	b Hughes	35
M. A. Lynch	c Gatting b Hughes	3
Intikhab Alam	c Butcher b van der Bijl	34
D. J. Thomas	b Hughes	4
R. D. Jackman	b Daniel	5
S. T. Clarke	not out	3
†C. J. Richards	run out	0
	b 1, lb 5, w 1, nb 7	14
Total (60 overs)		201

BOWLING	O	M	R	W
Daniel	12	3	33	2
van der Bijl	12	0	32	1
Selvey	12	5	17	2
Hughes	11	0	60	3
Emburey	12	2	34	1
Gatting	1	0	11	0

Fall: 1-26, 2-52, 3-59, 4-109, 5-123, 6-185, 7-186, 8-195, 9-201

MIDDLESEX

*J. M. Brearley	not out	96
†P. R. Downton	c Clarke b Knight	13
C. T. Radley	c and b Thomas	5
M. W. Gatting	b Jackman	24
R. O. Butcher	not out	50
G. D. Barlow		
J. E. Emburey		
V. A. P. van der Bijl		
M. W. W. Selvey		
W. W. Daniel		
S. P. Hughes		
	b 3, lb 11	14
Total (53.5 overs)	(for 3 wkts)	202

BOWLING	O	M	R	W
Jackman	11	1	31	1
Clarke	8.5	1	29	0
Knight	10	2	38	1
Thomas	12	0	38	1
Intikhab	12	0	52	0

Fall: 1-44, 2-57, 3-121
Umpires: H. D. Bird and J. G. Langridge.
*Captain; † Wicket-keeper.

but Edmonds came late into the attack. Men were clustered round the batsman and with six overs remaining, Edmonds found the edge of Perry's bat and Downton took the catch. Middlesex were Champions.

Their final fixture, at Canterbury, was drawn, and they returned to London for the Gillette Cup Final the next day. They had brushed aside Ireland, Nottinghamshire, Worcestershire and Sussex with contemptuous ease in the earlier rounds and now met Surrey who had challenged them so strongly in the County Championship.

This was the last year that the 60-over competition was sponsored by Gillette. Put in to bat, Surrey struggled for runs against van der Bijl and Daniel who, not fully fit, bowled well within himself. Hughes and Selvey offered no respite. Twenty-six runs came in the first hour before Clinton clipped Selvey off his legs into the hands of Radley. Emburey continued the tight hold on the Surrey batting, but Roope, Smith, beautifully caught by van der Bijl running back towards the pavilion and taking the ball over his shoulder, and Intikhab, 34 in 33 minutes, gave some panache to the innings and Middlesex faced a target of 202.

Brearley was soon in command, and the second Gillette triumph was as assured as the first. Downton stayed long enough to give the innings a firm foundation. Radley, for once, went cheaply, well caught and bowled off the last ball before tea. Gatting hit heartily before cross-batting wildly, but Butcher pulled and drove sweetly as the game passed out of Surrey's reach.

Butcher's 50 came off 41 balls, but it was Brearley who was man of the match for an innings of total authority and for captaincy of dignity and intelligence.

On the Sunday, Middlesex travelled to Bournemouth and with Brearley hitting 50, they beat Hampshire by five wickets to finish third in the John Player League. The Middlesex record for 1980 surpassed that of any county since the inception of the four competitions.

Inevitably, the following season had to be something of an anti-climax. Vincent van de Bijl did not return. His replacement was Jeff Thomson. The Australian fast bowler was not selected for Kim Hughes' touring side, and Middlesex offered him a one-year contract. It was a move that evoked much criticism although it was not in contradiction of existing rules. Some saw it as a cynical gesture, one more associated with the mercenary attitudes of top football clubs who would buy success at any price, in this instance at the cost of the development of young players who might have hoped for a first-team place. There were members who resigned on the issue, but Brearley maintained that Middlesex were acting within the laws and that Thomson was of value in the example he set to younger players.

As it transpired, the debate was irrelevant. Thomson was injured and played in only six Championship matches. What his presence did mean was that when Middlesex took the field for the first match, against Essex at Lord's, their side was composed of eleven Test Players, a unique event. The eleven were Brearley, Downton, Radley, Gatting, Butcher, Barlow, Emburey, Edmonds, Selvey, Thomson and Daniel.

The strength of that side is staggering, but Middlesex were unable to call on them throughout the season. Brearley was recalled to the England captaincy to lead the 'phoenix from the ashes', and Gatting, Downton and Emburey all played against Australia at different times. Test calls gave the opportunity to blood Norman Cowans for a couple of matches, Kevan James for one, and to play two reserve wicket-keepers, Colin Metson and Chilton Taylor. Unfortunately, Taylor was not registered, and Middlesex lost the seven bonus points that they had earned at Ilford.

An interesting, and successful, debutant was the 37-year old Irish slow left-arm bowler, Dermot Monteith. He was most impressive, and one could only wish that he had started his county career some 15 years earlier.

Colin Cook, born in Edgware, batted with confidence in six matches, but the young batsman to make the greatest advance was Wilf Slack. With Brearley on Test duty and Downton having dropped down the order, Slack was paired with Barlow to open the innings against Kent at Lord's in mid-July. Middlesex trailed by 117 on the first innings, but

Barlow and Slack shared an unbeaten stand of 367 in the second, a new Middlesex record. Barlow's 174 contained four sixes and 16 fours; Slack's 181 had three sixes and 20 fours. The stand lasted for 247 minutes. Later in the season both batsmen hit the highest scores of their careers, Barlow 177 against Lancashire, Slack 248 not out against Worcestershire. Their blend and understanding as a natural opening pair was to be Middlesex's biggest gain from the 1981 season, yet, the next year, when all but Edmonds and Gatting were available regularly, Barlow could not find his form and played in only four matches.

This was to be Mike Brearley's last season, and there was a determination that Middlesex should mark his farewell with a trophy. As they did not lose a match in any competition until the middle of June, it looked for a time as if they would win all four. That defeat was inflicted on Middlesex by Lancashire in the quarter-final of the Benson & Hedges Cup, and three defeats in the John Player League at the end of July and beginning of August cost them that title to Sussex, but Middlesex's final position of second was the highest that they have ever attained in the Sunday League. Two incredibly close victories saw the County qualify for the semi-final of the new NatWest Trophy, but Surrey gained ample revenge for former indignities with a 125-run win in a rain-affected match. That left only the County Championship.

By the end of May, Middlesex were ahead of Leicestershire, Sussex and Surrey, having won their first three matches. There was no relaxation in June even though they were thwarted by the weather at The Oval where Gatting played a mighty innings of 192. Daniel was bowling better than he had ever done, and Brearley's astute leadership was conjuring points from situations in which others would have been resigned to stalemate.

Defeat at Uxbridge by Leicestershire was followed by two wins over Nottinghamshire, and Middlesex entered August at the top of the table with Surrey in second place.

Surrey came to Lord's at the end of August. By this time, Leicestershire were in second place, 31 points behind Middlesex, but the Surrey challenge had by no means faded. It was Brearley's last match at Lord's and when he inspected the wicket he was convinced that it was so worn that it would take spin on the last afternoon. Fred Titmus, three months short of his 50th birthday, had called into the Middlesex dressing room for a cup of coffee. Brearley told Titmus his

MIDDLESEX *v* SURREY

Played at Lord's, 25, 26 and 27 August 1982

MIDDLESEX WON BY 58 RUNS

MIDDLESEX	FIRST INNINGS		SECOND INNINGS	
*J. M. Brearley	c Lynch b Monkhouse	43	c and b Needham	27
W. N. Slack	b Needham	79	not out	71
K. P. Tomlins	c Smith b Knight	9	c Thomas b Mackintosh	51
R. O. Butcher	c Knight b Needham	36	not out	0
C. T. Radley	c Richards b Mackintosh	40		
J. E. Emburey	b Mackintosh	13		
†P. R. Downton	c Clarke b Mackintosh	24		
P. H. Edmonds	hit wkt b Mackintosh	0		
N. G. Cowans	b Mackintosh	0		
W. W. Daniel	c Monkhouse b Mackintosh	3		
F. J. Titmus	not out	1		
	b 5, lb 13, nb 10	28	b 5, lb 1, nb 2	8
Total		276	(for 2 wkts dec)	157

BOWLING	O	M	R	W		O	M	R	W
Clarke	17	6	35	0		2	0	13	0
Thomas	25	14	43	0		3	0	16	0
Monkhouse	11	2	28	1					
Mackintosh	25	10	61	6		6	0	27	1
Needham	25	10	63	3		13	0	44	1
Knight	8	2	18	1					
Butcher						4	0	24	0
Lynch						6	0	25	0

1st inns: 1-84, 2-107, 3-173, 4-202, 5-240, 6-247, 7-247, 8-248, 9-273
2nd inns: 1-47, 2-146

SURREY	FIRST INNINGS		SECOND INNINGS	
A. R. Butcher	c Downton b Edmonds	82	c Brearley b Edmonds	1
G. P. Howarth	c Emburey b Daniel	112	c Cowans b Emburey	8
D. M. Smith	lbw b Cowans	19	lbw b Emburey	17
*R. D. V. Knight	not out	16	(5) c Butcher b Edmonds	7
M. A. Lynch	b Emburey	22	(4) c and b Edmonds	3
†C. J. Richards	not out	0	b Emburey	5
S. T. Clarke			c Cowans b Titmus	35
D. J. Thomas			c Slack b Titmus	7
A. Needham			c Cowans b Emburey	11
G. Monkhouse			lbw b Titmus	0
K. S. Mackintosh			not out	0
	b 7, lb 13, w 1, nb 1	22	b 6, lb 2	8
Total	(for 4 wkts dec)	273		102

BOWLING	O	M	R	W	O	M	R	W
Cowans	5	0	35	1				
Daniel	9	1	24	1	2	0	3	0
Edmonds	43	16	67	1	11	3	24	3
Emburey	43	11	76	1	13.3	2	24	4
Titmus	15	3	49	0	10	1	43	3

1st inns: 1-188, 2-233, 3-235, 4-272
2nd inns: 1-3, 2-13, 3-24, 4-40, 5-49, 6-70, 7-84, 8-100, 9-102
Umpires: C. Cook and Khizar Hayat.
Middlesex sealed the Championship with this victory.
*Captain; †Wicket-keeper.

assessment of the wicket and asked him to play. Titmus agreed and borrowed kit from his former colleagues.

Middlesex batted laboriously on the first day. Slack toiled five hours for his 79, and in the desperate attempt to gain a third batting point, Middlesex lost wickets. Mackintosh took three of them in four balls, and the intervening delivery was a no-ball. At the 100-over mark, Middlesex were 248 for eight.

Rain interrupted play on the second day, but Surrey seized the advantage as Howarth and Butcher were unbeaten with 180 on the board by the close. They added only eight more on the third morning before Butcher fell to Edmonds. Knight declared at lunch time, three runs in arrears.

Brearley, Slack and Tomlins hit briskly, but there seemed no hope of Brearley fashioning a victory from the situation. To general amazement, he declared and left Surrey 135 minutes in which to score 161, the tea interval having been abandoned. The declaration seemed generous to the point of foolhardiness. In spite of Brearley's assertion that the wicket would suit spin bowling, only five wickets had fallen to spin so far and two of those had come when batsmen were hitting out.

Daniel bowled only two overs, Cowans none. Edmonds and Emburey were soon operating in tandem. Edmonds took three of the first four wickets to fall and instantly Surrey were in trouble. The ball was spitting and turning, but Edmonds was forced to retire with a strained back.

Sylvester Clarke had been promoted in the order, and he came in at 49 for five. He hit three sixes and a four to score all 35 runs made while he was at the wicket. He fell to Titmus, caught at long-on by Cowans, and the veteran off-spinner quickly added the wickets of Thomas and Monkhouse. With 7.3 overs remaining, Emburey had Needham caught in the outfield, and Middlesex had won a sensational victory. It seemed part of an historical pattern which always threw up Surrey as the victims when Middlesex had the Championship in their sights.

This was the only match in which Titmus appeared during the season. He had finally retired. That he remained successful until the very end of a long, eminent career was due to his fitness, dedication and the classic simplicity of his action. A brief run to the wicket was ended with a hop and a pivot so that wrist, shoulder and hip were in unison. Allied to the economy and perfection of the delivery was a sharp intelligence which probed at the Achilles heel of every batsman on the county circuit.

In the wake of this sensational victory, Middlesex slumped at Hove where Green and Mendis, encouraged by Brearley's generous declaration, batted with great aplomb to set up a Sussex victory. In the meantime, Leicestershire had won their game in hand and the Middlesex lead was only two points so that the situation was tense when Hampshire came to Uxbridge. Brearley, his helmet falling on his wicket, Ellis and Gatting were out with only 22 scored, but Slack batted with great resolution. Butcher played with confidence and, at the close, Dermot Monteith, in his first match of the season, scored 36 hearty runs. Middlesex made 207, and Hampshire succumbed to Edmonds and Emburey for 178. A good crowd saw Middlesex bat with authority on the second day, and when Daniel bowled at a lively pace and Edmonds spun the ball eagerly the Champions-elect had taken the match by lunch time on the last day. Leicestershire had crumpled at Trent Bridge, and only four points were needed at Worcester for Middlesex to be confirmed as Champions.

It did not take Middlesex long to claim the necessary points. Norman Cowans, chosen for the tour to Australia, bowled very quickly and sent back both Worcestershire openers, Ormrod and Scott. Slack, one of seven bowlers used before lunch, had two wickets with his gentle medium pace, and shortly after ten minutes to three Warner lofted Emburey to Daniel at long-off. This catch reduced Worcestershire to 168 for nine and gave Middlesex their fourth bowling point and the Championship.

On the Tuesday morning, Mike Brearley turned a ball from Richard Illingworth through mid wicket to give Middlesex victory by ten wickets. He was clapped from the field on that misty morning, his last as captain of Middlesex.

The tributes were showered upon him. In *Wisden*, Terry Cooper wrote:

> So Brearley departed after a dozen seasons of captaincy, festooned with honours at Test and county level. The Middlesex successes were crammed into his final eight seasons, the necessary spade-work having been undertaken in the previous four years. In 1971 he inherited a side disunited and unsuccessful with, at times, an aversion to attacking cricket that was the despair of their dwindling supporters. Brearley restored purposeful cricket to Lord's, while winning four Championships (one shared) and two Gillette Cups. As the best county side of a generation they were a credit also to their coach, Don Bennett.

One of Brearley's chief qualities was his ambition. He is a man who wishes to do nothing unless he does it well, but his ambition was also able to recognise the ambition in others and he helped them to be realised without ever letting the individual's desires submerge the needs of the team. He was tough, but compassionate; demanding, but appreciative. He was purposeful and communicative. He left no doubt as to what he wanted and no doubt that he was going to get it. His judgment of the game was such that after the victory over Surrey at Lord's in his last season there were those who felt that had he lived in the Middle Ages he would have been executed for witchcraft.

He was the ideal teacher, the best of leaders, for he attempted to make his charges clear and independent thinkers as all good teachers should. That is a compliment which also has implicit in it a criticism, for it suggests a benevolent authority in which there may be a tinge of vanity. Inevitably, it is a characteristic which has its pitfalls, notably clashes with those who are or have become independent thinkers, one's best pupils.

Emburey and Brearley agreed to differ, but they maintained respect for each other. At times, the Edmonds – Brearley relationship came into open conflict. Clive Rice recalled an occasion when he clouted a short ball from Edmonds through mid-wicket at which the bowler immediately asked that a man be placed there. Brearley refused, saying that he would not set a field for bad bowling. An argument ensued which Rice found as embarrassing as anything he has ever witnessed on a cricket field. Brearley himself considered that he failed with Edmonds, that there was rarely a 'productive willingness to differ'. Brearley felt that: 'Edmonds rarely felt that I helped him or that my thinking enlarged his sense of his own ability. He felt – rightly, I think – that he would have done better, with his own Zambian upbringing, with a more abrasive, extrovert and physically tough captain, like Ian Chappell.'

For his part, Edmonds said that he was relieved when Brearley retired, but he was later to be quoted as saying that he (Edmonds) should be captain of England instead of Gatting. Incidentally, his record under Brearley, given all the circumstances, was as good as under anybody else.

No leader of an organisation is going to succeed with all those in his charge. No job of work will produce a group of people all of whom get on with each other all the time. The important thing is that the job is done, and in the years of Brearley's stewardship the job was done with more success than it had ever been done before.

Brearley's own reflections convey a satisfaction of a mission accomplished:

> By the time I retired, the management of the club had changed drastically. There was a realistic pay structure that was attractive to players. Overseas players were not paid any more than English players as they had been in the past. Four or five senior players served on the Cricket Sub-Committee so that the voice of the senior players was heard when it came to policy and decisions, and the younger players, too, were able to have their say.
>
> There was a much more friendly attitude between committee and players. Men like Mike Murray, Mike Sturt and Charles Robins were younger and closer to the players. They were easily approachable and willing to be challenged. They were friendly, and one could have a drink with them to chat over grievances or concerns. The divisions that had existed in the club in 1971 were no longer there.

And so the captain left with honour, awed respect and admiration, yet, in a sense, judgment of him had to be suspended, for what is success if your legacy is a vacuum?

GATTING AT THE HELM

THERE WAS NO VACUUM ON BREARLEY'S DEPARTURE. The cricket school at Finchley was now a flourishing sports centre offering amenities other than cricket nets. The Middlesex League had raised the standard of club cricket and young players were thriving in its competitive atmosphere. Not least it had raised the standard of fielding enormously. The Middlesex schools and youth programme was well organised and run with efficiency and enthusiasm. Ted Jackson, Jack Robertson and an army of schoolteachers had done fine work, and Don Bennett's achievements as county coach were providing an example which was an inspiration to all. An energetic and sensitive committee had led the County into the later part of the 20th century with an awareness of economic and commercial necessities, yet they never allowed these considerations to blind them to the desires of their members. George Mann had followed the path of his father in becoming President where once he had been captain, and Mike Murray became chairman of the club, leading with perception and tact. Alvan Seth-Smith instigated a county annual which immediately asserted itself as among the best of yearbooks. Mike Selvey, a lion of a cricketer, left to become captain of Glamorgan, but Tim Lamb returned after a successful spell with Northants to take over as Secretary–General Manager. This proved to be an inspired appointment; Lamb quickly won a reputation as one of the most approachable, energetic and competent of county secretaries, destined, most feel, to hold high office in the administration of the game as his move to the TCCB in 1988 would seem to confirm. Where, 30 years earlier, Middlesex affairs had been conducted as a minor department of MCC, they were now conducted from the club's own offices to the rear of the pavilion by a staff committed to the County's needs. The club had at last achieved its independence, but had retained its special relationship with MCC.

In variety or after-dinner speaking, it is not always the quality of one's own performance that is of paramount importance. It is where one is on the programme. Brearley was a very hard act to follow. His successor, Mike Gatting, attained the Middlesex captaincy almost by default.

Phil Edmonds had been named as vice-captain after the retirement of Mike Smith, who was sorely missed as man and player. Edmonds, as we have indicated, was something of an eccentric, as was Brearley in the eyes of many people, but then eccentricity is only a term applied to those who have a positive and singular personality which does not always produce the expected response or the accepted action. Edmonds' reign had been short-lived, and he was succeeded by John Emburey, a tough, thinking cricketer who had a respect for Brearley and his ideas, but retained his own interpretation and solution to affairs and to men. Emburey's participation in the tour to South Africa sponsored by South African Breweries and made against the advice and wishes of the TCCB caused him to be banned from Test cricket for three years (which, in fact, came as a boon to Middlesex) and to lose the vice-captaincy of the County at a time when he was close to ascending to the premier position. These events projected Mike Gatting into the post of successor to Mike Brearley, who had always been one of his most ardent supporters and had certainly championed his claims as a Test batsman in face of opposition.

The directors of Middlesex operations—captain Mike Gatting and vice-captain John Emburey.
(Courtesy of Adrian Murrell)

In every way Gatting was very different from Brearley. There was in his own mind never any doubt that he would be anything but a professional cricketer. He was a good footballer, but cricket was his calling. He was a scholarship boy with The Cricket Society and later went on a Whitbread Scholarship to Australia. There were no academic ambitions, no other distractions. If Brearley was the officer who had decided to take a commission for a few years, Gatting was the company sergeant-major who had risen through the ranks.

He started with certain advantages. He inherited a good side who were used to winning. He was backed by an excellent organisation with a knowledgeable cricket committee under the chairmanship of Charles Robins, which supported with the strength, wisdom and assistance of former Middlesex cricketers who knew the county circuit and had tasted both success and failure. He had respect for his side and knew their capabilities and their individual foibles. He was straightforward, honest and fair and said from the start that the side would be picked on merit. He was respected by his side as a player and liked by them as a man.

At the wicket, Gatting is a formidable sight, but the threat to the bowler begins as soon as he comes down the pavilion steps. There is a bristling of energy in the body eager to be released. There is a swirling of arms and bat, and it is as if a miniature tornado is approaching, slowly but relentlessly, in a whirl of dust and movement. The bowler is presented with a stance so emphatic as to suggest not only that he shall not pass, but also that they will be driven back further than from whence they came and beyond. No Englishman in contemporary county cricket, save Botham and Gooch, is more capable of destroying an opposing attack.

Gatting's captaincy proved to be as uncomplicatedly positive as his approach to batting. From the start the sound of 'Come on, lads, let's get out there!' boomed from the Middlesex dressing-room. There was no visible crease in Middlesex cricket dividing the Brearley era from Gatting's reign, for by the end of May the County was in the first three in the Championship and was making somewhat bizarre progress in the Benson & Hedges Cup. The Championship ended as a straight contest between Middlesex and Essex, and the same two sides, the best in the country, met in the Benson & Hedges Cup final.

A soggy Saturday at The Oval saw Butcher and Gatting bat well as Middlesex scored 273 for seven in their 55 overs of their first Benson & Hedges game. Surrey were 63 for two off 20 at the end of the day, and, as rain prevented any more play, Middlesex won on the faster scoring rate. A week later, at Canterbury, in the one match which Middlesex played in their qualifying zone which went its full course, victory came by five wickets. The match against Glamorgan was transferred from Lord's to Uxbridge but still could not be played while the final zonal match against the Combined Universities at Lord's suffered the same fate. The quarter-final at Bristol produced only four overs of cricket in three days, and Middlesex went through to the semi-final on the toss of a coin, a solution which pleased no one. The semi-final against Lancashire at Lord's was played in gloom in a nearly deserted stadium. The visitors were all out in 31.5 overs, and Middlesex won by five wickets at ten to eight on a very grey evening.

By the time of the final on 23 July, Middlesex were leading the Championship and Essex were pressing them close. Arguably, it was the first occasion when the two best sides in England have met in a knock-out final. There were problems for Middlesex in that they had lost Roland Butcher before the final. He had been hit in the face by a ball from Ferris of Leicestershire, and his loss was to be deeply felt for the remainder of the season.

The weather had been fine in the preceding week, but there was a drizzle on the Saturday morning and play began 50 minutes late in steaming damp. Fletcher won the toss and asked Middlesex to bat.

John Lever, the Essex left-arm pace bowler, had undergone an operation only a week previously and there were doubts as to his fitness. Barlow compounded these doubts when he drove Lever through the off-side field for four three times in the left-armer's first three overs. Foster, at the other end, was bowling with great pace and menace, and in the fourth over Slack edged him to slip where Gooch took a magnificent one-handed catch low to his right.

Radley now joined Barlow and played an innings, initially unobtrusive, ultimately commanding, which was to win him the individual award. As ever, he moved onto the front foot, nudging, deflecting, always dictating the length. In the tenth over, he lost Barlow who had his middle stump knocked over by a ball from Foster which moved back quickly.

Gatting breathed customary pugnacity, but he was frustrated by accurate spells from Gooch and Turner. In the

*Graham Barlow. His ability
to begin the Middlesex
innings at a brisk pace was a
decisive factor in
Championship success.
(Courtesy of Mark Leech)*

29th over, anxious to increase a limping run rate, he went for an improbable third run after Radley had turned Gooch to the Mound Stand boundary. Foster chased and stopped the ball inches from the rope. He turned and threw in one movement, staight into the gloves of David East, and Gatting was out by a yard. Tomlins was lbw first ball, and Middlesex were in trouble.

When Stuart Turner's spell ended with the 36th over Middlesex were 93 for four, and Emburey was struggling to put bat to ball. But Emburey is a tenacious cricketer. He has willed himself into a batsman who, however unorthodox, is increasingly effective. He stayed, and with Radley crouching lower and lower and offering a defiance which was becoming increasingly belligerent, Middlesex survived.

Emburey was dropped at mid–off, but he was out in the 44th over by which time Radley had reached his fifty. Radley, too, had been dropped, and in the last 11 overs, he was to cajole Downton, Edmonds, Williams and Daniel to help him add 73 to the score. Middlesex reached 196. Radley was undefeated on 89. It was an innings of character and resilience, typical of Radley's cricket throughout his time with Middlesex.

It looked as if Essex meant to get the match over quickly. Hardie crashed Daniel for four in the first over of the innings, and the second, for Middlesex, was traumatic. Gatting set an attacking off-side field, but Cowans bowled short and three times Gooch bludgeoned him to leg for four. Twice he hit him for two. After ten overs Essex were 71 for no wicket with Gooch on 40.

Williams had replaced Cowans after two overs, and in the 12th over of the innings, Gooch drove him straight and mightily to the sight-screen at the Nursery End. The batsman aimed to drive the next ball, but edged to Downton who took a fine low catch. The slaughter had been temporarily halted, Edmonds applying the break, but at tea, Essex were 113 for one from 25 overs, and an Essex win seemed inevitable.

Five overs after the interval McEwan drove Edmonds low to mid-off. Fletcher dithered and was taken at silly mid-off, bat and pad, prodding forward at Edmonds. Nevertheless, with 23 overs remaining, Essex needed only 61 for victory and had seven wickets in hand.

Pont was dropped, and the 150 was reached. Williams, a cricketer of high quality as both bowler and batsman, but one of whom we have yet to see the best, bowled a bouncer to Pont who lost sight of it, was hit on the side of the helmet and dropped his bat on his wicket.

Hardie had become becalmed and, in desperation, flashed at Cowans in the 41st over. Turner and Pringle now found themselves confronted by a side and a captain who had gone onto the attack. Emburey induced strokelessness, but when Daniel had Pringle lbw to the first ball of 52nd over Essex needed only 12 runs from 23 balls.

Williams had left the field injured after bowling his quota of overs, and John Carr came on as substitute. Turner hit Cowans high to mid-on in front of 'Q' stand where, in the gathering gloom, Carr took a splendid running catch.

David East touched a ball to the fine-leg boundary and Essex were six runs away from victory with three wickets and more than two overs in hand. Next ball David East tried to pull Cowans hard over mid-wicket to the Tavern boundary for what would have been a crucial four. Gatting just got a hand to the ball and, spinning round, brought off a

BENSON AND HEDGES CUP FINAL
MIDDLESEX *v* ESSEX

Played at Lord's, 23 July 1983

MIDDLESEX WON BY 4 RUNS

MIDDLESEX

G. D. Barlow	b Foster	14
W. N. Slack	c Gooch b Foster	1
C. T. Radley	not out	89
*M. W. Gatting (capt)	run out	22
K. P. Tomlins	lbw b Gooch	0
J. E. Emburey	c D. East b Lever	17
†P. R. Downton	c Fletcher b Foster	10
P. H. Edmonds	b Pringle	9
N. F. Williams	c and b Pringle	13
W. W. Daniel	not out	2
N. G. Cowans		
	b 3, lb 9, w 4, nb 3	19
Total (55 overs)	for 8 wkts)	196

BOWLING	O	M	R	W
Lever	11	1	52	2
Foster	11	2	26	3
Pringle	11	0	54	2
Turner	11	2	24	0
Gooch	11	2	21	1

Fall: 1-10, 2-25, 3-74, 4-74, 5-123, 6-141, 7-171, 8-191

ESSEX

G. A. Gooch	c Downton b Williams	46
B. R. Hardie	c Downton b Cowans	49
K. S. McEwan	c Cowans b Edmonds	34
*K. W. R. Fletcher	c Radley b Edmonds	3
K. R. Pont	hit wkt b Williams	7
D. R. Pringle	lbw b Daniel	16
S. Turner	c sub (Carr) b Cowans	9
†D. E. East	c Gatting b Cowans	5
R. E. East	run out	0
N. A. Foster	b Cowans	0
J. K. Lever	not out	0
	lb 12, w 3, nb 8	23
Total (54.1 overs)		192

BOWLING	O	M	R	W
Daniel	11	2	34	1
Cowans	10.1	0	39	4
Williams	11	0	45	2
Emburey	11	3	17	0
Edmonds	11	3	34	2

Fall 1-79, 2-127, 3-135, 4-151, 5-156, 6-185, 7-187, 8-191, 9-192
Umpires: H. D. Bird and B. J. Meyer.
*Captain; †Wicket-keeper.

remarkable catch as the ball dropped behind him. His command and aggression in the field had been inspirational. Now he had fired the closing stages of the game with a stunning piece of fielding.

Daniel began the next over with a wide, but Ray East could make little of what followed. The fifth ball of the over hit him on the pad and squirted out on the off side. The batsman charged down the wicket and was run out by Radley who threw down the stumps from square on the off side. Lever played out the last ball so leaving five runs to be scored from the final over.

With his first ball, Norman Cowans, who had come back so bravely after his early mauling, yorked Foster. He had taken three wickets in four balls and Middlesex had won a famous victory. It was ten minutes before nine and night was already asserting itself.

Essex were to gain revenge by taking the Championship in the last game of the season when Middlesex's game at Trent Bridge was washed out after the metropolitan county had struggled to take four points. Actually, they had lost their way through August with only one victory as against three defeats, and Gatting, still in his infancy as a captain in spite of his remarkable success, had shown unnecessary caution.

This caution was, perhaps, excusable in the match with Essex at Chemsford where Middlesex were shot out for 83 in cloudy conditions on the Saturday. Essex took a first innings lead of 206, but with Barlow and Radley in control, Middlesex had virtually achieved parity by the end of the second day. The third turned to farce as Middlesex batted on to a variety of bowlers, doing a variety of antics, and made 634 for seven from 211 overs. Barlow, Gatting and Emburey hit centuries.

There was another disappointment in the NatWest Trophy semi-final. Middlesex had won their earlier matches with ease, although had Northants made better use of former Middlesex pace bowler Tim Lamb, his old colleagues would have found victory harder in the quarter-final. In the semi-final, Botham played out Emburey's last over to give Somerset a win with the scores level by virtue of having lost fewer wickets. Other counties would have welcomed the type of disappointment which would leave them winners of the Benson & Hedges Cup, runners-up in the Championship and semi-finalists in the NatWest Trophy. Under Gatting's leadership, Middlesex had shown no sign of lowering the standard of attainment that they had reached under Brearley.

Essex were to retain the Championship in 1984 and, although they finished third, Middlesex never mounted a serious challenge, losing too much ground in the first part of the season. All seemed well when Radley hit a hundred and Mike Selvey's Glamorgan were beaten by ten wickets in the opening match of the campaign, but not another win was recorded until Worcestershire were beaten at Uxbridge in the first week of July. The period of drought extended into the Benson & Hedges Cup where interest ended at the zonal stage.

The main problem was in the bowling. Norman Cowans continued his advance as one of the most attacking bowlers in the country. Always encouraged and sympathetically handled, he enjoyed his best season for the County, but Wayne Daniel's years of unrelenting pace and endeavour had taken a little toll and he was below his best. More disappointingly, neither Williams nor Hughes, who vied for the position of third seamer, could find consistency. Both had considerable pace and promise, but they remained erratic and, at times, expensive, yet both were spoken of as future Test players. It was the lack of decisive strike support for Cowans which made it more difficult to bowl sides out, the key factor in the Championship.

No criticism could be applied to Emburey and Edmonds who, on wickets that mostly offered no help to spin, continued to torment the best of batsmen. As a partnership they had now reached a status comparable to that of Laker and Lock in the 1950s. They were as effective in limited-overs cricket as they were in the first-class game, and their adaptability to the modern game was a tribute to their quality as bowlers and their commitment as men. In his three years exile from Test cricket, Emburey did not miss a Championship game for Middlesex and his batting had flourished to the extent that he was a recognised number six.

Demon bowler: tempestuous spirit—Phil Edmonds. Spin colleague John Emburey is in the background.
(Courtesy of Adrian Murrell)

Edmonds, too, reasserted his all-round qualities. At Swansea, where Middlesex were facing a Glamorgan total of 327, he went in at 198 for six, hit a career-best 142 and took his side to a first innings lead of 111. At Bournemouth, he took four for 67 and Hampshire were bowled out for 188. Rajesh Maru's career-best seven for 79 against his old county restricted the Middlesex lead to 52, but Edmonds countered with a devastating eight for 53, the best figures of his career, and Middlesex went on to win by seven wickets. This victory prompted the run which took them to third place.

The batting was always sound. In all matches, Gatting scored more than 3,000 runs. At Bath, shortly after he had been left out of the England side, he hit 258 in 276 minutes with eight sixes and 32 fours. This was the highest score made for Middlesex since Jack Robertson's triple century at Worcester in 1949. Butcher was restored to fitness and form. Slack was increasingly solid and productive, and Barlow teamed with him to make a balanced opening pair. Radley exuded all that was good and honourable in a county cricketer, and there was yet another personal triumph for him at Lord's.

So high had become Middlesex's expectations, John Player League apart which has never seemed to satisfy their corporate character or aspirations, that third place in the Championship without a serious challenge for the title was close to failure, but the late season run coincided with the closing stages of the NatWest Trophy.

Northumberland had proved no great obstacle in the first round at Jesmond, but the second-round match at Trent Bridge was a different story. Downton, showing the resolution which had won him back his England place, and Gatting put on 92 in 21 overs, and at 170 for two in the 43rd over, Middlesex were prospering, but Hadlee cut short the elation and the later batsmen floundered against Saxelby. All out in the last over for 228, Middlesex were disappointed.

Broad and Robinson added to the disappointment with an opening stand of 96, but Gatting used his resources well. He called up Slack for three overs, and it brought the wicket of Randall. Then, crucially, Edmonds and Emburey exerted a tight hold on the Notts batting. Their 24 overs cost only 52 runs, and they accounted for both openers. Notts had been cruising to victory; now they were frustrated. With three overs remaining and five wickets in hand, they needed 24 to win, but Daniel had Hadlee taken by Radley at short-leg, Gatting maintaining the attacking fields, and Hemmings was run out. Thirteen were needed from the last over, but Rice skied Cowans to fine leg where Williams took the catch, and Middlesex won by five runs.

Lancashire and Northants were brushed aside, and Kent were the opponents in the final.

Kent were without Alan Knott, who had an ankle injury, and Middlesex preferred Hughes to Williams. Tavaré won the toss and Kent batted.

Benson played one magnificent off-drive, and he and Taylor gave Kent the soundest of starts. Daniel and Cowans tended to bowl wide of the off stump, and the new ball was negotiated with ease. Taylor straight drove Cowans for four to bring up 50 in the 17th over, and all was going serenely until, in the 30th over, Benson leant forward to Emburey, held his pose and was stumped. In the next over, Taylor played across a ball from Slack, who once again proved an invaluable sixth bowler after Edmonds had been expensive.

Lunch was not so comfortable for Kent as they had earlier expected. The hundred came in the 34th over, but before the arrival of the 150, in the 47th, Aslett had been run out and Tavaré caught behind swinging wildly. Chris Cowdrey was gloriously positive and Ellison was busy, but Johnson was run out first ball, and the inexperienced Waterton could not plunder the last over. A total of 232 was a disappointment to Kent, particularly as Middlesex had not fielded at their best.

Barlow was the provider of panache, Slack of solidity in the opening partnership. They began confidently until Barlow swatted at Jarvis in the 12th over. Slack was bowled in the 20th, and Underwood began a fine spell by bowling Butcher in his second over. Gatting could not get going and, frustrated by Underwood, he hit Jarvis loosely into the hands of mid-on.

The crucial stand of the match came when Downton joined Radley. In fading light they added 87 in less than 15 overs. Radley hurried, scurried and seemed to find a space with every shot that he played. In the 56th over, he was caught at extra cover, attacking to the last, and Downton went the next over, taken at mid-off. Edmonds and Emburey were together with 16 needed off 23 balls.

A push here and a dab there brought the target nearer, but an excellent penultimate over by Jarvis who had Emburey dropped by Underwood left Middlesex to score seven off the last over, bowled by Ellison.

The first ball produced a leg-bye. Edmonds took a single square on the off side, and Emburey straight drove for two before taking one to cover. Edmonds squirted the fifth ball of the over to third man for a single, which levelled the scores. Ellison pitched the last ball well up, but it was a fraction shorter than he wanted and Emburey turned it gleefully to the square-leg boundary for four, or rather it was swallowed by the invading crowd. Emburey wheeled excitedly for the pavilion. Edmonds followed him. Gatting, in his second year as captain, again held a trophy aloft. Radley, playing in his sixth Lord's final, took the individual award for the third time.

NATIONAL WESTMINSTER BANK TROPHY FINAL MIDDLESEX *v* KENT

Played at Lord's, 1 September 1984

MIDDLESEX WON BY 4 WICKETS

KENT

N. R. Taylor	b Slack	49
M. R. Benson	st Downton b Emburey	37
*C. J. Tavare	c Downton b Daniel	28
D. G. Aslett	run out	11
C. S. Cowdrey	c Radley b Daniel	58
R. M. Ellison	not out	23
G. W. Johnson	run out	0
†S. N. V. Waterton	not out	4
D. L. Underwood		
T. M. Alderman		
K. B. S. Jarvis		
	b 10, lb 8, w 3, nb 1	22
Total (60 overs)	(for 6 wkts)	232

BOWLING	O	M	R	W
Cowans	9	2	24	0
Daniel	12	1	41	2
Hughes	10	0	52	0
Edmonds	5	0	33	0
Slack	12	2	33	1
Emburey	12	1	27	1

Fall: 1-96, 2-98, 3-135, 4-163, 5-217, 6-217

MIDDLESEX

G. D. Barlow	c Waterton b Jarvis	25
W. N. Slack	b Ellison	20
*M. W. Gatting	c Tavare b Jarvis	37
R. O. Butcher	b Underwood	15
C. T. Radley	c Tavare b Ellison	67
†P. R. Downton	c Cowdrey b Jarvis	40
J. E. Emburey	not out	17
P. H. Edmonds	not out	5
S. P. Hughes		
N. G. Cowans		
W. W. Daniel		
	lb 7, w 1, nb 2	10
Total (60 overs)	(for 6 wkts)	236

BOWLING	O	M	R	W
Alderman	12	0	53	0
Jarvis	12	1	47	3
Ellison	12	2	53	2
Cowdrey	12	1	48	0
Underwood	12	2	25	1

Fall: 1-39, 2-60, 3-88, 4-124, 5-211, 6-217
Umpires: H. D. Bird and B. J. Meyer.

The demands on a side which has maintained consistent success over a long period of time are enormous. In the first place, there are the followers who expect you to win everything, all the time, and who feel a sense of failure when that does not happen. In the second place, there are the opponents who have a greater urge to lower your colours than anybody else's and will give you nothing in the way of generous declarations or sporting chances.

By the beginning of the 1985 season, Middlesex had won eight trophies in nine years. The Brearley era was of the past; Gatting was firmly in control. Success had its attendant problems. In the summer of 1985, five Middlesex players – Cowans, Gatting, Downton, Edmonds and Emburey – appeared in the Test series against Australia, three of them in all six Tests, Edmonds in five. The strain on the resources of the club was enormous, but Middlesex had built so wisely and strongly that they could call on 13 capped players, all of whom had helped win the Championship in 1982, as well as include promising youngsters like Metson, Carr, Rose, Miller, Sykes and Brown, who hit a maiden century in the game against the Australians. Wilf Slack hit a double-century in that match.

The path to the semi-final of the Benson & Hedges Cup was almost as bizarre as it had been in 1983, but at Chelmsford, Essex defended a small total with some stirring out-cricket. Gatting fell to a marvellous catch by Lilley, and at one time four wickets fell in an over so that Essex won by 62 runs. Essex were Middlesex's bogey team, for they also won the second-round NatWest Trophy match at Chelmsford, this time by 84 runs. For once, though, Essex were out of the Championship race where Hampshire, not affected by Test calls, and Gloucestershire, who lost Athey on one occasion, were the main contenders.

Hampshire were early leaders with Middlesex in second place, but in a dreadfully wet summer only two matches had been won by the third week in June by which time they had dropped to third. A crucial performance had come at Bournemouth on 12, 13 and 14 June. Edmonds and Cowans were in the side, but the other three England selections were on Test duty, and Hampshire took a firm grip on the game. Nicholas asked Middlesex to make 265 in 63 overs on a wicket that was helping the bowlers. Marshall and Maru took three wickets each, and, with 29 overs remaining, Middlesex were 82 for eight. Hughes and Sykes, two of the 'reserves', batted throughout the 29 overs and put on 84, the highest stand of the match. It was an example of the defiance and self-belief which were so important to the Middlesex challenge for honours.

Three wins at the end of June and beginning of July kept Middlesex abreast of Hampshire and Gloucestershire, but a decisive win came in the first match of Uxbridge week in late July, for the second was ruined by rain. The win was important because all other games in the Britannic Assurance County Championship were drawn.

Northants were the visitors and were 93 for seven against the pace trio. Roger Harper hit 97 off 85 balls with eight sixes and seven fours and lifted them to 191. Middlesex lost their first four wickets for 147, but Radley and Downton took the score to 216 before the close and next day extended their stand to 289. Paul Downton reached a maiden first-class hundred, and Radley hit the first double-century of his career. Now in his 41st year, Radley's appetite for the game seemed undiminished. Few men have given as much to a county or to the game itself. Accumulating with nudges and pushes rather than flowing drives, he always kept the score moving when he was at the wicket. His double-hundred included a six, a five and 26 fours, and the stand with Downton, who hit 13 fours, lasted for 340 minutes. Emburey hit a violent 68, and Gatting declared at 567 for eight. Rain on the last day nearly brought Northants a reprieve, but Middlesex won just after tea time.

A barren August threatened the County's chances, but a ten-wicket win at Leicester, where Cowans took six wickets in the first innings and Daniel seven in the second, put them back on top and although there was a draw with Essex in a game that should have been won, Middlesex entered the last game at Edgbaston one point ahead of Hampshire, who had lost valiantly by one wicket to Northants when Harper drove Maru's last ball of the match for six.

The formula for the game at Edgbaston was the one on which triumph had been based for so long: brisk runs so that there is ample time to bowl the other side out twice. Batting first, Warwickshire were given a sound start by Lloyd and Dyer, but Williams dismissed them both and Emburey destroyed the middle order so that, having bowled out the home side for 187, Middlesex were batting by late afternoon. Slack and Brown gave the side a fine start. Gatting led the charge, and another violent assault by Emburey took Middlesex to a first-innings lead of 258. Gatting left his bowlers a day in which to bowl out the opposition for a second time. They did not need it.

Dyer and Lloyd again began confidently, but Edmonds extracted considerable turn from the wicket and bowled Dyer. Emburey lured Kallicharran down the wicket and left him floundering while Downton pulled off the stumping.

Paul Downton—a worthy member of a line of outstanding wicket-keepers. (Courtesy of Tony Edenden)

Lloyd was taken close in as the hawks crouched eagerly for their prey. Smith and Din delayed the celebrations for only a short while. Middlesex were Champions for the fifth time in ten years.

One might be excused for believing that for Middlesex there could be the boredom of an Alexander with no more worlds to conquer, but in professional sport each triumph brings a fresh excitement and the stimulation to repeat the achievement.

But there was to be no County Championship success in Gatting's fourth year of leadership. Gatting himself was to become captain of England, and Test calls, wear and injury began to have their effect.

The most serious injury was the back injury sustained by Graham Barlow. In the opening match of the 1986 season, he hit 18 and 52 not out against Derbyshire. He did not bat in the rain-ruined game with Leicestershire and missed the Glamorgan match. He was back for the holiday game with Sussex and hit 107 and 3. The next game, against Surrey when he scored 12, was to be his last. The back problem was so grave as to force his retirement. Three Test appearances with very modest returns have tended to obscure his worth as a cricketer from a wider public, but those who followed Middlesex in the 1980s will know how much he contributed to the club's success and how important a role he played in the triumphs. Cheerful, friendly, exuding vitality, he batted with an uninhibited aggression that was refreshing in an opener and blended well with the more cautious methods of Wilf Slack. To ally to his punishing left-handed batting, Barlow possessed a dynamic brilliance in the field. Menacingly, but smilingly, he attacked the batsmen from cover. He gave constant encouragement to the bowlers with the speed and safety of his fielding, and he gave Middlesex out-cricket an extra dimension.

Barlow's departure was the first signal that a great team was breaking up, that changes, however subtle and slight at first, were being made. Neil Williams, in whom so many hopes had been placed, was also laid low by a serious back injury, and the exciting young Angus Fraser was also troubled. These injuries and other factors mentioned sapped the strength of the side and the first Championship win did not come until the first days of August when Gatting hit a century, Daniel took eight wickets and Northants were beaten by an innings. Three more victories followed before the end of the season so that the County climbed to 12th. If this was a disappointment in comparison with the club's recent history in the Championship, the season as a whole was not, for once again Middlesex carried off one of the four major trophies.

They had a hundred per cent record in the zonal matches of the Benson & Hedges Cup, beating Surrey, Hampshire, Combined Universities and Kent. Gatting won the Gold Award in three of those matches. Butcher, Radley and Gatting batted finely in the quarter-final against Sussex, and Cowans produced a fierce burst to take three wickets in a match which went into the second day. Notts were swept aside with ease in the semi-final, John Emburey taking four for 22 in his 11 overs, and old rivals Kent were the opponents again in the final.

For much of the day the final smouldered uneasily, but in rain and darkness it ended in high drama and heroic deeds. Middlesex were asked to bat first in overcast conditions. Dilley began with a wide to Slack. It was a portent, for Kent were to give Middlesex $2\frac{1}{2}$ extra overs in wides and no-balls, unforgivable in limited-overs cricket and suicidal in the context of this match.

Slack began nervously and was close to being run out in the first over before being bowled in the third. The light was bad, and Miller's desire to get forward meant that he was taking many balls high on his body. Runs were not coming easily. The first boundary did not come until the sixth over when Miller edged Baptiste through the slip area.

The first ten overs brought 28 runs, and Chris Cowdrey made a double change, bringing on himself and Ellison. Twice in Chris Cowdrey's first over, Gatting slashed the ball over Graham Cowdrey's head at extra cover for four, and he later scythed Ellison past slip. It was Ellison who struck back for Kent, dismissing Gatting and Butcher with successive deliveries in the 20th over. Both men fell to catches by Marsh who had an impressive game behind the stumps. He claimed a third victim when Miller fell in the 31st over, and at lunch, after 34 overs, Middlesex were 89 for four.

The position was not a healthy one, but Radley, moving down the wicket to smother Underwood and to dictate the length at which he would play the ball, got the scoreboard ticking over. He reached his fifty in the 48th over, having batted with his usual good sense and composure. He had hit Underwood over the top and run him down to third man

BENSON AND HEDGES CUP FINAL
MIDDLESEX *v* KENT

Played at Lord's, 12 July 1986

MIDDLESEX WON BY 2 RUNS

MIDDLESEX

W. N. Slack	b Dilley	0
A. J. T. Miller	c Marsh b C. S. Cowdrey	37
*M. W. Gatting	c Marsh b Ellison	25
R. O. Butcher	c Marsh b Ellison	0
C. T. Radley	run out	54
†P. R. Downton	lbw b Ellison	13
J. E. Emburey	b Baptiste	28
P. H. Edmonds	not out	15
S. P. Hughes	not out	4
N. G. Cowans		
W. W. Daniel		
	lb 8, w 11, nb 4	23
Total (55 overs)	(for 7 wkts)	199

BOWLING	O	M	R	W
Dilley	11	2	19	1
Baptiste	11	0	61	1
C. S. Cowdrey	11	0	48	1
Ellison	11	2	27	3
Underwood	11	4	36	0

Fall: 1-6, 2-66, 3-66, 4-85, 5-131, 6-163, 7-185

KENT

M. R. Benson	c Downton b Cowans	1
S. G. Hinks	lbw b Cowans	13
C. J. Tavaré	c Downton b Daniel	3
N. R. Taylor	c Miller b Edmonds	19
*C. S. Cowdrey	c Emburey b Hughes	19
G. R. Cowdrey	c Radley b Hughes	58
E. A. E. Baptiste	b Edmonds	20
R. M. Ellison	b Edmonds	29
†S. A. Marsh	not out	14
G. R. Dilley	not out	4
D. L. Underwood		
	lb 9, w 8	17
Total (55 overs)	(for 8 wkts)	197

BOWLING	O	M	R	W
Cowans	9	2	18	2
Daniel	11	1	43	1
Gatting	4	0	18	0
Hughes	9	2	35	2
Emburey	11	5	16	0
Edmonds	11	1	58	3

Fall: 1-17, 2-20, 3-20, 4-62, 5-72, 6-141, 7-178, 8-182
Umpires: D. J. Constant and D. R. Shepherd.
*Captain; †Wicket-keeper.

when the spinner threatened to dampen the innings, and he had followed these shots with a cover drive and a pull over mid-wicket off the same bowler. Initially Downton, and then Emburey, had also collected runs briskly to give the Middlesex innings a greater sense of urgency.

Radley was brilliantly run out by Marsh who threw to the bowler's end, and Baptiste bowled Emburey, but Hughes and Edmonds plundered well, and the total of 197 left the game wide open.

The Middlesex bowling was tighter than Kent's had been at the outset, and Benson struggled until he was caught behind in the ninth over. Daniel generated a lively pace and captured the vital wicket of Tavaré who sliced the ball to Downton. Next over Hinks was lbw to Cowans, and at 20 for three in 13 overs, Kent were in some despair.

Chris Cowdrey attempted to revive his side, but he was astonishingly caught right-handed by Emburey at wide slip. He tried to run the ball down to third man, but Emburey dived to his right to hold the ball inches above the ground. The catcher's feet punched the air in jubilation. Taylor had become becalmed and when the tea break came after 35 overs Kent were 71 for four and the game looked dead.

Taylor fell straight after tea, hitting rashly at Edmonds, but Baptiste and Graham Cowdrey revitalised the Kent innings. The younger Cowdrey, in particular, was in exciting form. He had square cut Edmonds for four in the first over after tea and followed this with a delightful assortment of shots, including a six over mid-wicket off Edmonds to bring up the hundred in the 43rd over. Baptiste enjoyed a couple of lives, but he tried to cut a ball that was too close to him and was bowled. He and Graham Cowdrey had added 69 in 12 overs. Ellison maintained the tempo and 37 runs came in four overs, but Graham Cowdrey's exuberant innings ended when he hit a full toss into the hands of mid-wicket. The rain was now driving down quite forcefully, and Kent needed 19 from two overs. Edmonds was bowling with intelligence and control, and he struck a decisive blow when he bowled Ellison in the penultimate over. Ellison had hit 29 off 18 balls.

The last over arrived with Kent needing 14 runs and Hughes bowling to Marsh, one of the heroes of a memorable match. Marsh missed the first ball, but took two off the second. The third was pulled high into the Grand Stand for six. This meant that six runs were needed from three balls. Hughes produced an excellent delivery, pitched right up in the block hole, and Marsh did well to survive. He scrambled a single from the next ball so that Dilley had to hit the last ball of the match for six if Kent were to win. He pulled it hard to the Tavern boundary, but it was fielded cleanly and the batsmen ran two. Middlesex had won their tenth trophy in eleven seasons, a phenomenal performance.

As has been indicated, however, there were signs that the great side which had brought much of this success was in the process of breaking up. The committee was aware of this, and in their report they issued a warning:

> The sudden enforced retirement of Graham Barlow after only a few games reminded us that perhaps we are reaching the end of the 'Brearley era', the most successful period of our history, and moving into new ground. Whilst our two international spinners and Wayne Daniel remain a striking force we should maintain a challenge for all competitions, but when replacements are required we will need the patience of our members and supporters during the rebuilding period.

These were wise words of caution, and as if to symbolise that the end of an era had come Middlesex lost three of her trustiest servants in a short space of time. W. H. 'Tagge' Webster, batsman, Treasurer, Chairman of the cricket committee and President died, as did Arthur Flower who had served at Lord's for 34 years and saw the Club's administration grow from its office in a converted wooden hut to its present offices of splendour. The third to die was Bill Edrich, and one recalls with happiness his memorial service, for it throbbed with thanks for the life of one who had given so much joy to others. One knows that he was well pleased that the traditions which he and Denis Compton fostered were being continued by the latest generation.

The difficulties that Middlesex faced in 1987 were greater than had been anticipated, for Neil Williams was slow to regain full fitness and Norman Cowans missed most of the season following a hernia operation. The season was to be the last for Clive Radley, who retired after nearly a quarter of a century as a Middlesex player. A fine fielder, as befits such a magnificent team man, and the most effective of batsmen, Radley seemed to encapsulate all that was good in Middlesex cricket, or indeed in cricket in general: honesty, endeavour and good humour. Happily, he is to remain with the County as Second-Eleven captain and assistant coach.

At the end of the season, too, it was decided not to offer a new contract to Phil Edmonds. The County had already done much to enable him to pursue his other business activities, but it was felt that the limitations on his services that he wanted in his new contract would not be in the best interests of the Club, and so he departed.

In his time with Middlesex he was rarely out of the news, and on various occasions it was rumoured that he was to join Surrey, Lancashire, Hampshire, Sussex and Somerset. He did not. He stayed with Middlesex for more than 15 years and served them well. Tall and strong, brilliant in the field, Edmonds was a left-arm spinner of the highest quality. His independent spirit and something of a cheerfully eccentric, easy manner hid from some the fact that he was a dedicated and motivated professional. He played with fun and he loathed tedium, but he played hard to win.

He is a richly gifted cricketer and man, and if, towards the end, it seemed that the ostentation of his other interests began to intrude upon his cricket, that should not obscure the fact that he was among the most talented of players. He was his own man, but his colleagues liked him and the summation of one of them comes closest to the truth: 'Henri needs a wider canvass than cricket can provide.'

In conjunction with the injuries to Cowans and Williams and the Test calls on Edmonds and Emburey, Middlesex had to accept that Wayne Daniel was, perhaps, not quite the force he had been. Middlesex could no longer guarantee that their bowlers would account for a side twice in a day and a half with comparative ease, nor could they guarantee that their batsmen would score as quickly or reach a set target in the required time. Gatting's duties as England's captain made it hard for him to return for the odd game and produce a blistering century to order, and younger players were fighting to establish themselves in the side.

The 1987 Middlesex squad.
Back row: S. P. Hughes,
A. J. T. Miller,
K. R. Brown, G. K. Brown,
J. D. Carr, M. A. Roseberry,
A. Needham,
M. R. Ramprakash.
Middle row: D. Bennett
(coach), A. Jones (2nd XI
scorer), N. R. MacLaurin,
P. C. R. Tufnell,
J. F. Sykes, A. R. C. Fraser,
A. J. G. Fraser,
I. J. F. Hutchinson,
N.F. Williams,
N. G. Cowans, H. P. Sharp
(scorer).

The records will show that, in 1987, Middlesex failed to win a trophy for the first time in six years, yet it was a season of hope not of gloom. The departure of Edmonds heralded the arrival of Phil Tufnell, who bowled admirably at Canterbury and Chelmsford in the closing month of the season and promised to keep alive the Middlesex spin tradition, as did Sykes when his off-breaks were given an opportunity. They are both lively, bustling cricketers.

Though troubled by injury, Angus Fraser displayed a mature pace and control that augurs well for the future. He could form a lethal partnership with Norman Cowans who, one should remember, was still only 26.

Following Barlow's retirement, Andy Miller held a regular place as opening batsman, but he was injured against the Pakistan tourists and John Carr moved up to open with Slack. Carr gave the balance that Barlow had provided. An

eager stroke-player who would rather be batting than padded up waiting to go in, he stormed through the second half of the season, hit a century before lunch against Surrey at Lord's and emerged as one of the most exciting young batsmen in the country, and, like Barlow and Radley, a brilliant fielder.

Slack was the first batsman to reach a thousand runs. Keith Brown held a regular spot and grew in confidence with every match.

Ramprakash, still at school, batted with a freedom and joy that mark him as one who will follow the Middlesex tradition and bring delight when he is at the wicket. Roseberry, too, though yet flushed with the impetuosity of youth, has the strength and authority that will command an attack.

'The old order changeth, yielding place to new.'

Front row: W. N. Slack,
P. R. Downton,
C. T. Radley,
M. W. Gatting,
J. E. Emburey,
W. W. Daniel,
P. H. Edmonds,
R. O. Butcher.

TOMORROW'S WORLD

CHARLES ROBINS MAINTAINS that, although Middlesex County Cricket Club has been in existence for more than 120 years, it is the youngest Club in the Championship. He argues with justification, for Middlesex's total independence from MCC has only been effected within the last 30 years. The arrangement is an amicable one, but the changes were necessary as the structure and the emphasis in the game altered.

It is only in the past decade that the offices of President and Chairman have been separated so that the Club has a streamlined form of management which is able to cope with the increasing commercial pressures of the modern game. George Newman was the last all-embracing President.

Other things have remained constant. George Mann asserts that Middlesex have always had a policy not to stand in the way of a player who wanted to move because he felt that he would have better opportunities elsewhere. None has moved for financial reasons, nor for discontent with the Club's management, but simply in search of regular first-team cricket. Mann also argues that a reason for the County's continued success has been the blend of firmness and frankness in their management. On the playing side, as on the business side, the Club is well run, not least because of coach Don Bennett's sound judgement of players and of their potential. As Mike Brearley has pointed out, people want to play for Middlesex. This was clearly evidenced when Mike Roseberry chose to play for the metropolitan county when many others were vying for his services.

There is no longer a Middlesex Regiment. The Club has not the benefit of the influence of a Lord Lieutenant of the County, yet it has much else for which to be thankful.

As early as 1771, Middlesex and Hampshire met Kent and Surrey at Sevenoaks Vine, and 56 years later, on 21 May, on Harefield Common, 'a single wicket match took place between two gentlemen of Middlesex and Francis Trumper, a farmer of Harefield, who was to have the help of his dog'. The farmer won by two wickets.

'The dog always stood near his master when he was bowling, and ran after the ball when struck and returned with it in his mouth so quickly that the two gentlemen had great difficulty to run even from a long hit. The dog was a thoroughbred sheep dog.'

The three men and a dog on Harefield Common at the beginning of the 19th century bear little resemblance to Mike Gatting and his team proudly holding the Benson and Hedges Cup in the pouring rain at Lord's in July 1986, but there is, one feels, a spirit and vitality that links the two.

Middlesex have been fortunate in the number of ex-players who have been willing to administer the affairs of the Club once their playing days were over. A glance at the list of members of the present committee will show the great number who continue to serve the club for whom they once played. An attitude to the game has been established which excites and entertains. This positive approach has been perpetuated so that it has become the essential character of the Club.

It is a rich heritage, and one that those in whom the future of the Club lies should cherish proudly and securely.

BIOGRAPHICAL DETAILS OF MIDDLESEX CRICKETERS

NAME AND EXTENT OF CAREER	BIRTH-PLACE	DATE OF BIRTH	DATE OF DEATH
David Robert Abbey 1967	Edmonton	11.12.1941	
Ahsan-Ul-Haq 1902	Jullundur	16. 7.1878	27.12.1957
Frederick Russell Alexander 1951	Acton Green	4. 6.1924	17. 5.1984
James Stephen Alldis 1970	Paddington	27.12.1949	
Sir George Oswald Browning Allen 1921–1950	Belle Vue Hill, Australia	31. 7.1902	
William Burn Anderson 1891	London	12.11.1871	31. 1.1948
Thomas Angus 1956–1957	Gateshead	23.11.1934	
Rupert Anson 1910–1914	Marylebone	7.11.1889	20.12.1966
Richard Arden-Davis 1881	Malins Lee	31. 1.1855	29. 6.1917
William Scott Ashmore 1946–1947	St John's Wood	29.10.1929	
Bernard Gerard Wensley Atkinson 1933–1934	Crediton	11. 9.1900	4. 9.1966
Geoffrey Bean Atkinson 1930	Lambeth	29. 1.1896	1951
Nigel Samuel Mitford Atkinson 1923	Hong Kong	26. 7.1899	24.10.1966
John Cecil Atkinson-Clark 1930–1932	Kensington	9. 7.1912	2.10.1969
Lucas Henry Bacmeister 1889–1890	Islington	22.11.1869	23. 5.1962
Edward Peter Baily 1872	London	18. 1.1852	21. 1.1941
Clare Valentine Baker 1906–1912	Marylebone	23.11.1885	7.12.1947
George Dashwood Baker 1872	Compton-Martin	4. 3.1849	1879
Dennis Oliver Baldry 1953–1958	Acton	26.12.1931	
Graham Derek Barlow 1969–1986	Folkestone	23. 3.1950	
Freeman Frederick Thomas Barnardo 1939	Bombay	16. 5.1918	25.10.1942
Robert Barton 1851		1820	7.10.1866
Alfred Myddleton Bashford 1906	Wickhampton	23. 7.1881	31. 7.1949
John Bastow 1874–1877	Bromley-by-Bow	30.10.1850	1. 6.1927
Henry Alfred Bates 1909	Brentford	3.12.1880	1942
James Bates 1880	Paddington	10. 1.1856	7.12.1915
Lawrence Charles Villebois Bathurst 1894–1895	Gressenhall	4. 6.1871	22. 2.1939
Arthur Douglas Baxter 1938	Edinburgh	20. 1.1910	28. 1.1986
Robert Augustus Bayford 1861–1864	Albury	13. 3.1838	24. 8.1922
Philip Ian Bedford 1947–1962	Friern Barnet	11. 2.1930	18. 9.1966
Cyril Asplan Beldam 1896	North Aylesford	15.10.1869	7. 9.1940
Ernest Asplan Beldam 1903–1907	Brentford	30. 6.1879	28.11.1958
George William Beldam 1900–1907	New Cross	1. 5.1868	23.11.1937

Ronald Victor Bell *1952–1954*	Chelsea	7. 1.1931	
Herbert Frank Benka *1933–1936*	Regent's Park	27.10.1909	22. 4.1970
Cecil Tristram Bennett *1926–1927*	Lambeth	10. 8.1902	3. 2.1978
Donald Bennett *1950–1968*	Wakefield	18.12.1933	
William Henry Benthall *1862–1868*	Westminster	3. 7.1837	4. 1.1909
Charles Bentley *1851*	Marylebone	28. 2.1819	2. 2.1891
William (Manstead) Benton	Chelsea	7.1873	17. 8.1916
Seton Robert de la Poer Horsley Beresford *1909*	Ireland	25. 7.1868	28. 5.1928
John Anstruther Berners *1904*	Westminster	23. 9.1869	2. 3.1934
Sydney Lionel Beton *1923–1928*	Paddington	22.11.1895	30.11.1972
Reginald Henshall Brindley Bettington *1928*	Merriwa, Australia	24. 2.1900	24. 6.1969
Morton Peto Betts *1872*	Bloomsbury	30. 8.1847	19. 4.1914
Robert Beveridge *1930–1934*	Paddington	16. 9.1909	
John Currey Bevington *1900*	Sydenham	6. 4.1872	4. 4.1933
Timothy Arthur Dent Bevington *1900–1904*	Ware	22. 8.1881	4. 5.1966
Donald (Albert) Bick *1954–1967*	Hampstead	22. 2.1936	
William Birch *1887*	Brentford	1863	1940
George Bird *1872–1877*	Crouch Hill	30. 7.1849	28.10.1930
Wilfred Stanley Bird *1905–1908*	Yiewsley	28. 9.1883	9. 5.1915
Arthur Theodore Bishop *1883*	West Ham	2. 9.1863	8. 9.1931
Christopher James Robert Black *1970–1973*	Johannesburg	15.12.1947	
Edward Vesey Bligh *1862*	Belgravia	28. 2.1829	22. 4.1908
John Boak *1873*	Edinburgh	27. 6.1837	29.10.1876
Kildare Dixon Borrowes *1882*	Exeter	21. 9.1852	19.10.1924
Bernard James Tindal Bosanquet *1898–1919*	Enfield, Middx	13.10.1877	12.10.1936
John Bowstead *1909*	Edenhall, Cumbld	14. 5.1872	17. 1.1939
Joseph William Box *1866–1868*	Bermondsey	1842	2.10.1873
Edward Hugh Bray *1895–1906*	Kensington	15. 4.1874	27.11.1950
Horace Brearley *1949*	Heckmondwike	26. 6.1913	
John Michael Brearley *1961–1983*	Harrow	28. 4.1942	
Hugh Richard Bromley-Davenport *1896–1898*	Capesthorne	18. 8.1870	23. 5.1954
Paul Wilson Brooks *1939*	Marylebone	1921	26. 1.1946
Gary Kevin Brown *1986*	Welling	16. 6.1965	
Keith Robert Brown *1984–1987*	Edmonton	18. 3.1963	
Sydney Maurice Brown *1937–1955*	Eltham	8.12.1917	28.12.1987
George Fairbrother Browne *1864*		1835	28. 5.1919
Clarence Napier Bruce *1908–1929*	London	2. 8.1885	4.10.1957
Charles Julius Brune *1866–1875*	Cuba	16. 4.1843	13. 1.1877
Frank Bryan *1891*	Amersham, Bucks	1853	11. 6.1923

Herbert William Bryant *1888*	Uxbridge	30. 6.1867	23. 2.1910
Edward Hastings Buckland *1885–1888*	Laleham-on-Thames	29. 6.1864	10. 2.1906
Francis Matthew Buckland *1877*	Laleham-on-Thames	27. 8.1854	7. 3.1913
Charles Francis Buller *1865–1877*	Colombo	26. 5.1846	22.11.1906
Charles William Lloyd Bulpett *1880*	Chertsey	18. 8.1852	11. 7.1939
Walter Henry Bunting *1877*	Cambridge	18. 6.1854	28.10.1922
William Burden *1851*			
Gerard Rodon Burge *1885*	Dinapore	9. 8.1857	15. 2.1933
Arthur Burghes *1876–1877*	London	8. 9.1848	1916
George Burton *1881–1893*	Hampstead	1. 5.1851	7. 5.1930
Geoffrey Cecil Burton *1930*	Hackney	14.12.1909	
Leonard Lionel Burtt *1921*	Fulham	1886	8.11.1942
Roland Orlando Butcher *1974–1987*	East Point, Barbados	14.10.1953	
Edward Montagu Butler *1885*	Harrow	3.12.1866	11. 2.1948
John Compton Butterworth *1925*	Samarang, Java	17. 8.1905	18. 3.1941
Reginald Edmund Compton Butterworth *1935–1937*	Samarang, Java	16. 8.1906	30. 5.1940
Robert Vere Buxton *1906–1909*	Westminster	29. 4.1883	1.10.1953
Charles Calvert *1865–1866*	Kneller Hall	21. 3.1833	7. 4.1905
John Maxwell Campbell *1900*	Kensington	3.10.1870	6. 3.1954
Ernest George Canning *1929–1931*	Marylebone	1902	
Robert Graham Caple *1959*	Chiswick	8.12.1939	
John Donald Carr *1983–1987*	St John's Wood	15. 6.1953	
Bertram Dudley Carris *1937–1939*	Flixton, Lancs	23.10.1917	
Harold Edward Carris *1928–1933*	Flixton, Lancs	7. 7.1909	29. 7.1959
Thomas Case *1864–1868*	Liverpool	14. 7.1844	31.10.1925
Charles Alexander Cater *1866–1867*	Liverpool	24. 1.1844	
William Catling *1864–1865*	Highgate	9. 9.1836	1899
J. Chalkey *1859*			
Arthur William Childs-Clarke *1923–1924*	Exeter	13. 5.1905	19. 2.1980
Harry Brodrick Chinnery *1899–1902*	Teddington	6. 2.1876	28. 5.1916
Jack Richardson Chisholm *1947*	Enfield	9.10.1924	24. 8.1977
Edward Austen Clark *1959–1976*	Balham	15. 4.1937	
Peter Clarke *1913–1914*		1882	12.1915
William (Benjamin) Clarke *1880–1884*	Old Basford, Notts	5.11.1846	18. 8.1902
Frank Leonard Clifford *1921*	London	29. 8.1891	13. 6.1982
Ernest George Clifton *1962–1966*	Lambeth	15. 6.1939	
Humphry Henry Cobb *1898–1901*	Kensington	12. 7.1873	13.12.1949
Leonard George Colbeck *1906–1908*	Hendon	1. 1.1884	3. 1.1918
A. Cole *1879*			

W. Cole *1863*			
William Ronald Collins *1982*	Hackney	29. 1.1868	10.12.1942
John Collinson *1939*	Sotterley	2.10.1911	29. 8.1979
Denis Charles Scott Compton *1936–1958*	Hendon	23. 5.1918	
Leslie Harry Compton *1938–1956*	Woodford	12. 9.1912	27.12.1984
Joseph Maurice Francis Connaughton *1939*	Paddington	1918	12. 2.1944
Alan Norman Connolly *1969–1970*	Skipton, Austr	29. 6.1939	
Arthur Trevenen Coode *1898*	St Helier, Jersey	5. 2.1876	28.12.1940
Colin Roy Cook *1981–1984*	Edgware	11. 1.1960	
Bransby Beauchamp Cooper *1863–1867*	Dacca, India	15. 3.1844	7. 8.1914
Rustom Sorabji Cooper *1949–1951*	Bombay, India	15.12.1922	
Terence Michael Cordaroy *1968*	Hampstead	26. 5.1944	
Harry Hemming Cornish *1893*	Westminster	1871	1918
Clement Edward Cottrell *1876–1885*	London	28. 5.1854	21. 1.1897
Frederick Ernest Covington *1936*	Kingston, Surrey	29.10.1912	
Norman George Cowans *1980–1987*	Enfield, Jamaica	17. 4.1961	
Maurice Edward Coxhead *1911*	Kensington	24. 5.1889	3. 5.1917
Thomas Craven *1850–1851*	Whitechapel	15. 3.1801	31. 3.1868
Cosmo Stafford Crawley *1929*	Chelsea	27. 5.1904	
Gordon Crosdale *1905*		14. 7.1880	12. 9.1954
Edward Crutchley *1947*	Paddington	2. 4.1922	18.10.1982
Gerald Edward Victor Crutchley *1910–1930*	Chelsea	19.11.1890	17. 8.1969
Thomas Cuming *1913*	Woolwich	21. 4.1893	18. 8.1960
Charles Morley Cunliffe *1897–1903*	Leyton	2. 9.1858	15.10.1884
Geoffrey Bourke Cuthbertson *1921–1927*	Hampstead	23. 3.1901	
John William Dale *1874–1878*	Lincoln	21. 6.1848	26. 6.1895
Hugh Lloyd Dales *1920–1930*	Lanchester, Durham	18. 5.1888	4. 5.1964
Lord Albert Edward Harry Mayer Archibald Dalmeny *1902*	Westminster	8. 1.1882	30. 5.1974
Lord Archibald Ronald Dalmeny *1929–1931*	London	1. 8.1910	11.11.1931
Arthur Raine Daly *1866*		1831	1. 2.1898
Arthur William Trollope Daniel *1861–1869*	London	3. 1.1841	26. 1.1873
Wayne Wendell Daniel *1977–1987*	St Philip, Barbados	16. 1.1956	
Maurice John Dauglish *1886–1890*	London	2.10.1867	30. 4.1922
Kenneth Brian Day *1959*	Hendon	19. 5.1935	19. 1.1971
Gustave Peter Saprine Delisle *1954–1957*	Basseterre, St Kitts	25.12.1934	
Reginald Patrick Deller *1951–1953*	Paddington	27. 3.1933	
Percy John De Paravicina *1881–1892*	Kensington	15. 7.1862	11.10.1921
Louis Norman Devereux *1949*	Heavitree, Devon	20.10.1931	

John Gordon Dewes *1948–1956*	North Latchford, Ches	11.10.1926	
Alfred John Day Diver *1850*	Cambridge	6. 7.1824	25. 3.1876
J. T. Dixon *1908*			
Alexander Graham Doggart *1925*	Bishop Auckland	2. 6.1897	7. 6.1963
Desmond Leonard Dolding *1951*	Oordegem, Belgium	13.12.1922	23.11.1954
Mordaunt Henry Caspers Doll *1912–1919*	Camberwell	5. 4.1888	30. 6.1966
Martin Paterson Donnelly *1946*	Ngaruawahia, NZ	17.10.1917	
Archibald Philip Douglas *1902*	Norwood Green	7. 6.1867	24. 1.1953
James Douglas *1893–1913*	Norwood Green	8. 1.1870	8. 2.1958
Robert Noel Douglas *1898–1905*	Norwood Green	9.11.1868	27. 2.1957
Sholto Douglas *1906*	Norwood Green	8. 9.1873	28. 1.1916
Paul Rupert Downton *1980–1987*	Farnborough, Kent	4. 4.1957	
Colin David Drybrough *1958–1964*	Melbourne, Austr	31. 8.1938	
Lord Alexander Frederick Dunglass *1924–1925*	London	2. 7.1903	
Frederick John Dunkley *1886–1888*	Chelsea	9. 9.1862	1901
Patrick Neville Durlacher *1921–1923*	Paddington	17. 3.1903	26. 2.1971
Frederick John Durston *1919–1933*	Clophill, Beds	11. 7.1893	8. 4.1965
James Thomas Eaglestone *1947*	Paddington	24. 7.1923	
Charles Hotson Murray Ebden *1905*	London	29. 6.1880	24. 5.1949
Philippe-Henri Edmonds *1971–1987*	Lusaka, N Rhodesia	8. 3.1951	
William John Edrich *1937–1958*	Lingwood, Norfolk	26. 3.1916	23. 4.1986
Philip George Edwards *1930–1933*	Hoxton	6.12.1906	3. 4.1987
Richard Gary Peter Ellis *1982–1984*	Paddington	20.12.1960	
John Ernest Emburey *1973–1987*	Peckham	20. 8.1952	
Henry John Enthoven *1925–1926*	Cartagena, Spain	4. 6.1903	29. 6.1975
Sydney Graver Etheridge *1908–1910*	New Barnet, Herts	3.11.1882	3. 9.1945
Maurice William Etheridge *1946*	North Hammersmith	24. 8.1916	

Name	Place	Born	Died
Alan Fairbairn *1947–1951*	Winchmore Hill	25. 1.1923	
Gordon Armytage Fairbairn *1919*	Logan Downs, Austr	26. 6.1892	5.11.1973
Colin Fairservice *1936*	Hadlow, Kent	6. 8.1909	
Norman George Featherstone *1968–1979*	Que Que, Rhodesia	20. 8.1949	
Robert Felton *1935–1948*	Streatham	27.12.1909	4.10.1982
Edwin Field *1904–1906*	Hampstead	18.12.1871	9. 1.1947
George Figg *1850*	Horsham, Sussex	13. 6.1824	20. 7.1888
Paul Bernard Fisher *1979*	Edmonton	19.12.1954	
Robert Allan Fitzgerald *1864*	Purley, Berks	1.10.1834	28.10.1881
Michael Flanagan *1873–1878*	Glen Colombkill	15. 3.1842	14. 1.1890
Cyril Pelham Foley *1893–1906*	Westminster	1.11.1868	9. 3.1936
Augustus Frank Justice Ford *1879–1882*	Sussex Sq, London	12. 9.1858	20. 5.1931
Francis Gilbertson Justice Ford *1886–1899*	Paddington	14.12.1866	7. 2.1940
Neville Montague Ford *1932*	Repton, Derbys	18.11.1906	
William Justice Ford *1879–1894*	Paddington	7.11.1853	3. 4.1904
Basil Samuel Foster *1912*	Malvern	12. 2.1882	28. 9.1959
Archibald John Burgess Fowler *1921–1930*	Marylebone	1. 4.1891	7. 5.1977
Thomas Seely Fox *1905*	Upton, Essex	23. 8.1878	3. 4.1931
Arthur Stopford Francis *1880*	Upminster	14. 6.1854	1.1908
Charles King Francis *1875–1877*	Upminster	3. 2.1851	28.10.1925
Francis Philip Francis *1881*	Upminster	15. 9.1852	18. 1.1926
Alastair Gregory James Fraser *1986*	Edgware	17.10.1967	
Angus Robert Charles Fraser *1984–1987*	Billinge	9. 8.1965	
John St John Frederick *1864*	London	6. 1.1846	10. 9.1907
Robert Alec Gale *1956–1965*	Old Warden, Beds	10.12.1933	
Michael William Gatting *1975–1987*	Kingsbury	6. 6.1957	
George Henry Bailey Gilbert *1851*	Cheltenham	2. 9.1829	16. 6.1906
Walter Raleigh Gilbert *1873–1874*	Strand, London	16. 9.1853	26. 7.1924
William Gilby *1872*	Leamington	26. 7.1834	19. 3.1905
James Gilman *1900–1901*	Marylebone	17. 3.1879	14. 9.1976
Cecil Argo Gold *1907*	London	3. 6.1887	3. 7.1916
Hilary Angelo Gomes *1973–1976*	Arima, Trinidad	13. 7.1953	
Charles Gordon *1851–1862*	London	25.12.1814	27. 7.1899
Bernard Charles Gordon-Lennox *1903*	Westminster	1. 5.1878	10.11.1914
Ian James Gould *1975–1980/81*	Taplow	19. 8.1957	

William Goulding *1851*	Enfield	3. 3.1813	11. 6.1878
Cyril Douglas Gray *1925–1927*	Hampstead	26. 4.1895	20. 2.1969
Lawrence Herbert Gray *1934–1951*	Tottenham	15.12.1915	3. 1.1983
Theophilus Greatorex *1883–1892*	Hyde Park	14.12.1864	27. 7.1933
Charles Ernest Green *1868–1879*	Walthamstow	26. 8.1846	4.12.1916
John James Green *1919*	Marylebone	1897	25.10.1960
John Constable Gregory *1865*	Marylebone	17. 8.1842	28. 6.1894
Arthur Wilfrid Michael Stewart Griffin *1910*	Iquique, Chile	19. 2.1887	29. 6.1962
Gerard Sandiforth Featherstone			
Griffin *1900–1903*	Fulham	1882	1950
Algernon Sidney Griffiths *1871–1872*	London	23. 5.1847	18. 4.1899
Robert Grimston *1850–1851*	Mayfair	18. 9.1816	7. 4.1884
John Lindsay Guise *1922–1934*	Calcutta	29.11.1903	
Churchill Hector Gunasekera *1919–1922*	Colombo	27. 7.1894	16. 5.1969
Alexander Astell Hadow *1872*	London	1. 6.1853	1. 6.1894
Edward Maitland Hadow *1883–1893*	Sudbury Hill	13. 3.1863	20. 2.1895
Patrick Francis Hadow *1873–1874*	London	24. 1.1855	29. 6.1946
Walter Henry Hadow *1870–1879*	London	25. 9.1849	15. 9.1898
Nigel Esme Haig *1912–1934*	Kensington	12.12.1887	27.10.1966
John Haines *1865–1867*	St Pancras	1825	1894
George John Gordon Hake *1948*	Sutton, Surrey	24. 8.1918	
Percy William Hale *1900*	Kensington	1874	8. 1.1933
Warren Stormes Hale *1893*	Sudbury, Suffolk	1862	5. 2.1934
Charles Hall *1867*	Islington	16.10.1842	1900
Ernest Austin Halliwell *1901*	Ealing	7. 9.1864	2.10.1919
Richard Bisset Halliwell *1865*	Bloomsbury	30.11.1842	9.11.1881
Kenneth Brand Harper *1910*	S Kensington	8. 8.1891	21. 1.1961
William John Roy Harrington *1946–1948*	St John's Wood	30. 1.1915	
Michael John Harris *1964–1968*	St Just-in-Roseland	25. 5.1944	
William Philip Harrison *1906–1911*	Barnet, Herts	13.11.1885	7. 9.1964
George Edmead Hart *1926–1939*	Harlington	13. 1.1902	11. 4.1987
Charles Musgrave Harvey *1859*	Hornsey	11. 5.1837	2.11.1917
Edmund Harvey *1872*	Islington	1850	23. 2.1902
Shearman Montague Haslip *1919*	Twickenham	13. 5.1897	4. 7.1968
Frederick Albert Hawkins *1927*	Wandsworth	11.12.1888	12. 9.1975
James Samuel Haycraft *1885*	Islington	1865	26. 3.1942
Arthur Haygarth *1850–1851*	Hastings	4. 8.1825	1. 5.1903
Herbert Bailey Hayman *1893–1901*	Hendon	5.10.1873	31. 7.1930
David Russell Hayward *1939*	Australia	7. 6.1920	21. 4.1945
John Reginald Head *1892–1898*	Hackney	15. 7.1868	15. 5.1949
Cecil Headlam *1902–1906*	London	19. 9.1872	12. 8.1934

George Hearne *1861–1868*	Chalfont St Peter	15. 5.1829	9.12.1904
John Thomas Hearne *1888–1923*	Chalfont St Giles	3. 5.1867	17. 4.1944
John William Hearne *1909–1936*	Hillingdon	11. 2.1891	14. 9.1965
Thomas Hearne *1859–1875*	Chalfont St Peter	4. 9.1826	13. 5.1900
Thomas John Hearne *1908*	Ealing	3. 7.1887	
Arthur Howard Heath *1878*	Newcastle-u-Lyne	29. 5.1856	24. 4.1930
George Lockwood Hebden *1908–1919*	Brentwood	16.12.1879	11. 6.1946
Martyn Carthew Hebert *1862*	Clapham	1841	1905
Robert Henderson *1872–1878*	Fulham	3. 5.1851	22. 9.1895
Denis Hendren *1905–1919*	Chiswick	25. 9.1882	29. 5.1962
Elias Henry Hendren *1907–1937*	Turnham Green	5. 2.1889	4.10.1962
Perceval Jeffery Thornton Henery *1879–1894*	London	6. 6.1859	10. 8.1938
Francis Anthony Hoste Henley *1908*	Woodbridge	11. 2.1884	26. 6.1963
F. Henry *1882*			
Allen William Henry Herbert *1875*	Hythe, Kent	20.10.1852	14. 9.1897
Herbert Henry Moore Herbert *1883*	Kensington	1863	1884
Robert Herkes *1978–1979*	Lincoln	30. 6.1957	
Robert Stephen Herman *1965–1971*	Southampton	30.11.1946	
Norman George Hever *1947*	Marylebone	17.12.1924	
Anthony North Hickley *1930*	Marylebone	10. 3.1906	5. 9.1972
John Arnold Einem Hickson *1894–1896*	Edmonton	1864	2. 1.1945
Thomas William Higginson *1960*	Esher	6.11.1936	
Richard Hamilton Hill *1921–1931*	Kensington	28.11.1900	5.10.1959
George Whiteside Hillyard *1886*	Hanwell	6. 2.1864	24. 3.1943
Charles Twysden Hoare *1875*	Mitcham	10.11.1851	22. 1.1935
George Langton Hodgkinson *1861*	Kentish Town	13.10.1837	16. 2.1915
William Ernest Johnstone Holdship *1894*	Auckland, NZ	15. 2.1872	unknown
Ronald William Hooker *1956–1969*	Lower Clapton	22. 2.1935	
Jeffries David Hopkins *1969–1972*	Bridgend, Glamorgan	23. 8.1950	
William Allen Horncastle *1883*	Edmonton	1864	1917
John Henry James Hornsby *1893*	Grantham, Lincs	18. 4.1860	9. 7.1926
William Herbert Francis Kenneth Horton *1927*	Brentford	25. 4.1906	31.10.1986
Neil Stafford Hotchkin *1939–1948*	Horncastle	4. 2.1914	
Cecil Geoffrey Howard *1930*	Hampstead Garden Suburb	14. 2.1909	

Charles William Henry Howard *1931*	Beckenham	7.11.1904	
George Howitt *1865–1876*	Old Lenton, Notts	14. 3.1843	19.12.1881
Simon Peter Hughes *1980–1987*	Kingston-upon-Thames	20.12.1959	
Joseph Harold Anthony Hulme *1929–1939*	Stafford	26. 8.1904	
John Hanbury Human *1935–1938*	Castle Ward, Northbld	13. 1.1912	
John Henry Sneyd Hunt *1902–1912*	Kensington	24.11.1874	16. 9.1916
Robert Norman Hunt *1926–1928*	Worsley, Lancs	24. 9.1903	13.10.1983
Robert Jack Hurst *1954–1961*	Hampton Hill	29.12.1933	
Gilbert William Hutchins *1890*	Knebworth, Herts	28. 2.1858	1902
Edward Ingram *1938–1949*	Dublin	14. 8.1910	13. 3.1973
Kevan David James *1980–1984*	Lambeth	18. 3.1961	
Malcolm Robert Jardine *1892*	Simla, India	8. 6.1869	16. 1.1947
Arthur Sannox Johnston *1886–1887*	Hornsey	16. 3.1863	8. 8.1929
Allan Arthur Jones *1976–1979*	Horley, Surrey	9.12.1947	
Keith Vaughan Jones *1967–1974*	Park Royal	28. 3.1942	
Peter Francis Judge *1933–1934*	Cricklewood	23. 5.1916	
George Harman Jupp *1867–1868*	Brentford	26. 2.1845	24. 2.1930
Anthony Kamm *1952*	Hampstead	2. 3.1931	
Henry Wynyard Kaye *1900*	London	21. 5.1875	21. 4.1922
Arthur Lock Kemp *1890–1894*	London	1869	1929
Nicholas John Kemp *1982*	Bromley, Kent	16.12.1956	
Percival Hepworth Kemp *1919*	Luton, Beds	2. 7.1888	14. 2.1974
Humphrey Neild Kent *1920*	Watford	2.11.1893	19. 4.1972
Eric Leslie Kidd *1910–1928*	London	18.10.1889	2. 7.1984
Edgar Thomas Killick *1926–1939*	Fulham	9. 5.1907	18. 5.1953
Horace David King *1936–1946*	Brentford	10. 2.1915	7. 3.1974
Roderick Calder Kinkead-Weekes *1976*	East London, SAf	15. 3.1951	
John Walter Knapp *1864*	Paddington	8. 3.1841	22. 6.1881
William Knightley-Smith *1952*	West Smithfield	1. 8.1932	31. 7.1962
Roger Kynaston *1850*	London	5.11.1805	21. 6.1874
Timothy Michael Lamb *1974–1977*	Hartford, Ches	24. 3.1953	
William Lambert *1874–1877*	Hatfield, Herts	19. 4.1843	4. 3.1927
John Douglas Algernon Langley *1937*	Northwood	25. 4.1918	
Amritt Harrichand Latchman *1965–1973*	Kingston, Jam	26. 7.1943	
George Law *1881*	Rochdale	17. 4.1846	30. 7.1911
Charles Lawrence *1861*	Hoxton	16.12.1828	20.12.1916
Patrick J. Lawrence *1964*	Roseau, Dominica	3.10.1942	

Michael Lutener Laws *1948–1950*	Finchley	12. 8.1926	
Frederick Lee *1863–1868*	Finsbury Sq,		
	London	11. 8.1840	13.11.1922
Frank Stanley Lee *1925*	St John's Wood	24. 7.1905	30. 3.1982
Henry (William) Lee *1911–1934*	Westminster	26.10.1890	21. 4.1981
John William Lee *1923*	Marylebone	1. 2.1902	20. 6.1944
Charles Frederick Henry Leslie *1881–1886*	London	8.12.1861	12. 2.1921
Edward Lester *1929–1930*			
Richard Percy Lewis *1898*	Marylebone	10. 3.1874	7. 9.1917
Frederick William Lillywhite *1850–1851*	Westhampnett	13. 6.1792	21. 8.1854
James Lillywhite *1851*	Hove	29.10.1825	24.11.1882
John Lillywhite *1851–1864*	Hove	10.11.1826	27.10.1874
David John Ling *1966–1968*	Enfield,	2. 7.1946	
Arthur Rieusett Litteljohn *1905–1914*	Hanwell	1. 4.1881	8.12.1919
Edward Salterne Litteljohn *1900–1914*	Hanwell	24. 9.1878	22. 1.1955
Gerald Edward Livock *1925–1927*	Newmarket	11. 7.1897	
Henry Kerr Longman *1919–1920*	Kensington	8. 3.1881	7.10.1958
Wilfrid Fraser Lord *1919*	Kolhapur, India	1. 8.1888	19. 9.1960
Geoffrey Robert Stuart Love *1920*	Islington	19. 4.1889	6. 2.1978
George William Lowles *1889*	Whitechapel	1865	1940
Arthur Charles Lucas *1877*	Lowestoft	22. 5.1853	14. 6.1915
Alfred Perry Lucas *1883–1888*	Westminster	20. 2.1857	12.10.1923
Charles James Lucas *1876–1877*	Clapham		
	Common	25. 2.1853	17. 4.1928
Robert Slade Lucas *1891–1900*	Teddington	17. 7.1867	5. 1.1942
Alfred Lyttelton *1877–1887*	London	7. 2.1857	5. 7.1913
Edward Lyttelton *1878–1882*	London	23. 7.1855	26. 1.1942
Norman McCaskie *1931–1932*	Kensington	23. 3.1911	1. 7.1968
Alastair McCorquodale *1951*	Glasgow	5.12.1925	
John Wyndham Hamilton McCulloch *1914*	Calcutta	4.12.1894	21.10.1915
John William McEwen *1884*	Dalston	25.11.1862	16. 2.1902
Gregor MacGregor *1892–1907*	Merchiston	31. 3.1869	20. 8.1919
Christopher Boyd William			
Magnay *1906–1911*	Marylebone	27. 3.1884	4. 9.1960
Henry John James Malcolm *1948*	Richmond,		
	Surrey	4. 7.1914	
Maurice Manasseh *1964–1967*	Calcutta	12. 1.1943	
Francis George Mann *1937–1954*	Byfleet	6. 9.1917	
Francis Thomas Mann *1909–1931*	Winchmore		
	Hill	3. 3.1888	6.10.1964
John Pelham Mann *1939–1947*	Byfleet	13. 6.1919	
Thomas Allen Mantle *1864–1872*	Kates Hill,		
	Worcs	31. 1.1840	29. 4.1884
Geoffrey Marks *1894–1898*	Croydon	15.11.1864	25. 8.1938

Dennis Alston Marriott *1972–1974*	Amity Hall, Jam	29.11.1939	
Edward Leverson Marsden *1897*	Hampstead	25. 7.1870	2. 7.1946
Charles Marshall *1866*	Cricklewood	20. 2.1843	25. 2.1904
Eric Martin *1919–1923*	Barnet, Herts	20. 5.1894	2. 5.1924
Marcus Trevelyan Martin *1870*	Barrackpore	29. 4.1842	5. 6.1908
Rajesh Jamnadass Maru *1980–1982*	Nairobi	28.10.1962	
John Alfred Massey *1927*	Hendon	1899	1963
Henry Maturin *1863*	Fanetglebe, Ireland	5. 4.1842	24. 2.1920
Frederick William Maude *1890–1896*	Plumstead	28. 2.1857	9. 2.1923
Cecil Reginald Napp Maxwell *1946*	Paddington	21. 5.1913	25. 9.1973
John Pole Mayo *1850*	Tanhurst Pk, Sy	12. 8.1822	23. 3.1899
Michael Edward Lovelace Melluish *1957*	Westcliff-on-Sea	13. 6.1932	
Henry Menzies *1891–1893*	Lambeth	28. 3.1867	7. 3.1936
William Gerald Merry *1979–1982*	Newbury, Berks	8. 8.1955	
Colin Peter Metson *1981–1986*	Cuffley, Herts	2. 7.1963	
Edward Mignon *1905–1913*	Kilburn	1.11.1885	14. 5.1925
Andrew John Trevor Miller *1983–1987*	Chesham, Bucks	30. 5.1963	
Henry Maynard Mills *1881*	Kensington	1847	13. 4.1915
Harold Aubrey Milton *1907*	Hackney Downs	15. 1.1882	14. 3.1970
Douglas Moffat *1864*	Cawnpore	31. 7.1843	27. 3.1922
Norman John Douglas Moffatt *1921–1925*	Edenhall, Scotland	13. 9.1883	11.10.1972
James Dermott Monteith *1981–1982*	Lisburn, Ireland	2. 6.1943	
Leonard James Moon *1899–1909*	Kensington	9. 2.1878	23.11.1916
William Robert Moon *1891*	Maida Vale	7. 6.1868	9. 1.1943
Eustace Charles Mordaunt *1891–1894*	Wellesbourne	6. 9.1870	21. 6.1938
Henry John Mordaunt *1889–1893*	Westminster	12. 7.1867	15. 1.1939
Richard Edwardes More *1901–1910*	Linley, Salop	3. 1.1879	24.11.1936
James Henry Morley *1865*	Herne Hill	20.12.1835	7. 4.1904
Geoffrey Dalgleish Morton *1950*	Acton	27. 7.1922	
Alan Edward Moss *1950–1963*	Tottenham	14.11.1930	
Roger Peter Moulding *1977*	Enfield	3. 1.1958	
George Mumford *1867–1872*	Ealing	1. 2.1845	12.11.1877
Bernard Leonard Muncer *1933–1946*	Hampstead	23.10.1913	18. 1.1982
Harry Raymond Munt *1923*	Paddington	31.10.1902	27.12.1965
John Thomas Murray *1952–1975*	N Kensington	1. 4.1935	
Michael Patrick Murray *19952–1955*	Westminster	14. 5.1930	

Harry Robert Murrell *1906–1926*	Hounslow	19.11.1879	15. 8.1952
Guy Greville Napier *1904–1913*	London	26. 1.1884	25. 9.1915
Andrew Needham *1987*	Calow, Derbys	23. 3.1957	
Robert Prynne Nelson *1932–1933*	Fulham	7. 8.1912	29.10.1940
Augustus Adolphus St John Marriott Nepean *1876–1877*	London	24. 6.1849	24. 1.1933
Charles Edward Burroughs Nepean *1873–1874*	Mayfair	5. 2.1851	26. 3.1903
Evan Alcock Nepean *1887–1895*	Mitcham	13. 9.1865	20. 1.1906
William Thomas Nevell *1936–1938*	Balham	13. 6.1916	25. 8.1978
John Harcourt Nevinson *1933*	Lausanne	2.11.1910	22. 8.1987
Douglas Leonard Newman *1948–1951*	Harringay	25. 6.1920	10. 9.1959
George Christopher Newman *1929–1936*	Paddington	26. 4.1904	13.10.1982
Stephen Cox Newton *1885*	Nailsea	21. 4.1853	16. 8.1916
Kenneth Iltyd Nicholl *1904*	Marylebone	13. 2.1885	2. 3.1952
Richard Williams Nicholls *1896–1904*	Crouch End	23. 7.1875	22. 1.1948
William Nicholson *1850–1865*	Upper Holloway	2. 9.1824	25. 7.1909
George Tait St Aubyn Nixon *1868–1870*	Neermuck, India	11. 8.1850	2.1913
Ernest John North *1923–1927*	Burton-on-Trent	23. 9.1895	24. 8.1955
Percy Northcote *1888*	Islington	18. 9.1866	3. 3.1934
John Ayscough Nunn *1926*	Hadley, Herts	19. 3.1906	6. 4.1987
Timothy Carew O'Brien *1881–1898*	Dublin	5.11.1861	9.12.1948
Valentine R. O'Connor *1908–1909*	Ireland	1878	1956
George Newland Osborn *1881*	Romford	1851	3. 3.1913
David Robert Osborne *1911*	Perth, Austr	29. 9.1879	1954
Cuthbert John Ottaway *1874*	Dover	20. 7.1850	2. 4.1878
David George Ottley *1967*	Worcester Park, Sy	23. 6.1944	
Harold Geoffrey (Owen) Owen-Smith *1935–1937*	Rondebosch, SAf	18. 2.1909	
John Haywood Oxley *1883*	Rotherham	1850	1917
Charles Carew Page *1905–1909*	Barnet, Herts	25. 4.1884	10. 4.1921
George Alfred Edward Paine *1926*	Paddington	11. 6.1908	30. 3.1978
Clayton Palmer *1904–1912*	Westminster	14. 7.1885	4.1956
Peter Howard Parfitt *1956–1972*	Billingford, Norfolk	8.12.1936	
John Parkinson *1863*	Knapthorne	1843	unknown
John Parsons *1863*	Oxford	27.12.1834	1912
Ashok Sitaram Patel *1978*	Nairobi	23. 9.1956	
Edwin Paul *1850*	Holloway	21. 9.1822	6.10.1858

Name	Place	Born	Died
Bernard Pauncefote 1868–1872	Cuddalore	28. 6.1848	24. 9.1882
Mehallasha Edulji Pavri 1895	Nausari, India	10.10.1866	19. 4.1946
Sydney Southgate Pawling 1894	Wallingford, Berks	6. 2.1862	23.12.1922
Cecil Arthur Lynch Payne 1905–1909	Dacca, India	30. 8.1885	21. 3.1976
Christopher John Payne 1968–1970	Hatfield, Herts	30.12.1947	
Meyrick Whitmore Payne 1904–1909	Fulham	10. 5.1885	2. 6.1963
Harold Edgar Pearce 1905–1907	Barnet, Herts	1. 4.1884	19. 5.1939
Hugh Pearman 1969–1972	Birmingham	1. 6.1945	
Roger Pearman 1962–1964	Lichfield	13. 2.1943	
Thomas Sherwin Pearson 1878–1885	Barwell, Leics	20. 6.1851	25.11.1935
Charles Urie Peat 1914	Edmonton	28. 2.1892	27.10.1979
Ian Alexander Ross Peebles 1928–1948	Aberdeen	20. 1.1908	27. 2.1980
George Perkins 1884	Ealing	1864	1933
Hylton Philipson 1895–1898	Tynemouth	8. 6.1866	4.12.1935
James Phillips 1890–1898	Pleasant Creek, Austr	1. 9.1860	21. 4.1930
Charles Carlisle Pilkington 1903	Woolton, Lancs	13.12.1876	8. 1.1950
Hubert Carlisle Pilkington 1903–1904	Woolton, Lancs	23.10.1879	17. 6.1942
George James Stuart Pitts 1914	St John's, Canada	6.10.1878	27. 7.1939
John Pocknee 1884	Brighton	1860	1938
Vivian Ralph Polley 1913	Fulham	22.12.1880	12. 2.1967
James Pollitt 1850	St Leonards	1826	unknown
Spencer Cecil Brabazon Ponsonby 1862	Mayfair	14. 3.1824	1.12.1915
Edward Pooley 1864–1865	Richmond, Sy	13. 2.1838	18. 7.1907
Stephen John Poulter 1978	Hornsey	9. 9.1956	
Alfred Peter Powell 1927	Marylebone	19. 8.1908	1985
James Alfred Powell 1926	Bloomsbury	5. 5.1899	1973
Leslie Roff Vincent Prentice 1920–1923	Melbourne, Austr	1887	13. 8.1928
Charles Henry Prest 1870	York	9.12.1841	4. 3.1875
John Sidney Ernest Price 1961–1975	Harrow	22. 7.1937	
Wilfred Frederick Frank Price 1926–1947	Westminster	25. 4.1902	13. 1.1969
Frank William Putner 1933–1934	Greenwich	26. 9.1912	
Clive Thornton Radley 1964–1987	Hertford	13. 5.1944	
Mark Ravin Ramprakash 1987	Bushey, Herts	5. 9.1969	
Geoffrey Lewis Raphael 1928	Westminster	10. 1.1910	12. 6.1986
Thomas Ratliff 1869–1873	Camberwell	31. 3.1836	unknown
John Thomas Rawlin 1889–1909	Greasbrough	10.11.1856	19. 1.1924
Tom Bokenham Reddick 1931	Shanghai	17. 2.1912	1. 6.1982
Edmund Reeves 1851	Kennington	1821	10.12.1906
Henry Adair Richardson 1869–1869	Bayswater	31. 7.1846	17. 9.1921
Arthur William Ridley 1882–1885	Hollington	11. 9.1852	10. 8.1916
Benjamin Roberson 1865–1866	Ware, Herts	12. 9.1832	6. 4.1874

Name	Place	Born	Died
James Harry Roberts *1892*	Anfield, Lancs	7.1864	11. 8.1911
James Robertson *1878–1891*	Edinburgh	10.11.1850	21. 3.1927
John David Benbow Robertson *1937–1959*	Chiswick	22. 2.1917	
William Parish Robertson *1900–1919*	Lima, Peru	5. 9.1879	7. 5.1950
Robert Victor Charles Robins *1953–1960*	Burnham, Bucks	13. 3.1935	
Robert Walter Vivian Robins *1925–1951*	Stafford	3. 6.1906	12.12.1968
Charles Robson *1881–1883*	Twickenham	20. 6.1859	27. 9.1943
Clayton Graeme Wynne Robson *1926*	Bareilly	3. 7.1901	
William Roche *1899–1900*	South Australia	20. 7.1871	2. 1.1950
George John Rogers *1850–1851*	Hackney	1. 5.1815	2. 9.1870
John Phillips Rogers *1891*	Hackney	1860	unknown
David Audley Moberley Rome *1930–1933*	Marylebone	14. 4.1910	20. 5.1970
Graham David Rose *1985–1986*	Tottenham	12. 4.1964	
Michael Anthony Roseberry *1986–1987*	S Hylton, Durham	28.11.1966	
Charles Hoadley Ashe Ross *1875*	Bath	22. 7.1852	5. 2.1911
Hamilton Ross *1876*	Grenada, WI	26. 8.1849	29. 3.1938
Nigel Patrick Dorai Ross *1973–1977*	Chelsea	5. 4.1953	
Reginald Routledge *1946–1954*	N Kensington	12. 6.1920	
Charles Robert Rowley *1872*	Marylebone	29.12.1849	5. 4.1933
Henry Royston *1850–1862*	Harrow on the Hill	12. 8.1819	30. 9.1873
Denis Leslie Russell *1928–1932*	Paddington	2. 7.1909	29.12.1986
Sidney Edward James Russell *1960–1964*	Feltham	4.10.1937	
William Eric Russell *1956–1972*	Dumbarton	3. 7.1936	
Edward Rutter *1862–1876*	Hillingdon	3. 8.1842	4. 2.1926
Edward Henry Pearse Salmon *1878–1879*	Madras	24.12.1853	1. 2.1907
J. Saunders *1891*			
Clifford Allen Saville *1914*	Tottenham	5. 2.1892	8.11.1907
Stanley Herbert Saville *1910–1928*	Tottenham	21.11.1889	22. 2.1966
Reginald Oscar Schwarz *1901–1905*	Lee, Kent	4. 5.1875	18.11.1918
Lord George William Montagu-Douglas Scott *1888*	Bowhill, Scotland	31. 8.1866	23. 2.1947
Stanley Winckworth Scott *1878–1893*	Bombay	24. 3.1854	8.12.1933
William Jerman Scott *1894–1895*	Hartley-Wintney	4. 4.1864	18. 7.1920
Michael Walter William Selvey *1972–1982*	Chiswick	25. 4.1948	
Timothy Selwood *1966–1973*	Prestatyn	1. 9.1944	
John Joseph Sewell *1863–1867*	Cirencester	10. 2.1844	8. 6.1897
Thomas Shackle *1868*	Hillingdon	28. 7.1834	12. 3.1887
Rowland Allen Shaddick *1946–1947*	Hackney	26. 3.1920	
Harry Philip Hugh Sharp *1946–1955*	Kentish Town	6.10.1917	

Cloudesley Brereton Sharpe *1923*	Hampstead	5. 2.1904	
Edward Domett Shaw *1882*	Passage West,		
	Cork	5.10.1860	5.11.1937
John Charles L. Shenton *1888*	Bethnal Green	1862	26. 1.1900
John Shepperd *1959–1960*	Willesden	8. 5.1937	
Noel Benjamin Sherwell *1925–1926*	Hendon	16. 3.1904	29.12.1960
James Morton Sims *1929–1952*	Leyton	13. 5.1903	27. 4.1973
Challen Hasler Lufkin Skeet *1920–1922*	Oamaru, NZ	17. 8.1895	20. 4.1978
Wilfred Norris Slack *1977–1987*	Troumaca, WI	12.12.1954	
Arthur Frederick Smith *1874–1877*	Regent's Park	13. 5.1853	18. 1.1936
Bertrand Nigel Bosworth Smith *1895*	Harrow	20. 6.1873	19. 2.1947
Cedric Ivan James Smith *1934–1939*	Corsham, Wilts	25. 8.1906	9. 2.1979
Charles John Smith *1868–1876*	Marylebone	19. 1.1849	8. 5.1930
Lewis Alfred Smith *1934–1937*	Brentford	12. 7.1913	12. 9.1978
Michael John Smith *1959–1980*	Enfield	4. 1.1942	
Albert Henry Percival Snow *1875–1876*	Bedford	9. 8.1852	5. 4.1909
William John Blair Soppitt *1887*		1857	29.10.1910
George Spillman *1886*	Strand	24.10.1856	18. 4.1911
Allan Ivo Steel *1912*	Toxteth, Lancs	27. 9.1892	8.10.1917
Frederick Steele *1877–1879*	London	14. 5.1847	22. 1.1915
Greville Thomas Scott Stevens *1919–1932*	Hampstead	7. 1.1901	19. 9.1970
Alexander Lamont Stewart *1880*	Port of Spain	2. 6.1858	17. 2.1904
James Marshall Stewart *1880*	Glasgow	9. 8.1861	20. 7.1943
Richard William Stewart *1966–1968*	Portland, Jam	28. 2.1945	
Haycroft Stirling *1932–1933*	Barnet	8. 2.1908	7. 5.1952
Andrew Ernest Stoddart *1885–1900*	Westoe,		
	Durham	11. 3.1863	4. 4.1915
John Hubert Stogdon *1899–1907*	Harrow	25. 4.1876	17.12.1944
George Strachan *1870–1871*	Prestbury	21.11.1850	29.12.1901
Alfred Hugh Stratford *1877–1880*	Kensington	5. 9.1853	2. 5.1914
Charles Thomas Studd *1879–1884*	Spratton	2.12.1860	16. 7.1931
George Brown Studd *1879–1886*	Netheravon,		
	Wilts	20.10.1859	13. 2.1945
Herbert William Studd *1890*	Tidworth,		
	Wilts	26.12.1870	8. 8.1947
John Edward Kynaston Studd *1878–1884*	Netheravon,		
	Wilts	26. 7.1858	14. 1.1944
Michael Ormonde Cleasby Sturt *1961–1978*	Wembley	12. 9.1940	
Desmond Ford Surfleet *1931–1933*	Dublin	5. 2.1912	
Manfred John Susskind *1909–1910*	Johannesburg	8. 6.1891	9. 7.1957
Edmund George Gresham Sutton *1868*	Marylebone	12.10.1844	7.10.1903
John Lassam Swann *1949–1951*	Ealing	3.10.1926	
Ernest William Swanton *1937–1938*	Forest Hill	11. 2.1907	
Edward Henry Sweetland *1927*	Westminster	25. 4.1903	18. 7.1978

Name	Place	Date	Date
James Frederick Sykes 1983–1987	Shoreditch	30.12.1965	
Alfred Tabor 1872	Trent, Middx	24. 2.1850	16.12.1925
Arthur Sydney Tabor 1872–1874	Trent, Middx	9.11.1852	14.10.1927
William Clifton Tabor 1862	Bloomsbury	13.12.1842	24. 5.1867
Arthur Ralph Tanner 1920–1927	Bromley, Kent	25.12.1889	16. 8.1966
Francis Alfred Tarrant 1904–1914	Fitzroy, Austr	11.12.1880	29. 1.1951
Chilton Richard Vernon Taylor 1981	Birkenhead	3.10.1951	
Herbert Taylor 1933	Accrington	22. 2.1910	
Stanley Shelbourne Taylor 1901	Islington	2. 3.1875	22. 7.1965
Thomas Clough Taylor 1850		1824	10. 7.1859
Charles Ashley Teape 1872	Blackheath, Kent	1844	1. 8.1925
Charles Mansfield Tebbut 1866–1870	West Ham	1840	27. 9.1898
Frederic John Napier Thesiger 1888–1892	London	12. 8.1868	1. 4.1933
Leopold Ernest Thomas 1893		16. 2.1865	28. 5.1937
Alexander William Thompson 1939–1955	Liverpool	17. 4.1916	
Leslie Baines Thompson 1946–1949	Brentford	12.11.1908	
M. Thompson 1866			
Jeffrey Robert Thomson 1981	Greenacre, Austr	16. 8.1950	
Charles Inglis Thornton 1875–1885	Llanwarne	20. 3.1850	10.12.1929
George Thornton 1893–1899	Skipton	24.12.1867	31. 1.1939
Percy Melville Thornton 1872	Mayfair	29.12.1841	8. 1.1918
Henry William Tilly 1954–1961	Edmonton	25. 5.1932	
Mark Tindall 1933–1938	Marylebone	31. 4.1914	
Frederick John Titmus 1949–1982	Kentish Town	24.11.1932	
Keith Patrick Tomlins 1977–1985	Kingston-upon-Thames	23.10.1957	
Barry Maurice Waller Trapnell 1946	Hampstead	18. 5.1924	
Thomas Edward Treloar 1872	St Austell	29.10.1846	unknown
Edward William Tritton 1864–1867	Marylebone	3. 8.1844	1.12.1901
Albert Edwin Trott 1898–1910	Abbotsford, Austr	6. 2.1873	30. 7.1914
Philip Clive Roderick Tufnell 1986–1987	Barnet, Herts	29. 4.1966	
Charles Molesworth Tuke 1882	Chiswick	23. 5.1857	24. 1.1925
Montague Turner 1863–1878	Acton	21. 9.1843	25. 1.1908
Nigel Frederick Turner 1937	Paddington	8. 8.1914	31. 1.1962
Richard Haynes Twining 1910–1928	Paddington	3.11.1889	3. 1.1979
Geoffrey Francis Uvedale Udal 1932	Holborn	23. 2.1908	5.12.1980
Vintcent Adriaan Pieter Van Der Bijl 1980–1981	Cape Town	19. 3.1948	
George Charles Vassila 1880	Richmond, Surrey	1857	1915
George Frederick Vernon 1878–1895	London	20. 6.1856	10. 8.1902
Martin Jeffrey Vernon 1974–1976	Marylebone	9. 7.1951	

Albert Edward Ernest Vogler *1906*	Swartwater, SAf	28.11.1876	9. 8.1946
Anthony Charles Waite *1962–1964*	Pinner	29. 5.1943	
Alfred Walker *1851–1859*	Southgate	8. 9.1827	4. 9.1870
Arthur Henry Walker *1859–1862*	Southgate	30. 6.1833	4.10.1878
Frederick Walker *1859*	Southgate	4.12.1829	20.12.1889
Isaac Donnithorne Walker *1862–1884*	Southgate	8. 1.1844	6. 7.1898
John Walker *1850–1866*	Palmers Green	15. 9.1826	14. 8.1885
John Walker *1879*	Harrow	1854	unknown
James George Walker *1886–1890*	Glasgow	9.10.1859	24. 3.1923
Russell Donnithorne Walker *1862–1877*	Southgate	13. 2.1842	29. 3.1922
Vyell Edward Walker *1857–1877*	Southgate	20. 4.1837	3. 1.1906
Arthur Christopher Walton *1957–1959*	Georgetown, WI	26. 9.1933	
Sir Pelham Francis Warner *1894–1920*	The Hall, Trinidad	2.10.1873	30. 1.1963
John James Warr *1949–1960*	Ealing	16. 7.1927	
William Richard Watkins *1930–1937*	Ealing	22. 6.1904	15.10.1986
Arthur Kenelm Watson *1890–1894*	Harrow	23. 3.1867	2. 1.1947
Ian Ronald Watson *1969*	Teddington	9. 6.1947	
Charles Johnston Bourne Webb *1902*	Bloemfontein	24.11.1874	18.11.1963
Sidney Webb *1897–1898*	Brompton	1. 2.1875	4. 4.1923
Alexander Josiah Webbe *1875–1900*	London	16. 1.1855	19. 2.1941
Herbert Ross Webbe *1875–1879*	London	18. 5.1856	9. 5.1886
William Hugh Webster *1930–1947*	Hackney	22. 2.1910	19. 6.1986
Cyril Mowbray Wells *1895–1909*	St Pancras	21. 3.1871	22. 8.1963
George Wells *1859–1864*	Whitechapel	2.11.1830	23. 1.1891
Lionel Seymour Wells *1898–1905*	London	3. 2.1870	26. 4.1928
Frederic Tristram Welman *1880–1888*	Taunton	19. 2.1849	30.12.1931
Herbert John Wenyon *1921–1924*	Canton, China	18. 4.1888	19. 8.1944
John Edward West *1885–1896*	Stepney	11.11.1861	14. 3.1920
John White Westhorp *1893–1894*	London	1868	24. 3.1935
Henry Weston *1910–1914*	Hurlingham	2. 1.1888	unknown
Jack Brian Wheatley *1925–1928*	Wandsworth	12.10.1903	29. 4.1982
Henry James William Wheeler *1864*	Gibraltar	27. 3.1840	29.10.1908
Walter Charles Wheeler *1873*	Newport, IOW	30.12.1841	10.10.1907
Philip Arthur Whitcombe *1948*	Kensington	23. 4.1923	
Luke Robert White *1946–1947*	Marylebone	15. 3.1927	
Robert Arthur White *1958–1965*	Fulham	6.10.1936	
Roger Frank White *1964–1966*	Perivale	22.11.1943	
Sidney Grayling White *1921–1923*	Staines	1892	1. 5.1949
William Harold Wignall *1934–1936*	Hendon	24.12.1908	4.1982
Anthony John Anstruther Wilkinson *1864–1874*	Mount Oswald	28. 5.1835	11.12.1905

William O'Brien Camac Wilkinson *1881–1882*	Sydney, Austr	15. 9.1857	2. 2.1946
Herbert Scott Williams *1890*	Woolland, Dorset	4. 9.1860	30.11.1942
Neil Fitzgerald Williams *1982–1987*	Hopewell, WI	2. 7.1962	
William Williams *1885–1902*		12. 4.1861	14. 4.1951
Arthur Edward Wilson *1932–1933*	Paddington	18. 5.1910	
T. Wilson *1880*			
Arthur Henry Winter *1866–1867*	Clapton	4.12.1844	31.12.1937
Gerald Esdaile Winter *1900*	London	29.11.1876	17. 1.1923
William Winter *1873*	Clapham Green	24. 4.1843	22. 8.1905
Frederick Winterburn *1883*	East London	10.12.1857	21. 4.1926
John Wisden *1859–1863*	Brighton	5. 9.1826	5. 4.1884
John Wormald *1910–1912*	Mayfair	23. 2.1882	13.11.1957
Harold Douglas Wyatt *1905–1909*	Enfield	12. 1.1880	24.11.1949
Hugh James Wyld *1900–1901*	Kensington	16. 4.1880	9.12.1961
John Albert Young *1933–1956*	Paddington	14.10.1912	

GROUNDS USED BY THE COUNTY

			First-class Record				
	First	*Last*	*P*	*W*	*L*	*D*	*T*
Lord's	1850	1987	1120	450	270	399	1
Southgate	1859	1859	1	1	0	0	0
Caledonian Road, Islington	1864	1868	16	10	4	2	0
Lillie Bridge, West Brompton	1871	1871	1	0	0	1	0
Prince's	1872	1876	18	3	10	5	0
Chiswick Park	1887	1887	1	0	1	0	0
Hornsey	1959	1959	1	0	1	0	0
Uxbridge	1980	1987	15	8	2	5	0
Enfield	1 NWB match only in 1982						

NOTES:

1. The home game *v* Surrey in 1870 was played at The Oval because the West Brompton ground was unfit (Middlesex lost).

2. The home game *v* Nottinghamshire in 1939 was played at The Oval because Lord's was required for the Eton *v* Harrow match (Middlesex lost).

3. The home game *v* Somerset in 1977 was played at Chelmsford as Lord's was being prepared for the Gillette Cup Final. The game had been postponed in order to play the Gillette Cup semi-final which had not been played on the proposed dates due to rain (match drawn).

4. Middlesex have played several matches against MCC at Lord's which are regarded as 'away' matches and so not included above.

5. Gentlemen of Middlesex *v* Gentlemen of England at Islington 1865 is excluded.

CAREER RECORDS OF MIDDLESEX PLAYERS IN FIRST-CLASS GAMES FOR THE COUNTY

Name	Inns	NO	Runs	HS	Avge	100s	Runs	Wkts	Avge	Best	5wI
Abbey D. R.	2	0	14	12	7.00	0	23	0	—	—	0
Ahsan-Ul-Haq	5	0	54	25	10.80	0	19	0	—	—	0
Alexander F. R.	3	0	15	8	5.00	0	—	—	—	—	—
Alldis J. S.	4	1	7	4*	2.33	0	37	1	37.00	1/33	0
Allen G. O. B.	210	28	4667	155	25.64	4	8668	420	20.63	10/40	27
Anderson W. B.	2	0	2	2	1.00	0	—	—	—	—	—
Angus T.	11	5	49	18*	8.16	0	353	23	15.34	4/81	0
Anson R.	43	4	849	97	21.76	0	228	10	22.80	5/59	1
Arden-Davis R.	2	0	14	14	7.00	0	—	—	—	—	—
Ashmore W. S.	3	3	18	15*	—	0	115	3	38.33	2/37	0
Atkinson B. G. W.	15	0	268	95	17.86	0	648	18	36.00	4/97	0
Atkinson G. B.	4	1	4	2*	1.33	0	24	0	—	—	0
Atkinson N. S. M.	2	0	41	39	20.50	0	147	12	12.25	5/16	1
Atkinson-Clark J. C.	12	0	116	66	9.66	0	13	1	13.00	1/13	0
Bacmeister L. H.	14	4	50	15	5.00	0	557	23	24.30	4/41	0
Baily E. P.	2	0	7	4	3.50	0	—	—	—	—	—
Baker C. V.	46	5	586	53	14.29	0	—	—	—	—	—
Baker G. D.	2	0	5	5	2.50	0	—	—	—	—	—
Baldry D. O.	84	5	1155	61	14.62	0	342	11	31.09	4/60	0
Barlow G. D.	385	57	11640	177	35.48	23	66	3	22.00	1/6	0
Barnardo F. F. T.	1	0	0	0	0.00	0	—	—	—	—	—
Barton R.	2	0	11	6	5.50	0	—	—	—	—	—
Bashford A. M.	4	0	27	14	6.75	0	29	1	27.00	1/12	0
Bastow J.	10	2	118	35	14.75	0	—	—	—	—	—
Bates H. A.	3	0	18	10	6.00	0	—	—	—	—	—
Bates J.	2	0	9	8	4.50	0	—	—	—	—	—
Bathurst L. C. V.	13	2	67	36	6.09	0	265	17	15.58	6/20	2
Baxter A. D.	4	2	17	7	8.50	0	232	5	16.40	3/80	0
Bayford R. A.	7	0	190	92	27.14	0	2	1	2.00	1/2	0
Bedford P. I.	64	18	722	75	15.69	0	3370	103	32.71	6/52	4
Beldam C. A.	4	2	34	12	17.00	0	.14	1	14.00	1/14	0
Beldam E. A.	61	5	1133	105	20.23	1	—	—	—	—	—
Beldam G. W.	172	13	4796	155*	30.16	7	2063	76	27.14	5/28	3
Bell R. V.	5	2	24	17	8.00	0	498	15	33.20	5/80	1
Benka H. F.	19	1	292	58*	16.22	0	200	5	40.00	2/44	0
Bennett C. T.	4	0	48	17	12.00	0	—	—	—	—	—

Name	Inns	NO	Runs	HS	Avge	100s	Runs	Wkts	Avge	Best	5wI
Bennett D.	590	120	10274	117*	21.85	4	19790	748	26.45	7/47	22
Benthall W. H.	12	1	201	46	18.27	0	19	0	—	—	0
Bentley C.	2	0	0	0	0.00	0	—	—	—	—	—
Benton W. M.	3	1	25	19*	12.50	0	—	—	—	—	—
Beresford S. R. D. H.	3	0	22	13	7.33	0	—	—	—	—	—
Berners J. A.	2	0	5	5	2.50	0	—	—	—	—	—
Beton S. L.	46	10	688	49	19.11	0	—	—	—	—	—
Bettington R. H. B.	23	3	605	95	30.25	0	1590	54	29.44	6/76	2
Betts M. P.	2	1	39	25*	39.00	0	—	—	—	—	—
Beveridge R.	57	19	352	49	9.26	0	1350	41	32.92	6/66	2
Bevington J. C.	2	0	8	6	4.00	0	—	—	—	—	—
Bevington T. A. D.	7	1	81	32*	13.50	0	69	3	23.00	3/21	0
Bick D. A.	189	31	2136	67	13.51	0	6328	229	27.63	5/22	5
Birch W.	4	1	6	4	2.00	0	95	2	47.50	2/28	0
Bird G.	23	2	223	31	10.61	0	—	—	—	—	—
Bird W. S.	17	2	154	57	10.26	0	—	—	—	—	—
Bishop A. T.	2	2	0	0*	—	0	76	2	38.00	2/72	0
Black C. J. R.	26	1	400	71	16.00	0	649	13	49.92	3/51	0
Bligh E. V.	2	1	11	11	11.00	0	—	—	—	—	—
Boak J.	2	0	19	11	9.50	0	37	1	37.00	1/20	0
Borrowes, K. D.	7	0	39	20	5.57	0	—	—	—	—	—
Bosanquet B. J. T.	200	13	6593	179	35.25	13	7271	268	27.13	8/53	19
Bowstead J.	2	0	21	16	10.50	0	—	—	—	—	—
Box J. W.	7	1	33	17	5.50	0	—	—	—	—	—
Bray E. H.	30	3	252	39	9.33	0	—	—	—	—	—
Brearley H.	4	0	55	24	13.75	0	—	—	—	—	—
Brearley J. M.	485	68	15985	173*	38.33	29	119	1	119.00	1/6	0
Bromley-Davenport H. R.	46	7	739	69*	18.94	0	603	15	40.20	3/20	0
Brooks P. W.	1	1	44	44*	—	0	—	—	—	—	—
Brown G. K.	2	0	17	14	8.50	0	—	—	—	—	—
Brown K. R.	52	7	1250	102	27.77	1	64	3	21.33	2/7	0
Brown S. M.	549	39	15050	232	29.50	20	80	3	26.66	2/19	0
Browne G. F.	1	0	8	8	8.00	0	—	—	—	—	—
Bruce C. N.	100	8	2959	149	32.16	3	—	—	—	—	—
Brune C. J.	33	6	354	41	13.11	0	755	34	22.20	6/66	2
Bryan F.	2	0	0	0	0.00	0	—	—	—	—	—
Bryant H. W.	12	3	71	38	7.88	0	—	—	—	—	—
Buckland E. H.	15	0	254	51	16.93	0	499	27	18.48	5/15	1

327

Name	Inns	NO	Runs	HS	Avge	100s	Runs	Wkts	Avge	Best	5wI
Buckland F. M.	10	1	153	36*	17.00	0	339	15	22.60	4/39	0
Buller C. F.	44	4	870	105*	21.75	1	32	0	—	—	0
Bulpett C. W. L.	2	0	13	13	6.50	0	61	1	61.00	1/35	0
Bunting W. H.	6	1	2	2*	1.20	0	107	0	—	—	0
Burden W.	2	0	15	11	7.50	0	—	—	—	—	—
Burge G. R.	2	0	1	1	0.50	0	58	5	11.60	5/46	1
Burghes A.	11	1	245	104	24.50	1	82	0	—	—	0
Burton G.	176	54	946	34	7.75	0	9079	529	17.16	10/59	43
Burton G. C.	2	0	1	1	0.50	0	—	—	—	—	—
Burtt L. L.	4	1	78	50	26.00	0	9	1	9.00	1/8	0
Butcher R. O.	330	31	9537	197	31.89	15	159	4	39.75	2/37	0
Butler E. M.	4	1	37	17*	12.33	0	—	—	—	—	—
Butterworth J. C.	2	0	17	13	8.50	0	—	—	—	—	—
Butterworth R. E. C.	23	0	379	59	16.47	0	242	10	24.20	3/11	0
Buxton R. V.	18	1	344	76	20.23	0	15	0	—	—	—
Calvert C.	12	1	171	33	15.54	0	30	1	30.00	1/30	0
Campbell J. M.	2	0	2	2	1.00	0	—	—	—	—	—
Canning E. G.	60	7	791	85	14.92	0	—	—	—	—	—
Caple R. G.	2	1	29	17	29.00	0	131	3	43.66	2/46	0
Carr J. D.	77	10	2347	156	35.02	3	609	16	38.06	6/61	1
Carris B. D.	20	1	283	65	14.89	0	60	0	—	—	0
Carris H. E.	58	2	1039	72	18.55	0	44	2	22.00	1/5	0
Case T.	19	1	432	116	24.00	1	—	—	—	—	—
Cater C. A.	4	0	22	20	5.50	0	—	—	—	—	—
Catling W.	12	7	53	24*	10.60	0	150	18	8.33	5/29	1
Chalkley J.	3	1	40	30	20.00	0	—	—	—	—	—
Childs-Clarke A. W.	16	3	258	58*	19.84	0	280	7	40.00	2/72	0
Chinnery H. B.	14	0	288	100	20.57	1	31	0	—	—	0
Chisolm J. R.	2	0	14	12	7.00	0	33	1	33.00	1/15	0
Clark E. A.	332	39	8595	149	29.33	6	1822	58	31.41	5/61	2
Clarke P.	13	4	47	13*	5.22	0	563	20	28.15	4/52	0
Clarke W. B.	33	9	182	33	7.58	0	1317	68	19.36	7/51	6
Clifford F. L.	2	2	0	0*	—	0	7	0	—	—	0
Clifton E. G.	29	16	128	25	9.84	0	—	—	—	—	—
Cobb H. H.	14	4	157	55*	15.70	0	—	—	—	—	—
Colbeck L. G.	20	2	134	46	7.44	0	—	—	—	—	—
Cole A.	4	0	36	21	9.00	0	40	3	13.33	3/29	0
Cole W.	2	1	6	6*	6.00	0	—	—	—	—	—
Collins W. R.	2	0	0	0	0.00	0	—	—	—	—	—
Collinson J.	4	0	85	34	21.25	0	—	—	—	—	—
Compton D. C. S.	485	49	21781	252*	49.95	67	14124	477	29.61	6/63	16

Name	Inns	NO	Runs	HS	Avge	100s	Runs	Wkts	Avge	Best	5wI
Compton L. H.	389	46	5781	107	16.85	1	569	12	47.41	2/21	0
Connaughton J. M. F.	1	1	16	16★	—	0	39	3	13.00	3/19	0
Connolly A. N.	44	14	180	26	6.00	0	3320	126	26.34	6/39	6
Coode A. T.	1	0	4	4	4.00	0	—	—	—	—	—
Cook C. R.	18	2	393	79	24.56	0	—	—	—	—	—
Cooper B. B.	11	1	366	89	36.60	0	—	—	—	—	—
Cooper R. S.	12	1	216	54	19.63	0	—	—	—	—	—
Cordaroy T. M.	3	0	104	81	34.66	0	—	—	—	—	—
Cornish H. H.	2	0	7	6	3.50	0	27	0	—	—	0
Cottrell C. E.	24	2	287	46	13.04	0	951	37	25.70	5/68	2
Covington F. E.	9	2	142	83	20.28	0	—	—	—	—	—
Cowans N. G.	95	17	771	66	9.88	0	6447	301	21.41	6/31	14
Coxhead M. E.	2	0	6	6	3.00	0	15	1	15.00	1/9	0
Craven T.	4	0	10	4	2.50	0	—	1	—	—	0
Crawley C. S.	1	0	0	0	0.00	0	—	—	—	—	—
Crosdale G.	4	2	30	17★	15.00	0	—	—	—	—	—
Crutchley E.	4	0	28	14	7.00	0	—	—	—	—	—
Crutchley G. E. V.	86	8	1384	145	17.74	2	477	19	25.10	2/5	0
Cuming T.	2	0	17	16	8.50	0	—	—	—	—	—
Cunliffe, F. H. E.	24	4	275	62	13.75	0	1068	36	29.66	5/99	1
Cuthbertson G. B.	25	3	235	58	10.68	0	—	—	—	—	—
Dale J. W.	14	0	166	41	11.85	0	13	0	—	—	0
Dales H. L.	173	13	4297	143	26.85	8	188	4	47.00	2/28	0
Dalmeny Lord A. E. H. M. A.	3	0	49	22	16.33	0	7	0	—	—	0
Dalmevy Lord A. R.	2	0	29	29	14.50	0	26	0	—	—	0
Daly A. R.	1	0	0	0	0.00	0	26	1	26.00	1/26	0
Daniel A. W. T.	25	1	597	87	24.87	0	12	0	—	—	0
Daniel W. W.	185	86	1043	53★	10.53	0	15052	683	22.03	9/61	22
Dauglish M. J.	15	3	102	46★	8.50	0	13	0	—	—	0
Day K. B.	—	—	—	—	—	—	—	—	—	—	—
Delisle G. P. S.	99	9	1935	130	21.50	2	—	—	—	—	—
Deller R. P.	3	3	4	3★	—	0	127	2	63.50	1/35	0
De Paravicini P. J.	101	12	1306	77	14.67	0	433	11	39.36	3/27	0
Devereux L. N.	2	0	43	32	21.50	0	—	—	—	—	—
Dewes J. G.	102	8	3589	139	38.18	10	10	1	10.00	1/0	0
Diver A. J. D.	2	0	31	19	15.50	0	—	—	—	—	—
Dixon J. T.	2	0	7	7	3.50	0	22	0	—	—	0
Doggart A. G.	4	1	96	38	32.00	0	111	2	55.50	1/23	0

Name	Inns	NO	Runs	HS	Avge	100s	Runs	Wkts	Avge	Best	5wI
Dolding D. L.	1	1	0	0★	—	0	—	—	—	—	—
Doll M. H. C.	32	4	488	102★	17.42	1	191	1	191.00	1/40	0
Donnelly M. P.	2	0	39	25	19.50	0	5	0	—	—	0
Douglas A. P.	2	0	38	34	19.00	0	—	—	—	—	—
Douglas J.	277	20	7669	204	29.84	13	672	17	39.52	5/98	1
Douglas R. N.	68	6	1390	93	22.41	0	—	—	—	—	—
Douglas S.	2	0	30	16	15.00	0	—	—	—	—	—
Downton P. R.	208	43	5012	126★	30.37	4	5	0	—	—	0
Drybrough C. D.	94	33	929	59★	15.22	0	5722	206	27.77	7/94	7
Dunglass Lord A. F.	3	0	23	19	7.66	0	81	4	20.25	2/23	0
Dunkley F. J.	21	4	58	11	3.41	0	1170	49	23.87	6/42	4
Durlacher P. N.	4	0	43	27	10.75	0	—	—	—	—	—
Durston F. J.	434	127	3569	92★	11.62	0	25877	1178	21.96	8/27	65
Eaglestone J. T.	17	0	247	61	14.52	0	—	—	—	—	—
Ebden C. H. M.	4	0	49	34	12.25	0	—	—	—	—	—
Edmonds P. H.	311	57	5037	142	19.83	2	20755	879	23.61	8/53	39
Edrich W. J.	658	65	25738	267★	43.40	62	9975	328	30.41	7/48	10
Edwards P. G.	5	2	12	10	4.00	0	140	1	140.00	1/35	0
Ellis R. G. P.	19	0	318	55	16.73	0	—	—	—	—	—
Emburey J. E.	269	56	4987	133	23.41	2	16943	738	22.95	7/36	38
Enthoven H. J.	190	18	4478	139	26.03	6	3927	100	39.27	5/29	2
Etheridge S. G.	12	2	81	22	8.10	0	—	—	—	—	—
Etherington M. W.	4	1	23	14	7.66	0	114	5	22.80	3/23	1
Fairbairn A.	32	4	728	110★	26.00	2	2	0	—	—	0
Fairbairn G. A.	6	0	144	72	24.00	0	369	12	30.75	5/154	1
Fairservice C.	8	0	97	41	12.12	0	19	0	—	—	0
Featherstone N. G.	344	34	8882	147	28.65	8	3477	137	25.37	5/32	3
Felton R.	18	0	496	171	27.55	1	121	2	60.50	1/4	0
Field E.	10	1	234	107★	26.00	1	—	—	—	—	—
Figg G.	2	1	0	0★	0.00	0	—	—	—	—	—
Fisher P. B.	2	0	6	6	3.00	0	—	—	—	—	—
Fitzgerald R. A.	1	0	0	0	0.00	0	—	—	—	—	—
Flanagan M.	27	9	85	14	4.72	0	936	52	18.00	6/76	1
Foley C. P.	94	10	1258	72	14.97	0	26	1	26.00	1/14	0
Ford A. F. J.	27	3	280	45	12.66	0	1336	95	14.06	7/32	7
Ford F. C. J.	168	7	4650	160	28.88	10	2191	87	25.18	6/56	2
Ford N. M.	2	0	11	11	5.50	0	—	—	—	—	—
Ford W. J.	12	0	245	75	20.41	0	56	2	28.00	1/15	0
Foster B. S.	15	1	157	35	11.21	0	—	—	—	—	—
Fowler A. J. B.	32	13	133	21	7.00	0	1097	41	26.75	5/29	1

Name	Inns	NO	Runs	HS	Avge	100s	Runs	Wkts	Avge	Best	5wI
Fox T. S.	—	—	—	—	—	—	—	—	—	—	—
Francis A. S.	4	0	81	26	20.25	0	—	—	—	—	—
Francis C. K.	15	2	104	45	8.00	0	829	31	26.74	4/44	0
Franics F. P.	1	0	0	0	0.00	0	—	—	—	—	—
Fraser A. G. J.	3	2	32	19★	32.00	0	165	8	20.62	3/46	0
Fraser A. R. C.	29	6	215	38	9.34	0	2033	63	32.26	4/48	0
Frederick J. S.	1	0	9	9	9.00	0	—	—	—	—	—
Gale R. A.	398	12	11234	200	29.10	13	1525	46	33.15	4/57	0
Gatting M. W.	307	48	12794	258	49.39	33	2808	114	24.63	5/34	2
Gilbert G. H. B.	4	0	40	17	10.00	0	—	4	—	4/?	0
Gilbert W. R.	16	1	261	49	17.40	0	66	2	33.00	2/47	0
Gilby W.	2	1	9	5★	9.00	0	84	2	42.00	2/70	0
Gilman J.	8	1	100	34	14.28	0	—	—	—	—	—
Gold C. A.	2	1	0	0★	0.00	0	—	—	—	—	—
Gomes H. A.	63	9	1199	93★	22.20	0	923	23	40.13	4/22	0
Gordon C.	6	0	41	19	6.83	0	—	—	—	—	—
Gordon-Lennox B. C.	1	0	0	0	0.00	0	—	—	—	—	—
Gould I. J.	119	18	2109	128	20.88	1	1	0	—	—	0
Goulding W.	4	1	14	6	4.66	0	—	—	—	—	—
Gray C. D.	25	1	563	81	23.45	0	30	2	15.00	2/7	0
Gray L. H.	233	119	772	32	7.42	0	14485	600	24.14	8/59	26
Greatorex T.	10	1	84	44★	9.33	0	—	—	—	—	—
Green C. E.	59	2	859	65	15.07	0	88	3	29.33	2/27	0
Green J. J.	1	0	3	3	3.00	0	129	2	64.50	2/97	0
Gregory J. C.	5	0	108	39	21.60	0	—	—	—	—	—
Griffin A. W. M. S.	2	0	2	2	1.00	0	56	0	—	—	0
Griffiths G. S. F..	22	2	372	88★	18.60	0	—	—	—	—	—
Griffiths A. S.	4	1	43	26	14.33	0	—	—	—	—	—
Grimston R.	6	0	35	11	5.83	0	—	—	—	—	—
Guise J. L.	90	8	1840	127	22.43	2	700	25	28.00	4/20	0
Gunasekera C. H.	55	11	644	88★	14.63	0	2160	75	28.80	5/15	4
Hadow A. A.	2	0	27	18	13.50	0	24	2	12.00	2/24	0
Hadow E. M.	94	8	1280	56	14.88	0	917	37	24.78	4/24	0
Hadow P. F.	8	1	101	37	14.42	0	—	—	—	—	—
Hadow W. H.	67	4	1436	217	22.79	2	1462	103	14.19	8/35	9
Haig N. E.	630	39	12289	131	20.79	11	24264	931	26.06	7/33	41
Haines J. A.	4	0	13	5	3.25	0	—	—	—	—	—
Hake G. J. G.	1	0	2	2	2.00	0	84	1	84.00	1/84	0
Hale P. W.	2	0	29	26	14.50	0	—	—	—	—	—
Hale W. S.	7	1	77	36	12.83	0	—	—	—	—	—
Hall C.	2	0	12	7	6.00	0	—	—	—	—	—

Name	Inns	NO	Runs	HS	Avge	100s	Runs	Wkts	Avge	Best	5wI
Halliwell E. A.	I	O	I	I	1.00	O	—	—	—	—	—
Halliwell R. B.	28	4	332	38*	13.83	O	—	—	—	—	—
Harper K. B.	5	O	31	28	6.20	O	—	—	—	—	—
Harrington W. J. R.	14	2	108	45	9.00	O	317	13	24.33	6/57	I
Harris M. J.	121	14	3371	160	31.50	6	85	2	42.50	1/4	O
Harrison W. P.	45	5	953	156	23.82	I	71	I	71.00	1/34	O
Hart G. E.	304	31	5711	121	20.91	4	1082	21	51.52	3/64	O
Harvey C. M.	I	O	36	36	36.00	O	—	—	—	—	—
Harvey E.	2	O	O	O	0.00	O	—	—	—	—	—
Haslip S. M.	5	O	41	13	8.20	O	275	12	22.91	3/12	O
Hawkins F. A.	2	I	19	19	19.00	O	—	—	—	—	—
Haycraft J. S.	2	O	5	5	2.50	O	—	—	—	—	—
Haygarth A.	6	I	36	20*	7.20	O	—	—	—	—	—
Hayman H. B.	154	11	3593	152	25.12	3	75	2	37.50	2/19	O
Hayward D. R.	I	O	2	2	2.00	O	5	I	5.00	1/5	O
Head J. R.	8	I	82	43	11.71	O	—	—	—	—	—
Headlam C.	14	4	171	44	17.10	O	—	—	—	—	—
Hearne G.	29	5	481	72	20.04	O	—	—	—	—	—
Hearne J. T.	630	223	4598	65	11.29	O	38167	2093	18.23	9/32	171
Hearne J. W.	744	73	27612	285*	41.15	71	33291	1438	23.15	9/61	88
Hearne T.	96	5	1799	146	19.176	2	2836	2048	14.10	6/12	12
Hearne T. J.	—	—	—	—	—	—	—	—	—	—	—
Heath A. H.	2	I	4	4*	4.00	O	7	O	—	—	O
Hebden G. L.	44	7	677	101	18.29	I	96	O	—	—	O
Hebert M. C.	2	O	14	14	7.00	O	35	3	11.66	2/25	O
Henderson R.	28	3	243	28	9.72	O	1833	97	18.89	7/100	10
Hendren D.	16	2	109	23	7.78	O	104	3	34.66	1/19	O
Hendren E. H.	928	119	40302	301*	49.81	119	2065	39	52.94	5/43	I
Henery P. J. T.	114	9	1495	81*	14.23	O	190	11	17.27	5/56	I
Henley F. A. H.	5	O	33	11	6.60	O	229	3	76.33	2/93	O
Henry F.	2	I	5	5*	5.00	O	52	2	26.00	2/16	O
Herbert A. W. H.	2	I	21	19*	21.00	O	—	—	—	—	—
Herbert H. H. M.	2	I	I	I	1.00	O	—	—	—	—	—
Herkes R.	5	3	O	0*	0.00	O	93	6	15.83	6/60	I
Herman R. S.	83	28	453	40*	8.23	O	5754	196	29.35	6/32	4
Hever N. G.	10	7	19	8*	6.33	O	448	14	32.00	5/26	I
Hickley A. N.	2	O	27	22	13.50	O	—	—	—	—	—
Hickson J. A. E.	3	I	O	0*	0.00	O	—	—	—	—	—
Higginson T. W.	3	2	30	15*	30.00	O	24	I	24.00	1/24	O
Hill R. H.	56	4	832	71	16.00	O	—	—	—	—	—
Hillyard G. W.	5	2	11	6	3.66	O	51	I	51.00	1/20	O
Hoare, C. T.	2	O	I	I	0.50	O	—	—	—	—	—

Name	Inns	NO	Runs	HS	Avge	100s	Runs	Wkts	Avge	Best	5wI
Hodgkinson G. L.	1	0	22	22	22.00	0	—	—	—	—	—
Holdship W. E. J.	5	0	21	15	4.20	0	—	—	—	—	—
Hooker R. W.	442	71	8222	137	22.16	5	13957	490	27.46	7/18	16
Hopkins J. D.	5	0	8	4	1.60	0	—	—	—	—	—
Horncastle W. A.	2	0	11	8	5.50	0	72	3	24.00	2/39	0
Hornsby J. H. J.	2	0	4	4	2.00	0	14	0	—	—	0
Horton W. H. F. K.	3	0	10	8	3.33	0	—	—	—	—	—
Hotchkin N. S.	8	2	107	41*	12.83	0	—	—	—	—	—
Howard C. G.	6	0	25	12	4.16	0	—	—	—	—	—
Howard C. W. H.	12	2	123	29	12.30	0	—	—	—	—	—
Howitt G.	72	19	322	49	6.07	0	3397	213	15.94	7/38	17
Hughes S. P.	111	38	815	47	11.16	0	8060	283	28.55	7/35	8
Hulme J. H. A.	346	45	8015	143	26.62	12	3223	89	36.21	4/44	0
Human J. H.	63	3	1703	144	28.38	3	155	3	51.66	1/9	0
Hunt J. H. S.	68	6	1256	76*	20.25	0	1915	72	26.59	5/60	2
Hunt R. N.	10	3	138	81*	19.71	0	453	5	90.60	3/32	0
Hurst R. J.	123	53	635	62	9.07	0	5948	245	24.27	8/65	6
Hutchings G. W.	2	0	9	7	4.50	0	25	0	—	—	—
Ingram E.	19	3	177	28	11.06	0	815	26	31.34	3/7	0
James K. D.	13	4	193	34	21.44	0	399	20	19.95	5/28	1
Jardine M. R.	9	1	102	32*	12.75	0	—	—	—	—	—
Johnston A. S.	6	1	24	10	4.80	0	—	—	—	—	—
Jones A. A.	50	12	193	33	5.07	0	3421	135	25.34	6/89	6
Jones K. V.	155	37	2031	57*	17.21	0	6519	241	27.04	7/52	7
Judge P. F.	14	7	76	19*	10.85	0	521	21	24.80	5/27	2
Jupp G. H.	12	0	132	47	11.00	0	—	—	—	—	—
Kamm A.	2	0	3	2	1.50	0	—	—	—	—	—
Kaye H. W.	5	0	117	76	23.40	0	—	—	—	—	—
Kemp A. L.	3	0	10	6	3.33	0	13	0	—	—	0
Kemp N. J.	6	2	121	46*	30.25	0	180	4	45.00	2/53	0
Kemp P. H.	2	0	43	38	21.50	0	—	—	—	—	—
Kent H. N.	2	0	0	0	0.00	0	29	1	21.00	1/13	0
Kidd E. L.	104	77	1848	150*	19.05	2	1053	44	23.93	4/39	0
Killick E. T.	71	6	2338	206	35.96	5	31	0	—	—	0
King H. D.	9	1	69	26	8.62	0	—	—	—	—	—
Kinkead-Weekes R. C.	1	1	4	4*	—	0	—	—	—	—	—
Knapp J. W.	1	0	3	3	3.00	0	—	—	—	—	—
Knightley-Smith W.	47	2	863	64	19.17	0	72	0	—	—	0
Kynaston R.	4	0	71	37	17.75	0	—	—	—	—	—
Lamb T. M.	44	13	548	77	17.67	0	2031	67	30.31	6/49	4

Name	Inns	NO	Runs	HS	Avge	100s	Runs	Wkts	Avge	Best	5wI
Lambert W.	14	3	112	34*	10.18	0	54	1	54.00	1/14	0
Langley J. D. A.	2	0	5	5	2.50	0	—	—	—	—	—
Latchman A. H.	183	49	1950	96	14.55	0	11032	400	27.58	7/91	18
Law G.	4	0	51	19	12.75	0	—	—	—	—	—
Lawrence C.	1	0	78	78	78.00	0	86	10	8.60	5/38	2
Lawrence P. J.	4	1	19	14*	6.33	0	186	6	31.00	3/52	0
Laws M. L.	6	2	7	3	1.75	0	—	—	—	—	—
Lee F.	6	0	64	25	10.66	0	18	1	18.00	1/8	0
Lee F. S.	3	1	57	42	28.50	0	29	0	—	—	0
Lee, H. W.	666	45	18594	243*	29.94	35	11064	340	32.54	8/39	7
Lee, J. W.	1	0	0	0	0.00	0	46	0	—	—	0
Leslie C. F. H.	35	2	482	141	14.60	1	29	3	9.66	2/15	0
Lester E.	11	4	41	13	5.85	0	10	0	—	—	0
Lewis R. P.	3	1	11	9	5.50	0	—	—	—	—	—
Lillywhite F. W.	6	3	11	6	3.66	0	—	11	—	6/?	1
Lillywhite James	4	1	9	5	3.00	0	—	5	—	3/?	0
Lillywhite John	8	1	143	28	20.42	0	69	1	69.00	1/46	0
Ling D. J.	15	3	174	40	14.50	0	386	7	55.14	3/24	0
Litteljohn A. R.	41	8	621	76*	18.81	0	1593	78	20.42	8/69	7
Litteljohn E. S.	120	9	2832	141*	25.51	5	25	1	25.00	1/11	0
Livock G. E.	6	2	110	38	27.50	0	—	—	—	—	—
Longman H. K.	19	2	336	66	19.76	0	—	—	—	—	—
Lord W. F.	3	2	8	8	8.00	0	177	3	59.00	3/50	0
Love G. R. S.	2	0	2	2	1.00	0	39	0	—	—	0
Lowles G. W.	2	0	3	3	1.50	0	—	—	—	—	—
Lucas A. C.	4	0	40	16	10.00	0	—	—	—	—	—
Lucas A. P.	21	3	400	97	22.22	0	97	2	48.50	1/17	0
Lucas C. J.	5	0	46	24	9.20	0	23	0	—	—	0
Lucas R. S.	120	7	2055	185	18.18	1	171	1	57.00	2/44	0
Lyttelton A.	61	2	1656	181	28.06	3	74	0	—	—	0
Lyttelton E.	24	4	518	113	25.90	1	6	0	—	—	0
McCaskie N.	4	0	30	26	7.50	0	—	—	—	—	—
McCorquodale A.	3	0	22	21	7.33	0	292	3	97.33	2/62	0
McCulloch J. W. H.	3	0	18	14	6.00	0	—	—	—	—	—
McEwen J. W.	5	0	13	8	2.60	0	126	4	31.50	3/37	0
MacGregor G.	286	39	4846	141	19.61	2	—	—	—	—	—
Magnay C. B. W.	4	0	17	9	4.25	0	2	0	—	—	—
Malcolm H. J. J.	6	1	139	76*	27.80	0	6	0	—	—	—
Manasseh M.	8	2	128	29	21.33	0	111	3	37.00	2/11	0
Mann F. G.	147	9	3403	116	24.65	3	45	2	22.50	2/16	0
Mann F. T.	472	39	10656	174	24.60	8	172	2	86.00	1/15	0
Mann J. P.	23	1	419	77	19.05	0	42	1	42.00	1/42	0

Name	Inns	NO	Runs	HS	Avge	100s	Runs	Wkts	Avge	Best	5wI
Mantle T. A.	40	3	458	46	12.37	0	582	27	21.55	4/30	0
Marks G.	4	2	31	17	15.50	0	—	—	—	—	—
Marriott D. A.	13	7	51	12	8.50	0	746	24	31.08	5/71	1
Marsden E. L.	1	0	3	3	3.00	0	68	1	68.00	1/45	0
Marshall C.	2	0	83	50	41.50	0	—	—	—	—	—
Martin E.	25	4	325	63	15.47	0	—	—	—	—	—
Martin M. T.	2	0	15	12	7.50	0	—	—	—	—	—
Maru, R. J.	16	3	147	25	11.30	0	766	23	33.30	4/30	0
Massey J. A.	1	0	17	17	17.00	0	—	—	—	—	—
Maturin H.	2	0	9	6	4.50	0	—	2	—	2/?	0
Maude F. W.	4	0	18	12	4.50	0	33	0	—	—	0
Maxwell C. R. N.	7	0	52	26	7.42	0	—	—	—	—	—
Mayo J. P.	2	0	1	1	0.50	0	—	—	—	—	—
Melluish M. E. L.	2	0	4	3	2.00	0	—	—	—	—	—
Menzies H.	7	3	47	18*	11.75	0	—	—	—	—	—
Merry W. G.	16	10	42	14*	7.00	0	1447	45	32.15	4/24	0
Metson C. P.	31	9	426	96	19.36	0	—	—	—	—	—
Mignon E.	186	70	977	34	8.42	0	10658	410	25.99	7/28	27
Miller A. J. T.	69	7	1916	111*	30.90	1	10	0	—	—	0
Mills H. M.	2	0	10	10	5.00	0	—	—	—	—	—
Milton H. A.	5	0	52	45	10.40	0	—	—	—	—	—
Moffat D.	1	0	25	25	25.00	0	—	—	—	—	—
Moffat N. J. D.	19	4	312	55*	20.80	0	—	—	—	—	—
Monteith J. D.	13	2	98	36	8.90	0	614	24	25.58	5/60	2
Moon L. J.	104	7	2616	135	26.96	5	24	0	—	—	0
Moon W. R.	1	1	17	17*	—	0	—	—	—	—	—
Mordaunt E. C.	7	0	16	11	2.28	0	22	1	22.00	1/14	0
Mordaunt H. J.	13	0	81	17	6.23	0	212	6	35.33	2/32	0
More R. E.	56	8	1010	120*	21.04	2	1703	55	30.96	4/55	0
Morley J. H.	2	1	25	19	25.00	0	—	—	—	—	—
Morton G. D.	3	2	1	1	1.00	0	97	0	—	—	0
Moss A. E.	329	141	1234	40	6.56	0	21556	1088	19.81	8/31	59
Moulding R. P.	1	1	26	26*	—	0	—	—	—	—	—
Mumford G.	4	0	4	2	1.00	0	39	1	39.00	1/6	0
Muncer B. L.	127	17	1944	85	17.67	0	648	23	28.17	3/11	0
Munt H. R.	—	—	—	—	—	—	28	1	28.00	1/28	0
Murray J. T.	761	105	15251	133*	23.24	11	134	4	33.50	1/1	0
Murray M. P.	10	1	149	44	16.55	0	3	0	—	—	0
Murrell H. R.	467	58	6033	96*	14.75	0	44	0	—	—	0
Napier G. G.	33	4	292	25	10.07	0	1327	54	24.57	7/68	1
Needham A.	12	3	164	33	18.22	0	545	12	45.41	4/96	0
Nelson R. P.	14	0	192	81	13.71	0	48	1	48.00	1/15	0
Nepean A. A. S. M.	5	1	61	19	15.25	0	53	1	53.00	1/24	0

Name	Inns	NO	Runs	HS	Avge	100s	Runs	Wkts	Avge	Best	5wI
Nepean C. E. B.	4	0	31	25	7.75	0	—	—	—	—	—
Nepean E. A.	78	12	1481	71	22.43	0	3059	161	19.00	8/48	8
Nevell W. T.	21	4	173	32*	10.17	0	677	24	28.20	3/38	0
Nevinson J. H.	9	5	6	3	1.50	0	369	4	92.25	2/20	0
Newman D. L.	17	1	238	29	14.87	0	—	—	—	—	—
Newman G. C.	80	7	1780	112	24.38	3	299	10	29.90	3/48	0
Newton S. C.	6	0	32	16	5.33	0	—	—	—	—	—
Nicholl K. I.	3	0	0	0	0.00	0	—	—	—	—	—
Nicholls R. W.	99	10	1487	154	16.70	1	—	—	—	—	—
Nicholson W.	8	0	65	19	8.12	0	—	—	—	—	—
Nixon G. T. S.	6	0	71	54	11.83	0	—	—	—	—	—
North E. J.	28	7	215	80	10.23	0	1198	45	26.62	4/18	0
Northcote P.	4	0	26	21	6.50	0	78	1	78.00	1/31	0
Nunn J. A.	5	0	72	25	14.40	0	—	—	—	—	—
O'Brien T. C.	268	19	7377	202	29.62	10	272	2	136.00	1/10	0
O'Connor V. R.	4	0	40	30	10.00	0	62	1	62.00	1/62	0
Osborn G. N.	4	1	9	6	3.00	0	105	4	26.25	2/32	0
Osborne D. R.	1	0	7	7	7.00	0	33	1	33.00	1/33	0
Ottaway C. J.	13	1	448	112	37.33	2	—	—	—	—	—
Ottley D. G.	9	1	109	30	13.62	0	—	—	—	—	—
Owen-Smith H. G. O.	43	3	993	77	24.83	0	2150	100	21.50	6/68	8
Oxley J. H.	4	0	10	5	2.50	0	—	—	—	—	—
Page C. C.	56	3	1423	164*	26.84	2	—	—	—	—	—
Paine G. A. E.	7	3	23	16*	5.75	0	356	11	32.36	5/77	1
Palmer C.	31	3	443	55*	15.82	0	—	—	—	—	—
Parfitt P. H.	665	84	21304	200*	36.66	46	6424	231	27.80	6/45	5
Parkinson J.	2	1	4	4*	4.00	0	—	—	—	—	—
Parsons J.	2	0	22	14	11.00	0	—	—	—	—	—
Patel A. S.	3	1	56	25*	28.00	0	55	2	27.50	2/55	0
Paul, E.	2	0	1	1	0.50	0	—	1	—	1/?	0
Pauncefote B.	13	1	287	94*	23.91	0	37	2	18.50	2/26	0
Pavri M. E.	1	0	19	19	19.00	0	79	1	79.00	1/53	0
Pawling S. S.	4	1	5	3	1.66	0	219	9	24.33	5/60	1
Payne C. A. L.	19	0	433	81	22.78	0	—	—	—	—	—
Payne C. J.	8	0	40	22	5.00	0	—	—	—	—	—
Paine M. W.	41	0	640	66	15.60	0	87	1	87.00	1/24	0
Pearce H. E.	9	1	169	46*	21.12	0	16	0	—	—	0
Pearman H.	5	1	121	61	30.25	0	112	0	—	—	0
Pearman R.	13	3	264	72*	26.40	0	—	—	—	—	—
Pearson T. S.	111	12	1816	88	18.34	0	623	22	28.31	5/36	1
Peat C. U.	7	3	24	13	6.00	0	369	10	36.90	3/88	0
Peebles I. A. R.	222	70	1361	58	8.95	0	12122	610	19.87	8/24	40

Name	Inns	NO	Runs	HS	Avge	100s	Runs	Wkts	Avge	Best	5wI
Perkins G.	2	0	0	0	0.00	0	—	—	—	—	—
Philipson H.	15	2	111	14	8.53	0	—	—	—	—	—
Phillips J.	144	42	1152	67★	11.29	0	4924	221	22.28	8/69	16
Pilkington C. C.	1	0	3	3	3.00	0	7	0	—	—	0
Pilkington H. C.	5	0	19	11	3.80	0	—	—	—	—	—
Pitts G. J. S.	2	1	14	14	14.00	0	165	6	27.50	3/36	0
Pocknee J.	2	0	8	5	4.00	0	—	—	—	—	—
Polley V. R.	8	4	18	5	4.50	0	382	10	38.20	3/49	0
Pollitt J.	4	0	21	15	5.25	0	—	3	—	3/?	0
Ponsonby S. C. B.	2	0	3	2	1.50	0	—	—	—	—	—
Pooley E.	9	0	75	21	8.33	0	—	—	—	—	—
Poulter S. J.	3	0	47	36	15.66	0	—	—	—	—	—
Powell A. P.	2	0	0	0	0.00	0	—	—	—	—	—
Powell J. A.	33	11	78	8	3.54	0	1814	62	29.25	8/72	2
Prentice L. R. V.	15	0	41	17	2.72	0	650	28	23.21	6/95	1
Prest C. H.	2	0	15	8	7.50	0	—	—	—	—	—
Price J. S. E.	190	79	902	41★	8.12	0	16440	734	22.39	8/48	25
Price W. F. F.	555	96	8300	111	18.08	3	—	—	—	—	—
Putner F. W.	15	2	159	80	12.23	0	86	2	43.00	2/42	0
Radley C. T.	813	132	24147	200	35.45	42	156	8	19.50	2/38	0
Ramprakash M. R.	14	3	321	71	29.18	0	1	0	—	—	0
Raphael G. L.	1	0	1	1	1.00	0	36	0	—	—	0
Ratliff T.	5	1	43	18	10.75	0	—	—	—	—	—
Rawlin J. T.	358	31	56.80	100	17.37	1	13277	659	20.14	8/29	35
Reddick T. B.	3	0	30	20	10.00	0	17	0	—	—	0
Reeves E.	2	0	66	57	33.00	0	—	—	—	—	—
Richardson H. A.	4	0	69	56	17.25	0	—	—	—	—	—
Ridley A. W.	27	1	527	136	20.26	1	181	7	25.85	2/21	0
Roberson B.	3	0	19	13	6.33	0	—	—	—	—	—
Roberts J. H.	1	0	35	35	35.00	0	—	—	—	—	—
Robertson J.	164	32	1333	62	10.09	0	6367	289	22.03	8/48	13
Robertson J. D. B.	745	39	27088	331★	38.36	59	2006	86	35.82	4/37	0
Robertson W. P.	157	10	3809	130	25.91	4	27	0	—	—	0
Robins R. V. C.	66	6	712	49	11.86	0	2434	73	33.34	7/78	3
Robins R. W. V.	378	24	9337	140	26.37	66	14907	669	22.28	8/69	38
Robson C.	23	4	246	51★	12.94	0	—	—	—	—	—
Robson C. G. W.	6	1	33	12	6.60	0	—	—	—	—	—
Roche W.	40	13	368	74★	13.62	0	1414	49	28.85	6/28	3
Rogers G. J.	6	0	46	26	7.66	0	—	—	—	—	—
Rogers J. P.	2	1	7	7★	7.00	0	—	—	—	—	—
Rome D. A. M.	6	0	56	32	9.33	0	11	0	—	—	0

Name	Inns	NO	Runs	HS	Avge	100s	Runs	Wkts	Avge	Best	5wI
Rose G. D.	8	1	93	52	13.28	0	419	16	26.18	6/41	0
Roseberry M. A.	22	4	444	70*	24.66	0	25	0	—	—	0
Ross C. H. A.	4	0	19	10	4.75	0	—	—	—	—	—
Ross H.	2	0	36	35	18.00	0	—	—	—	—	—
Ross N. P. D.	36	3	506	53	15.33	0	13	0	—	—	0
Routledge R.	96	17	1305	121	16.51	2	1880	38	41.57	4/29	0
Rowley C. R.	2	0	11	6	5.50	0	—	—	—	—	—
Royston H.	8	1	39	18	5.57	0	25	2411	12.50	6/?	1
Russell D. L.	39	3	448	66	12.44	0	189	12	15.75	7/43	1
Russell S. E. J.	105	8	2681	130	27.63	2	118	2	59.00	1/8	0
Russell W. E.	712	54	23103	193	35.11	37	643	10	64.30	2/46	0
Rutter E.	55	10	569	64	12.64	0	2626	155	16.94	7/47	14
Salmon E. H. P.	14	2	139	49	11.58	0	—	—	—	—	—
Saunders J.	3	1	16	7*	8.00	0	—	—	—	—	—
Saville C. A.	5	0	57	32	11.40	0	—	—	—	—	—
Saville S. H.	72	6	1220	76	18.48	0	50	0	—	—	0
Schwarz R. O.	25	3	378	74	17.18	0	184	7	26.28	4/39	0
Scott Lord G. W. M. D.	4	0	5	4	1.25	0	—	—	—	—	—
Scott S. W.	178	18	4176	224	26.10	4	199	3	66.33	1/15	0
Scott W. J.	5	0	12	11	2.40	0	—	—	—	—	—
Selvey M. W. W.	212	65	1835	67	12.48	0	15653	615	25.45	7/20	33
Selwood T.	31	4	441	41*	16.33	0	1	0	—	—	0
Sewell J. J.	13	2	350	166	31.81	1	—	—	—	—	—
Shackle T.	5	1	67	41*	1675	0	—	—	—	—	—
Shaddick R. A.	6	2	13	10	3.25	0	391	14	27.92	4/46	0
Sharp H. P. H.	266	28	6141	165	25.80	9	1628	50	32.56	5/52	1
Sharpe C. B.	5	1	5	3	1.25	0	109	1	109.00	1/18	0
Shaw E. D.	2	0	28	16	14.00	0	13	0	—	—	0
Shenton J. C. L.	2	0	8	5	4.00	0	—	—	—	—	—
Shepperd J.	5	2	29	13	9.66	0	167	4	41.75	3/35	0
Sherwell N. B.	3	1	37	32*	18.50	0	—	—	—	—	—
Sims J. M.	515	96	7173	121	17.11	3	31708	1257	25.22	9/92	77
Skeet C. H. L.	32	6	552	106	21.23	1	—	—	—	—	—
Slack W. N.	316	33	11337	248*	40.06	22	618	19	32.52	3/17	0
Smith A. F.	10	0	77	28	7.70	0	—	—	—	—	—
Smith B. N. B.	1	0	1	1	1.00	0	—	—	—	—	—
Smith C. I. J.	216	23	2977	101*	15.42	1	12001	676	17.75	8/102	39
Smith C. J.	6	1	36	13	7.20	0	—	—	—	—	—
Smith L. A.	5	1	35	21	8.75	0	263	6	43.83	2/52	0
Smith M. J.	664	77	18575	181	31.64	37	1857	57	32.57	4/13	0
Snow A. H. P.	8	3	9	3	1.80	0	308	22	14.00	5/35	2
Soppitt W. J. B.	2	0	15	10	7.50	0	159	5	31.80	5/159	1

Name	Inns	NO	Runs	HS	Avge	100s	Runs	Wkts	Avge	Best	5wI
Spillman G.	18	0	430	87	23.88	0	12	1	12.00	1/12	0
Steel A. I.	2	0	30	16	15.00	0	—	—	—	—	—
Steele, F.	17	3	22	6	1.57	0	615	34	18.08	5/22	1
Stevens G. T. S.	195	15	5434	170*	30.18	7	10556	385	27.41	8/38	16
Stewart A. L.	2	1	12	12*	12.00	0	50	2	28.00	2/33	0
Stewart J. M.	2	0	8	8	4.00	0	11	1	11.00	1/11	0
Stewart R. W.	35	11	98	19	4.08	0	3080	127	24.25	6/65	5
Stirling H.	3	1	4	3	2.00	0	195	0	—	—	0
Stoddart A. E.	300	9	9255	221	31.80	16	4038	141	28.63	5/78	2
Stogdon J. H.	24	1	492	101	21.39	1	—	—	—	—	—
Strachan G	4	1	67	33	22.33	0	161	5	32.20	3/37	0
Stratford A. H.	28	5	238	55*	10.34	0	1054	61	17.27	6/44	4
Studd C. T.	54	10	1241	105*	28.20	1	3370	200	16.85	8/71	21
Studd G. B.	47	2	959	104	21.31	1	5	1	5.00	1/5	0
Studd H. W.	1	0	3	3	3.00	0	23	1	23.00	1/23	0
Studd J. E. K.	18	0	122	28	6.77	0	73	4	18.25	3/32	0
Sturt M. O. C.	35	9	202	26	7.76	0	—	—	—	—	—
Surfleet D. F.	13	1	135	32	11.25	0	8	0	—	—	0
Susskind M. J.	10	0	99	38	9.90	0	7	0	—	—	0
Sutton E. G. G.	2	0	20	14	10.00	0	—	—	—	—	—
Swann J. L.	6	3	69	29*	23.00	0	220	6	36.66	3/39	0
Swanton E. W.	5	0	67	26	13.40	0	—	—	—	—	—
Sweetland E. H.	2	2	9	8*	—	0	—	—	—	—	—
Sykes J. F.	21	5	363	126	22.68	1	905	25	36.20	4/49	0
Tabor A.	2	0	49	42	24.50	0	—	—	—	—	—
Tabor A. S.	11	0	86	20	7.81	0	—	—	—	—	—
Tabor W. C.	2	1	15	15	15.00	0	5	0	—	—	—
Tanner A. R.	65	10	709	81*	12.89	0	1907	69	27.63	5/13	1
Tarrant F. A.	344	24	12169	250*	38.02	26	17518	1005	17.43	9/41	89
Taylor C. R. V.	3	0	25	19	8.33	0	—	—	—	—	—
Taylor H.	4	0	11	6	2.75	0	181	3	60.33	1/17	0
Taylor S. S.	3	0	24	16	8.00	0	—	—	—	—	—
Taylor T. C.	2	1	21	12	21.00	0	—	—	—	—	—
Teape C. A.	2	1	2	2*	2.00	0	42	4	10.50	4/38	0
Tebbut C. M.	9	1	38	10	4.75	0	—	—	—	—	—
Thesiger F. J. N.	11	1	164	60*	16.40	0	—	—	—	—	—
Thomas L. E.	2	1	0	0*	0.00	0	—	—	—	—	—
Thompson A. W.	317	30	7641	158	26.62	5	681	10	68.10	2/35	0
Thompson L. B.	4	2	16	13	8.00	0	248	5	49.60	3/50	0
Thompson M.	3	1	9	5	4.50	0	—	—	—	—	—
Thomson J. R.	6	1	63	35	12.60	0	522	23	22.70	4/66	0
Thornton C. I.	48	1	883	79	18.78	0	32	1	32.00	1/4	0
Thornton C.	52	8	1019	161	23.15	1	876	29	30.20	5/20	1

Name	Inns	NO	Runs	HS	Avge	100s	Runs	Wkts	Avge	Best	5wI
Thornton P. M.	2	0	3	3	1.50	0	—	—	—	—	—
Tilly H. W.	79	10	705	46	10.21	0	3181	126	25.24	6/33	4
Tindall M.	28	1	470	85	17.40	0	21	2	10.50	2/21	0
Titmus F. J.	931	171	17320	120	22.78	5	50223	2361	21.27	9/52	146
Tomlins K. P.	123	14	2883	146	26.44	4	326	4	81.50	2/28	0
Trapnell B. M. W.	2	2	11	8★	—	0	91	0	—	—	0
Trelor T. E.	2	0	10	6	5.00	0	27	1	27.00	1/27	0
Tritton E. W.	8	0	174	65	21.75	0	34	1	34.00	1/34	0
Trott A. E.	341	32	6253	164	20.23	6	20332	946	21.49	10/42	71
Tufnell P. C. R.	15	5	53	12★	5.30	0	1463	38	38.50	6/60	1
Tuke C. M.	10	8	25	8	3.12	0	505	15	33.66	3/38	0
Turner M.	53	8	544	82	12.09	0	—	—	—	—	—
Turner N. F.	1	0	0	0	0.00	0	43	2	21.50	2/38	0
Twining R. H.	54	5	1174	135	23.96	2	—	—	—	—	—
Udal G. F. U.	2	1	0	0★	0.00	0	58	1	58.00	1/40	0
Van Der Bijl V. A. P.	16	3	331	76	25.46	0	1290	86	15.00	6/47	5
Vassila G. C.	2	1	0	0★	0.00	0	37	0	—	—	0
Vernon G. F.	171	10	3648	106	18.93	1	—	—	—	—	—
Vernon M. J.	19	5	124	27	8.85	0	942	27	34.88	6/58	2
Vogler A. E. E.	2	0	87	52	43.50	0	91	5	18.20	4/71	0
Waite A. C.	12	7	53	29	10.60	0	610	17	35.88	4/25	0
Walker A.	7	2	8	4★	1.60	0	28	443	7.00	4/28	0
Walker A. H.	6	1	125	75★	25.00	0	49	3	16.33	3/49	0
Walker F.	3	0	31	13	10.33	0	—	—	—	—	—
Walker I. D.	257	19	6065	145	25.48	4	3151	152	20.73	6/42	8
Walker J. (1850–66)	13	0	102	43	7.84	0	55	1	55.00	1/55	0
Walker J. (1879)	2	1	6	6	6.00	0	26	0	—	—	0
Walker J. G.	77	2	1465	97	19.53	0	23	0	—	—	0
Walker R. D.	78	2	1678	104	22.07	1	2492	142	17.54	6/76	9
Walker V. E.	82	8	1310	87★	17.70	0	18151	20410	15.12	10/104	13
Walton A. C.	59	0	1279	83	21.67	0	—	—	—	—	—
Warner P. F.	571	50	19507	197★	37.44	46	198	4	49.50	1/4	0
Warr J. J.	344	90	2744	51	10.80	0	14592	703	20.75	9/65	24
Watkins W. R.	43	7	626	83	17.38	0	248	7	35.42	2/38	0
Watson A. K.	23	0	338	73	14.69	0	—	—	—	—	—
Watson I. R.	2	1	15	15	15.00	0	—	—	—	—	—
Webb C. J. B.	3	1	18	14	9.00	0	58	0	—	—	—
Webb S.	14	4	26	17	2.60	0	778	30	25.93	7/56	1
Webbe A. J.	430	44	9404	243★	24.36	7	1989	68	29.25	5/23	2
Webbe H. R.	39	3	723	63	20.08	0	—	—	—	—	—

Name	Inns	NO	Runs	HS	Avge	100s	Runs	Wkts	Avge	Best	5wI
Webster W. H.	67	7	1245	111	20.75	1	39	3	13.00	1/0	0
Wells C. M.	166	24	3383	244	23.82	4	7183	350	20.52	8/35	21
Wells G.	10	0	108	27	10.80	0	255	13	19.61	5/35	1
Wells L. S.	10	1	66	16*	7.33	0	4	0	—	—	0
Welman F. T.	27	11	138	41	8.63	0	—	—	—	—	
Wenyon H. J.	14	1	158	51*	12.15	0	71	2	35.50	2/31	0
West J. E.	127	13	1406	83	12.33	0	2052	82	25.02	6/31	4
Westhorp J. W.	11	0	97	39	8.81	0	123	3	41.00	1/7	0
Weston H.	27	7	402	79*	20.10	0	736	30	24.53	4/49	0
Wheatley J. B.	11	1	168	62	16.80	0	100	5	20.00	3/49	0
Wheeler H. J. W.	2	0	44	27	22.00	0	—	—	—	—	—
Wheeler W. C.	2	0	8	6	4.00	0	36	3	12.00	2/7	0
Whitcombe P. A.	3	1	15	8	7.50	0	154	7	22.00	3/60	0
White L. R.	4	1	29	14*	9.66	0	—	—	—	—	—
White R. A.	192	25	4140	108*	24.79	2	36	0	—	—	0
White R. F.	11	6	18	7*	3.60	0	518	17	30.47	4/79	0
White S. G.	3	1	23	20	11.50	0	33	0	—	—	0
Wignall W. H.	7	2	59	22*	11.80	0	77	1	77.00	1/19	0
Wilkinson A. J. A.	32	0	431	59	13.47	0	391	23	17.00	5/38	1
Wilkinson W. O. C.	8	2	164	52	27.33	0	116	8	14.50	4/49	0
Williams H. S.	2	0	1	1	0.50	0	—	—	—	—	—
Williams N. F.	91	24	1297	67	19.35	0	6554	206	31.81	5/15	3
Williams W.	46	6	332	39	8.30	0	560	17	32.94	3/37	0
Wilson A. E.	11	4	161	53*	23.00	0	—	—	—	—	—
Wilson T.	1	0	5	5	5.00	0	31	0	—	—	0
Winter A. H.	6	0	94	60	15.66	0	—	—	—	—	—
Winter G. E.	4	0	29	16	7.25	0	12	0	—	—	0
Winter W.	2	1	14	14*	14.00	0	—	—	—	—	—
Winterburn F.	5	1	19	8	4.75	0	—	—	—	—	—
Wisden J.	5	0	81	42	16.20	0	46	7	6.57	4/14	0
Wormald J.	33	1	548	61	17.12	0	—	—	—	—	—
Wyatt H. D.	6	1	67	23*	13.40	0	—	—	—	—	—
Wyld H. J.	9	2	82	35	11.71	0	42	2	21.00	1/10	0
Young J. A.	343	95	2124	62	8.56	0	22709	1182	19.21	8/31	70

RESULTS OF ALL INTER-COUNTY FIRST-CLASS MATCHES

(A = Abandoned without a ball bowled—not included in totals)

Year	DE	EX	GM	GS	HA	KT	LA	LE	NR	NT	SM	SY	SX	WA	WO	YO	P	W	L	D	T	Pos
1850												LL					2	0	2	0	0	
1851												–L					1	0	1	0	0	
1859				WW													2	2	0	0	0	
1861							No County matches															
1862							No County matches															
1863												–D					1	0	0	1	0	
1864			WW										WL				4	3	1	0	0	
1865	Cbs		W–				WL					DW					5	3	1	1	0	
1866	LW					WW				DW		WW					8	6	1	1	0	1st
1867										LL		LD					4	0	3	1	0	
1868						WL						WT	LW			WL	8	4	3	0	1	
1869												WL					2	1	1	0	0	
1870												LW					2	1	1	0	0	
1871												DW					2	1	0	1	0	
1872												LL		L–			3	0	3	0	0	
1873												WL		W–			3	2	1	0	0	
1874										LL		LW				WD	6	1	4	1	0	
1875										DL		LL				DL	6	0	4	2	0	
1876										DD		WT				LD	6	1	1	3	1	
1877										LD		LL				LD	6	0	4	2	0	
1878										DD		WD				WW	6	3	0	3	0	
1879		DD								DD		WW				LL	8	2	2	4	0	
1880		DL								LL		DW				WW	8	2	2	4	0	
1881		LD		–D						WD		WW				LL	9	3	3	3	0	
1882			WW			–W	LL			LD		WL				WL	11	5	5	1	0	
1883			WD			WW				DD		WL				LD	10	4	2	4	0	
1884			WD			WW				LL		LW				DD	10	4	3	3	0	
1885			LL			WL				LD		LL				WW	10	2	7	1	0	
1886			WW			WD				LD		LL				DL	10	3	4	3	0	
1887			DW			WD				LD		LW				WD	10	4	2	4	0	
1888			LW			LL	LL			WD		LL				WW	12	4	7	1	0	
1889			WD			AL	LW			LD		LL				WD	11	3	5	3	0	
1890			WL			LL	WL			WL		LL				LD	12	3	8	1	0	7th
1891			WD			LL	WW			WD	DW	WL	WL			LW	16	8	5	3	0	3rd
1892			WD			DW	WD			LL	WL	LL	WW			LW	16	7	6	3	0	8th
1893			LW			LW	WL			WW	WD	WW	LW			LL	16	9	6	1	0	3rd
1894			WD			DL	LW			WD	WW	WL	WW			LL	18	8	5	3	0	3rd
1895	DW		LD			WW	LW			WW	DD	LD	LD			LL	18	6	6	6	0	6th=
1896			WL			WD	WW			WD	WL	DW				LD	16	8	3	5	0	3rd
1897			DD			WL	DL			DW	DD	LL	WD			DD	16	3	4	9	0	7th=
1898			LD			WW	WL	WW		DW	DW	WD	WD			LW	18	10	3	5	0	2nd
1899			WW			WL	WD	WD		LW	WW	WD	WL			WD	18	11	3	4	0	2nd
1900	WD	LW				WL	LD	WL		LW	WW	WW	DD	DD		LL	22	9	7	6	0	7th=
1901	WL	DW				DW	DD			WD	WD	DD	WD			LD	18	6	2	10	0	2nd
1902	DD	DW				DW	AD			DW	LL	LL	LD			LL	17	3	7	7	0	12th
1903	AW	WW					AD	DD		DD	WW	WW	DD			WL	16	8	1	7	0	1st
1904	DW	DL				WL	DL			LW	WW	WD	WL			WD	18	9	4	5	0	3rd
1905	LD	LL				DW	DD			LD	WD	WL	WL			LD	18	4	7	7	0	11th
1906	DL	LL					LD	WW		LL	WL	LD	WL			LD	18	4	10	4	0	11th=
1907	DD	WW		DL	DW	DW				LL	WW	DD	WW			DL	20	8	4	8	0	5th
1908	DD	WW		DD		LA				DD	WW	WD	DL	DD		LD	19	6	3	10	0	4th
1909	WA	WW		DD		DL	DL			WD	LW	LD	DD	LW		DD	21	6	5	10	0	6th
1910	WW	WW	WW			LL	DD			DL	WW	DL	WW	DD		LW	22	11	5	6	0	3rd
1911	WD	WW	WW			LL	WL			LD	WW	WW	WW	WL		WD	22	14	5	3	0	3rd
1912	WD			DL	DW	LD				WD		DD	WD	WL	WD	WL	20	7	4	9	0	5th
1913	WD			WD	LL	DL				WD		WD	LW	WW	LD	DL	20	7	6	7	0	6th
1914	WW			WD	WL	DW				WW		DD	WD	WD	WW	DL	20	11	2	7	0	2nd
1919	DD			WD	DL	DW				DD		DL				DL	14	2	3	9	0	13th
1920	DL			WW	WW	WD				WL	WW	WW	WW	WW		DW	20	15	2	3	0	1st
1921	WW			WW	WL	DW				WW	DW	WL	WW	WW		WD	20	15	2	3	0	1st

Year	Results	P	W	L	D	T	Pos
1922	DD WW DW DL WL WL WL DL WW WW LD	22	10	6	6	0	7th
1923	DD WW LD DW LL DD DW LD WL WW LL	22	7	7	8	0	8th
1924	DW WL WW DW DD DW LW DD LW WW WD	22	11	3	8	0	2nd
1925	LW DD DD DW WW LW WW DD WW WD WW LD	24	12	3	9	0	6th
1926	WD WW DD DL DD WL WW LD WW DD DW DL	24	9	4	11	0	6th
1927	DW DW WD DL DL LD DD LD WD DD DL WD	24	5	5	14	0	9th
1928	DW LD DL DL DL WD WD DD WD DD WW LD	24	6	5	13	0	8th
1929	WW WD LL WD LW DD WL WL WW DW WD DL WD DL	28	12	7	9	0	6th
1930	DL LD LL DL LD DD DL DD DD DD LL DW WD LW DL	28	3	9	16	0	16th
1931	AD WD WD DL LL LD DD WD LD WL DD WL DD DD LD	27	5	8	14	0	11th
1932	DD WW WL DW LD WL DL DD DL LL DL DD WD LD	28	6	9	13	0	10th
1933	LW WL DD WW WL LL LL LD WL LL WL DD LL	26	7	14	5	0	12th
1934	WL DD WD LD DL WD WL WW DL DD WL DD LL WL	28	8	9	11	0	10th
1935	WW DW WD WL WW DD WW DD DL LL WW DL	24	11	5	8	0	3rd
1936	LD DW WD WD LD WD WD WD WD DW LD WW DL	26	10	4	12	0	2nd
1937	WW WL WL LW DW WD WW WW DW WW WL	24	15	4	5	0	2nd
1938	WW WW WD WL LD WW WL DL WW WW WD WL	24	15	5	4	0	2nd
1939	WL WW LL WW AW DW WW LW WW DL WD WD LD	25	14	6	5	0	2nd
1946	D- WW -W LW WW LW -L W- DW DW WL WW DW W- -W LD	26	16	5	5	0	2nd
1947	-W WL W- WW WW LD L- -W WW WW LL WW WW -W W- DW	26	19	5	2	0	1st
1948	DW -D DW D- W- DW DL DW -W W- W- WW WD WL WL LD	26	13	4	9	0	3rd
1949	WW W- DD -W -W WW DW WW W- D- -W LL DL DD WW DD	26	14	3	9	0	1st=
1950	D- D- DL -D LL LL WL DW DL -D WD LL DW LL WD LD	28	5	12	11	0	14th
1951	-D -D DD W- LD WW LD DD DD W- WW LD WL LL DL DD	28	7	6	15	0	7th
1952	WL LD L- WW WL WW LD -L WL DD -L LL WL W- WW DL	28	11	12	5	0	5th
1953	DD WD -D LL WW WW DD W- DT WD L- DL WD -W LW DD	28	10	5	12	1	5th
1954	-D -L LD W- WW LD DD WD DD W- WW LD DL DD WW DW	28	10	5	13	0	7th=
1955	D- W- WW -L WL LL LW WL WW -L WL LL DW WL WW LW	28	14	12	2	0	5th
1956	LW WW W- DW LW WL DL -W LW DW -D LL LW W- DD DD	28	11	9	8	0	5th
1957	LL WL -W WD WL LW LD A- LD WL W- LD W- -W LW LD	27	10	12	5	0	7th
1958	-D -D WD D- WD LW DD WD DD W- DW LL WD LD DD DD	28	7	4	17	0	10th
1959	L- L- DL -L LW WW WD WL DD -L WD DD WW WL DD WL	28	10	9	9	0	10th
1960	-D DD WW LD WL DW WD W- -W WD WW DL DL DW DD DD	28	12	4	12	0	3rd
1961	L- WL WD WW WD DL DD -W L- -W WW LW WD WW DL WW	28	15	6	7	0	3rd
1962	-L DL DD WL LD DL WD W- LD D- WW DL LD DD LD WD	28	6	8	14	0	13th
1963	DD WD D- WD LW LD WL -D WD WD -W DL LD D- DW DW	28	9	5	14	0	6th
1964	WW LW -D DW DD LD WW W- WL DW D- DD DD -D LL DL	28	9	6	13	0	6th
1965	-L -L DW W- DD DL WW WL DD W- DL LD DW DW DD DD	28	8	7	13	0	6th
1966	D- D- DD -W AL LD DD DD WW -D WW DL WD DA LD DL	26	6	5	15	0	12th=
1967	WD DD -D AL DT DL WD D- WL DD L- DD DD -D DW WD	27	5	4	17	1	7th
1968	WD DL D- DD DD WD DL -D LD WD WL L- WD WL DL	28	8	6	14	0	10th
1969	-D DD -L W- DD LL LD D- WL L- W- DL DD -D DD DD	24	3	7	14	0	11th
1970	D- DD D- -W DL WD LL -L DD -W -W LD DD D- D- WD	24	5	5	14	0	16th
1971	-D D- DD DW W- LD -D W- W- DL WL LW WL -D -D DL	24	7	6	11	0	6th
1972	W- -D -D -W L- DL W- D- L- D- -D DD WW -L DL	20	5	5	10	0	5th
1973	-D L- D- D- -D LW -D -D -L D- L- DL DW W- D- WT	20	4	5	10	1	13th
1974	W- -D -W -D W- DW L- L- D- D- -L WD DL -L -D WW	20	7	5	8	0	6th
1975	-D L- W- L- -W DW -L -L -W -D D- DD LL W- D- LW	20	6	7	7	0	4th
1976	W- WW -W -W L- WL D- L- D- -W DW WW -L -D -L	20	11	5	4	0	1st
1977	-L WD W- D- -D DL -W -L WW D- WD WD L- W- DW	20	9	5	8	0	1st=
1978	W- DL -W -W A- LL W- W- WW -W DW DL -L -D WD	21	11	5	5	0	3rd
1979	-D DW W- D- -D DD -L -W -D AD D- DD AD D- L- DL	20	3	3	14	0	8th=
1980	W- WW -W -L W- DD D- L- D- WD -W WD WD -D DW	22	10	2	10	0	1st
1981	-D DL W- D- -D DW -W -W -D DW D- WL AL W- D- WW	22	9	3	9	0	4th
1982	D- WD -W -D W- DW D- L- W- WW -W WD WL -W -W DD	22	12	2	8	0	1st
1983	WW DD W- -W W- -W DD W- LL -D L- WW DD WL -W AD	23	11	4	8	0	2nd
1984	-D LD WD DW WW DL -D -D DW L- -D LL LW L- W- W-	24	8	7	9	0	3rd
1985	D- DL -D D- -D D- DW WW LW DD DD WL -W WW -L	24	8	4	12	0	1st
1986	DL LL D- -W D- -D WD D- WL -L D- LD LD DW -L LD	24	4	9	11	0	12th=
1987	-L DD DD DL DL LD -D -L LD A- -D DL WW D- D- L-	23	2	8	13	0	16th

NOTES:

1. Middlesex's win under One-Day rules *v* Northants in 1939 included as Win.
2. Middlesex's loss under One-Day rules *v* Hampshire in 1950 included as Loss.
3. Middlesex's draw under One-Day rules *v* Essex in 1958 included as Draw.
4. Middlesex's loss under One-Day rules *v* Sussex in 1984 included as Loss.
5. Middlesex *v* Surrey Club 1864 is not included above.

RESULTS IN SUNDAY LEAGUE

Year	DE	EX	GM	GS	HA	KT	LA	LE	NR	NT	SM	SY	SX	WA	WO	YO	P	W	L	D	T	Pos
1969	L	L	W	W	L	L	L	A	W	A	W	W	L	W	L	W	14	7	7	–	–	7th=
1970	L	L	A	W	W	L	L	L	L	W	L	W	W	L	W	D	15	6	8	1	–	11th
1971	L	L	W	W	L	L	W	L	L	W	L	W	L	L	L	W	16	6	10	–	–	13th
1972	A	W	W	W	D	W	W	L	W	L	W	L	L	L	W	L	15	8	6	1	–	5th
1973	L	L	L	L	L	A	W	W	W	W	W	A	W	L	W	L	14	7	7	–	–	7th=
1974	W	W	W	W	L	A	T	L	W	W	L	L	W	L	L	L	15	7	7	–	1	8th=
1975	L	L	W	W	L	L	L	W	W	L	W	L	W	W	L	L	16	7	9	–	–	10th
1976	W	L	W	W	L	W	L	L	L	W	L	W	L	L	W	L	16	7	9	–	–	12th=
1977	W	L	L	D	L	W	W	W	W	L	W	L	W	W	W	D	16	9	5	2	–	3rd
1978	W	L	L	W	L	W	L	L	A	W	L	A	L	W	L	L	14	5	9	–	–	15th
1979	W	L	W	W	W	W	W	A	L	a	l	L	W	W	L	W	14	9	5	–	–	4th=
1980	L	L	W	L	W	L	W	A	W	W	W	W	W	L	W	W	15	10	5	–	–	3rd
1981	L	L	L	L	A	L	L	W	L	W	L	W	A	L	W	D	14	4	9	1	–	15th
1982	L	W	L	W	W	L	W	W	W	D	W	W	L	W	W	W	16	11	4	1	–	2nd
1983	W	W	A	L	A	W	L	W	W	L	L	L	L	W	W	L	14	7	7	–	–	8th=
1984	W	T	D	L	W	W	L	W	W	L	W	W	L	W	L	W	16	9	5	1	1	5th=
1985	W	A	L	W	L	L	W	W	L	L	D	D	W	L	L	D	15	5	7	3	–	12th=
1986	L	D	W	A	W	L	L	L	A	L	L	W	L	T	W	W	14	5	7	1	1	9th=
1987	W	W	W	L	L	L	L	W	A	A	D	L	W	A	L	L	13	5	7	1	–	10th=

(A—Abandoned without a ball bowled and not included in totals: D—No result matches where some play took place)

RESULTS IN BENSON & HEDGES CUP

1972 First in South Section; *Q/Final*: Lost to Gloucestershire.

1973 Fifth in South Section.

1974 Fifth in Midland Section.

1975 Second in South Section; *Q/Final*: beat Yorkshire; *S/Final*: beat Warwicks; *Final*: lost to Leics.

1976 Fourth in Group C.

1977 First in Group D; *Q/Final*; lost to Gloucestershire.

1978 Second in Group C; *Q/Final*: lost to Derbyshire.

1979 First in Group D; *Q/Final*: lost to Yorkshire.

1980 First in Group D; *Q/Final*: beat Sussex; *S/Final*: lost to Northants.

1981 Fourth in Group D.

1982 First in Group D; *Q/Final*: lost to Lancashire.

1983 Second in Group D; *Q/Final*: drew with Gloucs (won toss of coin); *S/Final*: beat Lancs; *Final*: beat Essex.

1984 Fifth in Group C.

1985 Second in Group C; *Q/Final*: drew with Worcs (won on striking rate in zonal matches); *S/Final*: lost to Essex.

1986 First in Group D; *Q/Final*: beat Sussex; *S/Final*: beat Notts; *Final*: beat Kent.

1987 Fourth in Group C.

RESULTS IN GILLETTE CUP/NATWEST TROPHY

1963 *1st Round*: beat Gloucs; *Q/Final*: lost to Northants.

1964 *1st Round*: bye; *2nd Round*: beat Yorkshire; *Q/Final*: lost to Surrey.

1965 *1st Round*: beat Bucks; *2nd Round*: beat Derbyshire; *Q/Final*: beat Sussex; *S/Final*: lost to Surrey.

1966 *1st Round*: bye; *2nd Round*: lost to Lancashire.

1976 *1st Round*: bye; *2nd Round*: lost to Sussex.

1968 *1st Round*: beat Essex; *2nd Round*: beat Surrey; *Q/Final*: beat Leicestershire; *S/Final*: lost to Warwickshire.

1969 *1st Round*: beat Bucks; *2nd Round*: lost to Notts.

1970 *1st Round*: beat Norfolk; *2nd Round*: beat Derbyshire; *Q/Final*: lost to Surrey.

1971 *1st Round*: bye; *2nd Round*: lost to Surrey.

1972 *1st Round*: bye; *2nd Round*: lost to Essex.

1973 *1st Round*: bye; *2nd Round*: beat Notts; *Q/Final*: beat Lancashire; *S/Final*: lost to Sussex.

1974 *1st Round*: bye; *2nd Round*: lost to Lancashire.

1975 *1st Round*: beat Bucks; *2nd Round*: beat Warwicks; *Q/Final*: beat Worcs; *S/Final*: beat Derbys; *Final*: lost to Lancs.

1976 *1st Round*: bye; *2nd Round*: lost to Lancashire.

1977 *1st Round*: beat Kent; *2nd Round*: beat Warwicks; *Q/Final*: beat Hampshire; *S/Final*: beat Somerset; *Final*: beat Glamorgan.

1978 *1st Round*: bye; *2nd Round*: beat Derbyshire; *Q/Final*: lost to Lancashire.

1979 *1st Round*: bye; *2nd Round*: beat Hampshire; *Q/Final*: beat Yorkshire; *S/Final*: lost to Somerset.

1980 *1st Round*: beat Ireland; *2nd Round*: beat Notts; *Q/Final*: beat Worcs; *S/Final*: beat Sussex; *Final*: beat Surrey.

1981 *1st Round*: bye; *2nd Round*: lost to Lancashire.

1982 *1st Round*: beat Cheshire; *2nd Round*: beat Lancashire; *Q/Final*: beat Gloucs; *S/Final*: lost to Surrey.

1983 *1st Round*: beat Cambs; *2nd Round*: beat Derbyshire; *Q/Final*: beat Northants; *S/Final*: lost to Somerset.

1984 *1st Round*: beat Northumberland; *2nd Round*: beat Notts; *Q/Final*: beat Lancashire; *S/Final*: beat Northants; *Final*: beat Kent.

1985 *1st Round*: beat Cumberland; *2nd Round*: lost to Essex.

1986 *1st Round*: beat Northants; *2nd Round*: lost to Yorkshire.

1987 *1st Round*: beat Durham; *2nd Round*: lost to Notts.

TEAM RECORDS

[1] HIGHEST AND LOWEST SCORE FOR MIDDLESEX AGAINST EACH COUNTY

Opponents	Highest	Year	Lowest	Year
Cambridgeshire	248 *at* Cambridge	1866	65 *at* Islington	1866
Derbyshire	456-9 dec *at* Derby	1949	29 *at* Chesterfield	1957
Essex	634-7 dec *at* Chelmsford	1983	61 *at* Lord's	1925
Glamorgan	484 *at* Lord's	1952	99 *at* Swansea	1957
Gloucestershire	573 *at* Bristol	1938	41 *at* Lord's	1879
Hampshire	642-3 dec *at* Southampton	1923	59 *at* Lord's	1956
Kent	488 *at* Tonbridge	1925	44 *at* Lord's	1891
Lancashire	501-3 dec *at* Lord's	1914	69 *at* Lord's	1933
Leicestershire	637-4 dec *at* Leicester	1947	41 *at* Lord's	1974
Northamptonshire	567-8 dec *at* Uxbridge	1985	62 *at* Wellingborough	1977
Nottinghamshire	621-9 dec *at* Nottingham	1931	32 *at* Lord's	1882
Somerset	596 *at* Lord's	1908	52 *at* Bath	1952
Surrey	563-9 dec *at* The Oval	1919	25 *at* The Oval	1885
Sussex	632-8 dec *at* Hove	1937	41 *at* Lord's	1924
Warwickshire	543-7 dec *at* Lord's	1920	62 *at* Lord's	1953
Worcestershire	623-5 dec *at* Worcester	1949	1954 *at* Lord's	1964
Yorkshire	527 *at* Huddersfield	1887	45 *at* Huddersfield	1879

The lowest total by Middlesex in all first-class matches is

20 *v* MCC (Lord's) 1864

(2) HIGHEST AND LOWEST SCORE AGAINST MIDDLESEX BY EACH COUNTY

Opponents	Highest	Year	Lowest	Year
Cambridgeshire	212 *at* Islington	1866	82 *at* Cambridge	1866
Essex	477 *at* Leyton	1929	64 *at* Lord's	1902
Glamorgan	478-5 dec *at* Cardiff	1985	83 *at* Swansea	1968
Gloucestershire	539 *at* Lord's	1928	31 *at* Bristol	1924
Hampshire	578 *at* Southampton	1928	35 *at* Portsmouth	1922
Kent	539-9 dec *at* Lord's	1928	⎰43 *at* Lord's	1953
			⎱43 *at* Dover	1957
Lancashire	484-8 dec *at* Manchester	1926	63 *at* Lord's	1891
Leicestershire	479-6 dec *at* Lord's	1932	65 *at* Lord's	1971
Northamptonshire	435 *at* Northampton	1964	58 *at* Kettering	1960
Nottinghamshire	596 *at* Nottingham	1887	40 *at* Lord's	1895
Somerset	523-9 dec *at* Taunton	1946	35 *at* Lord's	1899
Surrey	582-9 dec *at* The Oval	1919	35 *at* Islington	1869
Sussex	550-9 dec *at* Hove	1980	65 *at* Lord's	1894
Warwickshire	507-6 dec *at* Lord's	1927	55 *at* Lord's	1956

| Worcestershire | 436-9 dec *at* Worcester | 1951 | 62 *at* Worcester | 1960 |
| Yorkshire | 515-7 dec *at* Bradford | 1899 | 48 *at* Leeds | 1878 |

The highest totals against Middlesex in all first-class matches are
- 668 by West Indians (Lord's) 1939
- 612 by Oxford University (Prince's) 1876
- 603-5 dec by Rest of England (Oval) 1920

(3) HIGHEST SCORES IN LIMITED-OVERS COMPETITIONS

John Player League	270-5 *v* Gloucestershire *at* Lord's	1983
Benson & Hedges Cup	303-7 *v* Northamptonshire *at* Northampton	1977
Nat West Trophy/Gillette Cup	283-9 *v* Cumberland *at* Uxbridge	1985

(4) LOWEST SCORES IN LIMITED-OVERS COMPETITIONS

John Player League	23 *v* Yorkshire *at* Lord's	1974
Benson & Hedges Cup	73 *v* Essex *at* Lord's	1985
Nat West Trophy/Gillette Cup	41 *v* Essex *at* Westcliff	1972

INDIVIDUAL BATTING RECORDS

(1) DOUBLE-CENTURIES IN FIRST-CLASS MATCHES

Batsman	Score	Opponents	Venue	Year
S. M. Brown (2)	200	Kent	Canterbury	1949
	232★	Somerset	Lords	1951
D. C. S. Compton (5)	214★	Derbyshire	Lord's	1939
	202	Cambridge University	Cambridge	1946
	235	Surrey	Lord's	1946
	246	Rest of England	The Oval	1947
	252★	Somerset	Lord's	1948
J. Douglas (1)	204	Gloucestershire	Bristol	1903
W. J. Edrich (8)	248	Nottinghamshire	Lord's	1938
	222★	Northamptonshire	Northampton	1946
	225	Warwickshire	Birmingham	1947
	257	Leicestershire	Leicester	1947
	267★	Northamptonshire	Northampton	1947
	239	Oxford University	Oxford	1952
	211	Essex	Lord's	1953
	208★	Derbyshire	Chesterfield	1956
R. A. Gale (1)	200	Glamorgan	Newport	1962
M. W. Gatting (2)	216	New Zealanders	Lord's	1983
	258	Somerset	Bath	1984
W. H. Hadow (1)	217	MCC	Lord's	1871
J. W. Hearne (11)	234★	Somerset	Lord's	1911

J. W. Hearne (11) cont.	204	Lancashire	Lord's	1914
	218★	Hampshire	Lord's	1919
	215★	Warwickshire	Birmingham	1920
	202	Warwickshire	Birmingham	1921
	201	Gloucestershire	Gloucester	1922
	221★	Warwickshire	Birmingham	1922
	232	Hampshire	Southampton	1923
	245★	Gloucestershire	Bristol	1927
	223★	Somerset	Taunton	1928
	285★	Essex	Leyton	1929
E. H. Hendren (15)	201	Hampshire	Lord's	1919
	232	Nottinghamshire	Lord's	1920
	277★	Kent	Lord's	1922
	200★	Essex	Leyton	1923
	234	Worcestershire	Lords	1925
	240	Kent	Tonbridge	1925
	206★	Nottinghamshire	Nottingham	1925
	213	Yorkshire	Lord's	1926
	201★	Essex	Leyton	1927
	200	Hampshire	Lord's	1928
	209★	Warwickshire	Birmingham	1928
	232	Nottinghamshire	Nottingham	1931
	203	Northamptonshire	Lord's	1931
	301★	Worcestershire	Dudley	1933
	222★	Essex	Leyton	1933
E. T. Killick (1)	206	Warwickshire	Lord's	1931
H. W. Lee (4)	221★	Hampshire	Southampton	1920
	243★	Nottinghamshire	Lord's	1921
	200	Oxford University	Oxford	1929
	225	Surrey	The Oval	1929
T. C. O'Brien (1)	202	Sussex	Hove	1895
P. H. Parfitt (1)	200★	Nottinghamshire	Nottingham	1964
C. T. Radley (1)	200	Northamptonshire	Uxbridge	1985
J. D. B. Robertson (4)	229	Hampshire	Lord's	1947
	331★	Worcestershire	Worcester	1949
	201★	Somerset	Taunton	1951
	201★	Essex	Lord's	1957
S. W. Scott (1)	224	Gloucestershire	Lord's	1892
W. N. Slack (3)	248★	Worcestershire	Lord's	1981
	203★	Oxford University	Oxford	1982
	201★	Australians	Lord's	1985
A. E. Stoddart (2)	215★	Lancashire	Manchester	1891
	221	Somerset	Lord's	1900
F. A. Tarrant (3)	207★	Yorkshire	Bradford	1911

F. A. Tarrant (3) cont.	250★	Essex	Leyton	1914
	200	Worcestershire	Lord's	1914
A. J. Webbe (1)	243★	Yorkshire	Huddersfield	1887
C. M. Wells (1)	244	Nottinghamshire	Nottingham	1899

(2) CENTURIES IN JOHN PLAYER LEAGUE

Batsman	Score	Opponents	Venue	Year
G. D. Barlow (3)	104	Somerset	Bath	1976
	101★	Northamptonshire	Lord's	1977
	114	Warwickshire	Lord's	1979
J. M. Brearley (1)	109★	Somerset	Taunton	1980
R. O. Butcher (1)	100★	Gloucestershire	Lord's	1984
M. W. Gatting (2)	109	Leicestershire	Leicester	1984
	103★	Surrey	The Oval	1984
C. T. Radley (3)	133★	Glamorgan	Lord's	1969
	105★	Northamptonshire	Lord's	1975
	107★	Gloucestershire	Bristol	1982
W. N. Slack (1)	101★	Yorkshire	Lord's	1986
M. J. Smith (2)	103	Surrey	Lord's	1969
	110	Lancashire	Lord's	1971

(3) CENTURIES IN BENSON & HEDGES CUP

Batsman	Score	Opponents	Venue	Year
G. D. Barlow (1)	129	Northamptonshire	Northampton	1977
J. M. Brearley (1)	100★	Surrey	Lord's	1980
M. W. Gatting (1)	143★	Sussex	Hove	1985
P. H. Parfitt (1)	110	Essex	Lord's	1972
C. T. Radley (2)	103	Warwickshire	Birmingham	1975
	121★	Minor Counties East	Lord's	1976
W. N. Slack (1)	110	Somerset	Lord's	1987
M. J. Smith (1)	105	Minor Counties East	Lord's	1976

(4) CENTURIES IN GILLETTE CUP (NAT WEST TROPHY)

Batsman	Score	Opponents	Venue	Year
G. D. Barlow (1)	158	Lancashire	Lord's	1984
J. M. Brearley (1)	124★	Buckinghamshire	Lord's	1975
M. W. Gatting (1)	118★	Northamptonshire	Northampton	1986
P. H. Parfitt (1)	119	Nottinghamshire	Nottingham	1969
C. T. Radley (1)	108★	Worcestershire	Worcester	1975
W. E. Russell (1)	123	Surrey	Lord's	1968
M. J. Smith (1)	123	Hampshire	Lord's	1977

(5) CARRYING BAT THROUGH COMPLETED INNINGS

Batsman	Score	Total	Opponents	Venue	Year
G. D. Barlow (1)	44*	(83)	Essex	Chelmsford	1983
G. W. Beldam (1)	12*	(51)	Sussex	Lord's	1902
J. M. Brearley (1)	128*	(275)	Hampshire	Lord's	1976
S. M. Brown (1)	96*	(153)	Cambridge University	Cambridge	1948
H. E. Carris (1)	35*	(92)	Yorkshire	Bradford	1929
J. G. Dewes (1)	101*	(203)	Surrey	The Oval	1955
H. B. Hayman (1)	104*	(213)	Kent	Catford	1898
J. W. Hearne (1)	152*	(390)	Leicestershire	Leicester	1931
H. W. Lee (2)	80*	(212)	Essex	Leyton	1920
	52*	(132)	Essex	Lord's	1924
L. J. Moon (1)	62*	(136)	Essex	Leyton	1903
W. N. Slack (2)	72*	(195)	Worcestershire	Lord's	1985
	105*	(252)	Yorkshire	Leeds	1986
A. E. Stoddart (2)	216*	(372)	Lancashire	Manchester	1891
	195*	(327)	Nottinghamshire	Lord's	1893
F. A. Tarrant (4)	55*	(145)	Gloucestershire	Bristol	1909
	140*	(262)	Sussex	Lord's	1910
	207*	(378)	Yorkshire	Bradford	1911
	81*	(159)	Lancashire	Liverpool	1913
I. D. Walker (1)	47*	(126)	Surrey	Lord's	1884
P. F. Warner (7)	46*	(75)	Gloucestershire	Lord's	1898
	197*	(400)	Somerset	Lord's	1901
	73*	(168)	Yorkshire	Lord's	1901
	65*	(130)	Nottinghamshire	Nottingham	1907
	59*	(139)	Nottinghamshire	Lord's	1907
	102*	(201)	Surrey	Lord's	1909
	145*	(279)	Hampshire	Lord's	1920
A. J. Webbe (7)	97*	(201)	Nottinghamshire	Prince's	1875
	44*	(134)	Nottinghamshire	Nottingham	1876
	62*	(118)	Yorkshire	Sheffield	1882
	83*	(196)	Surrey	The Oval	1884
	63*	(119)	Oxford University	Chiswick Park	1887
	243*	(527)	Yorkshire	Huddersfield	1887
	192*	(412)	Kent	Canterbury	1887

(6) LIMITED OVERS (COMPLETE INNINGS DURATION)

John Player League

Batsman	Score	Total	Opponents	Venue	Year
J. M. Brearley (1)	109*	(241-6)	Somerset	Taunton	1980
C. T. Radley (1)	105*	(224-2)	Northamptonshire	Lord's	1975
W. N. Slack (1)	52*	(150-4)	Kent	Canterbury	1981

(7) CENTURY IN EACH INNINGS OF A MATCH

Batsman	Scores		Opponents	Venue	Year
B. J. T. Bosanquet (2)	136	139	Leicestershire	Lord's	1900
	103	100★	Sussex	Lord's	1905
D. C. S. Compton (1)	124	100	Lancashire	Manchester	1946
J. G. Dewes (1)	128	101	Sussex	Hove	1950
H. J. Enthoven (1)	123	115	Sussex	Lord's	1930
N. G. Featherstone (1)	127★	100★	Kent	Canterbury	1975
J. W. Hearne (1)	104	101★	Glamorgan	Lord's	1931
E. H. Hendren (3)	189	100★	Warwickshire	Birmingham	1931
	101	101	Kent	Lord's	1933
	104	101	Surrey	Lord's	1936
H. W. Lee (2)	163	126	Surrey	The Oval	1919
	124	105★	Lancashire	Lord's	1929
P. H. Parfitt (2)	105	101★	Nottinghamshire	Nottingham	1961
	122	114	Pakistanis	Lord's	1962
J. D. B. Robertson (1)	147	137	Sussex	Lord's	1948
A. E. Stoddart (1)	195★	124	Nottinghamshire	Lord's	1893

(8) CENTURY ON DEBUT FOR COUNTY

Batsman	Score	Opponents	Venue	Year
E. A. Clark	100★	Cambridge University	Cambridge	1959
A. Fairbairn	108	Somerset	Taunton	1947
I. D. Walker	102	Surrey Club	The Oval	1862

(9) 2,000 RUNS IN SEASON FOR COUNTY

Batsman	I	NO	R	HS	Av	100	Year
D. C. S. Compton (2)	35	4	2042	235	65.87	9	1946
	31	7	2467	246	102.79	13	1947
W. J. Edrich (3)	40	1	2000	161	51.28	7	1939
	33	7	2650	267★	85.48	10	1947
	55	4	2101	239	41.19	6	1952
M. W. Gatting (1)	31	9	2150	258	71.66	8	1984
J. W. Hearne (1)	35	8	2021	204	74.85	8	1914
E. H. Hendren (7)	35	5	2095	232	69.83	5	1920
	42	10	2669	200★	83.40	11	1923
	39	6	2006	240	60.78	6	1925
	34	4	2033	201★	67.76	8	1927
	38	5	2623	209★	79.48	12	1928
	48	8	2341	232	58.52	6	1931
	48	8	2514	301★	62.85	8	1933
P. H. Parfitt (1)	59	8	2007	165★	39.35	8	1961
J. D. B. Robertson (4)	45	3	2328	229	55.42	11	1947
	46	4	2622	201★	62.42	7	1951

Batsman	I	NO	R	HS	Av	100	Year
J. D. B. Robertson (4)	58	2	2203	162	39.33	2	1952
	53	2	2028	201*	39.76	4	1957
W. E. Russell (1)	56	5	2342	193	45.92	5	1964

INDIVIDUAL BOWLING RECORDS

(1) HAT-TRICKS

Bowler	Opponents	Venue	Year	
W. W. Daniel (1)	Lancashire	Southport	1981	
C. D. Drybrough (1)	Northamptonshire	Northampton	1964	(4 in 5)
F. J. Durston (2)	Cambridge University	Cambridge	1922	
	Oxford University	Oxford	1923	
P. H. Edmonds (1)	Leicestershire	Leicester	1981	
H. J. Enthoven (1)	Australians	Lord's	1934	
S. M. Haslip (1)	Nottinghamshire	Nottingham	1919	
J. T. Hearne (3)	Kent	Tonbridge	1896	
	Essex	Lord's	1902	(4 in 5)
	Warwickshire	Lord's	1912	
J. W. Hearne (2)	Essex	Lord's	1911	
	Essex	Leyton	1922	
T. Hearne (1)	Kent	Islington	1868	
A. E. Moss (1)	Gloucestershire	Lord's	1956	
I. A. R. Peebles (1)	Gloucestershire	Lord's	1932	
J. Robertson (1)	Australians	Lord's	1878	
R. W. V. Robins (2)	Leicestershire	Lord's	1929	
	Somerset	Lord's	1937	
J. M. Sims (1)	South Africans	Lord's	1947	
C. I. J. Smith (1)	Lancashire	Manchester	1939	
F. A. Tarrant (4)	Gloucestershire	Bristol	1907	(4 in 4)
	Surrey	Lord's	1909	
	Gloucestershire	Bristol	1909	
	Somerset	Bath	1911	
F. J. Titmus (1)	Somerset	Weston-Super-Mare	1966	
A. E. Trott (2)	Somerset	Lord's	1907	(4 in 4)
	Somerset	Lord's	1907	
	(twice in same innings)			
J. J. Warr (1)	Leicestershire	Loughborough	1956	
J. A. Young (2)	Northamptonshire	Northampton	1946	
	Lancashire	Lord's	1951	

LIMITED OVERS
Benson & Hedges Cup

Bowler	Opponents	Venue	Year
A. A. Jones (1)	Essex	Lord's	1977

(2) NINE WICKETS IN AN INNINGS

Bowler	Analysis	Opponents	Venue	Year
G. O. B. Allen (1)	10-40	Lancashire	Lord's	1929
G. Burton (1)	10-59	Surrey	The Oval	1888
W. W. Daniel (1)	9-61	Glamorgan	Swansea	1982
J. T. Hearne (3)	9-32	Nottinghamshire	Nottingham	1891
	9-68	Lancashire	Manchester	1898
	9-78	Yorkshire	Bradford	1908
J. W. Hearne (2)	9-82	Surrey	Lord's	1911
	9-61	Derbyshire	Chesterfield	1933
J. M. Sims (1)	9-92	Lancashire	Manchester	1934
F. A. Tarrant (5)	9-57	Yorkshire	Leeds	1906
	9-54	Lancashire	Manchester	1906
	9-41	Gloucestershire	Bristol	1907
	9-59	Nottinghamshire	Lord's	1907
	9-105	Lancashire	Manchester	1914
F. J. Titmus (2)	9-52	Cambridge University	Cambridge	1962
	9-57	Lancashire	Lord's	1964
A. E. Trott (1)	10-42	Somerset	Taunton	1900
V. E. Walker (2)	9-63	Sussex	Islington	1864
	10-104	Lancashire	Manchester	1865
J. J. Warr (1)	9-65	Kent	Lord's	1956

(3) FIFTEEN WICKETS IN A MATCH

Bowler	Analysis	Opponents	Venue	Year
G. Burton (1)	16-114	Yorkshire	Sheffield	1888
J. T. Hearne (3)	15-154	Nottinghamshire	Nottingham	1893
	16-114	Lancashire	Manchester	1898
	15-93	Somerset	Lord's	1904
A. R. Litteljohn (1)	15-189	Lancashire	Lord's	1911
F. A. Tarrant (2)	15-47	Hampshire	Lord's	1913
	16-176	Lancashire	Manchester	1914
F. J. Titmus (1)	15-95	Somerset	Bath	1955
A. E. Trott (1)	15-187	Sussex	Lord's	1901

(4) SIX WICKETS IN A LIMITED-OVERS INNINGS

John Player League

Bowler	Analysis	Opponents	Venue	Year
C. J. R. Black (1)	6-25	Surrey	The Oval	1971
R. W. Hooker (1)	6-6	Surrey	Lord's	1969

Benson & Hedges Cup

Bowler	Analysis	Opponents	Venue	Year
W. W. Daniel (2)	7-12	Minor Counties East	Ipswich	1978
	6-17	Sussex	Hove	1978

Bowler	Analysis	Opponents	Venue	Year
J. R. Thomson (1)	7-22	Hampshire	Lord's	1981

Gillette Cup/Nat West Trophy

Bowler	Analysis	Opponents	Venue	Year
W. W. Daniel (1)	6-15	Sussex	Hove	1980
R. S. Herman (1)	6-42	Surrey	Lord's	1968
K. V. Jones (1)	6-28	Lancashire	Lord's	1974
J. S. E. Price (1)	6-34	Surrey	The Oval	1971

(5) 125 WICKETS IN A SEASON

Bowler	R	W	Av	Best	5wI	Year
J. T. Hearne (2)	2354	145	16.23	8/55	17	1893
	1889	129	14.64	9/68	11	1898
R. W. V. Robins (1)	2735	133	20.56	8/69	7	1929
J. M. Sims (2)	2939	143	20.55	8/32	14	1939
	3284	126	26.06	7/38	9	1949
C. I. J. Smith (2)	2506	143	17.52	8/102	12	1934
	2169	136	15.94	7/35	8	1937
F. A. Tarrant (1)	2411	131	18.40	9/105	8	1914
F. J. Titmus (3)	2312	158	14.63	8/44	16	1955
	2821	125	22.56	7/39	6	1961
	2462	127	19.38	9/52	9	1962
A. E. Trott (2)	2398	150	15.98	8/91	15	1899
	3058	154	19.85	10/42	17	1900
J. A. Young (4)	2300	139	16.54	7/46	10	1947
	2423	131	18.49	7/47	7	1949
	2680	136	19.70	7/44	9	1951
	2984	142	21.01	6/40	5	1952

(6) 100 WICKETS IN A SEASON SINCE 1969

Bowler	R	W	Av	Best	5wI	Year
J. E. Emburey (1)	1983	103	17.88	6/13	14	1983
M. W. W. Selvey (1)	1929	101	19.09	6/26	8	1978
F. J. Titmus (2)	2512	100	25.12	7/81	6	1970
	2355	104	22.64	7/79	6	1971

HIGHEST WICKET PARTNERSHIPS

(1) FIRST-CLASS

FIRST WICKET

367*	G. D. Barlow and W. N. Slack	Kent	Lord's	1981
312	W. E. Russell and M. J. Harris	Pakistanis	Lord's	1967
310	J. D. B. Robertson and S. M. Brown	Nottinghamshire	Lord's	1947
306	P. F. Warner and J. Douglas	Nottinghamshire	Nottingham	1904
277	G. T. S. Stevens and E. T. Killick	Warwickshire	Lord's	1931

SECOND WICKET

380	F. A. Tarrant *and* J. W. Hearne	Lancashire	Lord's	1914
324	I. D. Walker *and* A. Lyttelton	Gloucestershire	Clifton	1883
324	S. M. Brown *and* W. J. Edrich	Warwickshire	Birmingham	1954
319	H. W. Lee *and* G. O. B. Allen	Surrey	The Oval	1929
315	A. W. Thompson *and* W. J. Edrich	Worcestershire	Dudley	1952
314	H. W. Lee *and* E. H. Hendren	Hampshire	Lord's	1928
277	W. J. Edrich *and* D. C. S. Compton	Leicestershire	Leicester	1947

THIRD WICKET

424★	W. J. Edrich *and* D. C. S. Compton	Somerset	Lord's	1948
375	J. W. Hearne *and* E. H. Hendren	Hampshire	Southampton	1923
338	J. M. Brearley *and* M. W. Gatting	Derbyshire	Derby	1981
318	C. T. Radley *and* M. W. Gatting	New Zealanders	Lord's	1983
304	W. J. Edrich *and* D. C. S. Compton	Gloucestershire	Lord's	1938
301	E. T. Killick *and* E. H. Hendren	Sussex	Hove	1928
296	W. J. Edrich *and* D. C. S. Compton	Surrey	Lord's	1946
287★	W. J. Edrich *and* D. C. S. Compton	Surrey	The Oval	1947
286	J. W. Hearne *and* E. H. Hendren	Somerset	Taunton	1928
267	W. J. Edrich *and* S. M. Brown	Oxford University	Oxford	1952
255	J. W. Hearne *and* E. H. Hendren	Somerset	Taunton	1934

FOURTH WICKET

325	J. W. Hearne *and* E. H. Hendren	Hampshire	Lord's	1919
304	D. C. S. Compton *and* F. G. Mann	Surrey	Lord's	1947
256	E. H. Hendren *and* F. T. Mann	Essex	Leyton	1923

FIFTH WICKET

338	R. S. Lucas *and* T. C. O'Brien	Sussex	Hove	1895
352	E. H. Hendren *and* W. F. F. Price	Worcestershire	Dudley	1933
289	C. T. Radley *and* P. R. Downton	Northamptonshire	Uxbridge	1985
285	E. H. Hendren *and* J. H. Human	Surrey	The Oval	1935
268	M. W. Gatting *and* J. E. Emburey	Essex	Chelmsford	1983
221	W. J. Edrich *and* A. W. Thompson	Northamptonshire	Northampton	1946
214	P. H. Parfitt *and* N. G. Featherstone	Gloucestershire	Gloucester	1971
208	J. Douglas *and* C. M. Wells	Essex	Leyton	1902
201	E. A. Beldam *and* G. W. Beldam	Somerset	Lord's	1904
200	E. H. Hendren *and* N. E. Haig	Nottinghamshire	Nottingham	1931

SIXTH WICKET

227	C. T. Radley *and* F. J. Titmus	South Africans	Lord's	1965
212	G. O. B. Allen *and* J. H. A. Hulme	Glamorgan	Lord's	1934
211	G. O. B. Allen *and* J. H. A. Hulme	Worcestershire	Lord's	1936
209	K. P. Tomlins *and* I. J. Gould	Worcestershire	Worcester	1978

SEVENTH WICKET

271*	E. H. Hendren *and* F. T. Mann	Nottinghamshire	Nottingham	1925
220*	J. T. Murray *and* D. Bennett	Yorkshire	Leeds	1964
182	D. Bennett *and* J. T. Murray	Glamorgan	Lord's	1961
169	J. W. Hearne *and* J. M. Sims	Kent	Gravesend	1933
167	A. J. Webbe *and* W. P. Robertson	Worcestershire	Worcester	1900
161	C. T. Radley *and* R. W. Hooker	Hampshire	Lord's	1967
159	D. C. S. Compton *and* W. F. F. Price	Essex	Lord's	1938
158*	F. T. Mann *and* N. E. Haig	Kent	Maidstone	1912
157	E. H. Hendren *and* G. T. S. Stevens	Nottinghamshire	Lord's	1920
155	P. F. Warner *and* R. Anson	Worcestershire	Worcester	1910
152	G. D. Barlow *and* V. A. P. Van Der Bijl	Nottinghamshire	Lord's	1980

EIGHTH WICKET

182*	M. H. C. Doll *and* H. R. Murrell	Nottinghamshire	Lord's	1913

NINTH WICKET

160*	E. H. Hendren *and* F. J. Durston	Essex	Leyton	1927
152	E. Martin *and* H. R. Murrell	Essex	Leyton	1919

TENTH WICKET

230	R. W. Nicholls *and* W. Roche	Kent	Lord's	1899
130	G. W. Beldam *and* C. Headlam	Surrey	Lord's	1902
122*	K. P. Tomlins *and* W. W. Daniel	Yorkshire	Lord's	1981
116	C. I. J. Smith *and* I. A. R. Peebles	Kent	Canterbury	1939
107	H. J. Enthoven *and* W. F. F. Price	Sussex	Lord's	1930
106	E. H. Hendren *and* G. E. Hart	Somerset	Taunton	1935

(2) JOHN PLAYER LEAGUE
FIRST WICKET

148	A. J. T. Miller *and* W. N. Slack	Yorkshire	Lord's	1986

SECOND WICKET

130	C. T. Radley *and* C. J. R. Black	Surrey	The Oval	1971

THIRD WICKET

146	G. D. Barlow *and* C. R. Cook	Gloucestershire	Lord's	1981
131	W. N. Slack *and* M. W. Gatting	Surrey	The Oval	1984

FOURTH WICKET

173	M. W. Gatting *and* N. G. Featherstone	Nottinghamshire	Lord's	1976
142	C. T. Radley *and* J. M. Brearley	Glamorgan	Lord's	1974

FIFTH WICKET

109 R. O. Butcher *and* J. E. Emburey Gloucestershire Lord's 1983

SIXTH WICKET

85 J. M. Brearley *and* P. H. Edmonds Somerset Taunton 1980

SEVENTH WICKET

90 C. T. Radley *and* P. H. Edmonds Gloucestershire Bristol 1982

EIGHTH WICKET

46 K. V. Jones *and* A. H. Latchman Somerset Bath 1970

NINTH WICKET

65 M. W. W. Selvey *and* J. E. Emburey Essex Southend 1977

TENTH WICKET

45 V. A. P. Van Der Bijl *and* R. J. Maru Kent Lord's 1980

(3) BENSON & HEDGES CUP
FIRST WICKET

103 J. M. Brearley *and* W. N. Slack Combined Universities Cambridge 1982

SECOND WICKET

209 M. J. Smith *and* G. D. Barlow Northamptonshire Northampton 1977
204 M. J. Smith *and* G. D. Barlow Minor Counties
East Lord's 1976

FOURTH WICKET

166* G. D. Barlow *and* M. W. Gatting Hampshire Southampton 1980
163 G. D. Barlow *and* M. W. Gatting Somerset Taunton 1980
136 C. J. Radley *and* H. A. Gomes Warwickshire Birmingham 1978

(4) GILLETTE CUP/NATWEST TROPHY
FIRST WICKET

143 K. P. Tomlins *and* W. N. Slack Cambridgeshire Wisbech 1983

SECOND WICKET

223 M. J. Smith *and* C. T. Radley Hampshire Lord's 1977

THIRD WICKET

123* C. T. Radley *and* N. G. Featherstone Worcestershire Worcester 1975

FOURTH WICKET

112 P. H. Parfitt *and* N. G. Featherstone Nottinghamshire Nottingham 1969

FIFTH WICKET

107   J. M. Brearley *and* G. D. Barlow   Warwickshire   Birmingham   1975
(BHC and NWT only minimum 100 included)

WICKET-KEEPING RECORDS

(1) SIX DISMISSALS IN AN INNINGS

Keeper	Total	Ct	St	Opponents	Venue	Year
L. H. Compton (1)	6	4	2	Essex	Lord's	1953
P. R. Downton (1)	6	6	0	Nottinghamshire	Lord's	1981
H. R. Murrell (1)	6	4	2	Gloucestershire	Bristol	1926
W. F. F. Price (2)	7	7	0	Yorkshire	Lord's	1937
	6	6	0	Warwickshire	Lord's	1938

(2) EIGHT DISMISSALS IN A MATCH

Keeper	Total	Ct	St	Opponents	Venue	Year
P. R. Downton (1)	8	8	0	Nottinghamshire	Nottingham	1981
I. J. Gould (1)	8	7	1	Somerset	Taunton	1980
J. T. Murray (3)	8	8	0	Glamorgan	Lord's	1960
	8	5	3	Yorkshire	Lord's	1961
	9	8	1	Hampshire	Lord's	1965
W. F. F. Price (1)	8	3	5	South Africans	Lord's	1935
M. Turner (1)	9	6	3	Nottinghamshire	Prince's	1875

(3) 70 DISMISSALS IN A SEASON

Keeper	Total	Ct	St	Year
L. H. Compton (3)	78	59	19	1947
	72	57	15	1949
	77	63	14	1951
J. T. Murray (7)	77	63	14	1956
	87	72	15	1957
	77	71	6	1958
	78	70	8	1959
	99	92	7	1960
	71	58	13	1964
	75	65	10	1965
H. R. Murrell (2)	78	54	24	1911
	71	63	8	1921
W. F. F. Price (6)	75	39	36	1921
	72	50	22	1931
	76	50	26	1934
	71	54	17	1936
	91	65	26	1937
	80	56	24	1939

(4) 400 DISMISSALS IN A CAREER

Keeper	Total	Ct	St	Years
J. T. Murray	1223	1024	199	1952–75
W. F. F. Price	937	627	310	1926–47
H. R. Murrell	778	517	261	1906–26
L. H. Compton	596	465	131	1938–56

FIELDING RECORDS

(1) FIVE CATCHES IN AN INNINGS

Fielder	Total	Opponents	Venue	Year
R. O. Butcher (1)	5	Australians	Lord's	1981
N. E. Haig (1)	5	Nottinghamshire	Lord's	1928
F. A. Tarrant (1)	6	Essex	Leyton	1906
V. E. Walker (1)	5	Surrey	The Oval	1865

(2) SEVEN CATCHES IN A MATCH

Fielder	Total	Opponents	Venue	Year
A. F. J. Ford (1)	7	Gloucestershire	Lord's	1882
F. A. Tarrant (1)	7	Essex	Leyton	1906

(3) 40 CATCHES IN A SEASON

Fielder	Total	Year
P. H. Parfitt (4)	46	1960
	46	1966
	45	1968
	43	1967

(4) 300 CATCHES IN A CAREER

Fielder	Total	Years
E. H. Hendren	561	1907–1937
C. T. Radley	486	1964–1987
P. H. Parfitt	452	1956–1972
W. J. Edrich	382	1937–1958
F. J. Titmus	378	1949–1982
J. W. Hearne	310	1888–1923
J. D. B. Robertson	301	1937–1959
R. W. Hooker	301	1956–1969

ALL-ROUND CRICKET RECORDS

(1) 100 RUNS AND 10 WICKETS IN A MATCH

R. H. B. Bettington

(1)	28	95	4-87	6-78	Sussex	Lord's	1928

B. J. T. Bosanquet

(3)	71	41*	6-109	4-61	Kent	Tunbridge Wells	1903
	141		5-112	5-136	Yorkshire	Sheffield	1904
	103	100*	3-75	8-53	Sussex	Lord's	1905

D. C. S. Compton

(1)	137*		6-94	8-80	Surrey	The Oval	1947

J. W. Hearne (6)

	54	88	7-83	4-104	Worcestershire	Worcester	1913
	106*		7-54	7-92	Essex	Leyton	1914
	83	39*	5-78	5-91	Essex	Lord's	1914
	79	28	6-74	4-73	Nottinghamshire	Lord's	1922
	140	57*	6-83	6-45	Sussex	Lord's	1923
	14	93	5-38	6-36	Gloucestershire	Lord's	1924

H. W. Lee (1)

	119		5-21	6-47	Sussex	Lord's	1920

C. T. Studd (1)

	105*		6-79	4-48	Kent	Canterbury	1883

F. A. Tarrant (2)

	152	11	7-93	5-56	Gloucestershire	Bristol	1908
	14	106*	9-105	7-71	Lancashire	Manchester	1914

A. E. Trott (2)

	123	35*	6-132	6-68	Sussex	Lord's	1899
	112		8-54	3-84	Essex	Lord's	1901

(2) 1000 RUNS AND 100 WICKETS IN A SEASON

	Runs	Av	Wkts	Av	Year
N. E. Haig (1)	1228	25.58	106	22.54	1929
J. W. Hearne (4)	1663	51.97	107	22.04	1913
	2021	74.85	114	21.42	1914
	1638	54.60	123	18.22	1920
	1252	46.37	103	19.48	1923
F. A. Tarrant (6)	1077	32.64	123	15.87	1907
	1234	47.46	103	18.12	1908
	1254	36.58	108	17.23	1909
	1295	30.24	123	15.82	1910
	1286	38.97	116	16.87	1913
	1743	51.26	131	18.40	1914
F. J. Titmus (4)	1267	26.96	102	24.53	1959
	1205	28.02	117	19.84	1960
	1579	35.89	125	22.56	1961
	1094	29.57	127	19.39	1962

TEST CAREER RECORDS OF MIDDLESEX PLAYERS

Name	Country	Years	M	Runs	Avge	Wkts	Avge
Allen G. O. B.	England	1930–47/8	25	750	24.19	81	29.57
Barlow G. D.	England	1976/7–77	3	17	4.25	—	—
Bosanquet B. J. T.	England	1903/4–05	7	147	13.36	25	24.16
Brearley J. M.	England	1976–81	39	1442	22.88	—	—
Bromley-Davenport H. R.	England	1895/6–98/9	4	128	21.33	4	24.50
Butcher R. O.	England	1980/1	3	71	14.20	—	—
Compton D. C. S.	England	1937–56/7	78	5807	50.06	25	56.40
Connolly A. N.	Australia	1964/5–70/1	29	260	10.40	102	29.22
Cooper B. B.	Australia	1876/7	1	18	9.00	—	—
Cowans N. G.	England	1982/3–85	19	175	7.95	51	39.27
Daniel W. W.	West Indies	1975/6–83/4	10	46	6.57	36	25.27
Dewes J. G.	England	1948–50/1	5	121	12.10	—	—
Donnelly M. P.	New Zealand	1937–49	7	582	52.90	0	—
Downton P. R.	England	1980/1–86	27	701	19.47	—	—
Durston F. J.	England	1921	1	8	8.00	5	27.20
Edmonds P. H.	England	1975–87	51	875	17.50	125	34.18
Edrich W. J.	England	1938–54/5	39	2440	40.00	41	41.29
Emburey J. E.	England	1978–87	46	1027	19.01	115	33.52
Ford F. G. J	England	1894/5	5	168	18.66	1	129.00
Gatting M. W.	England	1977/8–87	58	3563	40.95	2	128.00
Haig N. E.	England	1921–29/30	5	126	14.00	13	34.46
Halliwell E. A.	South Africa	1891/2–1902/3	8	188	12.53	—	—
Hearne J. T.	England	1891/2–99	12	126	9.00	49	22.08
Hearne J. W.	England	1911/2–26	24	806	26.00	30	48.73
Hendren E. H.	England	1920/1–34/5	51	3525	47.63	1	31.00
Killick E. T.	England	1929	2	81	20.25	—	—
Lee H. W.	England	1930/1	1	19	9.50	—	—
Leslie C. F. H.	England	1882/3	4	106	15.14	4	11.00
Lucas A. P.	England	1878/9–84	5	157	19.62	0	—
Lyttelton A.	England	1880–84	4	94	15.66	4	4.75
MacGregor G.	England	1890–93	8	96	12.00	—	—
Mann F. G.	England	1948/9–49	7	376	37.60	—	—
Mann F. T.	England	1922/3	5	281	35.12	—	—
Moon L. J.	England	1905/6	4	182	22.75	—	—
Moss A. E.	England	1953/4–60	9	61	10.16	21	29.80
Murray J. T.	England	1961–67	21	506	22.00	—	—
O'Brien T. C.	England	1884–95/6	5	59	7.37	—	—
Owen-Smith H.G.O.	South Africa	1929	5	252	42.00	0	—

Paine G. A. E.	England	1934/5	4	97	16.16	17	27.47
Parfitt P. H.	England	1961/2–72	37	1882	40.91	12	47.83
Peebles I. A. R.	England	1927/8–31	13	98	10.88	45	30.91
Philipson H.	England	1891/2–94/5	5	63	9.00	—	—
Price J. S. E.	England	1963/4–72	15	66	7.33	40	35.02
Price W. F. F.	England	1938	1	6	3.00	—	—
Radley C. T.	England	1977/8–78	8	481	48.10	—	—
Robertson J. D. B.	England	1947–51/2	11	881	46.36	2	29.00
Robins R. W. V.	England	1929–37	19	612	26.60	64	27.46
Russell W. E.	England	1961/2–67	10	362	21.29	0	—
Schwarz R. O.	South Africa	1905/6–12	20	374	13.85	55	25.76
Selvey M. W. W.	England	1976–76/7	3	15	7.50	6	57.16
Sims J. M.	England	1935–36/7	4	16	4.00	11	43.63
Slack W. N.	England	1985/6–86	3	81	13.50	—	—
Smith C. I. J.	England	1934/5–37	5	102	10.20	15	26.20
Stevens G. T. S.	England	1922/3–29/30	10	263	15.47	20	32.40
Stoddart A. E.	England	1887/8–97/8	16	996	35.57	2	47.00
Studd C. T.	England	1882–82/3	5	160	20.00	3	32.66
Studd G. B.	England	1882/3	4	31	4.42	—	—
Susskind M. J.	South Africa	1924	5	268	33.50	—	—
Thomson J. R.	Australia	1972/3–85	51	679	12.81	200	28.00
Thornton G.	South Africa	1902/3	1	1	—	1	20.00
Titmus F. J.	England	1955–74/5	53	1449	22.29	153	32.22
Trott A. E.	Australia	1894/5	5	228	38.00	26	15.00
	England	1898/9					
Vernon G. F.	England	1882/3	1	14	14.00	—	—
Vogler A. E. E.	South Africa	1905/6–10/1	15	340	17.00	64	22.73
Warner P. F.	England	1898/9–1912	15	622	23.92	—	—
Warr J. J.	England	1950/1	2	4	1.00	1	281.00
Webbe A. J.	England	1878/9	1	4	2.00	—	—
Young J. A.	England	1947–49	8	28	5.60	17	44.52

CAPTAINS OF MIDDLESEX

1864–1872	V. E. Walker
1873–1884	I. D. Walker
1885–1897	A. J. Webbe
1898	A. J. Webbe and A. E. Stoddart
1899–1907	G. MacGregor
1908–1920	P. F. Warner
1921–1928	F. T. Mann
1929–1932	N. E. Haig
1933–1934	N. E. Haig and H. J. Enthoven
1935–1938	R. W. V. Robins

1939	I. A. R. Peebles
1946–1947	R. W. V. Robins
1948–1949	F. G. Mann
1950	R. W. V. Robins
1951–1952	W. J. Edrich and D. C. S. Compton
1953–1957	W. J. Edrich
1958–1960	J. J. Warr
1961–1962	P. I. Bedford
1963–1964	C. D. Drybrough
1965–1967	F. J. Titmus
1968	F. J. Titmus and P. H. Parfitt
1969–1970	P. H. Parfitt
1971–1982	J. M. Brearley
1983–1987	M. W. Gatting

SELECT BIBLIOGRAPHY

F. S. Ashley-Cooper: *Middlesex CCC, 1900–1920* (Heinemann, London, 1921)

P. Bailey, P. Thorn and P. Wynne-Thomas: *Who's Who of Cricketers* (Newnes Books, Feltham, 1984).

W. A. Bettesworth: *The Walkers of Southgate* (Methuen & Co., London, 1900)

Mike Brearley: *The Art of Captaincy* (Hodder & Stoughton, London, 1985)

Norman G. Brett-Jones: *Middlesex* (Robert Hale, London, 1951)

G. B. Buckley: *Fresh Light on Eighteenth Century Cricket* (Cotterell & Co., Birmingham, 1935)

G. B. Buckley: *Fresh Light on Pre-Victorian Cricket* (Cotterell & Co., Birmingham, 1937)

Cyril P. Foley: *Autumn Foliage* (Methuen, London, 1935)

W. J. Ford: *Middlesex CCC, 1864–1899* (Longmans Green, London, 1900)

David Frith: *My Dear Victorious Stod* (Lutterworth Press, Surrey, 1977)

Nigel Haig: *Middlesex CCC, 1921–1947* (Middlesex CCC, London, 1948)

H. W. Lee and L. Thompson: *Forty Years of English Cricket* (Clerke & Cochran, London, 1948)

Ronald Mason: *Plum Warner's Last Season* (Epworth Press, London, 1970)

Arthur Mee: *The King's England: Middlesex* (Hodder & Stoughton, London, 1940)

Edward Rutter: *Cricket Memories* (Williams & Norgate, London, 1925)

Alvan Seth-Smith, ed: *Middlesex CCC Review 1980/81–1986/87* (Middlesex CCC, London)

H. T. Waghorn: *Cricket Scores, 1730–1773* (William Blackwood & Sons, London and Edinburgh, 1899)

H. T. Waghorn: *The Dawn of Cricket* (MCC, London, 1906)

Association of Cricket Statisticians: *First-Class Cricket Matches, 1864–1895*, 22 volumes

Benson & Hedges Cricket Year, ed. David Lemmon, Five volumes, 1982–86 (Pelham Books, London)

Pelham Cricket Year, ed. David Lemmon, Three volumes, 1979–81 (Pelham Books, London)

ACKNOWLEDGEMENT

The author would like to thank the President, Chairman, Committee and Staff of Middlesex County Cricket Club for their untiring help, advice and encouragement with this work. Their co-operation has been most gratefully appreciated.

Thanks are also due to the several players and ex-players to whom I have spoken and to those who were kind enough to write with comment and anecdote. Special thanks should be given to Stephen Green, Curator of the MCC Library and Museum, for his patience, wisdom and constant willingness to assist, to Mr and Mrs Len Grimsey for advice and encouragement, and to my wife, Val, who, as ever, has been unstinting in assistance and invaluable for advice and perceptive comment.

David Lemmon
Leigh-on-Sea, 1988

INDEX